THE
AIG
STORY

THE
AIG
STORY

MAURICE R. GREENBERG
LAWRENCE A. CUNNINGHAM

WILEY

John Wiley & Sons, Inc.

Published by John Wiley & Sons, Inc., Hoboken, New Jersey.

Published simultaneously in Canada.

Photos courtesy of Hank Greenberg.

For general information on our other products and services or for technical support, please contact our Customer Care Department within the United States at (800) 762-2974, outside the United States at (317) 572-3993 or fax (317) 572-4002.

Wiley publishes in a variety of print and electronic formats and by print-on-demand. Some material included with standard print versions of this book may not be included in e-books or in print-on-demand. If this book refers to media such as a CD or DVD that is not included in the version you purchased, you may download this material at http://booksupport.wiley.com. For more information about Wiley products, visit www.wiley.com.

Library of Congress Cataloging-in-Publication Data:

Greenberg, Maurice R.
   The AIG story / Maurice R. Greenberg and Lawrence A. Cunningham.
     p. cm.
   Includes bibliographical references and index.
     ISBN 978-1-118-34587-0 (cloth) – ISBN 978-1-118-51958-5 (ebk) – ISBN 978-1-118-51954-7 (ebk) – ISBN 978-1-118-51957-8 (ebk)
       1. American International Group, Inc.   2. Insurance companies–United States.   3. Insurance companies.   I. Cunningham, Lawrence A., 1962- II. Title.
   HG8540.A43G74   2013
   368.006'573–dc23

                                                                                    2012039474

Printed in the United States of America

10 9 8 7 6 5 4 3 2

From Maurice R. Greenberg

My wife, Corinne (Corky), is and has been supportive throughout my career during good times and bad and has been wonderful to bounce ideas off of. She has been a loving and loyal partner on this journey.

My children grew up as part of AIG during their youth. Jeff and Evan had successful careers at AIG and moved on to fulfill their own ambitions and hence have brilliant careers. Cathy is an outstanding physician and Scott is focused on investments. All my children were influenced one way or another growing up as part of the AIG family.

Shaké, my right hand on just about everything I did and do.

Mona, enormously competent and reliable, and together with Shaké, the best team anyone has ever had as assistants.

Ed Matthews, a close associate who was an investment banker and then a member of the AIG senior management, and personal friend.

Howie Smith, maybe the insurance industry's best financial executive, also a long-time close colleague and friend.

Bertil Lundqvist, who joined the team from Skadden Arps and was enormously helpful in the ensuing legal battles. Bertil has been invaluable in writing this book. He read draft after draft and made numerous suggestions. Most, if not all, were right on target.

David Boies, whose firm spearheaded the legal strategies following my leaving AIG, became a personal friend. His brilliance and loyalty were critical to me when I left AIG.

John Whitehead, a courageous friend who didn't hesitate to speak out when others feared to do so.

There are many more names that deserve individual mention, but it would consume pages. My thanks to so many loyal friends and colleagues who helped AIG become the largest insurance company in history. This book is a testament to them and what they accomplished—that will never change.

Contents

Chairman's Note   xi
Preface   xiii
Acknowledgments   xxi

Part One

Chapter 1   **Independence**   3

Chapter 2   **Innovation**   19

Chapter 3   **Succession**   31

Chapter 4   **Vision and Culture**   43

Chapter 5   **The Internationalist**   53

Chapter 6   **Raising the Iron Curtain**   63

Chapter 7   **Opening Trade in Services**   79

Chapter 8   **Reopening China**   95

Chapter 9   **The Life Business**   111

Chapter 10   **The Domestic Front**   125

Chapter 11   **Investments**   139

Chapter 12   **Governance**   149

Part Two

              Interlude   167

Chapter 13   **Hostile Change**   171

Chapter 14   **Restating History**   189

Chapter 15   **Civil War**   203

Chapter 16   **Saving the Starr Foundation**   213

Chapter 17   **Chaos**   223

Chapter 18   **Nationalization**   243

Epilogue   261
Notes   265
About the Companion Web Site   309
About the Authors   311
Index   313

Chairman's Note

In the late 1960s, a group of domestic and international insurance executives began to build American International Group, popularly known as AIG. We developed close relationships with some of the most interesting and successful business and world leaders of our time. We forged new trails throughout the world and helped pave the way for globalization. We assembled an innovative, loyal, and committed workforce without peer in the industry, which formed AIG's backbone. AIG became the largest insurance company in history with an unmatched record of growth and profit and a culture that attracted the best and the brightest.

Despite such achievements, in 2005 I became the target of an overzealous New York attorney general, Eliot Spitzer. He, along with a group of outside directors, lawyers, and accountants, coordinated to separate me from the company that we had built. Their aggression planted the seeds of AIG's near-destruction and loss of billions of dollars for shareholders, which included pension funds, and myriad other investors.

I was forced to fight heated battles with a company I led for almost 40 years. The battles cost more than $1 billion in legal fees and lasted five years. A new batch of managers, consultants, and advisers dismantled

AIG's traditions, culture, and internal controls. The company decimated its risk management systems and exposed itself to a liquidity crisis that would have been unimaginable during my tenure at the company. I sought to warn the new management about the dangers of the changes they had implemented, but my overtures were rebuffed.

When the financial crisis of 2008 blew up, AIG was at the heart of it. The government took control of the company and used it as a funnel to move capital to a dozen other financial institutions in "backdoor" bailouts.

C.V. Starr & Co., a much older company that had founded AIG, had always remained independent of AIG. It became the vehicle for me and several of my colleagues, who were either forced out of or left AIG, to begin building a new global property/casualty insurance company, and we are making significant progress in that new endeavor.

My schedule is packed. I travel extensively to countries where we had been doing business for decades and, frankly, I spend almost every waking moment working on this new exciting business.

I want to be sure that the record is complete about the building and near-destruction of AIG so I asked Lawrence Cunningham to collaborate with me to produce the book you are reading. It is a story of the building of AIG, along with the unvarnished facts of what occurred at AIG in a brief period of time after I was forced to leave. The U.S. government nationalized AIG despite there being so many alternatives it could have taken. Those alternatives would have led to a soft landing rather than the turmoil that ensued.

                                                              M. R. G.

Preface

The three-word name of the company starring in this book, *American International Group*, defines both the company and the book: a U.S. business, operating everywhere in the world, glued together by AIG's people. *The AIG Story* contributes instructive lessons drawn from its building and cautionary tales taken from its near destruction. AIG's uniqueness prevents its duplication, but America remains promising for business visionaries to pursue dreams.

Decades before "globalization," AIG opened markets in Mao's China; behind the Iron Curtain in the Soviet Union and its eastern European satellites during the Cold War; in Japan, Malaysia, and the Philippines; and throughout Latin America, the Middle East, and Africa—fighting nationalism and other evils along the way and fostering capitalism. The company's foundations were innovative domestic insurance operations assembled in the 1960s by Maurice R. ("Hank") Greenberg, along with a modest collection of insurance businesses created during the previous five decades by the legendary American business pioneer, Cornelius Vander Starr, from Shanghai in 1919 to Tokyo after World War II and across Asia in ensuing years.

In 1967, just before Starr died, he named Greenberg his hand-picked successor. Envisioning and implementing a new strategy for these diverse international ventures, Greenberg consolidated and rearranged the existing businesses, acquired and expanded new ones, and took most of the companies public in 1969, creating AIG. By early 2005, when Greenberg left as chairman and chief executive officer of AIG, it had grown into the world's largest insurance company and a leader in financial services.

Combining the entrepreneurial spirit of a private company with the discipline of a public one, AIG broke with many of the traditional practices of insurance companies that prevailed in the 1960s. It took a more creative approach to underwriting insurance, offering customers tailored terms to meet their needs and conducting more rigorous analysis of risks. Greenberg forged a culture committed to keeping expenses low and earning a profit from underwriting insurance, rather than relying on investment results from premiums received. Managers were accountable for the profit centers they ran, highlighted by a novel incentive compensation plan that enabled employees to earn AIG shares based on increases in AIG's earnings.

AIG's strategic growth plan hinged on creating a culture that valued product innovation. That culture was thriving by the early 1970s as the company pioneered insurance covering armies, kidnapping, oil pipelines and rigs, satellites, shipping, and other unusual risks, especially for companies that were expanding internationally during this period at the dawn of globalization. The plan included strengthening insurance operations overseas, where AIG turned the risks of operating in some foreign markets into opportunity, working in every corner of the globe.

With a business commitment to free markets and open trade, AIG mobilized to change the world's view of service industries. International conventions had long covered trade in goods, but countries discriminated against service providers such as AIG. The company led efforts by scores of other companies and successive U.S. trade representatives, from the Carter administration to the Clinton administration, finally winning in the World Trade Organization's financial services agreement. It recognized the economic importance of services and created an even playing field for them. Freer cross-border capital flow expanded financial markets worldwide, facilitating global economic growth.

The reopening of China for business is another important, illustrative, and profitable part of the strategic and tactical operation at AIG. Starr and other Americans were ousted from China in 1949 amid its civil war, followed by the nation's isolation from the world for several decades. After the thawing of China-U.S. relations in 1972, Greenberg undertook an arduous process that spanned from his 1975 overture through 1992. During that period and afterward, Greenberg visited China several times annually to get to know the country and build relationships with its political, diplomatic, and industrial leadership. His conviction was that a country of China's scale would not remain isolated from the international community. AIG became the first foreign insurance company licensed in China in the modern period.

AIG's strategy encompassed expanding the company's life insurance operations. This meant a commitment to enlarging the global life insurance businesses with roots dating to Starr's time, then leveraging the resulting expertise to grow operations abroad and bolster them at home. That, in turn, led to extending product innovation beyond traditional life insurance into a broader array of investment and retirement products.

With AIG's success in diversifying its domestic and foreign general and life insurance businesses, it won a coveted AAA credit rating. That enabled it to pursue the ultimate step in its strategic growth plan: to diversify earnings by expanding into other fields. This is illustrated by AIG's move into private equity, aircraft leasing, global infrastructure funds, and financial products to help businesses worldwide hedge business risks. In these fields, AIG's AAA rating provided a competitive advantage that made it easier to diversify its capital and earnings—which grew at steady and rapid clips, peaking in 2005 at nearly $1 trillion in assets and $11 billion in annual net income.

Greenberg embodied AIG's corporate culture and led by example, showing managers how to forge personal relationships into valuable business opportunities. Other insurance company CEOs would avoid the specifics of underwriting and often lacked knowledge of insurance business fundamentals, preferring to operate at higher levels of strategic direction. Greenberg learned the insurance business from the ground up—beginning as an underwriter trainee. From then on, Greenberg immersed himself in the details of the insurance business so that he knew exactly what challenges fellow managers faced and the solutions available to conquer them. An apt joke was that other insurance industry CEOs excelled at golf and drinking—but Greenberg was never good at either. He has excelled in the insurance business.

Leadership by example meant "being there": when business associates request assistance from headquarters, a CEO can always respond affirmatively by dispatching a deputy to provide it. Greenberg's first choice whenever responding to such requests was to go himself, along with the regional executive in charge. If a colleague needed high-level help in Chile, rather than send the executive vice president for Latin America alone, Greenberg preferred to fly down as well to assist. Moreover, Greenberg knew that many overseas economies operate differently than in the United States. The United States is open and decentralized, whereas many economies abroad tend to be more government dominated. Therefore, to manage business abroad requires demonstrating an interest in the foreign country and developing personal relationships with government officials there.

AIG's role as a leading American international insurance company frequently entailed intertwining its interests and affairs with those of the United States. In the broadest terms, AIG fought for open trade in dozens of countries and in several important global trade negotiations alongside U.S. trade negotiators. It joined forces with the U.S. government in numerous episodes fighting nationalism and despotism. On many foreign policy questions, U.S. government officials sought Greenberg's advice, which often meant debriefings following many of his international business trips.

AIG's employees made the company's culture distinctive. There were no employment contracts at AIG and compensation programs were long term, with most payoffs, which could be substantial, deferred until retirement. A large percentage of AIG employees held AIG stock, and most senior executives had virtually their entire net worth in AIG. In the resulting ownership culture, many employees considered AIG not just a job but a way of life: the adventure of building a large, prosperous business by underwriting risks when doing so was profitable, and avoiding them otherwise—everywhere from Boston to Beijing. AIG could not have been built without the tireless devotion of its many thousands of loyal employees over four decades. AIG's employees were its backbone.

In the late 1990s and early 2000s, AIG's triumphs culminated in the acquisition of additional insurance companies such as American General and Sun America. With the company on a solid footing everywhere in the world, Greenberg prepared to retire as CEO. He planned to step down from that role at the company's annual meeting in May 2005 and gradually hand the reins over to one of two successors who had been groomed for the job.

But the company was about to face damning reversals. With a few large-scale corporate debacles such as at Enron and WorldCom in the background, some prosecutors became overzealous; the big accounting firms grew paranoid about their own liability and survival. Many newly empowered outside directors believed themselves caught between their traditional duties and a heightened risk of prosecution and private litigation; and lawyers began advising directors that prudence dictated complying with prosecutorial wishes.

That combination of pressures, stoked by state officials in 2005, led AIG's directors to request Greenberg to resign from the company, which he reluctantly agreed to do in March 2005, just two months before he planned to step down and after four decades of service. A gut-wrenching series of battles ensued between Greenberg and the new management of his former company. The parties took several years to resolve the disputes. Combined legal fees exceeded $1 billion.

AIG would never be the same. The new board and chief executive officer became preoccupied, first with trying to justify their decision to seek Greenberg's resignation, and then with implementing numerous corporate governance reforms. They made a conscious decision to radically transform AIG from the top down, ignoring what made its corporate culture distinct. AIG's directors and senior officers lost control of the company. Its financial products division invested in increasingly risky and unhedged credit default swaps that committed it to post substantial collateral while insurance subsidiaries aggressively expanded a securities lending program on much riskier terms.

When a global financial crisis emerged in September 2008, at the heart of it were the contracts made by AIG's financial products division during the three and one-half years after Greenberg's departure. Mortgage-backed securities that financial institutions such as Goldman Sachs had warranted to AIG as "super senior" and rated AAA by the rating agencies were in fact super toxic and almost worthless at the time.

Amid the turmoil and confusion of the crisis, the U.S. government stepped in with billions of dollars in taxpayer funds and seized control of AIG. Although widely portrayed as a bailout of AIG, the facts were more complex. The government channeled a large portion of the funds, some $60 billion in all, not to help AIG but to save various large banks, including Goldman Sachs, paying them full price on contracts whose value was known to be a deep discount from that. After all, these contracts were not listed or traded on any organized exchange that revealed daily prices but were valued based on competing and divergent estimates by a small group of sophisticated firms involved in the market. The government's arrangement doomed AIG to repay these funds by selling many of the businesses that it had built over the previous decades.

Under Greenberg's tenure, the total market value of AIG's stock soared from several hundred million in the late 1960s to $180 billion— an increase of approximately 19,000 percent compared to a 700 percent increase in the Standard & Poor's (S&P) 500.[1] After these state and federal interventions, AIG's stock price first declined and then its value was massively diluted.

Some view favorably the changes made in corporate America over the past two decades by the "corporate governance" movement, especially the shift from vesting leadership authority in strong chief executives to favoring divided authority in outside directors and auditors backed by strong lawyers and governmental authorities. The story of AIG, a company ultimately taken over and run aground by a cadre of auditors, lawyers, outside directors, and government officials, conflicts with that view. Contrary to proponents of anointing such professionals as "gatekeepers" who police against corporate misconduct, the AIG story shows how such custodians ran amok.

Part One of this book is about building a business—developing the vision and promoting an innovative entrepreneurial culture riveted on risk management, cost control, and profitability. The examples come from the insurance industry, most from a time when vision concerned anticipating the effects of a global economy and execution entailed shaping the infrastructure for globalization. But the insights apply to all sectors and settings, as building excellent businesses means excelling at establishing relationships, creating products, and opening markets. Further, the book is about building an *American* business—based on private property, freedom of contract, open trade, and the rule of law. The stories highlight promoting such values abroad while addressing political risks and appreciating unique features in other countries necessary to succeed in international negotiations. AIG's distinctive value arose from scrapping the traditional operating manuals other companies adhere to in favor of context-driven decision making guided by strict accountability and reward mechanisms.

Part Two of this book is about the destruction of business. In the inapt guise of promoting "shareholder democracy," activists and regulators homogenized corporate America in recent years by imposing a one-size-fits-all governance model that often ignore the special cultures of particular businesses. The result has shifted power from corporate managers to an assortment of outsiders, including outside directors, auditors, and lawyers. Outside directors now control corporate boards, though they have vastly limited knowledge compared to inside directors. Outside lawyers, unschooled and inexperienced in business, take strong leadership roles for which many are unsuited. The risk of error and other costs can be great for corporate stakeholders. It may be time for a fresh look at whether the pendulum should swing back to more informed oversight.

At the same time, prosecutors wielded expanded powers over corporations, leveraging their influence by using these outsiders in campaigns against corporations and their employees, often in derogation of shareholder interests. The saga of AIG's near destruction is a reminder that the rule of law is not inevitable in America, where it can be undermined when citizens are supine in the face of official coercion.

There is a bright side to these stories of destruction, however, and the book ends on upbeat notes about the endless possibilities of business vision and entrepreneurship in America. After all, despite the upheaval AIG faced from 2005 through 2009, the business began to recover thanks to the outstanding employees of the company and the diversity of its insurance operations. AIG, though much smaller, returned from the brink of destruction. It may yet endure as one of the greatest American companies ever. Meanwhile, the problems and dangers revealed in the story of AIG's near destruction point to accessible cures: greater flexibility in corporate governance, more restraint by government officials, and alertness to the fact that political risk knows no borders.

This book is an account of an important American company whose story is intertwined with many political and economic milestones of the past half century. The book, through a selective series of vignettes, highlights the principles applied and the corporate culture developed when building AIG. There is no intention to chronicle day-to-day events, to be exhaustive, or to catalog all accomplishments, setbacks, or errors. The book aims to capture some of the excitement of building AIG; convey a sense of its distinctive strategies and culture; and identify some of the factors that caused its near-destruction.

Hank Greenberg led the building of AIG over a span of 40 years. These are his stories. To help him tell them, Greenberg asked Cunningham to collaborate in producing this book. The two spent several hundred hours together in more than 100 meetings or phone calls developing it. Based on these, Cunningham helped shape the narrative and architecture of the book, conducted research and inter-views, and drafted the text. Greenberg, during this time, was busy serving as chairman and CEO of the Starr Companies, building a new international financial services group. Greenberg and Cunningham then spent many more hours together in dozens of meetings reviewing and revising the manuscript. The result is a book told in the third person. But it is very much Greenberg's story and a personal one at that.

Acknowledgments

Helpful editing was provided by Ira Breskin; Fred, Marion, and Stephanie Cuba; Florence Davis; Stephanie Resnik; Arthur Schwartz; Richard Schwartz; and Adam Spilka. Helpful comments were offered by Kenneth Abraham, Lester Brickman, Michael Cassidy, Steve Charnovitz, Peter Henning, Thomas Morgan, William Placke, Michael Smith, and David Zaring. Cunningham interviewed 60 people in researching this book, some on condition of anonymity; he sought to interview a number of others who declined the invitation, including representatives of the law firm of Paul Weiss and the accounting firm of PricewaterhouseCoopers.

PART
One

Chapter 1

Independence

In 1952, days after returning as an officer in the U.S. Army in the Korean War, 27-year-old Maurice R. ("Hank") Greenberg was walking along William Street in Lower Manhattan.[1] Earlier that day, Greenberg had visited fellow alums of New York Law School. Needing a job to support his young family, he was considering practicing law, pursuing national service, such as at the FBI, or re-upping with the Army. Along William Street, Greenberg happened to pass the offices of the Continental Casualty Company, among the largest insurance companies of the day. Greenberg popped his head into the office to ask about job openings.

The personnel manager acted as if he had no time for the inquiry, giving Greenberg, barely out of uniform, the cold shoulder. Stoking his anger about how Americans largely ignored the Korean War, Greenberg stormed into the office of the branch vice president, Bob Vollreide, and told him he thought his personnel manager was a jerk. Vollreide seemed impressed with Greenberg's candor and even his judgment.

Intrigued, after a lengthy conversation, Vollreide offered Greenberg a job. Greenberg took it, beginning as an underwriter trainee. That day, Greenberg's career in insurance was launched.

Greenberg quickly learned that the insurance business was regulated by a state bureaucracy whose approval was often required before insurance products could be sold. He found out that backlogs in the filings at the New York State Insurance Department were often considerable and that many insurance managers accepted resulting delays as a matter of course. Greenberg thought such inefficiencies meant incurring unnecessary costs. He determined that the backlogs could be broken by developing direct relationships with state officials managing the approval process. He set out to meet those people and provide explanations that would speed the process.

An early example of the value of personal relationships in state regulation involved steps that eventually led to the creation of the American Association of Retired Persons, today's ubiquitous AARP. In that era, few elderly Americans had health insurance. Medicare did not exist and private coverage was scarce. An insurance broker from a small firm in Poughkeepsie asked Continental Casualty if it were possible to provide group-wide accident and health insurance for members of a New York association of retired teachers.

After researching the question, Greenberg could not find any provision of the applicable New York insurance law that specifically authorized it. So he inquired of his personal contacts at New York State's Insurance Department and successfully lobbied them to support legislation adding retired teachers associations to the list authorizing such "blanket" insurance.[2] That breakthrough attracted followers, including the National Retired Teachers Association, founded by Dr. Ethel Percy Andrus, a retired high school principal and proponent of the notion of "productive aging." Dr. Andrus soon broadened her mission beyond retired teachers to all elderly Americans, by founding AARP. Continental Casualty developed a novel mix of group health and accident products for many other customers as well.

In building such new products, Continental Casualty earned a reputation for being innovative, an uncommon trait in that era's insurance industry. In recognition of his leadership and lobbying skill, Greenberg became manager of a special risk division in New York and, working with Joe Norton, the regional vice president of the company's eastern U.S. region, handled the company's government relations there. Norton soon saw that Greenberg would likely find the operations side of the insurance business appealing. So Continental Casualty transferred him to world headquarters in Chicago and promoted him to assistant vice president. His portfolio included accident and health insurance for individuals and groups, as well as direction of the advertising department.

Combining these duties and building on Continental's earlier innovations, Greenberg and the chief actuary created a novel promotional effort marketing accident and health insurance to senior citizens, a market other companies had considered too small to bother with. The pitch would open enrollment to anyone who chose to participate within a stated period of time, from 15 to 30 days. The campaign would be initially offered in a test market using ad pages in the *Des Moines Register*. Greenberg and Continental's actuaries thought that a limited open enrollment period would work. They supposed that when many people join in a short period, they are likely to be a good cross-section of high and low risks; however, if enrollment without examination is open indefinitely, an excessive portion of high risks is likely.[3] This campaign proved them correct. The concept of open enrollment for limited times eventually became a staple in the field of accident and health insurance so widely recognized today.

Continental Casualty was unusually innovative compared to other insurance companies of this period, especially in the accident and health field. It had invented coverage of medical treatment for polio and other so-called "dread diseases."[4] Greenberg enjoyed this setting, winning the trust and confidence of the company's president, J. Milburn ("Mil") Smith, who became Greenberg's mentor. Smith, a prominent fixture of the insurance establishment, told Greenberg he valued his imaginative approach to insurance, especially pioneering innovative products and opening new markets. One year after his arrival in Chicago, Greenberg was promoted to vice president, the youngest person in Continental Casualty's history to earn that rank.

In 1960, Smith resigned from Continental Casualty due to a falling out with its chairman. He took a trip overseas to discuss business prospects. In Hong Kong, he called upon Cornelius ("Neil") Vander Starr,

a legendary American insurance entrepreneur who had built a collection of insurance agencies and companies around the world. Starr, a
California native, began building these businesses in Shanghai in 1919
when he was in his late twenties.[5] His business in China was prosperous
almost from the start, when Shanghai was a bustling international center
of commerce.

A flagship of Starr's early business was the American International
Underwriters (or AIU), a membership association of U.S. insurance
companies that held licenses to underwrite insurance in various countries, usually for other U.S. businesses. The AIU acted as agent for
members in markets where they held licenses. An American industrial
company, such as General Electric, needing insurance in Hong Kong,
could use the AIU to write a policy by an American insurer, such as
Fireman's Fund. Having AIU act as agent meant that the member
companies did not need to station substantial personnel or assets abroad
but could still engage in lucrative underwriting there. Each member, an
insurance company, had a percentage of the AIU pool by which its part
of payments and liabilities was derived.

Through the 1950s, Starr's businesses were primarily in Asia, though
he began planting the seeds for operations elsewhere around the world,
including Cuba, Lebanon, Pakistan, and selected countries in western
Europe. His companies acted as a general agent, writing commercial
policies for U.S. insurance companies within the AIU as well as writing
insurance directly in subsidiaries of Starr's Bermuda-based holding
company, American International Reinsurance Company (AIRCO).
Obtaining those franchises was an extraordinary achievement, considering the relatively slow means of transportation and communication in
those decades, when it could take months to transact business between
Asia and the States. For example, uncertainties about liabilities and
delays in payment arose because the AIU's policies and associated claims
would not necessarily become known to the insurers for months.

Besides salesmanship, Starr's achievements displayed his fierce
independence. He was able to work halfway around the world with
virtually no support from a home office in the United States. In building
the AIU and AIRCO, Starr attracted like-minded executives. They
were self-reliant internationalists who showed creativity and independence and a strong work ethic.[6]

Starr knew of Smith's independent, innovative approach to the insurance business. In a lengthy discussion on Smith's 1960 visit to Hong Kong, Starr said how much he admired many of Continental's insurance lines, especially its accident and health business. Starr, a visionary, predicted an increase in global trade and travel, convinced that it would lead to rising prosperity and thus demand for accident, health, and travel insurance outside the United States. Starr wondered whether Smith knew of any good executives who might be willing to open global markets for those products. Smith named Greenberg, referencing his entrepreneurship and knowledge of the insurance business.

Starr asked another favor of Smith. Starr, a divorced millionaire who never had children, developed a tradition of giving financial support to young people and encouraging them in their education and careers. Among the first of these was T. C. Hsu, the son of one of Starr's bankers in Shanghai. Hsu lost his father in the months before World War II when the Japanese military blew up the plane carrying him on a business trip. Starr put Hsu through college and graduate school in the United States and then hired him, forging a lifelong bond akin to father and son. A contemporary recipient was Chiharu ("Chick") Igaya, a Japanese Olympic skiing champion, who attended Dartmouth University on a scholarship that Starr had provided.[7] Starr described Igaya as a protégé and asked Smith if he could help find Igaya a spot in a U.S. insurance training program. Smith obliged.

Shortly thereafter, Starr sent an assistant to visit Greenberg in Chicago to probe whether he might be willing to leave Continental Casualty to join one of his companies. Greenberg made it clear that he was not interested in a move. Undeterred and sensing the need to reach out personally, Starr devised a plan to meet Greenberg. Smith had persuaded Greenberg to accept Igaya into his training program, and Starr used the cover story of visiting Chicago to catch up with Igaya as a way to meet Greenberg. Starr hosted Greenberg and his wife, Corinne, along with Igaya and his wife, for cocktails and dinner at Chicago's renowned Pump Room. Starr, known as a bon vivant, struck Greenberg as an interesting entrepreneur. But Greenberg, on the fast track at Continental, was not convinced that he should make a move. However, Continental was not the same after Smith's departure. Greenberg also had concerns about his career path, at a time when Jews rarely got top insurance company jobs.

For Starr's part, on his return from that trip to Chicago to meet Greenberg, he told Hsu, "I think I found the man."[8] As a result, Starr persisted, and the two had several more dinners. Finally, at a lunch meeting in New York, Starr offered an opportunity that was hard to resist: opening a new worldwide accident and health insurance business. Starr said: "We've talked many, many times and I hope you will decide to join us." Greenberg appreciated Starr's tenacity; the opportunity to open a new business abroad intrigued him, as his world travels with the Army had aroused a keen interest in international adventure and foreign policy. The next morning, Starr had the president of C. V. Starr & Company, William Youngman, call with the details.

Youngman, an old-school Bostonian and lawyer, did not impress Greenberg as an effective ambassador. Greenberg considered the offer Youngman presented on Starr's behalf to be laughable. He turned it down and Youngman did not budge. (It was not obvious whether Youngman was merely not communicating well or was not on board with Starr's enthusiasm.)

Later that day, as Greenberg packed his bags at his hotel room in preparation to return to Chicago, the phone rang. It was Starr. He apologized for how the offer Youngman delivered came across and reiterated his personal enthusiasm. Starr urged him to unpack, stay another night, and meet again with Youngman in the morning. Greenberg decided to give it a second chance and, as predicted, Youngman brought a more appealing offer the next day. The offer included appointment as a vice president of C. V. Starr & Company, the company at the top of Starr's organization. After some additional negotiation, Greenberg finally said yes and in December 1960 left Chicago, selling the family car on the way to the train station for the trip home to New York.

Other executives at C. V. Starr & Company and the AIU had mixed feelings about this new hire. Most, such as the towering Englishman Edwin A. G. ("Jimmy") Manton, president of the AIU, the flagship overseas operation, thought Greenberg was just another idiosyncratic Starr recruit. Although Starr certainly was very good at spotting executive talent, he also had a reputation for occasionally choosing protégés more accomplished as athletes than insurance executives. Others resented the hiring of Greenberg directly into the top ranks at

C. V. Starr & Company. They thought he should have to work his way up the ladder, starting out at the AIU or AIRCO.

Starr gave Greenberg a free hand to build the global accident and health insurance business. Greenberg chose Japan as his first market. There he would be assisted by Igaya, who had completed his training in Chicago, and Houghton ("Buck") Freeman, an American who was born in China, where his father had been an associate of Starr's. Freeman spent much of his life working in the insurance business in Asia, spoke several languages, and then was running the AIU in Japan.

Greenberg noticed that insurance companies in Japan were concentrating on property and casualty coverage—damage to things. They were neglecting accident and health insurance (locally referred to as the "third sector")—damage to people. The oversight seemed strange, given that Japanese culture is otherwise attuned to addressing accident and health risks.

On his first trip to Japan, visiting a Starr branch office in Osaka, Greenberg saw that virtually all the young schoolchildren wore yellow hats when crossing streets at intersections. Parents bought these so their children would stand out and accidents would be prevented. Greenberg found out that the yellow hats were made in a nearby factory. He made a proposal for a cobranding and comarketing venture. The two companies would jointly sell yellow safety hats along with insurance policies—and emblazon the hats with the insurance company's logo: AIU. Sales of one would boost sales of the other. The manufacturer readily agreed. Thousands of Japanese schoolchildren advertised for the AIU in an arrangement that put its new accident and health business firmly in the minds of the Japanese people.

The significant obstacle Greenberg faced in Japan was organizational. The existing Starr businesses in Japan, especially through the AIU, specialized in property and casualty insurance and serving U.S. military personnel stationed there.[9] AIU's agents resisted adding accident and health insurance to their offerings. They embraced specialization, focusing on one product line and brand; Greenberg argued the advantages of "cross-selling," offering multiple products to the same consumer targets. Meeting resistance, however, Greenberg resorted to hiring a team of salesmen, some of whom he had known when working at Continental Casualty, and others introduced to him by Freeman and Igaya. Greenberg spent his first two months at C. V. Starr & Company in Japan recruiting and training staff to launch this new insurance, teaching both marketing and underwriting skills.

Back in New York, Greenberg stayed in close contact with his top manager in Japan, Mickey Marcus, making creative use of the relatively limited communications technology of the era. Each week, they would exchange a cassette tape, recording their assessment of business progress and strategy. Decades before the advent of Skype, e-mail, or even faxes, this way of staying "current" was preferred to the existing alternatives of telephones, which were unreliable and expensive, or telexes, which were not always confidential.

Greenberg took every opportunity to let colleagues across the Starr organization know of this global initiative begun in Japan and the challenges ahead as he targeted additional territories. Robert White, a newly appointed recruit from Continental Casualty experienced in accident and health insurance, reported for his first day of work at C. V. Starr & Company's building at 102 Maiden Lane in Lower Manhattan, near today's South Street Seaport (the address of the building today is both 110 Maiden Lane and 80 Pine Street). Greenberg welcomed White by describing how much work there was to do. The first order of business was a meeting that morning of a group of senior regional executives. They would hear a lecture on accident insurance abroad.

As they hot-footed it down the hall to the meeting, White said, "Wonderful, I'd like to learn more about accident insurance abroad."

"Nonsense," Greenberg replied, "you're giving the lecture." Those assembled learned a great deal from White's remarks.

After Japan, Greenberg targeted Hong Kong. Again, market prospects were good, but Greenberg continued to face internal resistance. Starr's principal operation in Hong Kong was the American International Assurance Company (AIA), a large life insurance company. Its president, G. M. ("Barney") Hughes, was ambivalent about Greenberg's arrival. Hughes seemed concerned that asking his agents to sell accident and health insurance would reduce volume in his vaunted life insurance business.

Without bothering Starr, preferring to fight his own battles, Greenberg gave Hughes a choice: either his agency staff would cooperate and sell the two product lines together, or Greenberg would simply develop a division in Hong Kong using his own staff. Hughes remained obstinate for many weeks. However, Greenberg made sure that word of the early successes in Japan reached Hughes, and once the message was clear, Hughes went along. The new business prospered. Managers and executives company-wide soon began to see the value of cross-selling insurance products, such as offering life insurance and personal accident insurance together.[10] It was more profitable to diversify offerings and to sell multiple lines of insurance to customers than to focus on a particular type.

Given his global mandate, Greenberg took his new business to Europe as well, where organizational resistance again appeared. When Greenberg arrived in the Paris office one afternoon for a meeting, the president, Guy duSaillant, was dressed in a riding habit, having spent the business day with his horses. duSaillant, the brother-in-law of French president Valery Giscard d'Estaing, had to be taught the entrepreneurial aspects of business. He was a quick learner, fortunately, and the accident and health business in France prospered.

Greenberg found more spontaneous support from managers in Germany, especially Michael J. Faulkner, a native German-Jew who had escaped from Nazi Germany during World War II and joined the British Navy. He worked in government intelligence before joining Starr's companies. But Starr's businesses faced greater competition in Europe than in Asia. Many local insurers even used accident and health insurance products as "loss leaders." That is, they priced policies very low as a way to induce customers to buy additional coverage for other risks.

So Greenberg and his teams across Europe had to find creative solutions and concentrated on imaginative distribution channels: marketing health insurance through the Diner's Club charge card service in France, selling accident insurance at gas stations in Belgium, and leveraging existing business insuring U.S. military personnel stationed in Germany, where they expanded from automobile and life insurance into accident and health insurance as well.[11] Though the process was different, the result was the same as in Asia: the creation of profitable lines of business.

Greenberg and Robert White ran worldwide contests for employees of the personal accident business to stoke the competitive spirit.[12] Begun in December 1963, the result tripled the volume of insurance written. The contest capitalized on having developed an effective worldwide team of salesmen and underwriters for the global accident and health group. Among numerous regional prizes, the grand prize was a 10-day, all-expenses-paid trip for two to New York and the 1964 World's Fair. During the contest, Greenberg visited competing offices in the Far East, Southeast Asia, and Europe to share new business sources and promotional lessons that contributed substantially to continued record-breaking production.

After Greenberg opened the global accident and health business, Youngman offered a more challenging assignment. He was asked to take over as president of American Home Assurance Company, an ailing AIU member that Starr had acquired a decade earlier through AIRCO, his principal holding company. Using the AIU as an agent to place insurance abroad was a good business model for U.S. insurance companies in the early decades of the twentieth century. But as international business transactions grew, many U.S. insurers began to beef up their own direct operations overseas rather than rely on agents. If all AIU members did that, of course, Starr's business would shrink, so he acquired a majority stake in one member, which he promptly rebranded American Home Assurance Company.[13]

Fortuitously, Starr had the funding to acquire the stake because of the concurrent sale of another insurance company called U.S. Life. It did business in both the United States and the Philippines. Though U.S. Life set aside reserves to protect policyholders under Filipino law, the New York State Insurance Department declared that it had to establish additional reserves in New York. The cost of such double-reserving was a factor that led Starr to sell U.S. Life. With the proceeds, Starr acquired American Home, which was a multiline insurer licensed in 30 countries, as well as throughout the United States, and represented a 10 percent membership interest in the AIU.

By 1962, however, American Home faced significant problems, with high expenses and declining premium volume in its domestic insurance lines, which relied for business on hundreds of insurance agents around the country. Naturally, Greenberg wanted nothing to do with it. But given AIRCO's ownership of American Home and its importance as a member of the AIU, he reluctantly accepted the assignment, on the condition that be given free rein to address American Home's problems as he saw fit. Greenberg had specific ideas in mind for the turnaround.

To discern market trends, Greenberg and his team met with brokers. The brokers reported that commercial customers preferred to place insurance coverage with Lloyd's of London, the group of insurance syndicates based in London, which for centuries had been known for underwriting nearly any kind of risk imaginable. Greenberg decided to bring the capability of Lloyd's to America. American Home and the rest of the Starr organization would offer U.S. companies a corporate insurer in the United States prepared to cover the country's large-scale commercial risks and unusual risks traditionally covered only by Lloyd's and related reinsurance. Greenberg envisioned using the Lloyd's resources as a substitute for capital, which American Home did not have.

Starr gave Greenberg the green light. Despite that go-ahead, Greenberg's ideas met resistance, even among the entrepreneurial executives with whom Starr surrounded himself. Such resistance arose only a few weeks into Greenberg's tenure as president of American Home, when he did the unthinkable. Insurance rates had long been set by coordination among participants, including insurance trade associations, such as those that rate and price fire insurance risk. State insurance regulators supported these arrangements, and the insurance industry is exempt from federal antitrust laws under the McCarran-Ferguson Act of 1945, which reserves to states the authority to regulate insurance.[14] Greenberg withdrew American Home from these trade organizations, opting to set rates and other policy terms based on his company's independent judgment of risk. When his terms were competitive, he would tend to win business; when they were not, the risks were the kind he preferred not to underwrite anyway. That approach of tailoring policy terms to underwriting risk would eventually attract followers in the insurance industry, but the immediate response was howls of heresy.

Apropos for a "heretic," American Home bid on a contract to insure the property of the Catholic Archdiocese of Boston, a long-time client of Continental Insurance Company, an important member of the AIU. The chief underwriter at American Home helped make the bid using a tailored contract, with its own rate calculations, rather than the standard forms and prices other insurers had agreed to use. This was based on detailed examination of the locales of the church's various properties and related hazards. Another novel feature offered fire insurance with a "deductible" rather than the prevailing standard known as "first-dollar coverage." Under the prevailing standard, the insurer covered every dollar of losses and charged premiums accordingly. But a deductible meant that the Archdiocese would absorb the first $100,000 of losses and the policy would cover amounts greater than that. Premiums would be lower, as would commissions.

Executives at Continental Insurance, which held about 27 percent of the AIU pool, went ballistic. Its chairman, J. Victor Hurd, called Manton, the AIU president, complaining that American Home was stealing his business, reflecting the sense of entitlement and complacency among many insurance executives of the period. Hurd objected that this radical maneuver of using competitive pricing and deductibles in fire insurance was somehow going to ruin the insurance industry. Manton reported Hurd's call to Starr, cautioning that Greenberg could be damaging the organization, threatening to alienate AIU members, like Continental Insurance, which might opt to withdraw. Starr summoned a lunch meeting of his senior executives, including Greenberg and Manton, as well as Youngman and Gordon Tweedy, Starr's personal lawyer.

In the company's executive dining room in corporate headquarters at 102 Maiden Lane in New York, Greenberg felt as though he were in court on a witness stand charged with some grave crime. Manton, an old-fashioned insurance man whose career began in the 1930s working with Starr to build the AIU, insisted that their most important business objective was maintaining the AIU intact, calling it the centerpiece of the organization's history and a significant revenue source. Sustaining the AIU meant adhering to the accepted practices of its member companies, Manton argued. Greenberg contended that following those practices would doom American Home.

Greenberg explained his thinking, which he believed applicable not only to American Home but to other AIU members as well as the entire industry. We should not be tethered to outmoded practices, he said, whether the custom of rate-setting associations, the terms of our policies, or anything else. Take the agency system, for instance. Insurance agents worked for themselves in the field writing policies, yet they possessed the authority to bind the insurance companies they represented, including American Home. The quality of agents in a company's stable varied. Some carefully assessed and priced risks of the policies they underwrote, but many simply wished to maximize their short-term commissions rather than to conduct quality underwriting.

American Home's agents seemed to care more about commissions than quality. Greenberg envisioned moving American Home away from its reliance on agents in favor of setting its own underwriting standards and moving away from the personal lines that agents tended to underwrite in favor of commercial risks that tended to be identified by brokers. Using brokers, American Home could set and enforce strict insurance underwriting standards. It could rebalance the company's lines of business away from individual policies that agents typically wrote, to the more opportunistic underwriting of large-scale commercial risks for corporate customers. Properly executed, this would be a more profitable approach.

These steps would promote the cardinal principle Greenberg brought to the insurance business: to make a profit by underwriting insurance, not simply relying on the returns from investing premium payments received. Greenberg asserted that it was a mistake to rely on the prospect of generating income from investing money held between the time premiums are received and expenses and losses are paid (called "float" in the insurance field). The prospect of such investment income can lead insurance companies to compete too aggressively for business, ignoring the risk. The result is that expenses and losses absorb more than premiums received from year to year—an underwriting loss.

As Starr and the other executives listened in amazement to these radical ideas, Greenberg argued that the goal should be to make an underwriting profit, meaning keeping both losses and expenses low as a percentage of premiums. The percentage of premiums absorbed by expenses, called the "expense ratio," is an indicator of an insurance company's operational efficiency. It tends to be higher in agency businesses than for direct underwriters because agents have less incentive to control costs. At American Home in this period, the expense ratio ran to 42 to 45 percent, well above peers that operated in the range of 38 to 40 percent—still high because the peers all ran agency businesses. Having that much premium revenue absorbed by expenses was ruining American Home.[15] Ideally, Greenberg sought to slash the expense ratio to 30 percent.

Greenberg urged the importance of being open to all proposals to underwrite new forms of insurance and new ways of providing old forms—such as he was doing with the Boston Archdiocese. Product innovation was low on the insurance industry's priority list in those days, but Greenberg envisioned making it a top priority. In fact, one reason for the industry's opposition to innovations such as deductibles was how they reduced premium revenue. But clients, especially large organizations, preferred deductibles because they could readily absorb relatively small losses in the ordinary course of operations. It was the massive losses they wanted to insure against.

In the meeting with Starr's top executives, Greenberg reeled off other reforms he intended to make. At the top of the list was adding substantial reinsurance facilities. This refers to the practice of one insurance company buying policies from other insurance companies to recover part of the losses it suffers under its own policies. In addition to diversifying risk, it is sometimes cheaper to backstop insurance underwriting using reinsurance than to maintain capital to cover the losses, Greenberg explained. American Home needed reinsurance for its existing policies, moreover, simply because it was running out of capital.

Manton appreciated many of Greenberg's points but insisted that such innovations would not sit well with the traditional insurance companies that were AIU members. He again cautioned that retaining AIU members was essential to its continued success. As the AIU's president, Manton warned, changes like these could cause members to withdraw. In response, Greenberg reminded Manton that he was running American Home and that these changes were essential to its survival. To seal the case, he added that turning American Home around was also fundamental to the AIU in the long run: "Who will let us write insurance for them when we cannot write insurance profitably in our own company?"

With that, the two men simply could not reconcile their positions, which boiled down to whether to immediately favor the AIU or American Home. Given the stalemate, Greenberg wrapped up the lunch meeting by stressing that he needed a free hand to run American Home and thought that was the deal he had made with Starr and Youngman. He said if the deal had changed, he was not the man to run American Home, and excused himself from the executive dining room.

Back at their desks a short while later, Starr telephoned Greenberg. He asked him to steer the course at American Home as he thought best. In response, Greenberg proceeded to implement all these innovations at

American Home. The company moved from writing individual policies using agents to underwriting large commercial risks for corporations, using brokers. The controller made cost management a top
priority; the chief underwriter insisted on rigorous risk analysis and
calibrated pricing; and the team negotiated favorable reinsurance deals
to reinsure its entire book of business, including to Hurd's Continental
Insurance. American Home soon obtained a large reinsurance facility
from London in a deal, arranged by the large brokerage firm L. Hammonds, that provided substantial capital. Over time, that enabled it to
become a force in the domestic insurance industry.

American Home began to outperform other AIU member companies. Epitomizing the turnaround was the sharp reduction in the
expense ratio, cut from a high of 45 percent to a steady 31 percent.[16]
Assets more than doubled in four years by 1967, while revenue (technically called net premiums written) grew fivefold.[17] During this period,
Greenberg's strategy crystallized: acquire control of more AIU members
to focus on the direct underwriting of insurance, especially commercial
risks identified by brokers. Greenberg's goal was to control the AIU and
thus the destiny of the Starr organization. While continuing to grow
C. V. Starr & Company's global businesses in diverse insurance lines and
running American Home, Greenberg sought out new opportunities.

Chapter 2

Innovation

Discipline was not a hallmark of the American insurance industry of the 1960s. Greenberg set out to change that. He addressed a problem that plagued businesses across America in those days and seemed acute in the insurance industry: the "three-martini lunch." Agents, whose business was heavily based on entertaining prospects and clients, often drank during lunch, sometimes followed by a nap in the afternoon. Nor were brokers, managers, or executives immune to such habits. Underwriting quality, of course, suffered, ultimately reducing profits. Though lacking authority to control independent agents, for his own employees, Greenberg developed four simple and unambiguous rules: (1) do not drink at lunch; (2) if you drink at lunch, have only one; (3) if you have more than one drink at lunch, do not come back to the office that day; and (4) if you come back to the office after drinking more than one, do not come back to the office ever again.

Disciplinary rules extended well beyond those applicable to lunch-time libations, of course, encompassing underwriting profit, expense control, risk analysis, calibrated pricing, and error minimization. Discipline was imperative in making the acquisitions Greenberg and his team were about to negotiate.

Opportunity first knocked in early 1967, when a corporate raider named Louis Roussel bought 10 percent of the stock of the New Hampshire Insurance Company. New Hampshire held licenses in 27 countries, with leading positions in Europe, and represented a 15 percent share of the American International Underwriters (AIU). Roussel, a New Orleans banker, told the press he wanted to relocate the company from New Hampshire to Louisiana and to refocus its operations domestically rather than abroad. New Hampshire's chairman relayed this news to Manton, who promptly alerted Starr.

Starr called Greenberg, stressing that the loss of New Hampshire from membership in the AIU would be a significant blow to the organization. Aside from its substantial role in the AIU, Greenberg liked New Hampshire because of its strict underwriting standards. It boasted a record of never suffering an underwriting loss. Further, its expense ratio was low compared to other agency members, though still high by Greenberg's standards. Starr asked Greenberg to do whatever it took to prevent Roussel from taking over New Hampshire, including having American Home buy his stock. Greenberg upped the ante on this opportunity, envisioning not only buying Roussel's 10 percent, but having American Home gain control by acquiring additional shares on the open market or from incumbent management holding significant shares. In parlance that would be common in corporate America years later, Louis Roussel was preparing a "hostile takeover bid" for New Hampshire, and Greenberg was ready to play the "white knight."

Greenberg had met Roussel before, when the banker visited New York to peddle bonds for a Louisiana bank he was running. Few others in town bothered to meet Roussel, but Greenberg valued making new business contacts and was happy to get acquainted. Though Greenberg bought no bonds, he established a relationship. So Greenberg paid Roussel a visit, flying to New Orleans to catch up. At dinner, Roussel began to discuss his interest in New Hampshire, apparently ready to reveal his strategic plans. But Greenberg cut Roussel short, emphasizing his own interest in the company. He advised that going forward would involve a fight for control of the insurer. Both knew such competition would drive the bidding up. Greenberg offered to avert such profit-erosion by buying Roussel's 10 percent then and there. He asked Roussel to sleep on it that night and come up with a buyout figure. The next morning Roussel named a price and Greenberg accepted.

The price gave Roussel a profit on his stake. Though Starr and Youngman bickered about whether the price was fair, Greenberg was confident in his figure. Within a few weeks, New Hampshire's stock traded significantly above the deal's purchase price. Greenberg then negotiated with a grateful New Hampshire management the sale of enough additional shares to form a majority. This acquisition thus kept a valuable AIU member in the fold—an important goal, and the one Starr held dear. In addition, the transaction consolidated control of a business with the kind of attention to underwriting quality that Greenberg valued. And no radical operating changes were necessary.

A second opportunity to expand ownership over AIU members arose when National Union Fire Insurance Company of Pittsburgh ran into difficulties. A venerable firm controlled by the Mellon family and owned by citizens across Steel City, its president had tried to turn it around by entering into new insurance lines. To do that, National Union approached Colby & Hewitt, a Boston insurance brokerage firm held by the Hewitt brothers, which owned the Lexington Insurance Company, an insurer of unusual risks. It wrote insurance protecting cattle owners against rustlers, rock concert promoters against star laryngitis, salmon farmers from aquatic hazards, and sports stadiums against the risk that half-time contestants might actually make a basket from half court and win a large cash prize.[1] National Union bought Lexington, paying for it with a 20 percent block of National Union's stock.

By 1967, National Union was ailing nearly as badly as American Home had been, dragging the Lexington subsidiary down with it. Greenberg diagnosed National Union as having the same disease he had cured at American Home: heavy reliance on an agency system with high expenses and a whopping combined ratio (the percentage of premiums absorbed by both expenses and policy losses covered) of 114 percent.[2] Ideally, that figure should never exceed 100 percent. The danger to the Starr organization was familiar, too: National Union was also a long-time AIU member, with a 10 percent membership interest holding licenses in 30 countries. Starr was again concerned about the survival of the AIU; Greenberg wanted to own Lexington.

At a meeting in Puerto Rico of the Young Presidents Organization, a network of corporate leaders under 40 years old, Greenberg ran into one of the Hewitt brothers. The Hewitts were unhappy with how the family's National Union investment was performing, as its stock price sunk from $46 in 1964 to $17 by late 1967.[3] Sensing opportunity, Greenberg invited the Hewitt brothers to New York for lunch, joined by Starr, Youngman, and Manton.

Discussion turned to the stock. One brother asked what American Home would offer for it and Greenberg gave his answer. Oddly, Starr then piped up, cocking his lantern jaw: "That price is much too low. He's just trying to steal the company from you."

The two brothers were flabbergasted, as was Greenberg. They looked at each other, then at Greenberg, then back at each other and then tried to resume eating. The rest of the meal was awkward, as Greenberg sought to recover the negotiations from Starr's gaffe. The Hewitt brothers called Greenberg later that night, asking about Starr, "Is he for real? We're perfectly happy with the price you offered, which is a fair price." Greenberg quickly chalked up Starr's comment to his generous spirit and returned the Hewitts' attention to the business at hand.

Greenberg and the Hewitts agreed to close the deal at the price Greenberg proposed, transferring the 20 percent stake in National Union, along with considerable sway in its boardroom. The toehold persuaded Starr that nurturing the investment was desirable to protect its economic value and essential to preserve the company's overseas licenses for the AIU. Greenberg began to commute between New York and Pittsburgh on round-trip flights nearly every day for two months, offering assistance and discussing a deal to acquire majority control of National Union.

Back in New York in late 1967, Greenberg explained the opportunity to John J. Roberts, a seasoned international insurance executive then managing the AIU in Europe and the Middle East. He had become acquainted with the Starr organization in the Philippines as World War II ended and completed his tour of duty as a liaison Army officer in the Manila war crimes tribunals. Roberts, who had many friends on Wall Street, recommended that Greenberg retain Morgan Stanley, the investment bank, to develop and finance offers to buy more National

Union stock. Morgan Stanley's team would be led by partner Edward Matthews, whom Greenberg would later recruit to come work for him directly.

As Morgan Stanley began to value National Union, Greenberg prepared to obtain approval from American Home's board of directors. Most board members seemed supportive, but not all. When the board met, a few directors expressed doubts about the deal and signaled that they might oppose it. One, a prominent businessman whose opinions were influential, argued that American Home was doing well and that the company should build on that strength rather than venture into something new, especially given the uncertain state of National Union's business. Another director worried that acquiring an additional company would spread management too thin. Listening to these reactions at the board meeting, Greenberg was mentally preparing his response, ready to insist that the transaction must be done.

Before Greenberg could begin, Starr spoke up. He had become ill recently, was looking pale, and relying on an oxygen tank to aid his breathing. He had been sitting quietly, listening to the arguments on both sides when he rose to speak. "This is an important acquisition and I believe that it represents a very good value for us," Starr said in a weak voice as the room fell silent. "Hank has been doing an excellent job running American Home and building this business. He has negotiated a very good deal for us in this acquisition of National Union." Before concluding, Starr became emotional: "If you do not support Hank on this one and vote for the deal, I would advise Hank to leave the company and use his extraordinary talents where they will be appreciated." Starr sank down into his chair. The board voted unanimously to approve the acquisition of National Union.

For the National Union acquisition, Morgan Stanley, led by Matthews, arranged the funding. It created a new subsidiary, which it called American International Enterprises, and used it to obtain credit from Chase Manhattan Bank. Locating the shares was more difficult, as there was no central registry in that era for National Union shares. Following the standard practices of the day, Morgan Stanley bankers contacted brokerage firms that had sold small stakes in National Union to customers. Matthews and his several colleagues had the delicate task of persuading shareholders that the company was failing financially, yet they were being offered a decent price for their shares.[4] Those efforts delivered another 37 percent of the stock, bringing the total to a solid majority of 57 percent.

Starr's generous spirit, evident at the lunch table with the Hewitt brothers, showed in more amusing ways during the deal to acquire National Union. In Pittsburgh, commuting from New York, National Union provided Greenberg with car service—a vintage Checker taxicab driven by Bernie, the company's maintenance manager. Greenberg would invariably tip Bernie $10 or so (about $40-plus in today's dollars), depending on how much time travel to and from the airport took, significant tips for that era. After one National Union board meeting, Starr joined Greenberg in Bernie's Checker cab out to the airport. In those days, the company paid each director a stipend of about $100 per meeting— paid in cash tucked inside a paycheck envelope. Stepping out of the cab, Starr gave his packet to Bernie. Ever after, when Bernie picked up Greenberg at the airport, he asked, "When is Mr. Starr coming to town?"

American Home was about to report a substantial profit in 1967. Good news, of course, but also incurring a large tax bill at a time when the company's capital position still needed strengthening. Fortuitously, right at year-end, Greenberg got a call from Guy Carpenter, another legendary figure in the insurance industry whose name still graces the reinsurance firm he founded. Carpenter, with whom Greenberg developed a productive working relationship, reported an opportunity to acquire Transatlantic Company, which had a loss that, if acquired by year-end, would offset much of American Home's profit. The offering price was less than the tax savings, so American Home jumped at the opportunity, which the board quickly ratified, and the deal closed on time. Though not otherwise particularly substantive at the time, Transatlantic would serve as a useful reinsurance vehicle decades later.

American Home's rising profitability was due in large part to an organizational innovation Greenberg implemented called the profit center model, which would become a distinctive hallmark of all businesses in the organization. The concept refers to assigning full profit and loss responsibility for a business area to a single manager. At many insurance companies in the 1960s and 1970s, it was common for various departments to blame each other for business setbacks: agents blaming underwriting, underwriters blaming budgeting, the budget department blaming claims management—and so on. Greenberg decided that each manager should bear the full burden and earn the full benefits of his top-to-bottom operation across that business, whether underwriting, budgeting, claims—the whole insurance operation. In the profit center model, underwriting profit was the sole determinant of success. Managers responded, and a culture of expense management and underwriting rigor emerged.

To implement the profit center model, Greenberg held regular budget meetings: weekly with the handful of most senior executives, monthly with a larger group that oversaw the entire company, and quarterly with each manager. These meetings, which could last for hours, were a component of the company's internal audit function. Emerging problems could be identified promptly at the highest levels and solutions devised to correct them. All business functions were represented—actuarial, accounting, internal audit, underwriting—to review the budget plan thoroughly for the year-to-date. Managers thereafter lived with those budgets. That made accountability the essence of the profit center model.

The upshot was to grow people who understood the full range of the business, not merely parts of it. Due to the profit center model and this tight system of internal audit, employees across the organization—at American Home, National Union, New Hampshire, the AIU—energetically developed, tested, and promoted new products in niche areas to cover emerging risks. These companies insured everything from the boxer Muhammad Ali against accidental death during title bouts to the construction of the Washington, D.C., subway system, to a top-secret communications satellite called LEASAT that Hughes Aircraft built for the U.S. Navy.

One opportunity arose when the chairman of Marsh & McLennan, a leading broker of large-scale commercial risks, paid Greenberg a visit in 1968. He suggested venturing into a budding market in insurance covering corporate directors and officers (later called D&O insurance). Greenberg had a vague understanding of this concept, and it was just the kind of thing he liked to pursue: a novel niche product that could be priced reliably in relation to the risk, at a profit, and whose risk could be spread around to other firms using reinsurance. The Marsh executive explained that only a very small market in D&O insurance existed through Lloyd's.

Greenberg agreed that demand for D&O insurance in the United States would soon rise dramatically. So he promptly hopped a Pan Am flight to London to investigate. During the 1930s, Lloyd's introduced insurance to cover corporate directors for personal financial liability. At the time, corporations were prohibited by law to indemnify those officials for such costs. But there were not many grounds on which corporate officials could be held liable either. After all, directors were seen merely as business advisers; officers were rarely targets of lawsuits.[5] As a result, the insurance was not considered necessary.

In the late 1960s, attitudes toward corporate directors began to change as shareholders and governments came to insist that directors bear responsibility for corporate stewardship. Courts started to interpret laws more liberally to impose personal financial liability on directors and officers. Public sentiment swung in favor of the accountability movement after the 1970 failure of Penn Central Railroad, a collapse on a scale akin to that of Enron Corporation's disintegration three decades later, and leaving similar regulatory and legal changes in its wake.[6]

On his trip to London, Greenberg discovered that there was only one Lloyd's syndicate handling D&O insurance and the market was tiny. After a long meeting with the syndicate manager, the manager said he would be delighted if American Home would help develop the market, noting how its distribution system was vaster than anything London could match. The syndicate also agreed to reinsure related risks. American Home soon launched this groundbreaking D&O product. Experience over several years was required to fine-tune how to price this insurance, but underwriters gradually refined the pricing correctly and the product succeeded. American Home became the market leader in D&O insurance. As it and a half-dozen followers promoted the product, more directors and officers requested the coverage as part of their recruitment packages. The coverage soon became the industry staple that it remains today, when total industry premiums in the U.S. average $7.5 to $10 billion annually.[7]

The growth and wide-scale legitimacy of D&O insurance met some resistance and attracted controversy. Critics objected that coverage undermines the original objectives of the campaign to promote more active director oversight rather than having directors who merely provide advice.[8] American Home noted that corporate officials perform for a multitude of professional and personal reasons, and that the desire to avoid lawsuits is likely not the most important motivator. Some lawsuits, often those brought by lawyers working for contingent fees, are brought more for their settlement value than the merits warrant. In addition, the policies do not cover egregious behavior.[9]

Contemporary insurance firms promoted D&O policies through advertising. An amusing example, by the insurance broker Johnson & Higgins, ran in the *Wall Street Journal* in 1968. Warning of astronomical personal liability for directors, it depicted a board gathered around a table with a duck seated at the head. The caption: "Are you a sitting duck?"[10] The ad was a bit of Madison Avenue hyperbole, of course, as the perception of liability risk is often greater than the reality, enabling D&O underwriters to generate an underwriting profit reliably. Thanks to American Home executives, the tiny market they found in the late 1960s grew dramatically over the decades.

As American Home pioneered D&O insurance, underwriters else-where at 102 Maiden Lane were pioneering a variation on this coverage called errors and omissions (E&O) insurance. E&O insurance, which covers professional liability arising from mistakes and lapses, was initially launched for realtors and interior decorators. The product grew rapidly as National Union offered it to a broader range of professionals, from accountants, doctors, and lawyers to tanning salons, kidney dialysis centers, and travel agents.

The forces driving the expanding E&O market were familiar: as lawyers representing plaintiffs developed new theories of legal liability and judgments were rendered, people demanded new insurance coverage— and insurance companies developed it. As plaintiffs' lawyers grew increasingly aggressive, insurance policies, in tandem, became more cre-ative. Many types of coverage, especially professional malpractice insur-ance, became practically mandatory to cover legal risks. A pattern emerged: if a big lawsuit arose, posing a new legal theory and resulting in a big money judgment, underwriters at American Home, National Union, or New Hampshire would develop insurance to cover it.

American Home's team adapted rapidly to changing circumstances. On August 8, 1967, at 4:42 in the morning, two violent explosions awakened people across southwestern Louisiana.[11] The Cities Service Oil Company refinery had burst into a raging fire, caused by a leak in a butane line rendered explosive when a southwest wind blew gas towards a furnace in an adjacent area. The refinery, which looked like a large bomb had blown it up, was damaged beyond repair. The facility was insured by a pool of insurance companies that had underwritten the policy using the so-called *probable maximum loss* method. This method refers to the greatest forecast amount of loss from a property's destruction, assuming the proper functioning of protective devices, such as alarms, sprinklers, and fire departments. Actual losses to an insurance company covering the facility could exceed that amount, sometimes by substantial margins. At the Cities Service refinery, the engineers were wildly mistaken. The actual loss was twice the probable maximum loss, exhausting the insurance pool, and drying up capital for such risks.

Within hours of the explosion, Greenberg called Roy Williams, a smart young staff engineer, to discuss the loss and how C. V. Starr & Company might respond. First, the underwriting should change its key assumption, Williams said. Instead of probable maximum loss, underwriters should use the *maximum possible loss*, a much higher figure and therefore a more cautious calculation. An insurer adopting that position would know exactly how much it could possibly have to pay. Second, underwriters should work carefully with engineers and other technical experts to provide more rigorous analysis and evaluation of loss scenarios.

Greenberg ran these ideas by Manton, the insurance traditionalist who became persuaded by Greenberg's independent and innovative approach to the business. Manton also liked these ideas, so Greenberg named Williams president of a newly created company, called Starr Technical Risks Agency, Inc. A new profit center, it would apply those underwriting and engineering principles in acting as agent for a group of insurance companies writing insurance on petroleum-petrochemical risks in the United States and Canada.[12] The pool, officially announced on December 6, 1967, included both Starr companies and other U.S. insurance companies and was coordinated by American Home. Each member company had one seat on the pool's board of directors, giving each a voice at the governance table.

Starr Tech brought the AIU's vast global experience in underwriting and engineering oil risks to bear in running the pool. Though the AIU's previous energy projects were located overseas, Greenberg figured that, from a technical perspective, project differences were scant.

In fact, many overseas projects, particularly those in the Middle East, tended to be owned by the same oil companies, such as Cities Service, running stateside projects. In addition, the AIU then had decades of experience managing insurance pool operations. Starr Tech succeeded, gaining modestly at first and growing steadily thereafter. C. V. Starr & Company ultimately moved the business in-house, shifting from a pool/membership structure to direct underwriting of all the risks, backed by reinsurance.

With Greenberg on board, Starr's businesses were taking a new shape. Executives continued to exhibit the traits that Starr prized and Greenberg sought out: fresh-thinking, self-reliant individuals prepared to make necessary changes and to be creative. The new shape this team would build became even clearer as Starr began to discuss who should succeed him at the helm upon his retirement. His decision would lead Greenberg to create AIG—and continue to lead changes in the insurance industry.

Chapter 3

Succession

Aging and ailing in the late 1960s, Starr needed to identify a group of colleagues who could lead C.V. Starr & Company into the future. From among that group, his successor would be chosen. Through late 1967, Starr's senior executives met regularly to discuss the future of the organization, often gathering late into the night at Starr's tastefully decorated office at 102 Maiden Lane. Starr's heir apparent had long been Youngman. To lead the reorganization effort, Starr floated the idea to create a new post of AIRCO vice chairman and pondered whom to promote into it. Youngman was not sure such a new post was needed; if it were created, however, he was sure that Tweedy was the best choice and recommended him to Starr.

Starr asked Greenberg to accompany him from New York in the company plane for an AIRCO board meeting in Hamilton, Bermuda. During the flight, Starr seemed focused on preparing for the meeting while Greenberg attended to his own work. Starr gave no hint of what the trip would bring. At the board meeting, while Greenberg was working in a separate office nearby, Starr proposed that Greenberg should be AIRCO's new vice chairman. The board concurred. Though this disappointed Tweedy, it floored Youngman, who felt that Starr had rebuked his endorsement of Tweedy without giving him fair notice.

That evening, the senior executives were gathered with other AIRCO managers for a cocktail party at the Hamilton villa of Ernest E. Stempel, who had become the group's expert on life insurance. Starr stood, raised a glass of pink gin, and announced to the group that he had nominated Greenberg as AIRCO vice chairman and that the board had approved the nomination. The gathered crowd applauded, but the news caught everyone by surprise, flattering Greenberg, while embarrassing Youngman. Youngman pulled Starr aside to complain, suggesting that AIRCO was worth less than the price it traded for in the over-the-counter stock market.

Later that night, Starr asked Greenberg and K. K. Tse, his longtime accountant and top adviser, to come to his suite at the Bermudiana, a luxurious resort where Starr always stayed when in Hamilton. Clearly upset at Youngman's impertinence, Starr instructed Tse to assemble the financing needed to buy back Youngman's AIRCO shares. There was a concern: if Youngman were named Starr's successor, he was more likely to arrange to sell off the Starr organization, piece by piece, than to continue to reorganize and grow it. Starr was looking increasingly to the young Greenberg to lead C. V. Starr & Company into the future rather than pass the reins to Youngman or Tweedy. In response, Youngman began to take the cues; Greenberg gained increasing leadership responsibility and demonstrated his interest in creative, disciplined growth for the firm.

Youngman soon made official what had become a fait accompli. He reported his intention to seek early retirement from all his positions in the Starr organization. In a letter addressed to Starr, he wrote: "Things seem to be a little prickly between us, and no way am I going to fight with you. I've made a fortune and I think I'd better retire."[1] Youngman offered to sell his AIRCO shares to C. V. Starr & Company. Starr said he would consider the offer and asked the board to do the same. Stempel agreed to negotiate with Youngman about this. Before negotiations could be concluded, however, Youngman sold a significant block of his AIRCO shares to Victor Hurd of Continental Insurance—the rival, former insurer of the Archdiocese of Boston. Though Youngman claimed that he had first obtained Starr's permission, the other executives were dubious.[2] Some considered the sale a slap in the face. It was the first time a large block of AIRCO stock had been transferred outside of Starr's senior executive group.

The group endorsed Youngman's decision to retire and appreciated how it cleared the way for Greenberg's formal ascension. On August 16, 1968, the *New York Times* reported that both Starr and Youngman were retiring, though Starr would remain a director of C. V. Starr & Company, and Greenberg was its new president and chief executive officer.[3] Tweedy had been appointed chairman of C. V. Starr & Company (although he would shortly retire from that post). The position of chairman would remain vacant for many years, as Greenberg, at 43, felt he was too young for such a senior title.

One weekend in the early winter of 1968, Greenberg received a call at 6:00 A.M. from Starr's valet, Lin Yu-chuen. He said that Mr. Starr would like to see Mr. Greenberg. Both men were spending the weekend at their country homes in Brewster, New York, an hour north of New York City. Starr's home was nestled in his estate which he called Morefar, a name he excavated from his early days in China. When Starr had asked locals directions to a given destination around town, they invariably would tell him, in fractured English, that it was "more far." Equally whimsical is the business name used for the property: Back O'Beyond, Inc.

Starr, an avid tennis player, installed several tennis courts on the grounds, as well as a swimming pool. In 1964, Starr built a nine-hole golf course for his guests. The limited technology of the day resulted in fairways that approach flat greens surrounded by carved-in sand traps. In response to requests from guests, Greenberg oversaw the addition of the back nine, completed in 1974, using the more modern earth-moving equipment that cut through acres of forest to drive rolling fairways, contoured sand traps, shallow ponds, and undulating greens.[4]

Starr decorated the course with 30 bronze statues that represented a dozen sculptors, including the angular chanting singers of David Aronson, the voluptuaries of Chaim Gross and, his favorite, Milton Hebald, who specialized in figurative representation of human anatomy.[5] Off one pond lays a statue of a boy fishing; in a nearby sand trap, another boy flies a kite. Starr's friend, Helen Graham Park, an architect, observed that Starr "was vastly amused when someone accused him of building the golf course so that he could have the fun of decorating it."[6]

After Lin's call that winter weekend morning, Greenberg drove from his home up the hill to Morefar. He steered his car between the stone pillars marking the entrance to the estate, turning down a long lane that led to Starr's house. Lin took him to Starr's bedroom, where Starr lay in bed, ashen and frail. Starr asked Greenberg to sit by his bed.

"Hank," Starr said in a hushed voice, "I'm going to die shortly. I want you to know that I am at peace. I need not worry about the company's future any more. Now I know things are in good hands." Greenberg nodded, as a tear formed in his eye. Starr squeezed Greenberg's hand while Greenberg tried to comfort the man who had recruited him just eight years earlier and provided the opportunity of a lifetime. Starr had not said much in that last meeting, but Greenberg got the sense he said what he wanted to say.

Despite his condition, Starr was planning a trip to Hong Kong that winter of 1968. His doctors advised against it and even asked Greenberg and other close confidants to intervene. But Starr would rather have died on his way to Asia than sitting idly at home. He was scheduled to fly to Hong Kong on a December 21 flight. The day before that, however, Starr died in his apartment on the Upper East Side of Manhattan.[7] He left behind legions of devoted business associates and protégés worldwide, along with a few distant relatives and his estranged ex-wife.

Tse flew in from Hong Kong, met by Greenberg and Tweedy at John F. Kennedy Airport. On the drive into Manhattan, Tweedy, Starr's personal lawyer, explained that Starr's will named as executors of his estate the three of them, along with the other existing directors of C. V. Starr & Company, including Freeman, Manton, Roberts, and Stempel.[8] These directors were Starr's closest friends, each of whom he hand-picked for service, and entrusted them to administer his estate, valued at approximately $15 million (some $150 million in today's dollars).[9]

Tse asked about the interment. Starr wished to be cremated, Tweedy said, but had not indicated what to do with his ashes. Tse suggested reposing them at Morefar. After conferring with the other directors, the group agreed and chose a site atop a hill, deep into the estate, beyond what would become the fourteenth green of the golf course. The spot was within a grove of trees and overlooked a reservoir that had reminded Starr of China. Starr had long considered building a home there, so it seemed to be the natural place for Starr's ashes.

The entrance to the grove is flanked by two chiseled marble markers. Both are adorned, in Chinese and English, one with Starr's name and dates, the other: "The Spirit Never Dies." On one side of the grove, on a bluff, the memorial features a boulder under a 4×8 plaque with Starr's name and dates in raised letters. Nearby, fitted into natural stone jutting out of the mountain, is a bust of Starr, which Milton Hebald, his favorite sculptor, made from memory, perched toward the front of the rock. Friends who accompanied Greenberg to the Starr memorial remarked that his countenance, once there, would change. One observed: "He looks as if he is in church—or synagogue."

Before his death, Starr had been organizing a year-end celebration for some of his best friends and colleagues. That list included Freeman, Greenberg, Manton, Stempel, Tse, and Tweedy. The location was a hotel Starr had purchased in Stowe, Vermont, called Stowehof, a jewel of a cozy alpine New England inn. Though Starr had not taken up skiing until his mid-40s, his enthusiasm for sport and an interest in real estate led him to acquire a small ski resort in St. Anton, Austria, and what became one of the most famous resorts in the United States. Starr got into the business after he had taken ski lessons from the renowned Austrian skier Sepp Ruschp, who had immigrated to Stowe in 1936.[10]

Skiing at Stowe was a novelty in the period after World War II, when the mountain had a fledging business. Ruschp and Starr installed two new ski lifts and upgraded the dining facilities. For its era, the facility was state of the art and began to draw skiers to the region. By the 1950s, to showcase the results, they began to host high-profile events, including inviting the 1952 U.S. Olympic medalists to ski for a weekend. Starr's Mt. Mansfield Company was profiled in a 1955 *Sports Illustrated* cover story as the leading ski resort in the eastern United States.[11]

Thomas J. Watson, Jr., the CEO of IBM, also a skier and denizen of the Vermont slopes, offered to buy Mt. Mansfield Company from Starr. Though unwilling to part with such a magical retreat, which was a labor of love that lost money, Starr thought Watson's firepower worth a partnership. So he agreed to sell him a 20 percent interest.

At Starr's funeral, the C. V. Starr & Company directors discussed plans for New Year's Eve. They unanimously agreed that Starr would have wanted the big destination party he had planned to occur, even in his absence. So they all piled up to the slopes to pay another tribute to the man that they all continued to call Mr. Starr.

The outing mixed disaster with farce and tragedy. That weekend, government officials raided the resort, on a tip that it had been hiring illegal Austrian immigrants among the ski instructors. The staff, however, most of whom were Chinese, thought they were the targets. So they fled, leaving the executives to run the place themselves.

The next day, newly installed gondolas broke loose and tumbled along the trails, so Greenberg had to ski down the mountain to warn others and prevent injuries. One of the saunas erupted that night, causing a fire. At lunch the day after that, Greenberg sat with two children of the company's medical doctor, Richard McCormack. The kids were eagerly awaiting their father's arrival. A ski instructor soon whispered into Greenberg's ear that Dr. McCormack had suddenly passed away from natural causes. It was left to Greenberg to break this devastating news to the children.

It was as if the gods were rattling.

After Starr's death, Greenberg got a call from Tom Watson, owner of 20 percent of Starr's beloved Mt. Mansfield Company. Watson wanted to discuss buying the rest of Mt. Mansfield, suggesting that C. V. Starr & Company would not want to own the resort anymore. Greenberg said they should discuss that. When they met, Watson acted as if there were no question but that he was buying the company. Greenberg slowed the conversation down.

"I'd be happy to hear your offering price," Greenberg said. "But before you tell me, I want it to be the same price at which you'd be willing to sell."

Watson nodded at the buy-sell proposal and then made his bid. Greenberg turned the tables and repurchased Watson's 20 percent—and would spend the next two decades developing the property into one of America's leading resorts.

■ ■ ■

During 1967 and 1968, Greenberg had formulated a new vision for the reorganization of Starr's insurance companies—C. V. Starr & Company, AIRCO, the AIU, and the rest—and advisers were toiling at year-end to prepare the documents necessary to implement it. Greenberg's goal was to establish one substantial company with a strong U.S. identity that would translate into a unique franchise with a defined corporate mission. Combining the various agencies, companies, and subsidiaries would create significant savings by eliminating duplicative operations such as claims processing and combining them into a single unit. The structure would help attract capital, which the growing companies needed in increasing amounts, as well as the special breed of independent and innovative managers and executives Greenberg envisioned as its lifeblood. In addition, there were still minority shareholders in many of the companies in the group, including American Home, National Union, and New Hampshire. That meant occasional difficulties in deciding how to allocate new business—to the wholly owned or majority-owned companies, for example.

It was not easy to assemble such a diverse organization under a single corporate roof. There were a vast number of different enterprises in the Starr organization, with far-flung roots and structures in scores of countries. The organization was also therefore fragile, Starr having just died, a young Greenberg in command, and a mix of assets that might appeal to assorted insurance companies or takeover artists. Such an integration could not be accomplished all at once, but every phase had to be meaningful, and the company had to be protected throughout the transition from takeover risk. So Greenberg asked the largest shareholders, together owning about one-third of the total, to sign a shareholders' agreement restricting their right to sell shares outside the group. Most did so.

As a first step in the reorganization, in December 1968, the month Starr died, AIRCO transferred its assets—including shares in American Home, National Union, and New Hampshire, as well as the American Life Insurance Company (ALICO)—to the subsidiary Morgan Stanley had created to acquire National Union one year earlier, the one its creators called American International Enterprises. But Greenberg thought that "enterprises" sounded too speculative. Chewing it over with Matthews, still a partner at Morgan Stanley then, and reflecting that Starr and his team had always liked being part of a group, the name *American International Group* emerged, and AIG was christened.

The next step, completed in June 1969, was for AIG to acquire from the public all the shares of American Home, National Union, and

New Hampshire that it did not already own. Matthews and M. Bernard Aidinoff, a partner with the law firm of Sullivan & Cromwell, devised a way to do that in one fell swoop: AIG would offer shares in itself in exchange for all shares in each of those three companies, using a single offering plan circulated to all target shareholders. Dubbed a "triple exchange offer," the document describing the deal ran 200 pages, with a stack of exhibits—charters, licenses, projections, contracts—standing a foot tall.

The team's elaborate disclosure documents described the complex array of companies involved and how the valuations of each were made. The valuations resulted in a package of securities offered to each of the target shareholders: so many AIG common shares or other securities for so many shares of each target.[12] The offer worked; when AIG closed the triple exchange offer, it ended up owning 95 percent of American Home, 95 percent of National Union and 85 percent of New Hampshire. In second-step mergers, the remaining minority shares were acquired for cash, giving AIG total ownership of each.[13] As a result, AIG became a public company with a relatively large number of shareholders and its shares were registered with the Securities and Exchange Commission.

Planning to implement the operational side of the transaction had been under way for nearly two years. It involved melding the operations of the three companies as well as integrating ALICO, which operated life insurance businesses in scores of countries outside the United States. Senior executives responsible for each area coordinated their parts of the business and worked to develop an integrated control system across the global businesses. They agreed on how to combine branch offices, employee training programs, claims processing facilities, investment departments, and back-office operations. As a result of that extensive planning, when the deal was consummated, the worldwide business operation became one and went into operation with few noteworthy operational errors. AIG estimated the aggregate value of the 1969 triple exchange offer at $242 million (about $2 billion in today's dollars).[14]

In 1970, Greenberg led the same team that closed the 1969 triple exchange offer to design a further big step in the integration process. As a tribute to Starr, the business of the AIU was renamed Starr International Company (fondly called SICO, pronounced *cee-ko*); it was incorporated and most of its insurance assets put into a subsidiary. Those assets, along with most of C. V. Starr & Company's insurance assets, were then transferred to AIG in exchange for AIG shares. The assets left out of the transaction included Starr Tech and a few other small specialty agencies, in fields such as aviation and marine insurance, not suitable for the envisioned scale of the new public company.

In the 1970 exchange, SICO received AIG shares with a market value that far exceeded the book value of the insurance assets—in the amount of $110 million. SICO and its shareholders, who were the dozen top executives that Starr had installed in his organization, were legally entitled to that amount. But Greenberg made a bold proposal to his fellow SICO stockholders: that they should not keep that value entirely for themselves but rather set it aside in a legal structure designed to ensure that the core assets could not be extracted for personal use by SICO owners.[15]

The AIG shares would be put in a restricted account to be used for specific limited purposes, such as rewarding AIG employees and making investments as well as securing corporate control among the closely knit group to repel hostile takeovers by outsiders. These shares would be owned by a charitable trust rather than any individual person or corporation. The SICO shareholders unanimously agreed, solidifying a sense among themselves that they—Freeman, Greenberg, Manton, Roberts, Stempel, Tse, et al.—were a "band of brothers," fraternal partners in an exciting international insurance group inspired by the late Mr. Starr.

SICO not only used the shares for investment and other purposes, it also began a tradition of providing long-term incentives to AIG employees worldwide. Through a series of long-term profit participation plans SICO began in 1975, participants' long-term performance were tied directly to the engine that drove value for AIG shareholders: growth in AIG's earnings per share. Under each two-year plan, a participant could have AIG shares contingently set aside under a formula directly related to AIG's earnings. Participants became entitled to receive such shares upon retirement from AIG at the age of 65.

By tying the contingent, long-term reward from the SICO plan to increases in AIG's earnings, SICO developed a private company ownership mentality among outstanding employees in the public company. Participants could increase ownership in AIG without requiring AIG to issue stock, without diluting AIG's shareholders, and without costing

AIG anything. The arrangements nurtured a culture of long-term commitment and loyalty of employees to AIG that was distinctive among U.S. corporations. It also avoided the pitfalls of executive compensation practices that emerged in corporate America decades later, when executive compensation became skewed to create incentives for taking excessive short-term risk.[16]

AIG had no ownership of SICO, only SICO's board could approve transfers of the AIG shares it owned, and SICO's board always reserved the right to terminate the program for any reason. It would have terminated the program if AIG were ever required to treat the payments as compensation expenses on its books. SICO's board sought recommendations from AIG's senior corporate executives about which employees to reward and the SICO board had to obtain final approval of the recommendations by a vote of its voting shareholders. No one was guaranteed inclusion; even those participating in a given two-year plan had no assurance that they would be included in the next.

Though novel and perhaps inspired, the program had some parallels. Many entrepreneurs use their own stock to compensate employees of companies they own stock in, including Ray Kroc, founder of McDonald's.[17] The SICO program shared some features with what would later emerge after 1974 as employee stock ownership plans (ESOPs).[18]

At AIG, the program contributed to the spirit of the company in which employees and employer looked out for one another in an atmosphere of camaraderie and mutual loyalty. Through this program, many AIG employees became wealthy based on the value of their stock in AIG. To illustrate, at its creation in 1970, SICO's stake in AIG was worth about $110 million; by 2005 it was worth $22 billion—and throughout that time it had been regularly transferring meaningful numbers of its AIG shares to worthy AIG employees.[19]

Another advantage of this creative private/public structure was that it retained substantial control over AIG in SICO's management, protecting against the wave of hostile takeovers that swept through corporate America in the late 1960s.[20] SICO, after all, owned 30 percent of AIG's stock, a significant voting block against a hostile bid. Public companies can face periodic threats of unfriendly and unproductive battles for corporate control. During the 1960s, hostile bidders became increasingly imaginative. In the insurance industry, the prominent corporate takeover artist, Saul Steinberg, had used his relatively small company, Leasco, to win a hostile takeover battle for the estimable Reliance Insurance Company.[21]

And Greenberg still recalled an earlier visit to his office by Victor Hurd, that restive chairman of Continental Insurance. Continental had nearly 30 percent of the AIU pool and, after Youngman had sold his AIRCO shares to Continental, a stake in AIG. Hurd wanted to buy the rest of AIG. Greenberg thanked Hurd for the overture but declined, saying his company preferred to remain independent. Though Hurd left quietly, he was free to initiate takeover efforts, perhaps seeking private deals with other unfriendly shareholders to increase his stake. Accordingly, vesting substantial voting control of AIG in SICO offered a way to protect AIG from hostile bidders, whether Victor Hurd, Saul Steinberg, or anyone else.

The challenge of designing an effective structure for Starr's old collection of insurance businesses had been met. AIG's stock price quadrupled between May 1969 and August 1972. The company's vision was coming into focus and its culture coalescing around it.

Chapter 4

Vision and Culture

Growing an international insurance business requires people with a broad skill set: competitive, innovative, daring, risk savvy. The group must feel part of something important, not merely an organization, but a business team with a shared vision. AIG gathered together a large group of like-minded people sharing those traits and reinforcing their effects in colleagues.

There was no single trait that Greenberg looked for but these employees tended to fit a model type that he called the "white blackbird."[1] These were individuals with an entrepreneurial conviction and a unique tenacity to forge profitable change. At work, they pioneered the development of desirable products in a demanding environment that was based on innovation, political astuteness, market awareness and technical discipline. This entrepreneurial spirit would define AIG's culture.

Decades before *networking* became a household term, Greenberg invested substantially in developing relationships—with regulatory authorities, insurance brokers, customers, foreign ministers, other executives, and AIG employees. Personal relationships are essential to obtaining opportunities and overcoming obstacles. For AIG, Greenberg worked closely with insurance departments from New York to China to speed product approval and open new profit centers.

One relationship proved valuable in 1970 when AIG was looking for a new acquisition in Taiwan. Starr's longtime colleague, K. K. Tse, led the hunt. The Nan Shan Life Insurance Company was ailing financially but had a license in a locale poised for economic prosperity.[2] Tse, a Chinese citizen, was respected in Taiwan and paved the way for AIG to acquire Nan Shan, though it would take delicate negotiations. Above all, Tse knew, as a matter of culture, that it would be important for all constituents of Nan Shan to meet the top person of any company proposing to acquire it.

Tse introduced Greenberg to Nan Shan's board of directors and senior managers, and to Taiwan's prime minister, finance minister, and other officials. The prime minister, who had admired Starr and trusted Tse, advised on the legal and cultural steps they needed to follow. Government officials suggested having Tse become the nominal owner of the company, which could not be owned by foreigners. Tse then escorted Greenberg to meet owners of other local Taiwanese insurance companies, many of whom worked in tiny offices run by one or two people writing out contract policies by hand. Greenberg and Tse walked up countless back alleys and rickety stairs on the journey, talking to company after company, sipping tea and learning how to bridge cultural differences.

The painstaking personal effort worked. Within months of the start of the search, AIG acquired Nan Shan. Tse became chairman, and it steadily grew into the second-largest life insurer in Taiwan, adding a substantial profit stream to AIG. This success was possible only by the combination of Tse's excellent relationship with the leaders in Taiwan, Greenberg's commitment to meet and embrace them one by one, and the passion of Nan Shan's personnel in the field.

AIG developed passion in teams like that at Nan Shan in all of its businesses, from Taiwan to America, by stressing throughout the organization that AIG was a meritocracy. From AIG's inception, managers were trained that nothing but effectiveness mattered, so employees were hired, rewarded, and promoted without regard to other litmus tests, such as pedigree or politics. AIG invested heavily in employee training programs at all levels, in all countries. At training sessions, presentations would be made by AIG's top global executives, including Greenberg. These programs stressed professionalism, referring to the importance of good judgment, integrity, and personal responsibility.

Dominant traits of many of Starr's senior executives, which carried over to AIG, were deep desires to succeed and to excel, never to disappoint or come up short. There were no employment contracts at AIG, and employees would sink or swim on the merits. The company would try to reassign employees to match their abilities to the company's needs. That created incentives for employees and protection for the company from being bound to ineffective personnel. A sense of permanence and mutual loyalty was provided through the compensation program administered by SICO, where employees could earn substantial fortunes, though not liquid until retirement from AIG at age 65. Though many retired at that age, AIG welcomed people interested in working beyond the retirement age typical at other companies, and many did—including senior executives who worked productively well into their 70s and 80s.

Many of AIG's senior managers were former U.S. military officers—including Freeman, Greenberg, and Roberts. Most of these executives were influenced by this experience. The command-and-control hierarchy of military discipline, loyalty, and organization became part of AIG's culture. Managers and employees assumed that corporate directives would be followed. There was no hand-wringing and little debate. Once decisions were made, discussion or dissension down the ranks was essentially unheard of. Employees knew that the company's senior management would support them in the field, whatever danger might come.

AIG's culture of effectiveness was reinforced by the profit center model and the cardinal principle of earning an underwriting profit. That primary objective meant aggressive control of expenses and constant risk assessment. In a historic shift for the industry, emphasis allocated more corporate power to actuaries, statisticians, and underwriters, as headquarters made clear that the company valued such technical skills.[3] The industry began to employ models and data analysis in all lines, with pricing determined accordingly. There is no substitute for human judgment, and overreliance on data and models can mislead inexperienced analysts. So AIG relied on both the new science and the ancient art of underwriting proficiency.

AIG's culture was characterized by a relentless quest to be first—first to develop and launch products, first to open and grow markets, first in performance from earnings to growth to assets. The culture spawned a commitment to innovation unlike the culture at any other insurance company. People appreciated that insurance was a service that could not be patented, requiring constant invention, swift product introduction, and promotion, endlessly repeated. Creativity was ignited by paying close attention to trends and pockets of hazards where insurance was needed.

Headlines from the early 1970s told of harrowing tales from aircraft hijacking to kidnapping. Governments responded by investing in security; American Home developed an insurance product. During 1970 to 1972, hijackings were common. While a few posed serious threats of death or bodily injury, most exposed passengers to the more quotidian risks of diverted flights, an overnight hotel stay in an undesired destination and general aggravation. Hijackers were more often protestors rather than terrorists in those days and got away with transgressions due to the primitive state of airport security and prevailing sense that the risks centered on annoyance rather than destruction.[4]

The airlines had long used insurance to cover damage to aircraft, and AIG grew a substantial aviation division that wrote many of the policies.[5] The Nixon administration created a federal program to backstop this private insurance.[6] But no one was looking out for passengers. They were protected only when they had a claim against an airline for personal injuries. The costs of inconvenience to hijacked passengers had not been covered, although a frequent passenger complaint. So American Home created passenger insurance to compensate for inconvenience.[7]

This insurance enabled passengers, for a few dollars per ticket, to buy peace of mind for their flights, receiving compensation when costly and inconvenient diversions occurred. For distribution, American Home offered adding the product onto the accident and health policies of its existing customers. The company also developed relationships with the airlines through the ticket purchase process, making it easy for passengers to buy the insurance with their tickets. The innovation did not deter hijackings—improved security did that. However, the insurance comforted passengers, kept them traveling, and repaid some portion of the cost of flying in the unfriendly skies of the early 1970s.

In the quest to bring to the U.S. insurance coverage traditionally available only through Lloyd's of London, National Union developed protection for another problem beginning to ravage some Americans: kidnapping for ransom. Well-known kidnappings making front-page news in the early 1970s struck affluent targets such as the Getty, Hearst, and Bronfman families. On July 10, 1973, in Rome, the kidnappers of 16-year-old John Paul Getty III demanded a ransom of $17 million (about $83 million in today's dollars). The family balked, as Getty's grandfather and namesake, the oil tycoon, refused to pay. Negotiations only concluded four months later, after the captors severed one of the boy's ears and sent it to a local newspaper. The family reportedly paid $2.2 million for the return of the permanently traumatized lad.[8]

The elder Getty explained that his resistance to paying stemmed from concern that capitulation would encourage copycat kidnappings and add incentives for the period's wave of terrorist campaigns. Although a small market in kidnap and ransom insurance had existed at Lloyd's since the 1920s, U.S. demand for coverage grew in the early 1970s. Demand soared as domestic corporations expanded globally, increasingly placing factories and plants abroad, and often in countries where kidnappings recurred. Guerilla warriors in Colombia once abducted an American business executive stationed there and demanded millions in ransom from his employer—a fictionalized adaptation of which is retold in the 2001 film, *Proof of Life*.[9]

In response, National Union brought kidnapping and ransom insurance to the U.S. market. National Union's policies were offered both to families and to multinational corporations. It enlisted expert assistance in this dicey field by partnering with Clayton Consultants, a private firm specializing in kidnapping prevention, hostage negotiations, and rescue. Together with Clayton Consultants,[10] National Union trained customers in how to reduce the risk of kidnapping. The policies required both sides to keep their existence strictly confidential, lest the policy's existence encourage kidnappers to target the policyholder. The policies included an agreement to involve law enforcement authorities in any kidnapping that occurred.

As AIG built business from a diverse range of products in the 1970s, the company sought a way to shed some of the risk. Managers also wanted a way to assure plenty of capital to continually expand the insurance businesses. To achieve both objectives, in 1977, AIG led several other insurers to build a reinsurance company. For this task, they commissioned Transatlantic, the underutilized business acquired for a song back in December 1967, courtesy of Guy Carpenter.[11] The group of insurance companies together invested $100 million. AIG retained a disproportionate percentage of ownership compared to AIG's capital invested: AIG staked one-fifth of the capital investment but retained a two-fifths ownership interest. Renamed Trans Re, the company became a force in the market.

Though Greenberg earned a reputation as being a tough boss to work for, if something happened to an employee, he would assist in any way he could. If someone had grave health or marital problems or children with serious illness, he would make himself available and provide resources that might help. If an employee halfway around the world was in trouble, he would send a plane with aid. Creating such a sense of closeness in such a sprawling enterprise was difficult but worthwhile as it bred a powerful sense of loyalty among employees.

There were few secrets at AIG. When something happened—a covered catastrophe, a competitor's advance, a regulatory snafu—AIG managers knew Greenberg would hear about it. The sooner he knew about bad news, the better off those involved would be. Greenberg's wrath befell those who delayed or deceived, and he had no problems chewing out deviant personnel in front of their peers. Managers could always gauge the gravity of a situation by how quickly Greenberg called to give his impression of it.

Greenberg regularly called scores of executives to check in, even if only for a few minutes, though sometimes for much longer, to give his view of the state of things and ask others what they thought. Often, these overtures were intended less to add his two cents substantively than to make people aware that he knew what was going on. Greenberg demonstrated passion and a belief that presence meant something. He set an example of being there, never "mailing it in," so employees got the message that they could not mail it in either. Passion cannot be bestowed on employees, but demonstrating it can be contagious.

AIG was not an easy place to work and was certainly not for the complacent. There was a kind of self-filtering employee base: few who were not up for what AIG demanded would accept a job there in the first place, and those who found themselves unprepared quickly moved on. The investor and writer Phil Fisher once analogized corporate culture to a restaurant offering a menu that would attract or repel a certain kind of investor. AIG attracted competitive, type-A personalities.

Perhaps AIG's ultimate cultural distinction was its appeal to talented professionals.[12] Brian Duperreault, who began working at AIG in the early 1970s, rising to run the AIU for two decades before becoming CEO of ACE, a competitor, reflected on his years at AIG in an industry retrospective:[13]

> Professionalism and excellence were the standard and there was a certain relentlessness to it—a relentless desire for excellence and to be the best. [Greenberg] was an iconoclast too, so he was not going to do something that everybody else did. He was going to do something different. So there was this feeling of innovation, of changing the way things were done. That became the core ethos of the company and we all bought into it. We all thought about new products and changing how we approached the business, to try something innovative. Whether it was technology or products or sales, we felt we were supposed to change, not protect the status quo. That was the difference.

Greenberg said for the same retrospective:

> We [built] a great organization, a great team. One person doesn't do that. It was a team of many, many great people. It helped build a great culture in an organization that was best in class. It doesn't happen easily, and it doesn't happen in every company. We bred a lot of people for the industry. If you look around the industry a lot of people came from AIG.

Like Dupperault, at least a dozen AIG executives went on to serve as CEOs of other major insurance companies. Given its size measured by employee numbers, that yield put AIG among the leading progenitors of CEOs in corporate America, rivaling the likes of larger companies such as General Electric and IBM.[14] AIG alumni who became

CEOs elsewhere include two of Greenberg's sons, Jeffrey and Evan, who became CEO at Marsh & McLennan and ACE, respectively.[15]

In addition, a number of associated senior executives were inducted into the International Insurance Hall of Fame maintained by the University of Alabama. Begun in 1957, this honors some 100 insurance industry innovators, starting with Benjamin Franklin, who established America's first fire insurance company, and including Starr (1975), Greenberg (1989), and Manton (1999)—as well as Duperreault (2011).[16]

Complementing these executives and staff was a truly distinctive breed of AIG executive, epitomized by John Roberts, called the "mobile overseas personnel" or MOP. This group did service stints in numerous countries during their career, as many as 10 to 15, taking two-to-three year terms in each place. It was almost like the foreign service of the United States. They were corporate ambassadors who became legends within AIG. An experienced MOP could walk into any AIG office in the world, from Taiwan to Santiago, and know just about everyone. Having traveled widely, he could troubleshoot the thorniest problem successfully anywhere in the world, whether obtaining the release of colleagues captured by hostile governments or negotiating with customers perceived to have fabricated claims. The personality type could vary, from the diplomatic to the irascible, the elegant to the brusque. But they tended all to be wise, urbane, and multilingual—cowboys, pioneers, Indians, a cadre of colorful actors that made the company tick.

During the 1970s, AIG was growing: from Trans Re to Nan Shan and American Home and dozens of other businesses. One challenge was aggregating the financial and insurance information from the scores of countries and several different kinds of businesses (such as accident and health, life, property and casualty, or travel insurance) engaged in millions of transactions annually. Spearheading this task was Peter Dalia, the company's chief accounting officer from 1969 to 1985. Dalia spent the 1970s building an elaborate system of internal control over financial reporting and insurance reserve estimates.[17] Information had to be prepared in multiple formats, one complying with local practices in every locale where the company operated and a parallel set complying with U.S. laws and Securities and Exchange Commission requirements. Dalia established an audit committee, led by members of the board of directors and staffed by senior accounting officials. He divided AIG's operational world into 30 reporting regions, appointed controllers of each, and established foreign and domestic internal auditors to oversee everything. Dalia organized annual meetings for the regional controllers to discuss challenges and share solutions and sponsored regional seminars to assure adequate training and reviews.

In addition, Dalia formalized the existing internal audit systems to support the profit center model in every business unit, assuring that it worked to promote accountability as intended. Dalia created a system of budgetary reporting so that every region's financial statements were compared to the most recent budget, the next budget in relation to those financial statements, and so on. All these systems and controls not only enabled AIG to prepare reliable and relevant financial statements in accordance with local and U.S. accounting requirements, but to avoid surprises and assure managerial accountability for their budgets. Any prospective deviation between a budget and a financial statement was flagged beforehand and the manager summoned to account for it. AIG continued this impressive commitment to internal controls over the ensuing decades, both before and after passage of the Sarbanes-Oxley Act of 2002, which emphasized internal accounting controls in corporate America.

AIG's workforce grew considerably during the 1970s, with its New York City personnel alone spread over four buildings in Lower Manhattan, including the 102 Maiden Lane building, which Starr had acquired in 1947, and 90,000 square feet in the Cities Service (Citgo) Building nearby at 70 Pine Street. Just as it had been important to consolidate AIG's worldwide businesses and related controls, it was more efficient to put its 2,000 New York City employees under one roof in a new global headquarters. In the early 1970s, New York City was in the midst of a deep economic crisis, and corporations had been moving to the suburbs. Companies such as General Foods, IBM, and Pepsi had left, and several of AIG's fellow tenants at 70 Pine were considering departing, including Marsh & McLennan, Merrill Lynch, and Peat Marwick Mitchell. Citgo's chairman and president both passed away and the reigning CEO wanted to live in Tulsa, closer to corporate field operations.

A member of Citgo's board, a partner at Loeb Rhoades, in which C. V. Starr & Company had an investment, informed Greenberg of this situation. AIG saw an appealing opportunity, given its needs and the building's location, so long as the price was right. AIG told Citgo that unless the rent was lowered, AIG would move out or, alternatively, would buy the building. Citgo asked $34 million for a sale. It noted its recent $22 million overhaul and upgrading project—new air conditioning, elevators, and plumbing. AIG countered at $10 million, part cash, part financed. The deal closed at $15 million all cash, a big New York real estate transaction given the city's fiscal woes. Mayor Abraham Beame symbolized the significance by hosting the signing at a press conference in his office and informed the media he was "grateful" for AIG's commitment.[18]

AIG renamed 70 Pine the American International Building and moved into this venerable piece of the New York skyline, the last of the great prewar Art Deco towers, completed in April 1932. The timing of AIG's purchase, if not the event, marked the turning point for the city. Mayor Beame began to reinvigorate New York, and his successor, Ed Koch, amplified the effort, which dovetailed with the success of the memorable national campaign: "I love New York." The troubled New York of the 1970s turned into the prosperous New York of the 1980s.

The American International Building in Lower Manhattan soared 952 feet, making it the seventh-tallest U.S. building when AIG bought it, and third in New York, after other Manhattan landmarks the Empire State Building (1,250 feet) and the Chrysler Building (1,046 feet). The base at 70 Pine is of dark granite and the rest is brick, in tones that lighten as the tower rises, and where, at upper floors, every third brick is rounded instead of squared.[19] The landmark building's skyline drama is highlighted by massive floodlights from the 55th to the top (66th floor) where an enclosed room reached by a single small elevator offers sweeping panoramic views of New York City and beyond. The facility was tastefully decorated, from metal Art Deco butterflies in a vast two-story orange marble lobby, to rich mahogany furniture in the offices and conference rooms above. The senior executive suite was on the 18th floor, with offices housing Greenberg, Manton, and Roberts, along with furnishings that once belonged to Starr.

Seventy Pine became the professional home to many thousands of dedicated AIG employees, building the largest insurance company in the world. Greenberg had pulled a diverse set of companies together under a single corporate umbrella and united its New York–based employees under one roof. His vision of building a global insurance fortress was being realized.

Chapter 5

The Internationalist

With personal relationships so central to an international business, and the AIG commitment of managers engaging with counterparts, travel schedules were grueling. Throughout the 1960s and into the early 1970s, the preferred method of global travel for business executives was on Pan Am—like AIG, an American company pioneering the opening of global markets at a time when there were few multinational companies in the world. Many flights were satisfactory, but long-haul trips from New York to Moscow, Tokyo, or Beijing invariably entailed stops along the way. In that period, hotels for international business travelers were scarce, so Greenberg stayed in the guest homes that Starr had established in the cities where his companies did substantial business.

Starr had flown Pan Am for global flights, though for shorter and domestic flights he acquired, in 1952, the company's first corporate airplane, which traveled at 230 miles per hour, carried six and could fly for six hours, then a nonstop flight from New York to Chicago.[1] Range and speed were the most important features AIG looked for in corporate aircraft, which it needed for its executives in pretty much the same way that working Americans need a car: to get to work. AIG's early planes, in the 1970s, not only had limited range and speed, but were also cramped. This often meant that Greenberg and his wife, Corinne, who invariably accompanied him, slept head-to-toe on a pair of seats as they crossed the Aleutian Islands. When necessary, they would stop at the facetiously named "World Famous Weathered Inn" in Cold Bay, Alaska, an aptly named town that often seemed populated by as many polar bears as people.

Throughout the 1970s, on numerous lengthy international business trips, Greenberg developed relationships with government and business leaders vital to opening markets and building businesses abroad. He nurtured many of these into friendships and forged some of those into an impressive brain trust for AIG that constituted its International Advisory Board (IAB). Officially formed in 1981, the IAB boasted many active luminaries in foreign governments and international business who met annually with AIG's corporate directors and periodically with management.[2] Early members included Aritoshi Soejim, former Japanese finance minister and president of the leading Japanese corporate group, Nippon Hilton; Edwin Stopper, president of the prominent Swiss banking firm, Banque Leu; Yuet-Keung Kan, chairman of the Bank of East Asia; and Baron Leon Lambert, descendant of Baron James de Rothschild, and a pioneer of modern international banking.[3]

Greenberg tapped Henry A. Kissinger to be the chairman of the IAB. Kissinger was a fellow internationalist, a former professor who had served as both national security adviser and secretary of state for President Richard M. Nixon, before returning to civilian life to write books on international affairs and manage an advisory firm. Secretary Kissinger led IAB's formal meetings, held annually over two days, beginning with his overview of the world. Never using notes as he canvassed with penetrating lucidity, Secretary Kissinger would first explain how he saw the world, identify issues and trends, and compare how he would address contemporary challenges with how the incumbent U.S. government was approaching them. In his inimitable gravelly and accented voice, Kissinger would then turn to someone around the table, say Buck Freeman, and ask, "Buck, what do you think?" Freeman would opine.

Then John Roberts, for instance, would comment and the dialogue was off and running on the subject of U.S. foreign policy.

IAB meetings often featured distinguished guest speakers, who included many notables from the worlds of international finance, diplomacy, and business. Among the most memorable speeches was that given by Richard Nixon. The former U.S. president surveyed every region of the world in a riveting lecture that lasted more than one hour. Speaking without notes, Nixon demonstrated his unmatched ability to articulate a clear vision of his country's national interests, offering insights of value to all those assembled.

Another speaker was Ratan N. Tata, the prominent Indian businessman. Greenberg's relationship with Tata included the creation of a joint venture in India between Tata's companies and AIG.[4] India restricts foreign ownership of insurance operations, so it has always been difficult for AIG and other U.S. insurers to do business there. The joint venture with Tata opened the door for AIG to have high-level discussions, including with the country's prime minister, to change that. As a result, AIG received the first foreign insurance license from India, though with limited ownership. It received assurances that if and when the restrictions on foreign ownership were relaxed, AIG would be the first entitled to take advantage.

All IAB members were available to AIG for a wide range of consultations and other engagements to help solve problems or open doors. A good example involved the efforts of IAB member Moeen Qureshi, the international financier who once served as interim prime minister of Pakistan. One problem he helped AIG resolve had seeds sown on January 2, 1972. Zulfikar Ali Bhutto, newly installed prime minister of Pakistan, announced the nationalization of the country's banking and insurance sectors, including AIG's life insurance business run by its ALICO unit. Pakistan did not propose to pay any compensation for the taking, though the vast business representing nearly one million policies through 8,000 agents was valuable.

Negotiations for a fair price, begun by ALICO's senior executive in Pakistan, stalled. Other senior AIG executives from New York went to Islamabad to add pressure. They met with a stonewalling bureaucracy. After a month of fruitless efforts, the pursuit seemed futile. A few months later, Bhutto appeared in New York to give a speech to a meeting of the Foreign Policy Association, whose members include international business leaders with deep interest in U.S. foreign affairs, Greenberg among them. Advance copies of Bhutto's text indicated that topics would include an appeal to the gathering for making direct financial investments in Pakistan. Ahead of the speech, Greenberg ambled up to the speakers' table for a word with the prime minister.

"I'm Hank Greenberg, head of AIG, the company that used to own ALICO in your country. Your government recently nationalized my company, but we have not yet been compensated. I understand that you plan to appeal in your speech tonight for direct foreign investment from this audience. Knowing what I know, it will be difficult for me not to rise during the Q&A and share that information."[5]

Bhutto summoned an aide to his side and asked after the status of the AIG compensation determinations. The aide said he did not know the status but would look into it promptly. Greenberg thanked the gentlemen. The speech went off as prepared, and the government of Pakistan soon paid AIG for its confiscated assets. Bhutto, a controversial figure, was overthrown in 1977 and executed two years later at the direction of the country's Supreme Court. He had been found guilty of politically motivated crimes, including murder. After years of upheaval, Bhutto's daughter, Benazir Bhutto, in 1988 was elected prime minister, the first woman elected to head the government of a Muslim country, and a staunch ally of the United States.

Political turmoil consumed Pakistan, however, and Benazir Bhutto was turned out of office for an interim period. Throughout this turbulent time, AIG's executives remained in touch with Pakistani officials, expressing continued interest in reopening for business there. Benazir Bhutto was restored to office in 1993. As a member of the IAB, Greenberg asked Qureshi for help in reopening the country to AIG for business. Thanks to Qureshi, Greenberg met with Benazir Bhutto on one of her visits to the United States and repeated AIG's interest. The government returned ALICO's insurance license to AIG and the company resumed operations.

Greenberg saw early in his career the influential role that nongovernmental organizations, such as the Council on Foreign Relations and the Center for Strategic and International Studies, could play in international relations. In addition to gathering internationalists together to discuss global affairs, such organizations conduct research and host discussion forums. Greenberg joined these in the 1970s and provided leadership and financial support throughout his career. Among those he eventually led were the Asia Society, which he chaired for many years; the Council on Foreign Relations, where he served as vice chairman for many years alongside Peter G. Peterson as chairman, where the two developed a close relationship; the Peterson Institute for International Economics, on whose board he served for more than a decade; and the Center for the National Interest, which he helped to found and has chaired for many years.[6]

As a pioneering internationalist, Greenberg anticipated the influence such organizations could have, well before other international business executives did.[7] Thereafter, he tried to shape that influence.[8] In the 1970s, these organizations were of great utility to a dynamic international business organization such as AIG, whose leadership must have an abiding interest in the foreign policy of the United States, an active appreciation of international economics, and a deep curiosity about other cultures. These "think tanks" ascended into the role they have today at the pinnacle of policy formulation.

Greenberg's intense business and civic leadership resulted in numerous invitations to join advisory boards or committees formed by many governments and business organizations. U.S. presidents and cabinet members of both parties named him to boards concerning finance, intelligence, national defense, and trade. Abroad, he headed advisory boards to Hong Kong, the Philippines, and the mayor of Shanghai, and served on boards for the China Development Forum, the mayor of Seoul, and Tsinghua University. Among business organizations, he was chairman or vice chairman of many U.S.-foreign business councils, including those with ASEAN, China, and Korea.[9] The service, in which Greenberg remains very active, is a two-way street, where Greenberg contributes substantial knowledge and gains useful business information in return.

Frequent high-level international business trips yield valuable information about foreign policy issues and geoeconomic conditions. This is of great use not only to business executives and policy researchers but to government leaders. Dating to the 1970s, the U.S. government regularly debriefed Greenberg, on behalf of senior government officials, before and after many of his foreign trips.

Greenberg also perceived that while the foreign policy establishment of the 1970s in the United States tended to think of the world in *geopolitical* terms, the world would increasingly be defined in *geoeconomic* terms. With that inspiration, he created a research center within the Council on Foreign Relations devoted to the study of geoeconomic phenomena, which still today offers cutting-edge thought about topics such as energy, exchange rates, immigration, and trade. Much of that research, like much of AIG's entrepreneurship, focuses on thinking about contingencies: what would happen if . . . .

For an international business, such efforts to look around corners are crucial, though it is impossible for a business or consortium to prevent such events as war, nationalization, or expropriation. In a dramatic example, in early 1978, armed officials appeared at AIG's local office in Lagos, Nigeria. They announced that the government was seizing control of the company and would pay, as compensation, the par value of its shares of common stock. As any businessperson knows, however, par value, often merely $1 per share, is a nominal sum stated mostly for bookkeeping purposes. The actual value of the shares of a prosperous company, such as AIG in Nigeria, is vastly higher. The proposed compensation was a subterfuge, in violation of international law, which required paying a reasonable compensation for the nationalized assets.

The officials also took custody of Louis D. LeFevre, general manager in the Lagos office. His colleagues promptly reported this to AIG's New York office, where Greenberg immediately enlisted American diplomats for aid. His first call went to the office of Secretary of State Cyrus Vance and one of his top aides, Matthew Nimetz, who at once assigned staff to contact counterparts in Nigeria to assure LeFevre's safety and secure his release. President Jimmy Carter was planning a state visit to Nigeria, set for March 31 to April 3, 1978, to meet in Lagos with President Obasanjo. In an insightful measure, President Carter, a Georgia native, tapped for assistance an insurance executive from Atlanta, an African American whom Carter thought stood a greater chance of success negotiating the release and payment. It worked. Nigerian officials freed LeFevre and settled AIG's claim. AIG could not prevent such nationalization, but it could act quickly to mitigate losses and deter other governments from following similar courses of action.

AIG's leadership in international business and policy, and such battles against nationalization that it fought for itself on a number of occasions, equipped it to wage similar battles for customers. These customers were the hundreds of U.S. businesses that rapidly expanded internationally beginning in the late 1970s and early 1980s. They put substantial assets at risk abroad, often in developing countries lacking a history of private enterprise, commercial codes, or the rule of law. Political risk was great and these clients needed insurance against it. While other insurance companies were withdrawing from the market for political risk insurance, AIG widened its commitment.

Political risk insurance was a lousy business for companies with poor underwriting discipline. Yet it was a lucrative business for those, like AIG, that excel at assessing and pricing risk—as well as recovering losses—in environments where it had substantial direct experience. It was a delicate balance, akin to "underwriting a politician's mind," as some in the field described it. But AIG had long-standing operations in scores of countries run by employees—mobile overseas personnel (MOPs) and otherwise—who cultivated abiding relationships with national leaders. Using that knowledge, AIG wrote policies in many diverse countries covering risks ranging from government default on contracts to losses from expropriation of private assets. In those cases, AIG would first pay the customer's loss and then seek reimbursement from the foreign government. In the days before "globalization," enforcing such rights often required educating foreign officials and executives about contractual promises and commercial obligations.

An instance with international significance occurred in Peru in 1985. In July 1985, Alan García was elected president, after running on a nationalization platform. The next month, the Peruvian army stormed the facilities of Belco Petroleum, an American oil company. The troops seized its assets and ousted its personnel, putting them on planes bound for America. Total losses ran to $250 million, and the company filed a claim with AIG under its insurance policy covering political risks for a large portion. AIG paid Belco and then, exercising its rights under the policy, filed a claim with the government of Peru. AIG contended that the government's seizure was an expropriation under international and U.S. law entitling it, as successor under the policy, to fair compensation.

To enlist the powers of the U.S. government in such an exercise, AIG had to persuade several federal officials that the government's action was indeed an expropriation. If so, under American law then in effect, the United States could sanction Peru. Getting such a declaration was a protracted process that required sustained arm twisting. AIG had many supporters in the cause, in Congress, the White House, and industry, among insurers, and cabinet officials, but the politically charged nature of the episode limited their freedom of action. In the end, the U.S. government agreed with AIG and supported its right to sue the government of Peru.

The U.S. government also supported other formal sanctions, including blocking Peru's access to world capital markets, interfering with its right to participate in international events, seizing Peruvian assets held in the United States, and so on. The result was high-level pressure from the president of the United States and the secretaries of treasury and state. Though the pressure did not persuade García to relent, his immediate successor, Alberto Fujimori, was more ready to see the light.

At that point, several years after the initial taking, the International Monetary Fund and World Bank added pressure. They stressed that the Belco battle was a blemish on Peru's record. It had to be cleared up if Peru was to access financial capital in world markets. President Fujimori dispatched a delegation to meet with Greenberg and other AIG executives in New York, where they negotiated a deal in which Peru would repay AIG over several years. AIG's pact enabled the government and international banking authorities to resume ordinary economic relations with the country.

By surrounding himself with informed and intelligent internationalists and maintaining many reliable sources—within AIG, on the IAB, at the Council on Foreign Relations, and in other such organizations— Greenberg developed a sophisticated perspective on how to do business internationally. This was characteristic of only a small number of American executives during the period before globalization, confined to the few truly multinational companies of the period. AIG insured many ventures, in which companies often stumbled in analyzing risks, costing both themselves and AIG, directly under policies written and indirectly due to international frictions that follow costly mistakes. AIG underwriters around the world tried informally to educate customers in analyzing political risk and assessing international relations. But Greenberg eventually perceived the need to develop formal dynamic guidance for America's chief executives.

AIG hired Gerald Komisar, a U.S. government official whom Greenberg had known for many years to have good sources around the world. Komisar had been stationed in many different countries in a long career and was fluent in several languages, including Chinese. Greenberg asked Komisar to help educate customers AIG had insured to help them avoid making mistakes that lead to business disruption, insurance losses, and adverse political consequences. The idea was to assemble something like the "President's Daily Brief," the national security document provided to the U.S. president. Komisar came up with a budget and a plan and began publishing the *Executive Briefing Book*.

AIG distributed copies, usually published weekly with occasional special editions featuring hot topics, to top executives of its largest customers. They also gave it to members of the IAB, to which Komisar also made a presentation about the background of the project and the methods used in developing it. Komisar created the book by maintaining his contacts with government officials and business leaders around the world. He would respond to particular questions AIG's largest insurance customers might pose, as well as develop topic ideas himself—all geared to providing advice about how to do international business in light of unfolding global developments.

Political risk is not the only risk of operating an overseas business, of course, which also presents quotidian risks facing any business. Chief among these is foreign currency exchange risk, whose fluctuations can offset profits, as well as the risks of internal financial misreporting or human resources lapses. An example of the latter arose in Turkey. AIG had formed a joint venture, orchestrated by Greenberg, Manton, and Roberts, to write property and casualty policies with a local insurance business. Partners included a prominent family, and the president was a reputable man and former government regulatory official.

Barely a year into the venture, however, the financial reports submitted to 70 Pine seemed askew. The relationships among premiums written, earnings, and reserves did not match up. On a trip to the Middle East, Greenberg dispatched his internal auditors to Turkey ahead of his visit to discuss the matter. He and Roberts arrived in Ankara later in the evening. They were dining at a favorite spot when the auditors rushed in. The joint venture's building was afire—along with the accounting records. By the time emergency rescue teams arrived, the joint venture's Turkish president had fled and was hiding in his home and would not come out. The story suggests a sad truth: it is difficult to rely on a person's reputation as a basis for predicting future performance, though there is not much else to go on.

Some content for AIG's *Executive Briefing Book* came from Greenberg, of course, based on his extensive travels. Greenberg had always stressed to his chief pilot, Franklin Davis, the importance of speed and range for his international trips, and Davis, characteristic of AIG employees, worked hard to deliver on the goals. Above all, however, the crew put a premium on safety. Given the amount of flying Greenberg's business philosophy required him to do, it is unsurprising that there were many harrowing encounters, near-misses, and brushes with fate. But, throughout, Greenberg gave a standing order to Captain Davis that could never be countermanded: the pilots were in charge of all aviation decisions, no matter what Greenberg might say once airborne.

Overseas assignments for AIG employees offered the excitement of opening markets, addressing foreign cultural mores, and tackling unusual problems. Underwriting presented peculiar challenges because every country's political system is unique. Doing business in Rhode Island is not all that different from doing business in Virginia; doing business in Russia, however, is very different from doing business in Vietnam.[10] Thanks to Starr's pioneering endeavors, many of the early companies within AIG were first and foremost international businesses. Greenberg expanded on that legacy, tirelessly traveling the world in the era before globalization to open new markets for AIG.

In an interview for this book, Charlene Barshefsky, the former U.S. trade representative, quipped that "Greenberg traveled more and knew more foreign dignitaries than nearly any U.S. secretary of state."[11] When asked in an interview for this book to comment, former secretary of state Henry Kissinger said: "I concur and I would be among his rivals."[12]

Chapter 6

Raising the Iron Curtain

In March 1968, the Central Intelligence Agency (CIA) found out that the Soviet Union's military had lost a nuclear submarine, the *K-129*, in the Pacific Ocean about 750 miles northwest of Hawaii. The Soviets did not know exactly where the sub was, but the Americans did. The *K-129* carried nuclear weapons, codebooks, cryptology, and other Soviet technological secrets of great value to the American side in the Cold War. The CIA devised a covert operation to retrieve the sunken sub and its valuable cargo from the bed of the Pacific, 15,000 feet deep.

The CIA commissioned the private shipping company owned by Howard R. Hughes, the eccentric industrialist, to build a specialized vessel for the top-secret recovery. Called the *Glomar Explorer*, the vessel cost several hundred million dollars (more than a billion dollars in today's terms). The *Glomar Explorer* was tailor-made to travel stealthily from the West Coast of the United States out to the depths of the distant North Pacific, regularly patrolled by Soviet naval ships. Built to appear designed for deep-sea mining research, the vessel was constructed with a massive storage hold in its middle and outfitted with elaborate cranes.

No one, especially not the savvy Hughes, would undertake such an expensive clandestine mission, an audacious underwater feat, without insurance. But few insurance companies would agree to underwrite such unusual risks, likened to the same period's exploration of space and the moon landing, or to keep the venture strictly confidential.

Hughes and the CIA turned to AIG. To arrange the insurance contract, Greenberg hosted a meeting in his New York apartment, gathering Lawrence R. Houston, general counsel of the CIA, and senior executives from Hughes's company. Within a few hours, they agreed on the principal terms, and within days, their lawyers finalized a comprehensive maritime insurance contract that enabled the recovery mission to proceed.

In early 1974, Greenberg was in Hong Kong chairing an AIG board meeting when a secretary interrupted with an urgent phone call. A senior U.S. government official informed Greenberg that the *Glomar Explorer* story had leaked to the press. The *Los Angeles Times* was about to go public with it. At that, Greenberg reported on the project to the board. The story ran but did not name AIG.

It was never revealed what assets the United States recovered or how much their value had been compromised by the media leaks. But one thing was clear: AIG had played a pivotal role in an important matter of national security.[1]

The Soviet Union was among the more perplexing places where AIG and its forerunners operated. Greenberg's first glimpse into the Soviet bloc was in 1964 during the Cold War, just after he had begun working at C. V. Starr & Company. He and John Roberts took a trip to Moscow. Greenberg had read an article in an insurance journal reporting that the Soviet state insurance company, Ingosstrakh, provided automatic insurance coverage to travelers on the country's transport systems.[2] Greenberg perceived an opportunity to get a foot in the door of what he thought could become a large insurance market: reinsuring Ingosstrakh to relieve the company of some exposure.

Greenberg and Roberts obtained government clearance from both sides of the Iron Curtain to make the trip. Arriving by plane in Moscow, both men got a strange feeling from the airport's bleak and tense atmosphere, sensing that they were crossing enemy lines.

Driving in from the airport, as they passed through Lubyanka Square, the government-appointed escort, sitting in the front passenger seat, eyed the Americans in the mirror and, with a cockeyed grin, asked, "Do you know what that building is?"

"No," Greenberg said.

"But you must recognize it from your training program," the escort said mischievously.

Looking up at, and recognizing, the imposing KGB headquarters, Greenberg played along. "It looked different," he quipped.

The Soviet government put its guests up at the Rossia Hotel, the prison-like fortress where all foreign business executives stayed in those days in order for the government to keep close watch on them. The restaurant's menu boasted a rich array of wonderful dishes, none of which were actually served. When ordered, waiters told patrons *Nyet*— "No," signaling not that the restaurant was out of the item, but that it was never offered. Diners were left with an unmemorable choice of typical but cheerless dishes—borscht and black bread perhaps.

During the next day's business meeting about Soviet travelers' reinsurance, both sides kept the conversation playful. While discussing the proposal with one official, Greenberg noticed a photograph on his desk displaying a building in Havana, Cuba.

"That looks like the building where my company housed our Cuban operations," Greenberg said, "before we pulled out on the eve of Fidel Castro's revolution in 1960."

"That may be," the official replied. "Now it is the building where Ingosstrakh houses the Soviet Union's Cuban operations."

"Please take care of that building," Greenberg said. "We will get it back—*soon*."

Though Greenberg's prophecy remains unfulfilled, and he did not then obtain the Soviet travelers reinsurance business, the visit opened the door to Russia. American Home wrote an insurance policy covering the July 15, 1968, inaugural flight of Aeroflot from Moscow to New York and formed a joint venture to offer insurance to U.S. and European tourists visiting the Soviet Union.[3]

AIG executives habitually tried to anticipate world events and prepare to respond to them. Roberts tried to imagine what would happen if and when the Cold War ended. With this quest to "look around corners," Roberts supervised a team of young colleagues to develop new business in eastern Europe, behind the Iron Curtain. The team branded this new mission the Socialist Countries Division and established headquarters in Vienna.[4]

An early trip took them to Moscow, where their hosts included contacts at Ingosstrakh, the state insurance company Greenberg and Roberts had met on their first trip in 1964. They visited with executives from an American International Underwriters (AIU) client, Cleveland Crane Company, which was building a factory in Russia. Cleveland Crane had insurance contracts with both the AIU and Ingosstrakh. Using that as an opening for more direct business, Roberts persuaded his counterparts to sign a contract in which the AIU reinsured the risk Ingosstrakh had taken. Though the deal was not much in size or scope, AIG had established another valuable contact in the Soviet Union. Few foreign companies enjoyed that access, which would pay dividends as the Iron Curtain rose.

Roberts discovered that construction projects behind the Iron Curtain were essentially self-insured, though officials did not think of it that way. For example, the Hungarian government borrowed $50 million abroad to build a local factory. When the factory was totally destroyed by a fire, the state insurance company transferred $50 million to the state construction company to pay the loss. But the government still needed to repay the foreign lending market and borrow another $50 million. Roberts persuaded the Hungarian project managers that this practice was a mistake. His team argued that if the state was going to borrow foreign money to build, it should insure these projects externally as well—using the AIU. Ensuing discussions were halting, intermittent, and inconclusive, but the AIG team kept talking with the Hungarians and other eastern Europeans anyway, for the chance of future business; that chance would come, even before the West won the Cold War.

In the late 1970s and early 1980s, across eastern Europe, Roberts detected small changes in many capitals, signs of an increasing interest in private enterprise as an alternative to Soviet-style communism. Particularly in Budapest, Hungary, Roberts noticed the gathering groundswell: restaurants were starting to develop and were allowed to make money, rather than just participate in a pool; taxi drivers were beginning to earn their own income rather than having to share it with other cab operators.[5] Across eastern Europe, AIG managers encountered many pioneers, from the East and the West, seeking to trade, whether in insurance and other services or goods and manufacturing. They cultivated relationships with business entrepreneurs eager to do deals, and increasingly with diplomats and political figures who had open minds about open markets.

AIG's efforts led to high-level meetings, one of which brought Greenberg together with the president of Romania, Nicolae Ceauşescu in May 1982. A Romanian insurance commissioner had encountered Greenberg at a conference in Manila, where he debated the merits of different kinds of insurance companies: Greenberg argued for the corporate form, owned by shareholders, while his opponent argued for the mutual form, owned by policyholders. Intrigued by the corporate form—then alien to Romania—the commissioner invited Greenberg to visit Romania and meet government officials. At the airport, the insurance commissioner who greeted Greenberg surprised him by saying that President Ceauşescu wished to see him right away. Ceauşescu, a self-declared "ambassador for world peace" then at the height of his powers, had instructed deputies to treat the event as equivalent to a state meeting. They seated the two men in oversized chairs opposite each other, in a cavernous room at the presidential palace. Several AIG executives and numerous Romanian government officials looked on as television cameras captured the proceedings.

Ceauşescu asked Greenberg: "Why is the West pointing ballistic missiles at the East?"

Posing such a question of political and military strategy to a businessman was unusual. But it was the kind of topic Greenberg thought about often and understood.

"When the East stops pointing ballistic missiles at the West," Greenberg replied, "the West will stop pointing them at the East," marking a standoff that mirrored the tough stubborn stances taken by both sides in the Cold War.

The two canvassed headline subjects of the day. Besides war and peace, they debated forms of government and principles of international economics and trade. Ceauşescu quizzed Greenberg on his business interests in eastern Europe. Greenberg explained the efforts of AIG's Socialist Countries Division to develop reinsurance projects in selected nations, including Romania. By the end of the conversation, Ceauşescu had warmed to Greenberg. Afterwards, as Greenberg walked around Bucharest, then a dark capital city, he imagined the vast possibilities that lay ahead for the country.

The Socialist Countries Division opened doors for AIG executives to have discussions with top officials in Hungary and Poland in addition to Romania. Three of the larger countries in the Warsaw Pact, Roberts envisioned a four-partner company—with each country a partner—to provide reinsurance in all those countries. But squabbling complicated that, as the Romanians and Poles each insisted on holding the largest percentage. Roberts improvised a creative solution. He formed three separate companies, one for each country to own; he then created an AIG partnership with each one and tied the network together by a new agency called the "European American Underwriting Agency in Vienna." The deal was signed, and the companies—called Romanian American Managers, Hungarian American Managers, and Polish American Managers—became affectionately known within AIG as RAM, HAM, and PAM.

The agency's portfolio grew to include not only reinsurance of commercial risks in each country but primary insurance covering a wide range of specialty risks, in fields as diverse as aviation, construction, and marine. It continued to face challenges, such as reprisals that threatened employee safety during Polish General Wojciech Jaruzelski's repression of Poland's Solidarity movement. But it paved the road for AIG to win business in future years, and to nurture the embryonic desire among citizens behind the Iron Curtain for the rewards of private enterprise.

Back in the USSR, in 1978 and 1979, AIG built on its relationships to make another deal with Ingosstrakh (the state insurance firm), to jointly underwrite the insurance for the 1980 Summer Olympics, to be held in Moscow. The plan was aborted, however, as President Jimmy Carter announced that the United States would boycott the Olympics in retaliation for the Soviet invasion of Afghanistan. The executive order also prohibited U.S. companies, including AIG, from participating in the event, putting AIG out of the business.

President Carter viewed the Soviet invasion of Afghanistan as part of a wider regional conflict extending to neighboring Iran, where in early 1979 AIG employees faced a harrowing ordeal that foreshadowed the hostage crisis later that year. In a violent coup, waged in the name of Islam, a flock of mullahs seized control of Iran, deposing Mohammad Rezā Pahlavi, the shah, a U.S. ally. After the shah abdicated, the mullahs nationalized AIG's business.

AIG had established its business in Iran just five years earlier, after the shah had asked David Rockefeller to organize a seminar in Tehran on financial services, a topic just beginning to engage the interest of international officials. Rockefeller invited Greenberg to speak. At the seminar, Greenberg, along with Roberts, met several Iranian executives with whom AIG soon formed a joint venture, called the Iran American International Insurance Company. To run the business, AIG relocated Koshrow C. ("K. C.") Shabani, a prominent Iranian American working at New Hampshire Insurance Company. His impressive connections in Iran were useful for AIG during the shah's tenure. The business prospered.

Shabani's fate changed dramatically with the fall of the shah amid the Iranian Revolution of 1979. Upon nationalizing the joint venture, the Iranians accused Shabani of being a spy for the CIA and asserted that Greenberg was the director of CIA operations in the Middle East. They confiscated Shabani's passport and put him in a high-security prison under cruel conditions. Twice, the guards told Shabani in the middle of the night they were going to shoot him. They took him outside and blindfolded him. Then they shot bullets into the air, laughed, and returned Shabani to his cell.[6] Greenberg was in regular telephone contact with Shabani's wife in Tehran, using a direct phone link that the authorities could not intercept. He learned that Iranian police had broken into Shabani's home, where his wife and newborn son were staying. They traumatized the two, picking up the baby by the legs and threatening to kill the boy if the woman interfered with their demands.

From New York, Greenberg worked feverishly on a rescue mission, contacting every U.S. government agency that could possibly help. But after the violent overthrow of the shah, the U.S. government had no useful assets left in the country. Worse, on November 4, 1979, Iranian militants stormed the U.S. embassy in Tehran and took 70 Americans hostage. Despite determined efforts to free them (including a failed attempt at a military rescue), they would be held for the remainder of President Carter's term, only to be released after 444 days in captivity, once President Ronald W. Reagan succeeded Carter.

AIG was on its own to rescue Shabani. The only thing the U.S. government could do was issue a new passport for Shabani, which, though seemingly a minor detail, was indispensable. Rescuing Shabani would require exiting through a neighboring country by car. No country would admit him from Iran without a passport. AIG worked closely with the many friends it had made in Iran during the period it operated there, and they devised a unique plan of escape.

While the assistants and details must remain secret to protect those who gave aid, Shabani's release and transport from Tehran was accomplished without paying any bribes. At the border, Shabani and his family were greeted, passport in hand, by R. Kendall ("Ken") Nottingham, one of AIG's prominent mobile overseas persons (MOP). The ordeal had inflicted serious pain and suffering, evident from how Shabani's black hair had turned white. Back in the United States, Shabani resumed living in San Francisco, where AIG arranged for him to have an office and personal assistant for life.[7]

The Iranian Revolution did not come as a surprise. Shabani had alerted Greenberg to the risk ahead of time. Greenberg offered to remove Shabani to protect his family. Shabani said he wished to stay. Meanwhile, another manager in the life insurance business had not checked in with headquarters. Facing the overthrow, this man, an American, simply cut and ran. When Greenberg learned of his defection, he was furious. Greenberg caught up with him in back in the States shortly afterwards and fired him on the spot.

The upheaval in Iran kept AIG out of the country, while Greenberg and Roberts concentrated on developing relationships with leaders struggling to move their countries out from behind the Iron Curtain. In December 1982, for instance, the Hungarian finance minister, an avid hunter, invited Roberts and Greenberg on a hunting trip outside of Budapest.

Greenberg asked Roberts: "What sort of gift shall we bring for the finance minister?"

"In Hungary," Roberts observed, "there is a shortage of pretty much everything, so anything would be useful."

"I suggest hunting gear," Greenberg said, "perhaps some shotguns, rifles, and ammo."

Roberts and Greenberg procured those gifts and, along with their own munitions, cleared all the gear through customs in preparation for their flight into Budapest. Inclement weather required rerouting all Budapest-bound flights to Vienna, not far away, though on the western side of the Iron Curtain. After landing, Roberts and Greenberg loaded up a rented car and began their short journey back toward the Hungarian border.

Reaching the crossing at about 9:00 P.M., passports and other papers all were in order and the guard was about to wave the two through. But then another guard asked to see inside the trunk. As soon as he opened it, he said, "Come with me."

Greenberg tried to explain that the gear was for hunting, and much of it gifts for the finance minister. He asked the guard to please call the minister. The guard balked, as he considered the two Americans to be highly suspicious. His comrades eventually reached the finance minister and verified the story. Within two hours, the finance minister himself arrived at the border to welcome the two Americans and rescue their belongings.

The hunt the next day was a great success. Roberts nabbed a boar in the morning, and Greenberg shot a stag in the afternoon. The antler trophy, rising some four feet, remains prominently displayed above the fireplace in the club house at Morefar, Starr's estate in Brewster, New York. Mounted on a simple wooden base, a small metal plaque reads: "HUNGARY 12-7-82 MRG."

AIG's early investments throughout eastern Europe began to pay substantial dividends in the years after the Cold War ended and the Soviet Union dissolved. AIG steadily expanded its interests in all three countries where it had gained early footholds—Hungary, Poland, and Romania—using HAM, PAM, and RAM to write policies for multinational corporations doing business there, including Exxon and General Electric. It began general insurance operations in countries throughout the region, including the Czech Republic, Estonia, and Latvia, and developed reinsurance joint ventures elsewhere, including in Uzbekistan.

At an international gathering in Moscow of the U.S.-Russian Business Council in 1987, Greenberg chatted with Mikhail Gorbachev, the last president of the Soviet Union during the 1980s. Gorbachev had overseen the adoption of policies of openness that led the bloc to dissolve and move the former communist states haltingly toward capitalism and democracy. The two men were discussing America's immigrant history with a small group of other business and diplomatic guests at the Kremlin, a mix of American and Soviet leaders.

"I'm curious," Gorbachev asked of all the Americans in the group, "where are your ancestors from?"

Each guest answered as they and Gorbachev bantered about the significance of America's immigrant tradition. When it was Greenberg's turn, he said, "My great grandmother was actually from Russia." Expounding on the meaning Greenberg attached to this, he added, "She left this country with little money in search of a better life, and went to America. Two generations later, I have just arrived here in Russia from America on a private corporate jet. Which system do you think is better, the Soviet or American system?" President Gorbachev, though not exactly fond of the Soviet system, could scarcely acknowledge that in front of his Soviet comrades, so instead turned and walked away.

After the Cold War, AIG was eager to build on the relationships executives had developed in Moscow in the two previous decades and opened a representative office there. In 1994, it won a license to operate a full-scale insurance company, the Russian American Insurance Company, as a joint venture with Moscow's Stolichny Bank of Savings and Garant-Invest.

Russia's leadership changed after the dissolution of the Soviet Union. In 1991, Boris Yeltsin succeeded Gorbachev as president of Russia. Many in the United States offered assistance in the transition. E. Gerald Corrigan, of the Federal Reserve Bank of New York, advised Russian officials on financial matters. Corrigan in turn drew on the expertise of fellow American businessmen, including Greenberg, then serving on the New York Fed's board.

Yeltsin was poised to adopt an aggressive approach to economic reform, including the rapid transformation of how resources were allocated. Under this radical approach, however, some dark forces emerged as communist-era apparatchiks became oligarchs grabbing control of large chunks of the economy. Greenberg urged Yeltsin and other officials to take a more moderate approach, one that centered principally on adopting policies that would attract foreign investment into the country. This meant embracing the principles of private property, freedom of contract, and the rule of law. Greenberg believed

that it was important to help Russia attract the capital needed to res-
urrect its collapsed economy, rebuild its eroded infrastructure, and
establish a reliable banking system.

Corrigan and Greenberg met with Yeltsin; Russian oligarchs; Yuri
Skokov, a leading figure in Russia's national politics; and such American
participants as William B. Harrison, Jr., then vice chairman of Chase
Manhattan Bank. Greenberg proposed to create a private investment
bank, called the Russian American Investment Bank, to draw foreign
direct investment for infrastructure projects. Corrigan championed the
Russian-American Banking Forum and the Russian-American Enterprise
Fund, both to promote formation of capital to rebuild the country.
Meetings took place in the dachas of the Russian elite, country homes in
Moscow Hills, outside of the main city. Skokov let Greenberg use a guest
house in Moscow Hills next door to where Stalin's dacha had been.

Over hearty meals of caviar, herring, and sturgeon and prodigious vodka—like night and day compared to the cuisine served at
the Rossia Hotel in the 1960s—these men debated the future of the
country's economy: how markets would work, how resources would
be allocated, and, of greatest interest to AIG, what foreign businesses
would be permitted. As Yeltsin pushed his radical and rapid reforms, a
skeptical Duma (parliament) resisted, while oligarchs divided their
support. Those at the center of the communist party held a hard line
against capitalist tendencies.

The Russian oligarchs supported a bill pending in the Duma that
would confiscate the assets of foreign insurance companies and ban them
from operating in Russia. The bill's proponents portrayed foreign
insurance multinationals as exploitative capitalists who would cause
harm to the Russian people. In a meeting on this subject with the head
of the communist party, Gennady Zyuganov, Greenberg changed the
narrative.[8] He explained that foreign insurance companies had knowledge and expertise in underwriting insurance that would be good for
the Russian people. Russian insurance companies, however, controlled
by the oligarchs, lacked anything approaching this capability, and would
limit the amount and range of insurance for the Russian people.

Zyuganov appreciated this straightforward argument. It changed the
way he saw the issue. Foreign competition might be agreeable after all.
Though he did not throw his weight behind legislation that would have

liberalized rules on foreign ownership and investment, he did the next best thing: he announced that he would neither endorse nor oppose such measures but leave it to the conscience of each participant to decide accordingly.[9] At that, the pending confiscatory bill failed to pass in the Duma.

In international business negotiations, Greenberg preferred to make arguments in precisely such terms—what is good for the people of a nation. It was neither necessary nor desirable to make arguments at more abstract levels, such as whether capitalism or communism should be preferred. By thinking along the lines of what is best for a nation's people, Greenberg supposed that participants would be led to prefer capitalism to other forms of economic and political organization. In any event, Greenberg had put forth an argument for capitalism that even a communist could accept.

These efforts for a private investment bank in Russia, however, came at the wrong time. The rule of law in Russia was simply too vague to support the kinds of commitments inherent in the investment banking relationships that Corrigan and Greenberg envisioned. It was impossible to persuade Yeltsin to support the policies that would attract requisite foreign private investment. Although the oligarchs were enthusiastic about becoming investors themselves, they did not support the kinds of reforms necessary to protect outside investors. The Russian economy stagnated through 1995 and, as erstwhile satellite states of the Soviet Union broke free across eastern Europe, Russia defaulted on its sovereign debts in 1998. The ensuing crisis stoked Soviet-style appetites for order. In 1999, this brought to power Vladimir V. Putin, who reasserted substantial state control over the economy.

Despite the name "Cold War," the United States and the Soviet Union waged belligerent proxy battles during much of it. One hot spot was Vietnam, where the AIU had been in business for decades, writing a variety of insurance—automobile, fire, marine, and worker's compensation. Business expanded substantially with the escalation of the Vietnam War in the late 1960s and into the early 1970s. AIG became the primary insurer of the expansive contracting operations that President

Lyndon B. Johnson instituted, in which several large U.S. general contractors employed as many as 60,000 South Vietnamese citizens and left Vietnam with the largest number of functioning airfields per capita of any country in the world.[10]

The AIU provided a key but quiet role promoting U.S. foreign policy. In the battle between the communist North Vietnamese and the U.S.-backed South, military support on the battlefield came from ideologically aligned nations. North Korea aided the communist North Vietnamese, and democratic South Korea gave military support to the South and the United States. South Korea's alliance with the United States began by supplying noncombat forces in 1964. Then, from 1965 to 1973, the South Korean army sent many thousands of troops into harm's way for the U.S.-backed South Vietnamese. To contribute this aid, it was important for the government of South Korea to have insurance. It sought coverage for its troops in the case of accidental, noncombat, death. Not many insurers could be employed for such a complex mission. The AIU wrote the coverage.

During the Vietnam War, the AIU insured some of the U.S. vessels that supported troops in the waterways of the Mekong Delta, including boats carrying supplies to forward areas. U.S. naval patrols fought intensely against the Viet Cong and their surreptitious aides, maneuvering in junk and sampan boats along the rivers.[11] Amid one treacherous period, the percentage of U.S. supply ships destroyed steadily increased, as did the AIU's insurance losses. Greenberg, immersed in the details of the battles and related data, was stunned. On a regular trip to the AIU's Hong Kong office, he had a dinner meeting with colleagues from the AIU and from a Chinese insurance company run by good friends of K. K. Tse. During dinner, Greenberg mentioned this problem and wondered whether the company would be interested in reinsuring these vessels. Tse's friends were interested, and the two companies struck a deal.

In 1974, the tide in the war turned. Political support for the war within the United States had evaporated, and the executive branch, embroiled by the Watergate scandal, lost authority to sustain the commitment. Communist forces began to infiltrate Saigon in early 1975, putting AIU employees' lives in danger, as the United States ordered a troop withdrawal.[12] Henri Charoui, the Saigon manager, conveyed the concern to an annual meeting of AIU managers in

Hong Kong. Saigon was one of the company's oldest offices, staffed with about 60 people, mostly women and older men. It was a completely Vietnamese staff except for Charoui, who was French and had transferred from the Beirut office. Many had been with the company for a decade or more. In April 1975, communist forces from North Vietnam drove into South Vietnam, targeting Saigon.

True to AIG culture, the managers devised a rescue plan. They dispatched several MOPs to Saigon, including a claims manager, Patrick O'Rourke. Then based in Manila and previously in Beirut, O'Rourke had been in Saigon for his prior assignment handling claims for several years and knew many people there. On April 19, 1975, O'Rourke, along with Peter Hammer and Dick Ritter, both then serving in the AIU's Hong Kong office, strapped $5,000 in U.S. currency to their bodies, and caught one of the few commercial flights still going into Saigon. There were few planes flying out, but this group hoped to depart with their colleagues on a U.S. Air Force escort; they were also prepared to remain if necessary.

AIG executives in New York prepared a list of personnel likely to be endangered if they stayed in Saigon; they were to be promptly evacuated. Ultimately, six employees and their family members—a total of 27 people—needed saving as the North Vietnamese army marched in. The team arranged for a bus to round up the group from their homes, with Ritter physically hoisting most of them on board, as the driver slowed but did not stop the vehicle. The bus drove to the U.S. Embassy where the families were escorted to the rooftop and into a helicopter that whisked them to a U.S. Air Force jet awaiting at a nearby airfield.

There, Ritter joined the crew for an airlift to the U.S. Air Force base in Guam. The next day, O'Rourke escaped as well, catching an irregular flight first to Manila and then to Guam. The day after that, Saigon fell. In Guam, the 27 evacuees, along with Ritter, were consigned to a vast and chaotic refugee camp where they had to live for several days. O'Rourke contacted Tom Foster, the manager of Guam Insurance Adjusters, the claims office of the AIU agency in Guam. With intrepid cunning, Foster and O'Rourke found the AIU employees, including Ritter, and got them all released safely into their custody. Back in Saigon, the remaining staff kept the office open, and headquarters managed to pay their salaries and benefits.[13]

Vietnam remained under communist rule for many years, with the country nationalizing the company's assets. Concurrently with the end of the Cold War, however, reforms begun in the late 1980s softened the central grip, and the country took steps to renew economic growth. Amid that renewal, AIG returned to Saigon, now called Ho Chi Minh City. It obtained a life insurance license in 2000 and a general insurance license in 2005. This is an exquisite example—that AIG repeated in a dozen countries—of a process that recurs when opening international markets: initial prosperity, interrupted by upheaval, followed by eventual reopening for business.

On Tuesday, October 29, 2002, a fierce blaze erupted in the International Trade Center in Ho Chi Minh City,[14] a building that hosted many businesses, including a branch and training facility of AIG's AIA life insurance affiliate there. During the blaze, which raged for hours, the building's stairways collapsed, leading to the deadliest fire on record in Vietnam's largest city. All the personnel pulled together, with AIA managers going out of their way to save trainees. Despite efforts, among the dead were 24 AIA personnel and young trainees, some of whom had jumped from the roof to escape the inferno. Many employees suffered from severe burns. Vietnam then lacked the advanced medical facilities or doctors required to treat such critical patients.

From AIG headquarters at 70 Pine Street in New York, Greenberg began making phone calls to help. He arranged airlifts for victims to obtain advanced treatment at specialty hospitals in Singapore and Thailand. For those wounded so seriously as to forbid transporting, AIG flew expert physicians in from Bangkok. To oversee the effort, Greenberg enlisted a medical team from New York–Presbyterian Hospital, which houses one of the world's most sophisticated burn units, to fly to Ho Chi Minh City. Within 48 hours, senior AIG personnel from around the world were on site providing a full range of needed services—operational, medical, linguistic, and security. Bereaved families received personal support from AIA staff and professional crisis counselors.

Greenberg and his wife, Corinne, flew to Vietnam, along with AIG's international life insurance executive Edmund Tse, to provide moral support to the victims and their families. On November 16, they attended memorial services for those lost in the fire. Afterward, they visited hospitals where injured employees and trainees were being cared for. They learned both of harrowing escapes—one pair of trainees, a husband and wife, miraculously survived their jump from the roof—and of tragic ends—many lost their lives attempting to flee. Greenberg later met with Le Thanh Hai, chairman of the People's Committee (the local Communist Party leadership) to express condolences on the human toll of the tragedy.

The victims and their families were moved by Greenberg's presence. Government officials were inspired by AIG's humanitarian gestures, which extended not only to AIG's employees and trainees but to other victims. They were amazed that a CEO of a large multinational corporation would fly across the world and take such a deep interest in the well-being of local personnel. To Greenberg, such actions—which he repeated dozens of times throughout his career, whether responding to typhoons in the Philippines or the earthquake in Kobe, Japan, in 1995—were part of AIG's corporate culture, the right thing to do.[15]

With the growth of its global reach, AIG's MOPs, epitomized by Roberts, had earned a badge of honor. Citizens of the world, they were willing to relocate anywhere AIG needed them. Given the often-hazardous work of building an international business, especially an insurance business, these executives had to have an amazing sense of commitment and creativity and the will to be on the frontier, whatever the personal risk. Assignments often took AIG's people, especially its MOPs, into treacherous territory. Like soldiers of fortune, they and the company navigated such perils with skill and tenacity. The tenacity meant that the company commanded a presence in these countries when peace followed war and business returned to usual.

As an American company, moreover, AIG and its personnel were natural assets for the United States. AIG's value to the United States grew as AIG rose from a company of moderate scale in the 1970s to substantial size in the 1980s, and then to among the largest of global companies by the 1990s.[16] The alliance between AIG and the United States was clear in the international trade battles of those decades, particularly concerning trade in services.

Chapter 7

Opening Trade in Services

On a flight from New York to Tokyo one Sunday in the summer of 1978, AIG's pilot, Franklin Davis, was guiding the company's plane west toward the Pacific Ocean near King Salmon, in the southwest corner of Alaska. Given the limited range of aircraft in that period, the flight plan required several stops for refueling. That Sunday, the jet was battling sustained headwinds exceeding 200 mph, eating so much fuel that Davis advised Greenberg that they would need to add a refueling stop for their final leg on one of the Aleutian Islands in the North Pacific. Davis suggested Shemya Island, a small, ruggedly beautiful rock 200 miles east of Russia.

The Shemya airfield was run by the U.S. Department of Defense and closed to civilian aircraft. On the scheduled refueling stopover at King Salmon, Greenberg got out of the airplane and called Lieutenant General Eugene Tighe Jr. They knew each other from service on the

U.S. Defense Intelligence Agency Advisory Board, a group of distinguished Americans empaneled by the secretary of defense to advise on matters of national security. General Tighe told Greenberg he would look into getting him access to the Shemya airfield, which required Pentagon approval. Tighe pointed out that it may be difficult to contact anyone since it was a Sunday, but that he would try. He suggested that, in the meantime, Captain Davis proceed to airspace above the base. "If, when approaching, they break into you by radio," the general said, "then you'll know you've been cleared to land. Otherwise, you'll have to turn around and come back."

Davis proceeded toward Shemya but grew nervous as he heard nothing over the radio when coming within descending distance to the base. Then, to his relief, the Navy air traffic controller's voice broke over the radio directing him to head directly to Shemya. As the plane descended, Greenberg and Davis looked out the jet's window. Over the base commander's office was a sign reading "Welcome, Mr. Greenberg."[1]

The trade battles AIG fought from the 1970s through the 1990s became a metaphor of that trip to Tokyo: braving sustained headwinds but eventually being waved in and welcomed. Open international trade was essential to a company such as AIG since more than half its revenue was derived from overseas operations. International trade struggles had intensified throughout the 1970s. In 1970, President Nixon referred to a dangerous nationalism in many parts of the world.[2] AIG had battled the expropriation of its assets in a half-dozen countries, from Pakistan to Nigeria—and usually won. Worse, in that era, services such as insurance, as distinct from goods, were not generally treated as part of international trade. People long understood the value of open trade in tangible goods such as butter, cars, corn, or oil, but found it harder to grasp the value of open trade in services such as accounting, airline tickets, insurance policies, or credit cards. The international laws that promoted open trade in goods did not apply to AIG's businesses, which were in services.

U.S. officials did not even believe that services were a particularly important part of the domestic economy. In 1975, President Gerald R. Ford, grappling with the dual economic woes of high unemployment and high inflation, appointed Greenberg to the President's Advisory Committee on Trade Policy and Negotiations (ACTPN), as did every president thereafter until President George W. Bush.[3] ACTPN is a broad-based private-sector panel formed to assure that trade policy reflects a range of U.S. commercial interests. Greenberg seized the opportunity to educate fellow committee members on the importance of trade in services. True, the U.S. Trade Act of 1974 had referenced international trade as including services,[4] but this aspect of trade remained a blind spot. Such an education was important because the blind spot, which existed in other countries as well, cost AIG access to profitable markets; the education was also valuable because the blind spot showed that many American leaders misunderstood their own economy, as trade in services offered substantial opportunities for economic growth that were not being harnessed.

After President Jimmy Carter reappointed Greenberg to ACTPN, Greenberg explained the anomalies about trade in services to the president's aide, Robert Strauss, then the U.S. trade representative. For purposes of international trade and U.S. economic growth, Greenberg argued, rendering services is just as important and worthy of respect as selling goods. In fact, from the U.S. perspective, the economic value of the service sector had been steadily rising and would grow even faster in the next decade. Strauss said he was sympathetic to this concept. But he also explained that expanding the scope of international trade agreements was not likely feasible at the time, due to other priorities being debated on long-standing issues of dispute among U.S. trading partners. Still, Greenberg urged Strauss to raise the subject of discriminatory actions against service industries at international meetings on the General Agreement on Tariffs and Trade (GATT). Strauss agreed to do what he could, though he did not have high hopes.

Japan was AIG's largest overseas market and where it invested in one of the most valuable office buildings in the world. It was located opposite the Imperial Palace in the heart of Tokyo's financial district (Marunouchi) on Sotobori-Dori (Outer Moat Street). Starr had acquired the property for the site in 1946, when the American International Underwriters (AIU) opened for business in Tokyo. Starr believed that his companies should invest in each country where they operate to show a commitment to a permanent presence and dreamed of constructing a building in Tokyo for the AIU. Plans were years in the making, as officials kept changing the building code for no apparent reason. Completed a few years after Starr died, the 15-story structure overlooked the Imperial Palace plaza, with its trees, lawns, and fountains that stretch nearly a mile to the south.[5]

At the building's dedication ceremony in 1974 were many of Starr's friends and colleagues, including Freeman, Manton, Stempel, and Tse. Greenberg unveiled a bronze bust of Starr, made by Milton Hebald, the same artist who rendered the sculpture for the Starr memorial at Morefar, and whose other work adorns the golf course there. In Tokyo, the sculpture rested on a shelf of Italian white marble in the building's spacious lobby. At the height of the Japanese real estate market of the late 1980s, the AIU Tokyo Building could have been sold for more than $2 billion, real estate mavens said, and decades later in a down market retained that value.[6] But as Starr's colleagues saw it, AIG should never sell such a monument, which symbolized Starr's pioneering spirit and international vision and is *the* prime piece of real estate in Japan, of which AIG employees there were justly proud.

During the 1970s in Japan, AIG introduced new products and distribution techniques in the fields of accident and health that Greenberg had begun there in the 1960s, and built a booming business in travel insurance. Customers were low risk, given the culture of safety in Japan; and the incidence of false claims was modest, given its culture of honesty. These features kept expenses and paid claims low, translating into impressive underwriting profits. Yet AIG remained locked out of many lines of business by Japanese regulations. Japan's regulatory scheme divided insurance into three sectors: life; general, which included automobile and property and casualty insurance; and "other," which included accident and health insurance. AIG was limited to the "other" category—known as the "third sector."

As a result of regulatory protection, the large Japanese insurance companies dominated the first and second sectors. Regulation determined the pricing of products in those sectors and limited any flexibility companies might otherwise have. In the late 1980s, AIG repeatedly requested Japan's minister of finance to deregulate the first and second sectors and enable AIG to enter those fields and to set its own rates. Domestic insurance executives believed that it would never happen. In fact, domestic Japanese companies were eyeing the impressive profits AIG generated in the Japanese accident and health insurance market, the third sector. They wanted a piece of that business and urged government officials that any deregulation plan should begin there. AIG, alone among foreign insurance companies in this fight, insisted that deregulation should begin with the second sector—automobile and property.

As one might expect, the minister of finance favored Japan's domestic company preferences, reflecting a protectionist streak that then ran throughout Japanese business and government. The arguments officials made revealed an extreme conviction. When a glass manufacturer in Cleveland was refused authorization to export glass into Japan, authorities explained that "Japanese eyes cannot see through American glass." A U.S. grain exporter was told that "Japanese mouths cannot eat American grain." Due to the lack of a trade agreement, matters were even worse for companies selling services, as AIG did, rather than goods.

President George H. W. Bush, campaigning for reelection in 1992, knew that jobs and the economy were the most important things on Americans' minds. Yet he was renowned more for his foreign policy skills and experience, assets many believed had become less relevant after the end of the Cold War. In trade, however, foreign policy and the domestic economy combine. Trade would produce U.S. jobs and stimulate economic growth; expanding trade called for the kind of international diplomacy in which the president excelled.

To advance this mission, President Bush organized a lengthy trip to visit leading capitals of Asia in late 1991 and early 1992. With U.S. unemployment high and the economy sluggish, the goal on the domestic side was to highlight the importance of trade to American workers and national prosperity. Abroad, the president would urge trading counterparts to appreciate that the basic teachings of international economics make clear that trading partners enjoy mutual gains from trade. President Bush invited a group of American business executives to join him on the trip, Greenberg among them. The entourage traveled first to Australia and then on to Singapore, South Korea, and Japan, where the president promoted open trade and free markets.

AIG was then locked in a heated standoff with Japan's minister of finance over how to deregulate the insurance industry. It appeared that the authorities were prepared to deregulate, beginning by opening the third sector. During the presidential trip, at the widely reported Tokyo state dinner at which President Bush became ill,[7] Greenberg pressed the case to open the other sectors and made some headway. Deregulation would reduce costs and open competition, which would benefit Japanese consumers and, ultimately, the entire economy, he argued. Greenberg also made his case before the U.S.-Japan Business Council, and continued to work hard on behalf of AIG's trade agenda through organizations he belonged to, such as the Japan Society. President Bush's U.S. trade representative, Carla Hills, appealed to her Japanese counterparts on behalf of open trade generally and AIG's case in particular. Notwithstanding the considerable firepower of this comprehensive effort, negotiations dragged out for several months.

Back at home, though the president made an impressive showing on the campaign trail, the electorate was not convinced that he was the right leader for the next four years. The White House instead went to Bill Clinton. Fortunately for AIG, President Clinton also embraced principles of open trade. President Clinton appointed Mickey Kantor U.S. trade representative; Charlene Barshefsky served as Kantor's deputy and would later succeed him. Following the lead of Ambassador Hills, they adopted a firm stance on open trade and a hard line with Japan over insurance deregulation. Barshefsky coordinated these negotiations for the United States as they intensified throughout 1993.

Barshefsky found negotiating with the Japanese over trade matters to be both exhilarating and exhausting.[8] The Japanese had stamina and were willing to stretch meetings out in an attempt to wear interlocutors down. Barshefsky responded in kind. If the Japanese proposed adjourning a meeting after 12 hours, Barshefsky would insist on going for one more hour to hash out another point. If the Japanese agreed to grant two American licenses in the third sector, she would request three in the first and second sectors. After working around the clock one weekend, Barshefsky thought all issues concerning insurance deregulation across sectors were resolved and caught a plane from Tokyo back to Washington, D.C. Upon arrival in the United States, however, a colleague called from Tokyo to say the negotiations hit a glitch. Furious with the characteristic intransigence, she called the Japanese finance minister with an ultimatum: sign the deal as agreed or forget any concessions that the United States may have been willing to make. The minister acquiesced, and the deal was signed in 1994.[9] Ambassador Kantor immediately called Greenberg to report the victory.

AIG grew to be the largest foreign insurance company in Japan. Its successful fight to open the Japanese insurance market benefited the Japanese and their economy, as well as other U.S. insurance companies. Before deregulation, the large Japanese insurance companies were so entrenched that they had no incentive to respond to the needs or preferences of customers. Opening the markets unleashed the spirit of competition. That, in turn, stimulated the imagination of those formerly entrenched companies. Resulting were more products, better pricing, wider consumer choice, and swifter handling of claims. For American companies, it was a new market.

At the time, however, international trade law still did not recognize services as part of the global trading regime. GATT did not encompass services. Though U.S. policy supported open trade in services, the United States and AIG lacked the leverage usually available in trade disputes. It remained to convince world leaders to change these rules to open trade in services, too, just as the global community had long preferred trade in goods to be open.

Greenberg knew that another international business executive, James D. Robinson III, the long-time CEO of American Express, had also grown frustrated over international trade in services in the late 1970s. Countries around the world blocked access to markets for charge cards and other financial products offered by American Express. Discrimination took many forms against different service sectors. While Japan strictly controlled financial firms operated by foreigners, other countries imposed duties on imported computer software, which restricted the flow of financial information.[10] Some countries gave subsidized loans to national shipping firms or imposed quotas on foreign movies. Subtler tactics forbade a foreign accounting firm from using its international name. Other tools were blatantly protectionist, like the punitive landing fees that some governments imposed on foreign air carriers.[11]

In 1979, as Robinson became exasperated with failed attempts to access foreign markets, American Express created a team to fight back. But Robinson discovered, as AIG had, that no company acting alone could meet the challenge. After comparing notes about these problems, Greenberg and Robinson agreed to join forces and organize other companies in their cause. Assisted by senior aides, including by Ronald K. Shelp at AIG,[12] the men engaged counterparts at other large service companies, such as Citibank in banking, Pan American World Airways in aviation, and Peat Marwick Mitchell in accounting. They enlisted CEOs of other domestic companies, manufacturers and distributors of goods, and counterparts in other countries. In 1982, this group became the Coalition of Service Industries (CSI), which Greenberg chaired and he and Robinson led.

The CSI's mission was clear: equal treatment for services in international trade. That meant an even playing field, without discrimination between domestic and foreign companies, concerning establishing a business, accessing markets, and offering new products. Throughout its history, the CSI called upon successive U.S. trade representatives, all of whom understood the mission as in the national interest and worked avidly in support of it throughout the 1980s and 1990s.

In Washington, the CSI also won the support of many influential members of Congress from both parties and their staffs. Such support enabled the CSI to occupy a unique role on trade policy in Washington, as a member of an advisory committee on trade in services. The coalition used that role to urge global trade representatives to include trade in services on the GATT agenda. A breakthrough came quickly in 1982, when William Brock, the U.S. trade representative from 1980 to 1985, persuaded his counterparts in vital countries to add it to the November 1982 GATT ministerial meeting in Geneva. This was the first formal international recognition of the subject as legitimate.

Robinson traveled to India on several occasions during this period to meet with ministers of trade and finance. Attempting to explain the importance of trade in services, and how India's most valuable resource was its impressively educated and well-trained workforce, he would be met with blank stares.[13] Within decades India would, in fact, become a leader in many services. Consistent with AIG's persistent passion for "looking around corners," CSI members foresaw that future while others awakened to it much later.

Why was it so hard to bring people worldwide to understand the importance of trade in services? A principal reason was absence of statistics. Governments, including the U.S. government, maintained substantial data on the volume of trade in goods. None, however, kept reliable track of trade in services. No one could verify its importance, and few had the curiosity to ask. Among the first ambitions that the CSI had was to persuade the U.S. Bureau of Labor Statistics to measure trade in services.

The CSI reached that milestone in 1984, when amendments to the U.S. trade law mandated improved government data collection on trade in services.[14] The figures stunned those outside the service industries. Trade in services, it turned out, was a central piston of the economy: by the 1980s, 70 percent of the U.S. gross national product (GNP) and jobs were attributed to the service sector[15]; international trade exceeded $1 trillion, and one-fourth of that was in services.

In addition to the lack of statistics, the intellectual underpinnings had not been formed. Classical economists, from Adam Smith on, dismissed service enterprises to be of secondary importance. These economists worked in a world where the value of services was modest compared to goods and they were not traded in the same way. The CSI thus had to be more than a trade association committed to traditional political lobbying. It invested significantly in researching and developing an intellectual framework to think about services and in the context of international trade.[16]

Global demand for services was rising rapidly, mandating this rethinking. For the United States and other developed countries, liberalized trade in services would mean more jobs, more foreign trade income, and a strengthened global position. For all countries, it would mean enhanced technological achievements and blossoming in the broad field of intellectual property.

Members of the CSI began to participate in conferences on international trade, launching a serious dialogue among policy makers and scholars. The CSI, formed in the United States, spawned sister CSI organizations abroad. This growth eventually led to creation of an umbrella organization called the Global Services Coalition. It also propagated many kindred groups interested in promoting open trade generally and attracted the support of older groups, such as the U.S. Chamber of Commerce.

Checking this momentum were a few vocal opponents who resisted the CSI's and AIG's efforts, both in the United States and abroad. Developing countries, led by Brazil and India, objected to allowing large U.S. financial services companies to compete in their local markets, fearing those would drive local firms out of business. In response,

Greenberg repeatedly emphasized in his annual AIG chairman's letters and other high-visibility platforms that allowing such competition would help the economies of these developing countries as well.

Although the debate remains one of popular conversation, most economists and policy makers have embraced the notion, first argued as long ago as 1817 by David Ricardo, the influential classical economist, that gains from trading exceed losses for both developed and developing countries when countries specialize in what they do best.[17] True, it is not usually propitious to make radical, rapid shifts from a closed to an open economy, when it is difficult for people to make the inevitable transitions that trade shifts require.[18] In the long term, however, trade has proven to be a better route to prosperity than isolationism.

Despite the mounting proof of the benefits of open trade, it was still met with opposition at home. Environmentalists opposed trade agreements unless countries agreed to control pollution in particular ways; human rights advocates objected to deals with countries tolerant of forced labor. Supporters countered by arguing that such conditioning of trade agreements would mean no agreement at all, as countries reject the dictates of foreign governments over such domestic matters. AIG acknowledged that it may be distasteful, but campaigns to promote environmental protection and protect human rights are often more likely to succeed when trade is open. Trade produces economic wealth available to cover the costs of social and ecological progressivism. It also helps people to escape parochial viewpoints by thinking beyond their own borders and limitations.

By far the biggest obstacle to overcome on the road to open trade in services was nationalistic protectionism. Many countries had laws that limited foreign ownership of insurance businesses. In Malaysia, protectionist laws dated to race riots in 1969 when native Malays, called *Bumiputra* (meaning "son of the earth") protested against the longstanding control of their economy by the minority "overseas Chinese"— people of Chinese origin born in Malaysia. Rioters in the streets of Kuala Lumpur demanded reforms. Government responded with a law giving priority to *Bumiputra* in areas from hiring in the workplace to equity ownership of certain kinds of businesses, including foreign insurance companies.

Mahathir bin Mohamad, prime minister of Malaysia from 1981 to 2003, had been instrumental in developing the *Bumiputra* policy and setting these limits on foreign ownership. AIG had a large and profitable branch office in Malaysia that predated this law by decades, back to the period of British colonial rule that ended in 1946. Switching from full ownership of the branch to a subsidiary partially owned by Malays would cede capital and relinquish control. Mahathir and Greenberg would wrestle over this issue throughout his entire premiership, during periods that alternated between harmony and strife for the two men.

To achieve his own objectives, Greenberg always tried to identify the objectives his counterparts held and then meet them if possible. He determined that Mahathir's objective was identifying foreign investment. To help with that, AIG hosted dinners and receptions for Mahathir in the United States, where the prime minister and his aides could meet other U.S. business leaders and explain to them the advantages of investing in Malaysia. Mahathir had been a student of Henry Kissinger at Harvard University, so Greenberg invited Secretary Kissinger to accompany him on trips to Malaysia, to assist Mahathir and other ministers in finding economic opportunities for foreign companies in Malaysia.

On the merits, AIG argued that allowing it to operate in Malaysia would generate substantial benefits to the country because it would be an investor of "patient capital" locally. Especially for life insurance companies such as AIA, the business of insurance involves accumulating and husbanding large amounts of capital that must be invested for the long term in the locale. AIA may write an insurance policy for a 30-year-old citizen, receiving premiums, and be prepared to pay under the policy on any given day during a period as long as the next 40 years. The company must invest all the premiums it receives along such a lengthy time horizon, often in long-term government bonds. These bonds fund infrastructure, such as roads, bridges, and hospitals.

As a result of its advocacy, AIG in 1985 obtained the right to continue its own branch in Malaysia for a series of renewable five-year terms. As promised, AIG's Malaysia offices generated substantial benefits for the country and its people. The branch sustained a large number of jobs for Malays, native and otherwise, fielding 50,000 agents countrywide along with 2,500 employees. The employee training AIG provided produced an experienced cadre of senior executives and middle managers who would go on to serve other companies and governmental offices throughout Malaysia. With a substantial business value measured in billions of dollars, and profits reinvested in the country, AIG's branch contributed significantly to gross domestic product and spurred economic growth.

During this series of negotiations and renewals with Prime Minister Mathathir, Greenberg continued to push for ways to make the branch arrangement permanent. An opportunity arose in the mid-1990s during the World Trade Organization's negotiations on a global agreement on trade in financial services, including insurance. Due to the efforts of Greenberg, Robinson, and other members of the CSI, many countries in the World Trade Organization (WTO) agreed to reduce discrimination against foreign companies in service industries, including reducing or ending foreign ownership caps.

Throughout the administration of George H. W. Bush and the first administration of Bill Clinton, international negotiations over the financial services agreement had been tense. The United States refused to ratify several versions because, as Clinton's first U.S. trade representative, Mickey Kantor, noted and AIG agreed, the agreement remained too protectionist. In 1997, however, to seal the WTO's financial services agreement, the United States and the European Union brokered a grand bargain that many other countries supported—and so did AIG. In effect, the United States was willing to forego its unilateral power to punish unfair trade practices in order to secure fair access of its financial services firms to other markets. For AIG, this would mean a level playing field, which is all it wanted, no more and no less, as it flourished in competitive markets. In addition, the United States requested binding commitments on this point from the countries where service industries most desired access, such as Brazil, India, Japan, and . . . Malaysia.

The issue came to a head in the final days before the WTO financial services agreement was to be signed. The United States requested that Malaysia eliminate its foreign ownership restrictions, including those applicable to AIG. Malaysia countered by offering to modify its policy going forward to allow foreign ownership at 51 percent. But it also proposed that it be permitted to apply, to any company not then in compliance, an even lower percentage cap. This proposal was a clear attack on AIG, to which it solely applied because of its series of five-year exemptions. The United States, along with European allies, resisted and aggressively negotiated to persuade Malaysia to withdraw the proposal. The argument was simple: international trade agreements were intended to expand trade, while this proposal would curtail it by sanctioning a partial expropriation of foreign insurers.

President Clinton's second U.S. trade representative, Charlene Barshefsky, stressed that Malaysia was then *the* emerging economy among Southeast Asian countries.[19] Its positions were watched closely and often followed by its neighbors, such as the Philippines and Thailand. If Malaysia could get away with a regressive tactic in a trade liberalization deal, those countries might follow suit. The United States could not afford to let that example stand. Nor, of course, could AIG. Greenberg dispatched AIG's government relations officer, Oakley Johnson, to Geneva, where diplomats, officials, and trade representatives from scores of countries were gathered. They expected only to hammer out a few final details, but the Malaysia ownership issue remained a sticking point. Johnson's message raised the stakes: he informed Timothy Geithner, then a deputy Treasury Department official for international trade, that AIG could not support the agreement unless it addressed the Malaysia divestiture rule directly.

Ambassador Barshefsky's staff, along with Geithner and his colleagues, developed a compromise proposal to address what participants named the "AIG issue." They proposed a proviso that any WTO member, including the United States, would be allowed to discriminate against countries that forced the localization or expropriation of a foreign insurance company. To its credit, the European Union threw its weight behind this solution. Soon, most major countries supported it, too, as more in keeping with the open trade philosophy to which they had committed. For Johnson, this compromise solution was appealing, although it was not the pure renunciation Greenberg had sent him there to get.

Johnson informed the group that he could not give AIG's assent until he had spoken with Greenberg. Earlier that day, a Friday in December, Johnson had called to apprise Greenberg of developments, and let him know that they would need to speak the moment any breakthrough emerged. Greenberg would be aboard AIG's jet later that night and assured Johnson that it was outfitted with a newly installed telecommunications system so that he could talk on the phone while in the air—a novel technology at the time.

By 11:00 P.M. Geneva time, trade negotiators had all agreed to the U.S. compromise proposal on the AIG issue, and Malaysia finally capitulated. All that remained was securing AIG's support. U.S. delegates were leaning hard on Johnson for an answer. He rang the air phone, but the new system did not work. The international delegation was assembling in the hall. From Washington, Geithner's boss, Lawrence Summers, called Johnson directly, seeking the final go-ahead, noting that everyone was growing impatient. The government was eager to have AIG's support.

Johnson stood firm, insisting that he could not give AIG's support without getting clearance from Greenberg—and that he was trying earnestly to reach him but having technical difficulties. Geithner then arranged with his counterparts for a two-hour extension of the final deadline. Greenberg's assistant, Shaké Nahapetian, suggested that Johnson send a fax to the airplane, where it could be read on the pilot's screen in the cockpit. Johnson wrote out an imperfect summary of the situation and faxed it to the plane. Greenberg replied as expected: "I would prefer Malaysia to drop the divestiture rule entirely but if this compromise proviso is the best that can be done I will not hold up the agreement over it." With that, Johnson threw AIG's support behind the agreement and the ceremonial signing was undertaken at close to 3:00 A.M. local time.[20]

Greenberg resigned himself to further negotiations with the Malaysian government that he calculated would eventually lead to permanent resolution of the issue. Three years later, Greenberg returned to Malaysia to negotiate for another five-year renewal. Under the renewal, AIG maintained its commitment to sustain its investments in the country's infrastructure. In exchange, its historic branch would be unaffected by the foreign ownership laws until 2005.[21]

AIG fought for open trade in most countries in the world from the 1970s into the early 2000s, obtaining as a result many first-of-kind insurance licenses, including in Japan (1972), Romania (1979), Portugal (1986), Finland (1987), Italy and Turkey (both 1988), Uzbekistan (1994), Slovakia (1995), India (2000), and Vietnam (2000 and 2005).

Most were hard-won, and often partial, victories for open trade. Though differences existed among each country and every deal, they all shared a broad theme: AIG pioneering new markets. As the first mover, it often paid a substantial price for leadership in bruising struggles of politics, power, and unfair local competition; however, AIG reaped outsized rewards from the leadership position. It helped to enable driving AIG's business to become the largest insurance company in the world—probably in world history. By 2004, AIG had accreted substantial value for shareholders, reflected in its market capitalization of $180 billion.

In any difficult negotiation, tenacity is perhaps the most valuable trait: the will to stay the course and try repeatedly when pursuing an objective. The fuel of tenacity is conviction, meaning a belief in the rightness of one's cause. Equally important is empathy, understanding what your counterparty seeks, and reciprocity, helping to deliver that.

The end result was imperfect, but the grand bargain held, a triumph for open trade in services. The WTO agreement on trade in services defined new opportunities for the world: open access to markets, increased foreign ownership thresholds, and fair treatment to existing and prospective foreign companies in domestic markets.[22] Today, trade in services is a multitrillion-dollar global enterprise. All the traits Greenberg utilized in AIG's quest to open trade in services would also be critical in AIG's arduous 15-year effort to reopen China.

Chapter 8

Reopening China

In late 1991, a Paris gallery exhibited 10 imposing Chinese bronze window panels, each towering 10 feet and emblazoned with iconic serpents and raised floral designs. They had been looted by foreign armies during the Boxer Rebellion in 1900, pillaging the Baoyun Pavilion at the Summer Palace in Beijing. News of this exhibit reached T. C. Hsu, Starr's protégé who had become president of the Starr Foundation, the private foundation that received the bulk of Starr's estate. Hsu reported the exhibit to Greenberg, chairman of the Starr Foundation. The two set out to verify the panels' provenance, which held extraordinary national significance for China.

The Pavilion, built in the 1750s by the Jesuits on behalf of the Emperor Qianlong as a religious shrine for Buddhist monks, had been closed ever since the Boxer Rebellion, as the loss of those window panels amounted to a loss of face for the Chinese.[1] The Starr Foundation contacted China's minister of culture, offering to pay the costs of experts traveling to France to investigate. The experts confirmed that the window panels were indeed those missing from the Pavilion. The treasured national assets had been stolen by a French army officer in 1900.

The Starr Foundation, whose assets were concentrated in AIG stock that would enjoy a peak value exceeding $6 billion, made substantial philanthropic contributions to China. It bought the iconic window frames from the Paris gallery for $515,000 and arranged for their repatriation to China. A national rededication service followed in December 1993, broadcast throughout the country on television. Millions of grateful Chinese watched tearfully during the ceremony. It was the first time that any foreign organization had returned missing national Chinese artifacts to the homeland. Greenberg thought it was the right thing to do in a country where he and his company had developed important relationships during the toilsome process of reopening China for business, culminating in China's accession into the World Trade Organization (WTO).[2]

Starr had begun his insurance companies in China in 1919, and his businesses prospered there. In 1941, however, the Japanese army seized Shanghai, and its liquidators impounded all properties. Ahead of that, loyal Starr employees, led by K. K. Tse, managed to preserve the company's files, and even much of the furniture, and store them safely amid the chaos of the siege. When World War II ended, in 1945, Starr returned to his old office to find that his employees had reassembled it, furniture and files, much as it had been when the war began.[3] With the outbreak of civil war in China in the late 1940s, however, Starr's companies were again forced out of the country. China and the United States terminated all diplomatic and economic relations.

Greenberg kept a close eye on China. Through his many regular trips to Hong Kong to meet with AIU executives, he had developed good relationships with Chinese businessmen running insurance companies in Hong Kong. They were knowledgeable about China, yet exposed to the broader world by their base in a leading international trading hub. Greenberg learned a great deal about Chinese history and hopes. China had been isolated but was an ancient civilization whose people had accumulated immense wisdom and knowledge. And the Chinese people genuinely liked Americans and remained grateful for the U.S. military support protecting China from Japanese hostilities during World War II. As a result, Greenberg surmised that, with a massive population and an area of continental scale, China would not be isolated from the world or the United States for long.

These insights began to pay off when President Richard M. Nixon and his indefatigable national security adviser and later secretary of state, Henry A. Kissinger, quietly reopened the U.S. door to China. Their 1972 trip to China, the first by a sitting U.S. president, produced the joint Sino-American "Shanghai Communiqué" with Zhou Enlai and Deng Xiaoping stating, "Progress toward normalization of relations between China and the United States is in the interest of all countries." President Nixon and Secretary Kissinger held primarily geopolitical objectives; they embraced China as a counterweight to the Soviet Union's power, to gain advantage in the Cold War. For their gambit to pay off, however, it was important that American businesses embrace China to nurture commercial and cultural exchanges. AIG was well suited for the task at hand.

Inspired by Nixon and Kissinger's trip, Greenberg's initial overture was a letter to the People's Insurance Company of China (PICC), the state-owned monopoly insurance company. It proposed developing a new insurance business together. Officials responded belatedly, eventually sending a "Welcome to China" kit, asking for more information about Greenberg's intentions. He wrote back explaining that he would like to visit China, bringing his wife, Corinne, along with Freeman and Manton, and their wives.

The PICC embraced this overture and invited the group to come. Ahead of the November 1975 trip to China, Greenberg provided a detailed business plan and proposal. Arriving in Beijing that month, Mao's Cultural Revolution was everywhere in evidence. Monochrome uniforms of drab blue, brown, or gray were the standard dress. There were few cars but thousands of wobbly bicycles crowding the streets, flanked by dense crowds of pedestrians. Few hotels could be found, certainly no five-star offerings, and only one remotely "Western." Foreign visitors to China were rare then, and citizens found the white skin of these visitors alien. People stared at the Americans as if they were from another planet.

Late one afternoon, the AIG executives met with Sung Guohua and other state insurance officials designated by the PICC to represent it. In a plain office off Tiananmen Square, the Americans explained the concept of reinsurance, a policy that one insurance company offers another to backstop some of the primary risk. Because China did not grant licenses to write primary insurance policies to foreigners, reinsurance was the only plausible path to launching an insurance enterprise there. A reinsurance franchise would provide a way to learn about the local business, develop knowledge of regional conditions, and build valuable relationships—the essence of successful business.

The Chinese officials seemed open-minded and showed interest in the venture, apparently having decided beforehand to make commitments. Within two hours, AIG had secured an agreement on a mutual reinsurance deal and to handle marine claims for each other. That was a modest business proposition but a symbolic milestone: the new era's first formal insurance contract between companies of the two countries and a basis for continuing discussion. It was the start of the relationship that would lead to a steadily expanding series of hard-won business deals for AIG in China.

After making that deal, PICC officials escorted the AIG group to dinner and an evening of sightseeing. Sung introduced the AIG team to *maotais*, the traditional toasting drink in China. R. W. Apple of the *New York Times* once wrote that the 130-proof beverage "smells a lot like JP-4, the stuff that powers the engines on *Air Force One*, and it is only slightly more drinkable."[4] Americans became familiar with the drink, too, used in the same period's toasts between President Nixon and Premier Zhou and between Secretary Kissinger and Vice Premier Deng Xiaoping. On AIG's outing, hosts and guests took turns making toasts, moving around the table, each time everyone imbibing a full small glass of the stuff. Sobriety was impossible. On the menu, bear paws were offered, thick slabs of animal fat, and other curious foods foreign to the Americans. Into the night, the new friends took in the landmarks of Beijing and its bustling commercial past, which contrasted with its monochrome present, though that was about to change.

Thanks to the U.S. political leadership, including Presidents Ford and Carter as well the chief of the U.S. Liaison Office to China, George H. W. Bush, formal reopening of U.S.-Chinese diplomatic relations occurred in 1978. Throughout this period, Greenberg and Freeman made regular semiannual trips to China, leading to winning AIG's first representative office there, in Beijing, in 1980. Shortly thereafter, PICC and AIG formed a joint venture, the China America Insurance

Company. It would write general insurance for companies involved in U.S.-China trade. AIG operated the joint venture for a decade, while its personnel gained the trust and confidence of their Chinese partners, including high-ranking government officials. The 1980 contracts were important steps in the right direction, though the PICC continued to write all domestic Chinese insurance. More work remained to open China's insurance markets entirely. "You have to spend as much time trying to open markets for the future as you do running markets for today," Greenberg advocated at the time.

By the 1980s, Shanghai, once a busy seaport brimming with cosmopolitan life, known as the "Paris of the Orient," was in disrepair. To help revive it, the Atlanta real estate developer, Jack Portman, formed a joint venture with Kajima Corporation, a Japanese construction and engineering company. They planned to build a world-class downtown complex to anchor what they believed was the great city's prosperous future. Called the Shanghai Center, and located on Nanjing Road in the heart of town, it would feature a five-star hotel, luxury apartments, offices, shops, restaurants, and a sophisticated conference facility. Slated to be the largest real estate development project in Shanghai, Portman needed $30 million in equity capital for the $175 million project. He turned to AIG, which provided it in exchange for an ownership stake in the joint venture as well as a long-term ground lease of the property.

Construction began in 1986 and continued steadily, with 32 stories completed within the year. At that time, dramatic demonstrations promoting democratic reforms erupted in Beijing's Tiananmen Square. They were met by government force and ended with a large number of demonstrators dead. Political upheaval rocked the country, along with the international condemnation that followed. Amid these tragedies, many real estate developers halted work on construction projects across China. In Shanghai, Zhu Rongji, the mayor in the late 1980s who would later serve as vice premier and premier of China, gave a nationally televised speech distancing his city from the tragic events and stressing his government's unwillingness to use military force of this kind. At the Shanghai Center construction site, work proceeded without interruption, as AIG and its partners were assured that, after the temporary interruption, China would continue on its path of gradually reopening.

AIG even increased its equity stake in the project and guided it to its grand opening in March 1990. The hotel, the Portman Ritz-Carlton, was a trailblazer, followed during the 1990s by many more hotels, restaurants, shops, and art galleries. In recognition of AIG's commitment to China, Greenberg twice obtained extensions of its ground lease on the Shanghai Center, the final expiration date set for 2020.

As mayor of Shanghai, Zhu supported liberalizing the Chinese economy and was particularly interested in attracting foreign private investment. While he was mayor, his efforts included streamlining the approval processes for projects, an enthusiasm that earned him the nickname "one-chop Zhu." One problem was that the government buildings were spread out across various parts of the city. Getting approvals required documents to be submitted for signature and certification to numerous ministries in different areas, a cumbersome and costly process that turned off many foreign investors. To redress that, just after the Shanghai Center was completed, Mayor Zhu eyed the undeveloped land across the Whampoo River, called Pudong, stretching thousands of acres. He aimed to develop the property and modernize the bureaucracy by consolidating its government offices. Zhu also believed that the development would become an appealing commercial center in his vision of transforming Shanghai into a financial powerhouse on the scale of Hong Kong, rooted in the heart of China's mainland.

To attract the necessary foreign capital and to plan projects such as the Pudong development, Zhu created the International Business Leaders Advisory Council (IBLAC). He asked Greenberg to be IBLAC's first chairman to lend it the credibility and leadership it would need, including helping recruit companies as members. Greenberg gladly accepted and served two terms. Subsequent chairmen included Rick Wagoner, former head of General Motors, and Lord James Prior, the British diplomat and businessman whom Greenberg also had tapped to serve on AIG's International Advisory Board.

Thanks to such leadership, IBLAC remains a formidable force in Shanghai, contributing steadily and significantly to the city's development over more than two decades. Of greatest importance is how IBLAC concentrated entirely on assessing and helping to meet the needs of Shanghai and its citizens—it was not a forum to define what AIG and other companies wanted, but, instead, what the city required. IBLAC's meetings, inaugurated in March 1990 in the Shanghai Center, gathered the world's foremost leaders in business and government. They held a series of meetings in 1990 and 1991 that focused on every aspect of the dream to transform Shanghai into a world-class twenty-first-century city. IBLAC engaged experts to address ports, industrial development, infrastructure, environmental impacts, trade relations, and, of course, financial services. Government officials from across China attended, making copious notes that they would take back to their own cities to stimulate local action plans.

For funding, council members stressed the importance of securing long-term commitments to sustain the ambitious visions they shared for Shanghai. Greenberg highlighted the advantage that AIG brought to this part of the vision. Life insurance is a rich source of long-term capital, he explained, referencing his concept of "patient capital." Modern China had never encouraged the nation's life insurance business to fund infrastructure. Before World War II, families tended to be large and essentially self-insured against death; for several decades afterward, the state bore the burden; and more recently, Chinese law limited the size of families, and the state had begun to look to the private sector for solutions. So Greenberg made a win-win proposal: grant AIG a license to sell life insurance in China and it would pool capital collected there to invest in local long-term projects.

Mayor Zhu was receptive to this proposal, which both made clear economic sense and supported his vision. Equally important, it was backed by a man who understood China well and represented a business with ancestry in China dating back to 1919. AIG was years ahead of any other insurance company in going to China—most did not begin to imagine the economic opportunities available there until the mid-1990s, two decades after Greenberg's first overtures. Even when other companies followed suit, their CEOs made fewer trips to China to meet with officials or executives compared to Greenberg. In addition, many CEOs would dispatch deputies to meetings in China. Though CEOs may not have intended any slight, such gestures profoundly misunderstood important aspects of Chinese culture that Greenberg knew. The Chinese government sought to deal with the top person at any company wishing to do business in China. Seeing the number two or three would not suffice.

In China, Greenberg was so identified with AIG that the two were practically synonymous.[5] Greenberg had more autonomy than many CEOs, as AIG's governance structure gave him latitude that other corporate boards would not routinely grant to their chief executives— Greenberg was a classic "strong CEO." In addition, Chinese officials saw that Greenberg had considerable influence with their counterparts in Washington policy circles.[6] That cachet, combined with two decades of personal presence in China, made AIG an excellent candidate to receive China's first insurance license issued to a foreign company. As mayor of Shanghai, Zhu reported his support for granting AIG an insurance license at the November 1991 IBLAC meeting. The mayor characterized the grant as a test case. The business would be 100 percent owned and operated by AIG—no need for a joint venture with PICC or another Chinese entity and no imposition of foreign ownership limitations. It would, however, be limited to Shanghai, as that was the only province within Zhu's jurisdiction as mayor.

Even that influence, of course, was checked by other Chinese officials, including some in the PICC. Many of Zhu's colleagues believed that his support for awarding a license to AIG, a foreign company, amounted to "selling out China."[7] Unlike during its past, when Mao or another single leader's declarations bound all, the new China was governed by a more consultative group of nine or so more or less coequal leaders (known as the Politburo Standing Committee). For several months, Zhu had been working back channels in China to win group support for his proposal to grant AIG the license. In that effort he had enlisted China's ambassador to the United States and United Nations, Zhu Qizhen.

In August 1992, Premier Li Peng was to be in New York to visit Ambassador Qizhen and assorted dignitaries, including David Rockefeller. The ambassador contacted Greenberg, who had just arrived in Switzerland from the United States, and said he could arrange for Greenberg to have five minutes to meet the premier. Few would relish the idea of immediately turning around to fly back across the Atlantic for a five-minute meeting, even with Premier Li. But Ambassador Qizhen persuaded Greenberg to hop the AIG jet back to New York.

Greenberg reiterated to Premier Li how life insurance is a long-term business and related the concept of "patient capital" that AIG offered. In

that spirit, he assured the premier that AIG would not take any dividends out of China for at least 10 years. This orientation appealed to the
premier because of the long-term view so engrained in Chinese culture.
At the end of the meeting, which lasted 45 minutes, Premier Li
promised to consider granting AIG its insurance license. True to his
word, Li later consulted with the country's other leaders, and AIG
received its license on September 30, 1992.

After receiving the license, AIG opened its new offices in the
Shanghai Center. AIG's reopening of China for business quickly
became the most successful AIG start-up venture ever. And, once again,
AIG and the United States were in lock-step: 1992 was also the year
when the United States conferred "most-favored-nation" status upon
China. That endorsement, elevating a trading partner to top rank, was a
big step toward China's eventual entry into the WTO. AIG's 1992
license, the first granted to a foreign-owned insurance company,
allowed it to operate a 100 percent–owned insurance company.

AIG's business would be regulated by the People's Bank of China
(PBC). AIG executives arranged for PBC's officials to take a trip with
them to see AIG's operations in other Asian markets: Hong Kong,
Malaysia, Singapore, and Thailand. The lesson AIG hoped to convey
was how its operations helped local economies and how the added
foreign competition aided the domestic insurance industry. After all, for
a company to succeed in international business, it must give as well as
get, and show the host government that its presence benefits the
country's people.

To launch the new business, American International Assurance
Company (AIA) managers were advised by the old China hand, Buck
Freeman, on general insurance, and Edmund Tse on life insurance.
They recruited experienced underwriters and accountants, brought
many AIA employees from Hong Kong, and hired the rest of the staff
from among large pools of local applicants. Nysco Shu, a veteran
manager from AIG's Nan Shan subsidiary in Taiwan, trained the new
life insurance staff. Nysco and his colleagues had that rare chance,
claimed only by true pioneers, of defining the Shanghai life insurance
market since it had scarcely existed. Nysco explained his task in historic
terms: "We were opening not just the Chinese market; we were
opening the Chinese mind."[8]

In China, insurance sales teams were paid on salary, a fixed cost that can lock in high expenses. AIG introduced an agency system instead, in which individuals wishing to earn money could learn to sell insurance policies, compensated on a commission basis. That attracted employees from many walks of life, including doctors, engineers, and lawyers. For the company, this approach helped manage costs. The model thus suited both employer and employee and led to expanding business, which spelled new jobs for the economy, profits for the company, coverage for risks and losses of Chinese citizens, and the accumulation of capital for investment.

The team started by selling simple, cheap accidental death policies. Later, they gradually increased the complexity and cost of offerings, ratcheting up the sophistication of both the sales force and customers. Entrepreneurship blossomed. Agents even developed favorite marketing techniques, such as, when pitching life insurance targeted to a particular company, sell it to the boss first; selling to the rest of the staff becomes easy.[9] For general insurance, training proved more difficult. The products—which included marine and property and casualty insurance—are more complex and founded on concepts alien to domestic Chinese. The staff needed to be taught to think about and analyze a risk, and then translate that into an insurance policy that could be sold at a price delivering an underwriting profit.

After three years of operation, participants—American and Chinese— saw that the vision was being realized. Carla Hills, the U.S. trade representative from 1989 to 1993 and AIG corporate board member from 1993 to 2006, explained that with its 1992 license, AIG demonstrated that competition in the insurance business—even from foreigners— benefited China and its economy. PICC and other state agencies gradually responded by picking up the slack in their organizations. PICC eventually copied AIG's incentive compensation programs, so that PICC employees were paid only when they wrote policies. Premier Zhu observed that not only did AIG prosper but "our local insurance companies also learned many operational and management skills from AIG. [T]hey too grew faster than before."[10]

In December 1996, AIA moved into offices at the impressive neo-renaissance structure at No. 17 The Bund, the grand *North China Daily News* building—where Starr had opened his first small agency generations earlier. Then owned by the Shanghai Bund Buildings Transformation Corporation, the asking price for a sale was too high. Greenberg quipped that he was "not prepared to pay $45 million for a museum." But AIA signed a 30-year lease for the eight-story 102,000-square-foot structure.[11] AIA renovated the building and consolidated its many offices around town in the modernized space. A permanent photo exhibition illustrating the early days of the American International companies in China was unveiled at the grand reopening of No. 17, then renamed the AIA Building.[12]

AIG's Shanghai success suggested that it was time to expand. Again, of course, AIG met governmental resistance. As Premier Zhu would later recount, despite how AIG prospered and helped Chinese insurance companies prosper:

> When AIG wanted to set up branches in other regions, there was still considerable resistance. Even though I was by then already a Vice Premier, I was still unable to meet Mr. Greenberg's requests. He grumbled that the wait was long enough to turn a young girl into an old lady.[13]

Waiting was not exactly what Greenberg did, as he persisted actively in seeking ways to gain access to additional Chinese markets. Greenberg pointed to AIG's success in Shanghai to persuade the authorities to license AIG in Guangzhou, the commercial center of South China, for a life insurance business. Guangzhou was appealing both for its large size and its proximity to Hong Kong, making it easier to move AIG employees between the two cities. AIG repeated the business model that had succeeded in Shanghai: recruiting and training a first-class workforce capable of conducting rigorous underwriting. The Guangzhou business flourished just as the Shanghai business did.

Despite meeting a constant bias in favor of domestic and state-owned businesses in China, AIG continued to leverage its diplomatic channels to push against restrictions and obtain additional licenses. But the best that seemed to be offered were opportunities for AIG to form joint ventures with either SOEs or Chinese-owned insurers. Neither avenue was appealing. What AIG wanted most was a nationwide license for a business that it owned 100 percent. The promise of this outcome arose at the same time that China was courting the international community, and the United States, for accession into the World Trade Organization.

Along with Secretary Kissinger and kindred diplomatic pioneers, Greenberg believed in the future of U.S-China relations. China's membership in the WTO would increase its sense of responsibility in international affairs, especially in trade. So Greenberg took an active role in bringing China into the WTO. China's accession into the WTO, according to Kissinger, marked a "crucial" return of China to world affairs and credits Greenberg with playing an "important role" in that feat.[14] AIG urged U.S. policy makers to grant China the annual renewal of most-favored nation status, which had become a political ritual during the 1990s. AIG argued that U.S.-China trade was so integral to the U.S. economy and to global peace and security that domestic politicians should separate it from other issues, such as political change and human rights.

Others, notably Kissinger, had long argued that trade should not be held hostage to other objectives because success in promoting other objectives is more likely when the issues are treated separately.[15] Kissinger's experience taught him that it is better to use soft diplomacy than apply formal public pressure. In his service inside and outside of government, Secretary Kissinger said it was easier to persuade officials to undertake reforms, from democracy to human rights, in private discussions than by public hectoring.

After much debate, the U.S. leadership accepted this view, epitomized in May 1994 when President Clinton renewed most-favored-nation status for China and announced that U.S. policy would no longer tie China's trade status to change in other areas. As chairman of the U.S.-China Business Council, Greenberg cheered: "If we only did business with the countries that share our views, we wouldn't be doing business in very many places overseas."

AIG worked tirelessly urging the U.S. government to embrace China openly and urging the Chinese government to reciprocate.[16] As chairman of IBLAC and head of AIG, Greenberg coordinated efforts with U.S. Trade Representative Charlene Barshefsky. She firmly backed and actively campaigned for open trade with China throughout her tenure from 1997 to 2001. Other insurers, particularly those in Europe, were suspicious of AIG's ambitions. They thought that AIG stood a good chance, given its leadership and connections, of being licensed throughout China, rather than merely by province or city, and to have

100 percent ownership. And this seemed to be the case. At a meeting that Greenberg arranged with Zhu, now premier, and Chen Yuan, governor of the China Development Bank, Premier Zhu said he understood that if China were admitted to the WTO, then AIG would receive a nationwide, 100 percent–owned insurance license in China.

By early 1999, the groundwork for China's admission into the WTO seemed to have been laid as the United States signaled its strong support. Greenberg had been discussing China's WTO interest with President Clinton's advisors and successive treasury secretaries, Robert Rubin and Lawrence Summers. It appeared to be U.S. policy to back China's admission to the WTO. In a speech on April 7, 1999, President Clinton indicated that he endorsed China's admission. With great expectations and high hopes, Premier Zhu traveled to the United States a few days after that speech. The centerpiece of the trip was a state visit to Washington, where Premier Zhu was the guest of President Clinton at a White House dinner for 224 dignitaries. In the receiving line, President Clinton introduced Premier Zhu to Greenberg, prompting the premier to say, "I know Hank," as he threw his arms around his old friend. The warm bear hug led the *Washington Post* to report that Greenberg was "the guest Zhu seemed most pleased to see."[17]

A week later, on April 13, Premier Zhu headed north to give a speech at the Economic Club of New York. Greenberg shared the dais with the premier in a roomful of distinguished financial executives, including many from leading international insurance companies. During the speech, Premier Zhu repeated the assurances that he had been giving, that AIG would be granted a national 100 percent–owned license upon China's entrance into the WTO. The assembled competitors cringed. European executives, in particular, let the premier know the next morning that they would object to such favorable treatment for AIG unless they, too, could win nationwide licenses with 100 percent ownership.

At the same time, the mood in Washington was cooling. Questions arose about whether Congress and even Vice President Al Gore, backed by labor and running for president, would support President Clinton's decision to champion China's admission into the WTO. Participants had expected the president to announce a final favorable decision but were disappointed to learn that, in the face of such domestic pressure, Clinton caved. Greenberg and the CEOs of other

U.S.-based global companies tried to persuade Rubin and Summers to get the president to reconsider, but by then it was too late, as Zhu had already continued his journey with a stop in Canada before heading home. Premier Zhu returned to China without a final deal. Some months later, at a dinner at Tsinghua University, Premier Zhu informed Greenberg that he was no longer able to assure the national license they had been discussing. He cited the power struggles of Chinese politics and noted that even President Jiang was no longer committed to the issue. President Clinton's turnabout had made it more difficult for Premier Zhu and President Jiang to maintain party enthusiasm for seeking admission to the WTO, let alone offering concessions to get there. In addition, European insurance companies continued to pressure the Chinese government not to grant anything to AIG unless they were treated the same way.

As WTO negotiations continued, Greenberg maintained the dialogue with Premier Zhu as well as other Chinese officials to support the licenses that AIG preferred—100 percent–owned nationwide licenses. But Greenberg now encountered stronger pushback. In one case, he confronted the good-cop, bad-cop routine, a negotiating technique known worldwide. Playing the bad cop was a senior official overseeing commerce, Madame Wu Yi. A tough negotiator whom Greenberg knew well and admired, Wu firmly delivered to Greenberg the bad news: China could not grant AIG a nationwide license, citing the most-favored-nation principle's restrictions on the country's flexibility. Greenberg challenged this stance, recounting the repeated assurances that he had been receiving. To lower the rising temperature in the room, Wu suggested that Greenberg take a walk around the grounds—a common tactic of international negotiations.

Upon returning from the walk, Wu had departed, but Premier Zhu appeared, prepared to play good cop. True, the premier said, Wu was correct about the inability to deliver nationwide licenses. But, he added, it did seem possible that AIG could be awarded some number of additional branch licenses. Greenberg replied by urging Zhu to give the nationwide possibility one last chance, by directing that Chinese trade negotiators have another round of talks with Ambassador Barshefsky. Those discussions, however, quickly hit a wall.

In the end, AIG pressed for and obtained additional provincial licenses, including in the large and valuable market of Beijing, as well as in Dongguan, Jiangmen, and Suzhou. AIG won many unique successes and firsts in China—the first representative office; the first joint venture; the first license; the only 100 percent ownership; the first to receive two, then three, four, five, and six licenses; and so on—but did not get everything it fought for. Of course, Greenberg nevertheless supported China's joining the WTO, as he personally believed that it was of great value to China and in the national interest of the United States, making it incontestable, even by companies whose own negotiations ended in partial disappointment. In 2001, after 13 years of negotiations, China joined the WTO; the next year, AIG opened offices in Beijing.

In March 2005, Chinese officials bestowed on Greenberg the coveted Marco Polo Award, given to an American businessperson distinguished for contributions to improving relations between the United States and China. Greenberg has also been named an honorary citizen of Shanghai, one of a handful of Americans to be so honored.

Trade and investments between the United States and China have grown substantially since the historic reopening of China to the West.[18] As with any relationship between major powers, there is friction and mutual concern about how trade is conducted. The countries have swapped allegations of improper activities. The United States accused China of "dumping" products below their cost and failing to protect property rights. China has accused the United States of unfairly imposing tariffs on selected Chinese imports. Such trading in accusations recurs in international dialogues but often yields the same result: cordial dead-ends and enduring frictions that hamper improving the overall relationship.

A bolder approach is warranted, and both countries are prepared for it today. China and the United States should open negotiations for a free trade agreement between them. Negotiations will be protracted and punctuated by impasses, but instead of trading accusations and meeting dead-ends, by discussing concerns in the context of a formal negotiation driving toward an agreement, the chances of success are substantially improved. While agreement on some issues may prove impossible, progress on others is all but certain and will create a productive trade climate. Greenberg believes that China is prepared for such an agreement and that it is in U.S. national interest. A free trade agreement is far superior to a trade war.

Chapter 9

The Life Business

Property and casualty insurance exposed AIG to Mother Nature's vicissitudes: earthquakes, floods, and tsunamis. The business is also volatile as a result of myriad other factors from the vagaries of interest rates to the uncertainties of litigation. A property and casualty insurance company can generate an underwriting profit for several years only to face a massive loss due to such circumstances. It is therefore desirable to diversify such risks by entering into businesses that operate in different ways. In comparison, life insurance is stable, at least so long as premiums received are invested conservatively, and in any event the variability in life insurance is usually different in both kind and time compared to property and casualty. The two lines together, therefore, provided an optimal mix for AIG, especially as it diversified its life insurance business across the world and in many product lines.

Starr built small branch life insurance operations throughout Southeast Asia beginning in the 1930s. Ousted by China's new rulers in 1949, Starr relocated his Asian base of operations to Hong Kong under the new name, American International Assurance Company (AIA).[1] AIA followed a company-wide business model whereby mobile overseas personnel (MOPs) were dispatched to recruit local staff and provide professional training so they would view their jobs as careers. Agents, preferably paid variable commissions, fanned out nationwide to educate people about life insurance and tailor products to suit customer needs.

The company reinvested capital in infrastructure projects benefiting the national economy—bridges, dams, hospitals, houses, roads, and schools. As soon as it became feasible, each local company committed capital to construct its company-owned office buildings in leading cities to demonstrate its permanence, reliability, and scale. AIA's buildings were designed according to ornate architectural plans and advanced engineering standards, achieving landmark status. At dedication ceremonies, the company's local executives would beseech the nation's leader—prime minister, president, king, or the like—to officiate. Critical in every life insurance operation abroad is sensitivity to local economic conditions, being sure that capital is invested patiently, including by avoiding temptation to invest in high-yield instruments that tend to be both risky and volatile. After all, life insurance companies serve as trustees of policyholders' funds.

In the Philippines, AIG's flagship company was Philamlife, short for Philippine American Life Insurance Company. Starr had begun a life insurance business in the Philippines in the mid-1920s, though it was disrupted by World War II. Fortunately, just as the Japanese army marched on Manila in December 1941, Starr's loyal colleagues, Clayton L. Seitz, a regional manager, and Werner Stamm, an accountant, stored most of the company's records.[2] That helped the company resume business after the war ended. Postwar rebuilding of the country required cooperation between the United States and Filipino governments, collaboration between governments and business, and the commitment of Filipino citizens. As always, personal relationships proved critical: Starr became friends with General Douglas MacArthur, who oversaw the country on behalf of the victorious allies, and Paul V. McNutt, a popular American diplomat, appointed ambassador by President Harry S. Truman.[3]

After Ambassador McNutt stepped down from that post, Starr persuaded him to serve as Philamlife's chairman. This proved to be shrewd recruiting. An initial challenge to building an insurance company after the war was a lack of insurance consciousness among citizens. The chaos of war and its aftermath left many policyholders across the country undercompensated for destruction. Reviving trust in insurance was vital, and Starr thought that Ambassador McNutt's popularity among Filipinos made his name a badge of trust for the company. To run the operation, Starr and Ernie Stempel, head of Starr's life insurance operations, recruited Earl Carroll, a colorful character who had become a local hero among the prisoners at Santo Tomas camp, where the Japanese had interred prisoners during the war. Philamlife attracted prominent and capable Filipinos as senior executives, who in turn hired and trained an impressive legion of insurance agents and managers to blanket the country's 7,107 islands and build the business.

The sales strategy targeted the middle class, from farmers to merchants, using agents knocking on doors selling small policies and collecting premiums. Filipinos, struggling to move themselves and their country from poverty to prosperity, cherished financial security. Without many banks or investment alternatives such as stocks, bonds, or mutual funds, life insurance was an attractive way to amass savings. Many Filipinos so prized their investments in Philamlife that they hung framed copies of their policies on their living room walls.

From its inception, a basic premise of Philamlife was to invest its capital in ventures that would accelerate the county's economic development.[4] In addition to financing infrastructure projects, Philamlife supported agriculture and industries like cement making, food processing, oil refining, and pharmaceuticals. These civic-minded commitments went beyond typical capital investment to include free annual health exams for policyholders and such steps as circulating mobile x-ray units to administer free tuberculosis tests.

In Manila, Starr constructed Philamlife's first building in 1961, designed by local architect Carlos D. Arguelles, and featured in both *National Geographic* and *Time*.[5] Known locally as "The House of Savings," one graceful feature stood out for its role in the public sphere: a rounded marble tunnel off the lobby opened into an acoustically sophisticated 800-seat auditorium. The auditorium staged a variety of public artistic and civic events, from symphonies and operas to government and United Nations programs.[6]

Greenberg took a trip to the Philippines shortly after the 1965 election of Ferdinand Marcos as president, and the two would work closely together in the Philippines for the next two decades. Greenberg developed an abiding relationship with President Marcos, though punctuated by disagreement and eventual disillusionment. One sour note in the early days concerned the House of Savings, which Philamlife owned outright (and so epitomized Philamlife that the company was also known as the House of Savings). Although a treaty between the United States and the Philippines, called the Laurel-Langley agreement,[7] committed each country to respecting ownership rights of the other's companies, Marcos fixed on another domestic law restricting ownership of real property by foreign companies. Greenberg objected that the restriction Marcos invoked was specifically targeted to *Japanese* companies—not American companies.

The two had been discussing this for many months, Greenberg understanding Marcos's motivation but resisting given the importance of real estate assets to a life insurance business as well as the symbolic importance of the company's headquarters. Greenberg thought that a resolution was all but concluded. He was shocked when Marcos confronted him at a state dinner in the Malacañang Palace, stating that the deal was off and that Philamlife would have to share ownership in the building with a Filipino partner. Greenberg was livid, and, though he tried not to make a scene, the two soon raised their voices at one another, drawing the attention of many guests in the dining room.

Normally, guests at a state dinner do not depart before the president leaves. That night, however, Greenberg left immediately after this heated discussion, which few in the room could miss despite Greenberg's best efforts at decorum. The Greenbergs drove to the nearby airfield and boarded their plane for Hong Kong, where they spent the night. The next morning, the U.S. ambassador, Henry Byroade, called Greenberg. President Marcos wished them to return to the Philippines. Upon their return, Marcos proposed a resolution. In the end, President Marcos conceded Greenberg's argument.[8]

In those early days, Greenberg and President Marcos maintained a collegial enough relationship that Marcos would invite Greenberg to play *pelota*, an ancient court sport similar to handball. The fast-paced game puts players in close physical proximity with one another. Greenberg joked with Stempel, who joined one of the games, that they had to be careful how close they got to Marcos, as he was invariably accompanied by military aides.[9]

While visiting the Philippines in 1966, Marcos invited Greenberg to the Malacañang Palace for breakfast. Greenberg's relationship with Marcos entailed giving practical advice and counsel. On arrival, it was impossible to miss the oversized flowers spread ungainly in the middle of the dining table. As Greenberg approached, a Filipino colleague, Cesar Zalamea, put his index finger to his lips, nodding his head to direct Greenberg's attention to the flowers. Duly warned of a tape recorder in surreptitious use, Greenberg watched his words.

Marcos entered the room and the men sat down to eat and chat. After a short while, Marcos casually remarked, "I am thinking about introducing mutual funds into the Philippines. What do you think of that?"

"We have evaluated whether mutual funds would be appealing to citizens here," Greenberg said. "We have determined that, at least at present, there is not enough demand to make a fund succeed. What makes you think about this?"

"I have a particular businessman in mind who has proposed the idea. I wanted to see if you and Philamlife would be interested in a joint venture or partnership with him."

"We usually don't prefer joint ventures or partnerships," Greenberg explained, "but who is that?"

"Bernie Cornfeld," President Marcos replied.

Greenberg almost choked on his mango.

Marcos continued. "He's selling mutual funds throughout Europe and Asia and wants to break into our country."

"We don't want to have anything to do with that," Greenberg replied, "and neither should you."

Cornfeld was among the most controversial figures in global finance at the time, peddling American mutual fund interests across the world in a company called Investors Overseas Services.[10] Pitched to small investors, Cornfeld appeared to have grown it into a billion-dollar enterprise. But it eventually collapsed and was taken over by another infamous financier of the age, Robert Vesco. Cornfeld was investigated for securities fraud and settled charges by agreeing to wind up or sell all his U.S. operations. His ventures abroad prospered for a few years before failing in 1970. Legal disputes battled him the rest of his life, and he never made a comeback.[11] Marcos, who trusted Greenberg's judgment, heeded the advice to stay away.

Greenberg never learned who bugged that dining room or why, but eavesdropping on him and his entourage had become standard. One defense often employed when traveling: at the last minute, he would switch hotel rooms with AIG's pilots and crew.

During the 1970s, the Philippines was marked by corruption, lawlessness, and a sputtering economy. Feeling imperiled, Marcos desperately clung to power even as his grip loosened. To maintain control, his staff allowed a rumor to flourish that an insurgent group was conspiring to start a communist insurrection. As such rumors swirled, Marcos considered declaring martial law. President Marcos dispatched his brother-in-law, a top aide, to run the proposal for martial law by Greenberg. Marcos hoped that, given Greenberg's connections in Washington, Greenberg would be able to forecast the official reaction. Greenberg told the interlocutor he could not make such a prediction and advised him to ask the U.S. government himself. Greenberg then promptly reported the pending despotism to State Department officials. Marcos declared martial law the next day, which he maintained through 1981.

President Marcos lurched from one national crisis to another. Marcos stood for reelection as president in 1981, shortly after lifting martial law, and won, in part because the opposition boycotted the election in protest. The domestic economy returned as a sore spot in Marcos's third term. To address this, in 1983, Marcos radically devalued the Filipino peso, a move that reduced Philamlife's capital position and income, reversing years of profitability. But net damage to AIG was offset by the broader diversification of its businesses around the world that its people had been relentlessly pursuing. By 1983, such diversification had diminished the relative weight of operations in the Philippines.[12] At the same time, the situation in the Philippines continued to decline.

Benigno S. Aquino Jr. had been a presidential candidate against Marcos during the period of martial law, but subsequently left the country to teach for several semesters in the United States. As he was planning a return to the Philippines to run for the presidency again, rumors circulated that his life might be in jeopardy. Ignoring the warnings, he flew back to Manila. After disembarking from his plane, while walking down the gangway, an assassin killed him. Some citizens pointed the finger at senior officials in the Marcos administration. Government officials denied the murder charges without investigation. Public furor erupted, becoming by February 1986 the potent "People Power Revolution."

Although President Marcos planned to seek a fourth term in the presidency, people had lost confidence in his leadership and were eager for change. This turn of events concerned the United States and AIG. Both had invested substantially in the country and both felt a responsibility to people in the Philippines. The United States had important military bases there—Clark Air Base and Subic Bay Naval Base. Many Filipino citizens thirsted for independence from the United States, and thus some preferred to have U.S. forces withdraw. Presidential leadership was needed to explain why military withdrawal was not in the national interest and why the close alliance with the United States was essential. From AIG's perspective, Philamlife was not only a prosperous business but an important Filipino corporate citizen. Its interests and presence in the Philippines ran deep. It had built a large employee and policyholder base, helped people accumulate savings (it was the "House of Savings"), contributed significantly to the development of the national economy, and projected and sustained a positive image of America in the popular Filipino mind.

In April 1985, a senior U.S. government official contacted Greenberg to ask if he would talk to President Marcos about foregoing another term. U.S. government officials believed that Greenberg's knowledge of the Philippines and relationship with its leadership positioned him better than anyone to make this overture. It was always delicate for one country to intervene in another country's domestic politics and thorny for the U.S. government to enlist the aid of private citizens in such an intervention. To arrange the meeting, Greenberg reached out to Roberto ("Bobby") V. Ongpin, a top aide to Marcos then serving as minister of trade and industry.

Visiting Manila in May 1985, Greenberg was joined in the effort by Admiral Robert L. J. Long, retired U.S. commander of the Pacific, and John S. Reed, chairman of Citicorp, which also had a significant presence in the Philippines dating to the early twentieth century.[13] The men flew in separately, meeting at the Manila airport in the late afternoon before heading to the Malacañang Palace for dinner. When they arrived, it was clear that Marcos had become gravely ill. After the meal, while sipping tea, Greenberg took up his task. Turning toward Marcos, Greenberg cleared his throat: "Mr. President, we have known one another for a long time. I need to speak frankly with you about something."

Marcos, who looked bloated, was having difficulty breathing, as Greenberg continued, "Are you feeling okay?"

The president's expression was blank, replying that he felt fine and his health was not of concern.

Greenberg leaned forward over the table, clasping his hands before him, saying, "As you know, running for office is strenuous. Given your health, is it really a good idea to run for president of the Philippines again?" Marcos assured Greenberg that he had the strength, brushing off the suggestion.

Greenberg persisted. "Why not step down at the top of your game? It would be a shame if you were to run and lose. Why would you do that?"

Marcos was resolute, telling his interlocutors: "Gentlemen, I'm going to run and win. And I have plenty of support, here and in the United States."

"But many will be skeptical about whether you won fair and square," Greenberg cautioned.

Reed repeated the plea in different words, adding that international investors were becoming anxious for an orderly succession in the Philippines.

"You'll see. Don't worry about these matters," Marcos said.

The cavernous dining room in the palace was still, as Greenberg concluded the conversation. "I think it would be a mistake," he said.

Throughout 1985, the U.S. government continued efforts to convince Marcos not to run again. Efforts included personal diplomacy by Nevada Senator Paul Laxalt. The senator, who consulted with Greenberg ahead of his mission, visited with Marcos in October 1985.[14] Despite winning Marcos's trust and confidence, however, Laxalt could not dissuade Marcos from going ahead with the election either.

The official results of the February 1986 election declared Marcos the winner by a wide margin. But, as Greenberg had warned, opponents and some international observers questioned the integrity of the results. Members of his own cabinet turned on Marcos as well. Marcos soon capitulated, renouncing the presidency, being airlifted from the palace by helicopter to assure his safety. President Reagan arranged for sanctuary in Hawaii, where Marcos lived in exile until his death in 1989.

The Philippines continues to be a valued U.S. ally and strategic interest, and an important member of the Association of Southeast Asian Nations. In 1997, with Philamlife prospering, the company moved from the old Philamlife building built under Starr's direction to a 46-story office tower in Manila's Makati City built under Greenberg's direction.[15] The Philamlife Tower, soaring 656 feet, remains among the tallest buildings in Manila. The massive building is modern in technology—with high-speed elevators, security card access, a gym, and a helipad—and contains a private dining and social club on the top floor that is among the most sought-after spots in town. Attesting to the role Philamlife has played in the country, on a later trip to the Philippines, Greenberg was happy to see that half the members of the cabinet of President Benigno Aquino III were former senior executives of Philamlife, as was a recent ambassador to the United States, Jose L. Cuisia Jr. Philamlife continues to be a very important entity in the Philippines.

AIG's distinctive buildings, in Manila and a dozen other cities around the world, stood as symbols of community and permanence. The architecture reflected each site's national culture,[16] tailored to environments as varied as Hong Kong; Beirut, Lebanon; Havana, Cuba;[17] and Karachi, Pakistan.[18] In the 1960s, Starr proposed expanding operations in Bangladesh, the eastern region of Pakistan. Bangladesh was and remains among the world's most populous yet poorest nations. To lift vast numbers of people out of poverty, Starr believed it was desirable to create a life insurance business there—along with a new building. One executive, Richard Rhodebeck, was opposed, referencing the country's uncertain political and economic future.[19] Rhodebeck concluded: "The building will be built only over my dead body." Starr replied, "Okay, we'll call it the 'Rhodebeck Memorial.'" Throughout his business dealings, Starr always kept his witty acerbic side.

One asset that every American International company leveraged abroad was its "red, white and blue" American identity. The word *American*—American Home, American International, American Life

Insurance Company (ALICO), or any of dozens of AIG companies—signaled the fortitude of the United States. Because selling life insurance overseas involved marketing values identified with the United States—savings, safety, and security—agents were trained to promote these associations.

ALICO targeted markets in Latin America, Europe, the Middle East, and Japan. By 1971, ALICO had $1 billion of life insurance in force—an amount Greenberg thought modest compared to what was possible. He asked Stempel and the energetic Ken Nottingham, an MOP, to make it happen. They reorganized ALICO along AIG's profit center model. They decentralized its operations by creating regional vice presidents, general managers, and branch offices in different countries. They increased cross-selling of products, among them an offer to add a personal accident and health policy to every life insurance plan. ALICO's customers found this appealing, and it drove substantial underwriting profits. The reorganization succeeded: the business grew more than eightfold within a decade, and ALICO became one of the largest international life insurance companies in the world, operating in 60 countries through 70,000 agents.

ALICO operated in a dozen Latin American countries, where the company had planted roots in the 1950s, when the region was an economic dynamo compared to Asian and European economies decimated by war. Following a model akin to that of AIA, ALICO targeted less developed markets, dispatched experienced managers to create a local company, adhered to local customs, recruited talented locals, and let them build the business, with profits reinvested in the local economy.[20] Its products started out simple, just whole life. As the economy and market matured, the product line became more complex, adding annuities and, ultimately, retirement and pension programs. However, the environment in most of Latin America was never ripe for AIG to establish a leading life insurance business there as it clearly had in Asia.

ALICO's efforts in Europe faced different challenges, as AIG lacked the first-mover advantages arising from introducing customers to the value of life insurance. It faced sophisticated competition using powerful entrenched distribution systems. Germany, for example, boasts large, strong trusted life insurance companies tied to major banks. Still, ALICO innovated in Europe, penetrating markets with creative distribution techniques: direct marketing in Germany, specialty products in France, and cobranding deals in the United Kingdom. It also found its familiar first-mover advantages in southern Europe, in Portugal, Italy, Greece, and Spain (long before others dubbed those four countries the "PIGS") and, after the Cold War, in eastern Europe, especially Hungary, Poland, and Romania.

Innovation meant tailoring products to meet local needs and tastes. In the Middle East, ALICO's agents concentrated on basic whole life insurance in small offices throughout the region: Jordan, Kuwait, Lebanon, Saudi Arabia, Syria, and Turkey. In Japan, ALICO pursued advanced financial products such as annuities and pensions marketed using direct mail, in retail stores, by credit card, and over the phone. In 2000, AIG bought Chiyoda Mutual Life Insurance, and in 2003 GE Edison Life Insurance—heavily negotiated deals between Greenberg and GE's CEO, Jeffrey Immelt, that made AIG a top 10 Japanese life insurance company.

AIG was also a pioneer in developing business in Africa. It built prosperous operations in many parts of that continent in such countries as Kenya, Nigeria, and South Africa. However, its overtures were ahead of their time in some places, notably Uganda. There, in the early 1970s, AIG formed a joint venture run by Louis D. LeFevre, the MOP who also faced harrowing challenges in Nigeria. In Uganda, LeFevre was obliged to operate under the vicious rule of military dictator Idi Amin, who reigned from 1971 to 1979 with brutal force.

Greenberg visited the country on a trip to South Africa with John Roberts. They stayed at the Kampala International Hotel—a name that sounded better than it was, where thieves prowled and danger lurked at every turn. The American ambassador hosted a party for Greenberg and AIG at the hotel, located in the heart of Kampala, the nation's capital, on the hotel's top floor.

After passing through the receiving line, Greenberg and Roberts and their wives observed two senior Ugandan officials and their wives standing along the rail of the rooftop. They appeared to be dropping glasses off the roof and then laughing after they dropped. Asked what they were doing, the ambassador reluctantly confessed that they were seeing if they could hit passersby below. The atrocious behavior was a microcosm to the horrors of Amin's Uganda—where AIG did not remain for long.

In the United States, Starr had invested briefly in the life business before World War II in U.S. Life. That had been one of his trademark companies before selling it, due to duplicative regulations, to the company where Greenberg got his first job with Mil Smith, and the proceeds of which he used to acquire American Home. Decades later, a successful life insurance business in the United States gave AIG a basis for expanding into the more sophisticated retirement planning products. These had become the central business of Sun America, the financial services company run by Eli Broad.

In 1998, Broad offered to sell the company to AIG. Decades earlier, Broad had founded a home-building company, Kaufman and Broad Home Corporation, in Los Angeles (the company was later renamed KB Home). The home-building business is notoriously cyclical. To diversify it, Broad acquired Sun Life Insurance Company of America, a life insurance company less sensitive to the business cycle.[21] As the 1980s dawned, however, Broad found that small life companies like his could not beat their larger rivals. Broad decided that Sun Life should carve a new niche. Demographic trends—rising private wealth along with declining support from public programs such as Social Security—pointed to increasing need for retirement planning.

Sun Life wound down its life businesses and ramped up its investment lines, first moving into annuities and later mutual funds. It built a network of independent financial planners, nearly 10,000 nationwide. Broad changed the company's name to Sun America and rebranded the business. The effort succeeded: by 1998, Sun America had become a leader in asset accumulation products. For AIG, synergies appeared: Sun America's domestic distribution prowess would boost AIG's domestic life insurance business, and AIG's unmatched international capabilities would give Sun America's retirement-planning businesses new fields to plow abroad. AIG bought 100 percent of Sun's common stock, paying in AIG shares worth $18 billion. Within one month after Broad broached the possibility, the deal was approved by both corporate boards and signed in late August.[22] In addition to the mutual product and distribution synergies, the fit between AIG and Sun America was strong for less tangible but important reasons: the companies shared an entrepreneurial culture, a commitment to expense control and a focus on the bottom line.

Similar attributes made American General Corporation, among the largest life insurance companies in the United States, an attractive target. On March 12, 2001, Prudential plc, the massive British life insurance company, and American General announced that they had signed a merger agreement. American General shareholders would receive shares in Prudential, then worth $50 per share, valuing American General at $27 billion. The deal would rank among the largest transatlantic financial mergers and redefine the global life insurance industry. In response to their perception that Prudential was overpaying, traders dumped Prudential's shares on the London Stock Exchange, driving the deal's value to American General down to $40 per share by April 3.[23]

Greenberg learned of these developments while meeting with company executives at a weekend retreat. Sensing opportunity, they acted that same day. They enlisted professional advisers in law and investment banking to consider the possibility of AIG's making a bid for American General, a company that Greenberg knew well and had long admired. The lawyers spent the weekend reviewing the necessary steps, and the bankers prepared a valuation analysis. The advisers presented results to AIG on Monday, and the team formulated a tentative plan, arranging for an AIG board meeting to get input and approval.

After the board meeting, Greenberg called American General's chairman and CEO to say that AIG was interested in acquiring the company. Greenberg said AIG was prepared to pay $46 per share in AIG stock, $25 billion in total.[24] The next day, AIG made that unsolicited offer public and sent American General a formal letter outlining terms. Within one week, on April 9, American General's board agreed to recommend AIG's bid to its shareholders and cease supporting Prudential's offer. A formal agreement was signed a month later.

Prudential could not match AIG's offer and it sued, claiming AIG had wrongly interfered with its contract. That was a losing argument, however, and Prudential withdrew it after a court declined to block the AIG–American General deal. Instead, Prudential pointed to a provision in its agreement with American General calling for American General to pay Prudential a break-up fee of $600 million if it terminated in favor of a better bid. American General paid the fee, and AIG acquired the company on August 29, 2001, paying stock then valued at $23 billion.[25]

Acquiring American General cemented the achievement of AIG's long-standing strategic objective of diversifying earnings through an expanded life insurance presence in the United States. The deal, the largest in AIG's history, added a sizable retirement savings business that would bolster Sun America's position in that market. In addition, American General had been growing its consumer finance business, which some AIG divisions abroad had been developing as well. Owning American General created new opportunities for AIG's other units to cross-sell products, in the United States and overseas. It enabled consolidating back-office operations to slash expenses. American General increased AIG's earnings by 10 percent.

From the small world department: American General then owned U.S. Life, the domestic life company that Starr had owned in the 1940s before selling it to Mil Smith's company due to duplicative regulation, now returned to the family under Greenberg's watch. Traced to humble beginnings, by 2005, AIG was the largest life insurance company in the world—and the life business was AIG's largest segment, enjoying more than $9 billion in annual earnings[26] from 70 countries through 175,000 agents.[27]

Chapter 10

The Domestic Front

D ays after September 11, 2001, in the Roosevelt Room of the White House, President George W. Bush and his senior advisers met with chief executives of six of the nation's leading insurance companies. Their goal: to avert an international calamity. They needed to ensure that the world's commercial aircraft fleet would not go idle for lack of insurance. Under typical aviation insurance contracts, the insurer can cancel the policy on seven days' notice, after the occurrence of a designated event, including terrorist acts. After the 9/11 attacks, aviation insurance companies immediately sent cancellation notices to customers worldwide. And without insurance, airplanes could not fly. As of midnight September 18, 2001, most of the world's commercial aircraft would be grounded.

As an emergency measure, the richest countries—including the United States, members of the European Union, and Japan—announced temporary governmental insurance programs to provide coverage in the absence of private insurance. Those short-term programs were mere

Band-Aids, however, and unaffordable for many governments. Green-berg proposed creating an industry-wide pool of capital to supply aviation insurance. This would provide a long-term, private-sector solution. After explaining this to the president and the other executives, Greenberg left the White House. Within four days, AIG formed a $1 billion insurance fund, supplying a $200 million share of it directly. The world's planes kept flying and a global crisis was quietly averted.[1]

Another way AIG responded to 9/11 was to conduct a compre-hensive global analysis of calamitous risk such as terrorism. To spearhead this project, AIG enlisted Gerald Komisar, the former government official who for many years had been producing AIG's *Executive Briefing Book* for executives of its largest customers. Komisar developed a security risk index, ranking 140 countries on a scale of 1 to 5. The scale incorporated various risks, including terrorism, coup, insurrection, violent strike, and other upheaval. No country ever earned a 1, the lowest score, signaling absence of risk. The index was a directive to AIG's insurance underwriters: with a rating of up to 3, the underwriter could proceed at his own discretion; 4 required asking a supervisor; 5 required going to corporate headquarters, usually to Greenberg's office. The results were color-coded and designed to be simple and easy to use, despite the intensive underlying data and complex analytical process required to reach the conclusion.

After any catastrophe, insurance markets adjust. Claims consume capital, prices rise, and insurers must replenish capital or obtain rein-surance. AIG took advantage of that cycle after the terrorist attacks of September 11. It formed Allied World Assurance Company, a joint undertaking with Chubb, (with investments from Goldman Sachs and Swiss Re) to underwrite high-dollar coverage in several fields, including directors and officers (D&O) and errors and omissions (E&O). AIG sent more managers into the new business than Chubb did, as many Chubb executives hesitated out of concern that Allied World would operate in the same lines of business as Chubb, increasing competition for itself.[2] While it was difficult for Chubb to overcome this resistance to "can-nibalization," AIG managers did not resist. They tended to embrace competition, even between companies under the same corporate roof.[3]

AIG employees assigned to particular subsidiaries or divisions understood that they ultimately were part of AIG, not Allied World,

American Home, National Union, or Lexington. Managers and underwriters appreciated that in some sense they were competing with colleagues at other units. But it was not as if they were competing with a particular company or for a given account. They were competing broadly in the wider marketplace. The philosophy was simple: the more boats you have in the ocean, the more fish you will catch. In any event, as Greenberg would remind employees, they did not own stock in American Home, National Union, Lexington, or Allied World, but in AIG.

AIG's competitive culture, reinforced by its preoccupation with earning an underwriting profit, enabled it to avoid hazards that devastated some revered competitors. Excruciating examples arose from the explosion of tort liability during the 1980s and 1990s.[4] Many insurers wrote policies, in fields ranging from environmental liability to medical malpractice, in order to earn premiums for investment while paying insufficient regard to the risks. Resulting losses not only erased the premiums and gains but sent AIG competitors into insolvency or reorganization.

AIG withdrew from the market when prices were low compared to risks, while competitors fought for business, and reentered when prices rose and an underwriting profit could be earned, when competitors retreated. Competitors failed to stress the importance of underwriting profit. True, insurers can make considerable income from investment—as AIG did. But at AIG an underwriting profit was the first priority and senior management broadcast that message to the troops. That command-and-control approach enforced discipline at AIG, enabling it to grow and amass capital while rivals shriveled or perished. Being ahead of the competition in product innovation and being widely diversified internationally were also great advantages.

■ ■ ■

At AIG, competition among rivals was not limited to insurance markets but extended into the public policy arena, where AIG's business compelled it to take positions on matters of national interest. AIG fielded a strong public policy and government relations team. Among debates they influenced were those concerning the environmental hazards caused by previous generations, known as Superfund cleanups. AIG had entered the environmental insurance business through a company acquired in 1968, Commerce & Industry Insurance Company (C&I), which would be run by an outstanding manager named Elmer N. Dickinson Jr. It was a state-of-the-art specialty writer of "highly-protected" fire risks—meaning insurance on buildings constructed using the ultimate in protective methods. Designed to reduce the risk of destruction by fire, protections included superior construction, advanced smoke sensors, and rapid-response sprinklers. High-tech buildings qualified for lower insurance premiums; underwriting the insurance is also specialized, involving inspection and analysis by structural engineers.

C&I thereafter launched an environmental insurance business, expanding its inspection and engineering capabilities. C&I underwriters engaged the technical expertise of engineers knowledgeable in chemistry, geology, hazardous materials and waste management. By the 1980s, as AIG had grown into a substantial insurer of environmental risks, the country awakened to a painful reality: for generations, industry had been contaminating the environment without appreciating the costs, especially by letting chemicals leach into water systems. The timing of C&I's success in this field, ironically, retaught an old lesson about the insurance business. Unlike in most businesses, insurers do not know production costs at the time products are made. Instead, they write coverage with a sense of future claims (probability and magnitude) but predictions prove inaccurate. In addition, unanticipated forces intervene, such as when judicial attitudes change, national priorities shift, or both—as happened concerning environmental risks during the 1980s and 1990s.

Several dramatic hazardous waste disasters—such as New York's Love Canal catastrophe in which 20,000 tons of buried chemical waste was linked to large-scale miscarriages, birth defects, and cancer—stirred Congress to pass the Superfund law in 1980.[5] Hastily drafted and quickly passed, Superfund radically changed the nation's approach to cleanups by stating tight rules. Companies that dealt with hazardous waste became liable for costs even if their actions were entirely legal at the time and they had not been negligent or deliberate. Minor contributors became liable for entire cleanups if no other contributors could be found—called "joint-and-several" liability. Superfund established "retroactive liability," making companies responsible for actions that occurred even before the law was passed—when the lion's share of the damage from hazardous waste occurred—and there is no statute of limitations. The retroactive liability even exposed current owners or operators to liability for actions of predecessors.

Under Superfund, the Environmental Protection Agency (EPA) makes a list of hazardous sites targeted for cleanup. It then hunts for potentially responsible parties who might be required to pay. The EPA directs those parties to clean up the site, or else conducts its own remediation and sends those parties the bill. When the EPA names potentially responsible parties, the parties often respond by challenging the EPA in court; finding additional parties to pay, who might likewise lodge a court challenge; and scouring old insurance policies for language saying the activity was covered. This latter maneuver was called "insurance archeology."

Insurance companies also fought in court, arguing that the old policies did not cover pollution. The oldest policies—some dating back decades before the 1970s when ecology became a national priority—had vague language about coverage, but insurers contended it did not cover the kinds of risks that had emerged. Since the companies had not set premiums under those old policies in anticipation of such risks, they had not collected funds for them. Beginning in the early 1970s, insurers added explicit policy language to encompass "sudden and accidental" events which, they said, excluded the hazardous waste problems that involved gradual pollution over many years.[6] Many courts nevertheless held against the insurance companies, finding that the policies did cover these losses.[7]

The EPA named thousands of national priority sites where average cleanup costs per site ran to $40 million, translating into gargantuan sums totaling hundreds of billions of dollars. The legal expenses of sorting out who was responsible consumed many additional billions of dollars. In some instances, attorneys' fees exceeded the clean-up costs. The result was a flawed system to address a serious problem, as Superfund had done more to generate administrative costs than to actually clean up the nation's hazardous waste sites.

Reformers suggested ways to reduce litigation and increase money available for cleanup. Ending the rules of retroactive liability and joint-and-several liability would reduce litigation, but would not generate resources to pay for the problem. Reformers proposed various funds, such as one to be created by industry and insurance companies who would contribute according to their current size—a "deep pocket" approach. For AIG, that was problematic because of the relative size of its business before the 1970s when most pollution occurred and in the 1990s when the fund was to be established. AIG's market share was comparatively modest in the earlier period but substantial since it had built C&I. Under most of the fund proposals, AIG would be forced to shoulder a disproportionate amount of costs compared to premiums received.

So AIG proposed a different approach, called a National Environmental Trust Fund.[8] It would impose a small surcharge on all commercial insurance policies, with proceeds used to pay for cleanups. The trust fund would eliminate the unfairness of retroactive and joint-and-several liability and save the billions of dollars being lost in litigation. The theory was simple: this was a societal problem and the solution should be societal as well. Other insurance companies disliked this proposal, worried that policymakers would soon believe that charging insurers was the new way to handle all society's costly problems.

After a decade of dismal results under Superfund, in August 1993 senior officials in the Clinton administration summoned top officers of eight large insurance companies, including AIG, Hartford, Nationwide, and Travelers. At this meeting, the government, backed by most of the insurance executives present, endorsed creating a pool funded by insurers based on their size. Greenberg repeated AIG's objection that under this proposal it would pay a very large share due to its current industry dominance though when the activities in question occurred and policies at stake were written, it held a smaller relative share. The meeting lasted seven hours. As it drew to a close, the officials asked whether the group could all agree, particularly whether AIG would support it. Greenberg said no, repeating support for the National Environmental Trust Fund. With that, the meeting—and the hope for both concepts—ended.

Superfund survives, imperfect though it is, leaving costly litigation in its wake. While the bulk of the policy fight occurred during the 1980s and 1990s, and the costs of environmental cleanup have been declining, the number of claims remains high. Many billions of dollars of reserve liabilities linger on the balance sheets of U.S. insurance companies. Whether those reserves accurately reflect the actual costs is unknown, because it is notoriously difficult to estimate such reserves. Indeed, until the Superfund era, there were no systematic accounting standards governing environmental liabilities, either of industrial companies or insurers. Even using the most thorough estimating techniques, the accuracy of existing reserve liabilities will not be known for many years to come.

■ ■ ■

During the 1990s, billions of dollars of costs were also the stakes in lawsuits fought about responsibility for asbestos-related disease. Asbestos is a composite of silicate minerals that has been used in many applications for centuries, primarily because of its fire-retardant properties. Widespread modern commercial use dates to the late 1800s when Johns Manville used it in construction insulation, and to the 1940s when the U.S. military installed fire protection in naval ships. Applications multiplied through the 1970s—to scores of uses in ubiquitous building materials from bricks to pipes to drywall as well as automobile brake linings.

When scientists discovered that inhalation of asbestos fibers can cause serious illness, including lung cancer, a litigation explosion followed. Lawyers filed hundreds of cases claiming tens of billions of dollars. Medical screening, however, could not distinguish reliably between those who were ill and those who were not or between those whose illness was caused by asbestos rather than other carcinogens.[9] The result was large numbers of complex claims that were costly to administer and prone to high error rates. The cases were so lucrative for lawyers and medically complex that fraud arose in many forms, as patients concocted claims with the help of doctors and lawyers submitted falsified evidence.[10] Old-fashioned litigation failed to resolve the asbestos problem.

The Supreme Court urged Congress to create a national administrative solution.[11] It would be a "wholesale" approach to the problem rather than the case-by-case "retail" approach of courts. Participants generally agreed that a systemic approach was desirable, including a national screening standard, a fair claims process and a fund to cover costs. They disagreed on the details. Not only did various interest groups oppose each other, but many groups differed among themselves, including insurers.

A coalition of insurers—ACE, Hartford, Liberty Mutual, State Farm, and Travelers—embraced the idea of a government-administered fund. Each would contribute significant capital, but exposure would be capped at their contribution. Such a system of paying up front in exchange for a cap on liability is ordinarily an appealing way to resolve exposure uncertainties such as this. But AIG, along with one other dissenter, Chubb, perceived problems. The fund approach would set aside many insurance policies on which policyholders had paid substantial premiums to cover liabilities such as these. Disagreements arose about whether policyholders were better off in the fund or under their own policies. AIG and Chubb preferred finding an industry-based solution rather than a governmentally administered fund.

Despite concerns, AIG and Chubb initially joined the coalition of other insurance companies, attempting to shape debate and work toward a better proposal. At a pivotal meeting of the chief executives of these larger insurers, Chubb's chief executive sent his vice chairman, John Degnan, to join Greenberg in opposing the coalition's majority. At the meeting, which was scheduled for two hours, Greenberg spoke first. He spent 20 minutes explaining why AIG could not support the fund proposal. During ensuing discussion, however, it appeared clear that the others would not budge.

So AIG and Chubb turned their attention to Washington, where Congress was developing proposals to address the asbestos problem. They joined a group of manufacturing, construction, energy, and smaller insurance companies to create the Coalition for Asbestos Reform (CAR), to fashion alternatives.[12] Every lobbyist was eager to get the ear of Bill Frist of Tennessee, Senate majority leader, whose position would be influential. This was not an easy appointment to set up, with waiting times up to several weeks. Degnan called Greenberg to discuss this and noted the need to meet with Frist sooner, not later. Within days, Greenberg had a meeting set with Frist. Degnan explained: "In Washington policy formulation circles, when Hank Greenberg spoke, people listened."[13] At the meeting, Greenberg and Degnan made a strong case and Frist seemed receptive, but they did not get an immediate answer.

By early 2005, the other insurers had persuaded Senators Arlen Specter and Patrick Leahy, who sponsored legislation to create a special fund to handle asbestos claims. Named the Fairness in Asbestos Injury Resolution (FAIR) Act, their bill would establish a national administrative agency to handle claims arising from asbestos illness based on a fund, of at least $140 billion, established by contributions charged to manufacturers and users of asbestos and their insurers.[14] AIG and Chubb opposed the complex bill, nearly 400 pages long.

CAR explained that the FAIR Act left hundreds of smaller companies worse off than under the judicial case approach, comparing what they relinquished under their policies with what they had to pay into the fund. CAR objected that the bill shifted costs from larger to smaller companies, as the bill's complex formula meant relatively low maximums on larger companies and relatively high minimums on smaller ones. CAR also objected that the legislation did not correct the severe weaknesses in the medical screening process or establish required medical criteria.

When the bill finally reached the Senate floor, the call was close. The vote was scheduled in the evening. Just ahead of it, Senator Daniel Inouye's wife became ill and he could not appear on the Senate floor. He tried frantically to find a proxy to render his "yea" vote but could not find one in time. The legislation failed by a single vote.[15] Thanks in part to the accidents of health, AIG could claim a victory in its hard-fought campaign.

■ ■ ■

As the cases of Superfund and FAIR illustrate, AIG preferred private market solutions to those promulgated by government. This philosophy pervades the United States, and can be found in many historical examples of businesses responding to national crises. In particular, the preference for private market solutions is exemplified by the story of a century-plus-old company that AIG acquired in 1999: the Hartford Steam Boiler Inspection and Insurance Company (HSB), which was created in the wake of an 1865 explosive fire aboard the massive steam ship *Sultana* while she was plying the Mississippi River.[16] The vessel, under commission of the U.S. War Department, carried 2,400 Union soldiers heading home after being held as Confederate prisoners of war. In one of the largest maritime accidents in U.S. history, the S.S. *Sultana* sank near Memphis, killing some 1,800. The cause: three of the ship's four boilers exploded.

Boiler explosions had become common during the industrial expansion of the latter nineteenth century. Insufficient attention was paid to inherent risk of explosion or how to manage that risk. The sinking of the *Sultana* stimulated a group of entrepreneurial engineers to create HSB. Its mission, in addition to pooling resources to cover losses when they occurred, was to manage risk to prevent losses. HSB would set minimum manufacturing and maintenance standards for boilers. Only boilers produced and maintained in accordance with established standards would be insurable. The engineers believed that their commitment to such standard setting, along with rigorous insurance underwriting, would be more effective than government regulation. Their efforts proved correct.[17]

HSB cemented its niche to become the dominant insurer of commercial equipment nationwide, while simultaneously developing a substantial engineering business focused on risk management. By 1999, HSB had an excellent underwriting record with impressive technical capabilities. Its professional team excelled in evaluating risks and preventing losses. The company provided advice and coverage directly to commercial operators as well as reinsurance to hundreds of property and casualty insurance companies nationwide. HSB was AIG's kind of insurance company: a niche business employing legions of highly skilled professionals committed to earning an underwriting profit.

Had there been more HSBs mitigating the hazards of modern life, whether in the workplace or elsewhere, the country might have avoided its costly experiment of redressing contemporary accidents by tort laws, both judge-made and statutory, another policy fight in which AIG participated. Unlike vast administrative systems—such as Superfund, FAIR, and alternatives—traditional tort law addresses one party battling another over which should be responsible to pay the costs of a given mishap. In the early 1960s, the typical tort case involved a car accident.[18] U.S. law's general approach was to assign responsibility for accidents to those who caused them. The point was to compensate victims and deter wrongdoing by making the blameworthy pay.

Thereafter, Americans became more familiar with tort cases involving products liability, medical malpractice and toxic health harms. From the 1960s to the late 1990s, liability expanded on many such fronts due to a broadened sense of what constitute abnormally dangerous activities and a greater preoccupation with safety. A new regime emerged in which liability arose for more kinds of actions to target more possible defendants and procedures emerged to aggregate claims on mass scales in the modern "class action." In addition, damages increasingly went beyond pure compensation to encompass escalating sums for "pain and suffering."

A public policy debate rolled out of the courtrooms and law school classrooms into the world of media, politics, and even pop culture—in such films as *Erin Brockovich* and *A Civil Action*. Known as the "tort wars,"[19] proponents of the new regime insisted that paying victims was the top priority and that those profiting from risks—and their insurers— should pay, even when fault could not be established in the traditional manner. Those opposed to growth in scope and size of liability judgments urged reforms that would curtail the excesses. AIG stood firmly for tort reform.

The debate was legitimate—and remains important—yet escalated into exercises of mutual myth-making.[20] Sparring partners portrayed the same data and identical cases in opposite lights. Critics said there are many frivolous tort cases winning runaway jury verdicts while proponents stressed that the percentage is small and awards often slashed on appeal. After a customer of McDonald's scalded with its piping-hot coffee won a large tort settlement, critics said the case epitomized a system out of control, while proponents objected to that view as overlooking questionable practices at the fast-food chain.[21] In a 1986 speech, President Reagan referenced the case of a man using a telephone booth when a drunk driver crashed into it and ridiculed a resulting lawsuit against the phone company that California's top court allowed to proceed.[22] Tort critics hailed the speech as highlighting a system off the rails, while defenders criticized omissions in the tale, including that the booth was poorly designed and dangerously located and all the court had said was a trial ought to be allowed, not that the phone company was responsible. (The case eventually settled on undisclosed terms.)

Mutual demonization was also a motif of the tort wars. Plaintiffs' lawyers characterized defendants as villains and their insurers as conspirators in a grand scheme to exploit powerless Americans. Corporate America, by and large the target of such attacks, would respond in kind, painting the plaintiffs' bar in particular as a cabal of mendacious pillagers. Greenberg used such strong language in a speech at the Chief Executives Club of Boston College in February 2004.

The rhetoric of the tort wars has calmed down, though disagreement persists about how much broader tort liability and damages became during recent decades.[23] Yet there seems to be a consensus that the tort reformers won on several important issues, as many reform laws were enacted in the past decade and the volume of tort litigation has fallen.[24] Perhaps the most striking specific change is the widespread adoption of statutory ceilings on the permissible level of damages awarded for "pain and suffering."[25] What's most important in these debates, however, as suggested by AIG's position on asbestos reform, is not so much which advocacy group wins or loses, but finding ways to channel fair compensation to the injured without overpaying the undeserving.[26]

■ ■ ■

A final domestic policy debate on which AIG sought to lead was the approach to regulation of the insurance industry. For largely historical reasons, since 1945, under the McCarran-Ferguson Act, American insurance companies have been regulated by the states, not the federal government. In many lines of insurance this is an appealing regime. States oversee insurance companies doing business in their locales where the state has an interest in promoting insurer solvency and establishing industry-supported funds to cover for insolvent firms. These state laws, focused on the individual customer and based on consumer-protection motives, are attractive for automobile, homeowners, and life insurance products serving that clientele.

But the 50-state regime is unnecessary for large-scale commercial insurance targeted to corporate customers, such as industrial policies covering property and casualty losses or directors' and officers' liability. These sophisticated customers do not need the protection of state solvency regulations or industry pools to pay claims of insolvent com-panies. They can investigate the solvency and reliability of the insurers they consider doing business with and often prefer to apply their own judgment in the exercise than delegate to state authorities. For those insurance companies, AIG advocated an alternative national charter. Such a system would significantly reduce costs of regulation and com-pliance, because there would be a single supervisory authority in Washington rather than 50 separate state overseers. Despite the logic of this stance, broad coalitions of state governments and local insurance departments blocked any chance of persuading Congress to consider such an initiative.

AIG's engagement with domestic policy issues of the day was vital because of the vast scale of its business. It did not win every position, and not every policy debate was exciting, but AIG was always at the table and its victories translated into real gains for the company, the insurance industry, and its customers. While many other CEOs considered them extracurricular affairs, Greenberg saw participation in these activities as central to running AIG's business, and real gains to AIG resulted. Investing AIG's increasing gains posed a more exciting challenge, as AIG ventured into new fields of business.

Chapter 11

Investments

I n 1993, Peter G. Peterson, the renowned financier and cofounder
of the Blackstone Group, invited Greenberg to invest in the pioneering firm. AIG bought a direct 7 percent stake, for $150 million,
among the few outside positions ever taken in the private company.
The participation of AIG, with its reputation for skilled risk analysis and
financial astuteness, helped Peterson attract other investors to Blackstone's funds. Blackstone eventually owned companies boasting some
100,000 employees and 10 years later went public. Blackstone's initial
public offering raised $30 billion. AIG's share was worth $2.1 billion,
which yielded it a compound annual growth rate exceeding 30 percent.
In addition to the pleasure of playing a key role developing Blackstone,
one of its era's great financial successes, it was a lucrative way to invest
AIG's growing capital.

AIG began to accumulate substantial corporate capital in the 1980s,
which grew to enormous sums through the 1990s and early 2000s.
Investment of AIG's capital was always handled separately from the

insurance operations that generated the underwriting profits that drove this capital accumulation. Unlike other insurance companies, success for the insurance executives was defined solely in terms of insurance operations, rather than in terms of the yield on investments. Owing to the growth capital from insurance underwriting, the investment operation became increasingly important.

Reflecting the quality of AIG's businesses, the credit rating agencies assigned it the best possible rating: AAA. Such a rating was a badge of capital strength only few American companies enjoyed. The AAA rating enhances a corporation's position in any financial transaction, from borrowing on more favorable terms to guaranteeing commitments without needing to post collateral. Greenberg defended the AAA rating vigorously. It was common knowledge around AIG that anyone who jeopardized the rating would walk the corporate plank. AIG sought to use its AAA rating in existing businesses and to scout for other opportunities where it would yield economic gains.

One chapter in the search for rewarding investments occurred in the spring of 1990. James D. Wolfensohn, the prominent banker who later became president of the World Bank, called Greenberg about a potential acquisition for AIG. The target was International Lease Finance Corporation (ILFC), a pioneer in commercial aircraft leasing. It then owned 100 planes that it leased to airlines around the world. To grow, it needed capital. Wolfensohn wanted to know if AIG would supply it. Greenberg did not know much about the aircraft leasing business, but AIG was a large insurer of airlines and he knew a lot about aviation.

Leslie Gonda, ILFC's chairman, hosted a meeting in Los Angeles with Greenberg and Ed Matthews, then AIG's vice chairman of finance, along with Gonda's son, Louis, and Louis's friend, Steven Hazy. Gonda explained that, in 1946, he had emigrated from Hungary to escape the communist takeover, moving first to Venezuela and later to Southern California. Hazy's parents, also Hungarian, had left their native land to flee the 1956 uprising in Budapest.

Aside from their Hungarian heritage, the three shared an entrepreneurial streak and a passion for aviation. Hazy had spent some time working at Hughes Airwest and then consulted to the industry. Through resulting contacts, in 1973, Hazy discovered a DC-8 aircraft on sale for $2.2 million from National Airlines of Miami. Gonda heard of a Mexican airline hunting for a plane to use on a new route from Los Angeles to Acapulco. Putting the two concepts together, Hazy and the Gondas acquired the DC-8 and leased it to the airline. The economics worked, producing positive cash flow that enabled the trio to repeat the transaction profitably. They bought a series of turbo-prop planes from Hughes on the cheap—$250,000 each—and leased them to capital-short airlines in Africa.

In the early years, the trio scouted for planes they could acquire at a low price and bought only when a leasing deal was in place. That required persuading airlines about the appeal of the aircraft operating lease. Airlines had conventionally bought their own planes or swapped them with each other under temporary leases to handle seasonal travel fluctuations. The significant capital required to buy planes had to be internally generated or borrowed. The idea of airlines leasing from independent third-party owners was new. Most of the trio's early customers were airlines based in Africa, Asia, and Latin America, starved for capital and attracted to leasing.

Success in those regions enabled pitching to larger airlines in Europe and the United States, where capital was available but costly. In 1977, the three bought their first brand new jet, a Boeing 737, and promptly leased it to Britannia Airways. As business boomed, ILFC increasingly bought new planes, boosting credibility with industry heavyweights. In 1988, ILFC ordered 130 new planes from Boeing. Though Hazy and the Gondas saw more growth ahead, they needed substantial capital and firepower to propel it. Hence the overture to AIG, Leslie Gonda explained.

Greenberg and Matthews liked the story, the pitch, and the men. ILFC faced few competitors, had demonstrated an eye for acquiring quality used aircraft for retrofitting and had established a reputation for excellent customer service. Further, many of ILFC's customers were located in places where AIG had a strong presence, from eastern Europe and Russia to the Middle East and China. Investing capital in the aircraft leasing business, with ILFC's proven track record, was an appealing way to extract value from AIG's AAA rating, prodigious capital resources and balance sheet strength.[1]

In 1990 AIG bought ILFC for $1.2 billion in cash and stock. The trade journal *Aircraft Leasing* made the transaction its cover story under the headline "Deal of the Year," editorializing that "AIG will gain a balanced portfolio of quality assets, a predictable stream of earnings, plus an experienced management team with proven aircraft lease placement and remarketing capabilities." Bringing a smile to Greenberg's face, the story opined that AIG's acquisition of ILFC was "a bargain."[2]

When AIG acquired ILFC, Matthews estimated the optimal size of its fleet at 400, a considerable expansion. But by 2004, Hazy had grown the fleet well above that ambitious level. It seemed the only thing Hazy loved more than airplanes was buying airplanes. To curb that passion, AIG adopted an internal control rule: ILFC was not allowed to buy a new plane without AIG corporate approval. At AIG, such controls were part of the corporate culture to assure discipline and consistent risk assessment. By 2004, ILFC estimated that one of its aircraft took off or landed somewhere in the world every 15 seconds.[3]

As a corporate practice, AIG invested substantial capital in countries where it did business that needed funds to build infrastructure. In the early 1990s, it became clear to Greenberg that, in the decade ahead, some $2 trillion of infrastructure investment would be needed across Asia, Central Europe, the post-Soviet Commonwealth of Independent States, and Latin America.[4] The need was driven by increased economic activity, growth, and privatization. For instance, as more people in Malaysia bought cars, the number of vehicles on the streets of Kuala Lumpur mushroomed, creating need for new and better highways. Similarly, as China's economy expanded, the country needed a massively larger electricity grid to power it. As the economies of Latin America grew and living standards rose, countries needed new airports, communications networks, energy projects, highways, port refurbishment, and utility construction.[5]

AIG's global operations gave it substantial experience with investing in and insuring such infrastructure projects—such as pipelines in the Middle East and airfields in Vietnam. Greenberg perceived that funding for such projects could be obtained from institutional investors seeking opportunities to diversify their investments in higher-yielding undertakings. Infrastructure funds were the way to match demand and supply. For advice, Greenberg consulted Moeen Qureshi, who would later become Prime Minister of Pakistan and a member of AIG's International Advisory Board.[6]

Qureshi had been a senior official at the World Bank, where he commanded deep knowledge of the needs of developing countries and financing opportunities especially in the infrastructure field. When Qureshi left the World Bank in 1992 to begin a private-sector career, he had signed an agreement with a large international bank to pursue a joint venture. Before the deal was executed, however, Qureshi was diagnosed with cancer and the bank broke off the deal. Qureshi went to see Greenberg about this at AIG's offices. After listening to the story, Greenberg urged that beating cancer had to be Qureshi's top priority and offered to help in any way he could. Greenberg also assured Qureshi that, after he won that battle, they would become partners in infrastructure funding. Qureshi did win that fight and, as promised, the two embarked on a series of large, productive and profitable infrastructure products spanning a decade.

Greenberg and Qureshi started with Asia. Their initial goal was to raise a $500 million fund to be used in accordance with each country's government priorities in infrastructure development, aware that there were specific opportunities in telecommunications, transportation, power, and oil and gas.[7] AIG was the lead investor, committing $100 million, and had the right to name the fund. The leadership and naming were designed to help attract additional investors. To draw more lead investments, Qureshi suggested calling upon distinguished heads of state and corporate executives.

One intriguing suggestion: to solicit the prime minister of Singapore, Lee Kuan Yew, widely known as "Harry" Lee. Greenberg had known Lee for many years while overseeing AIG's life insurance company in Singapore. Lee, who had led the transformation of Singapore since its 1965 separation from Malaysia, had a close relationship with Henry Kissinger. Greenberg asked Secretary Kissinger to contact Lee and discuss the fund. That conversation paved the way for Qureshi to meet with Lee. They hoped to get a commitment from Singapore in the range of $50 to $100 million.

Lee grilled Qureshi on the fund: its size, the investments it would make, and its duration. Qureshi highlighted AIG's unique ability to assemble capital, plan projects, and control risks through its project management capabilities. This fund was an exceptional vehicle, from the perspectives of both investors staking capital and countries where projects would be built. The next morning, Lee's senior staff officer informed Qureshi that the prime minister wished to play a major role in the fund, on the condition that Singapore be designated as a lead investor and recognized as a naming sponsor. Qureshi explained that AIG had already claimed those roles and that he could not change that without first consulting Greenberg. But, he advised, "If Singapore really does something enormous, such as investing half the fund, I would certainly report that to him."

A day later, Lee's senior officer informed Qureshi that Singapore was prepared to invest $250 million if it could be a lead investor. After getting that news from Qureshi, Greenberg called Lee and agreed that Singapore would be the lead investor, committing $250 million, and AIG would be the naming sponsor, staking $100 million. That combination enabled Qureshi to increase the fund's size to $1 billion, expanding the scope and type of infrastructure projects in which the fund could invest. Launched in 1996, it was called the "AIG Asia Infrastructure Fund." Its success promoted formation of a successor a year later, also attracting $1 billion, called AIG Asian Infrastructure Fund II.

Though not every investment was profitable, the funds delivered above-average returns for investors. By the early 1990s, Manila, for example, had become a bustling metropolis boasting the wonders of contemporary cosmopolitan life—along with some of its headaches, particularly traffic jams. In response, the AIG Asian Infrastructure Fund enabled town planners to create the Metro Manila Skyway, a two-level 12-lane toll road that relieves congestion around the city.[8] Other investments were used to build a toll road in China, which the fund later sold, plus a Chinese port, telecommunications in Korea, cement manufacturing in India, and power plants throughout the region.[9]

In addition to the two Asian Infrastructure Funds, AIG formed an African infrastructure fund; an Indian equity fund; a Latin American fund, in partnership with GE Capital Services; and an Overseas Private Investment Corporation fund for direct equity investments in private businesses in Russia and the Baltics. These funds invested in various infrastructure projects as well as in gas, mining, oil, water treatment, and environmental protection.

While innovations in infrastructure financing proliferated during the late 1980s and early 1990s, the wider world of financial innovation was taking off as well. When handled properly, tools such as interest rate swaps and even credit default swaps contribute efficiency to the economy. When designed poorly or misused, however, they can be destructive. AIG created a division to focus on these products, which pioneered financial product innovation. This division began with a phone call Greenberg received in late 1986, from Abraham A. Ribicoff, a retired U.S. senator from Connecticut working as a special adviser in the law firm of Kaye Scholer.

"Hank, there is a young man I think you should meet," Senator Ribicoff said. "He is a creative finance guy looking to develop new business in financial products. His name is Howard B. Sosin, now at Drexel Burnham Lambert."

"If he is a friend of yours, I'd be happy to meet him," Greenberg told the ex-senator.

Greenberg invited Sosin to meet with him and Matthews at 70 Pine Street. Sosin proposed developing an interest rate swap business. Because AIG used these devices in managing its own financial risks, Matthews was familiar with the business. The product would attract customers wishing to hedge exposure to interest rate fluctuations. Some have loans requiring payment of a fixed rate, when a floating rate would be cheaper or more convenient, and vice versa. AIG would be a reliable go-between for such parties because its balance sheet strength, attested by its AAA credit rating, made it trustworthy in capital markets. Counterparties would have justifiable confidence that AIG would pay its debts when due.

Greenberg and Matthews believed that launching this product with Sosin was a strategic opportunity to put AIG's AAA rating to profitable use. They invited Sosin back for another meeting to discuss more details, this time inviting along Dean Phypers, the chief financial officer of IBM who had been on AIG's board since 1975, who had additional expertise in financial instruments.

Phypers opined that the business Sosin proposed was exotic compared to AIG's traditional insurance businesses and that part of Sosin's presentation was complex and confusing.[10] But, Phypers continued, if kept on a tight leash, the proposed business would fit well as part of Greenberg's broader tenets of risk management by broadening AIG's earnings base.

By the end of the meeting, Greenberg and Matthews had concluded that a financial products division would enable AIG to capitalize on its strengths, particularly its sophistication in assessing and managing risk. Ahead of the curve, AIG anticipated that companies would increasingly use specialized financial contracts to hedge exposure to business risks, from interest rate and currency exchange fluctuations, regulatory mandates, and cyclical gyrations. For example, banking regulations required commercial banks offering customers lines of credit to keep capital reserves to provide credit. For a fee, AIG could commit to funding such lines of credit, especially for large amounts that were unlikely to be drawn.

In the discussions, Sosin suggested creating a joint venture, called AIG Financial Products (later abbreviated as FP). Sosin would contribute skills and recruit experienced employees, mainly from Drexel; in turn, AIG would contribute capital resources, managerial oversight, and the prestige of its AAA rating. The business would create customized products for large corporate clients wishing to hedge financial risks. FP's financial resources and sophistication would enable it to serve as a market intermediary, providing hedges to one group of customers and, in turn, hedging those positions with another group of counterparties.

FP's business took off quickly, earning $38 million in its first half year of operations in 1987. As the hedging market burgeoned, FP opened offices in Hong Kong, London, Paris, and Tokyo, in addition to maintaining its original space in Connecticut. In 1993, however, Sosin and AIG parted ways over differences of opinion on matters ranging from accounting to controls and operations. The disagreements were so fundamental that maintaining the joint venture was impossible. One example: FP mostly wrote large long-term contracts with profit flowing over periods as long as 25 years. AIG wanted to book the profits accordingly, in incremental amounts annually over that 25-year term. In contrast, Sosin wanted to recognize all the profits from any given contract right away, when a contract was made. Sosin was right that FP's long-term contracts were fully hedged, so trading profit would be realized so long as the other side did not go belly up. But AIG, adhering to conservative accounting, did not want to record or pay profits today that were really tomorrow's profits.[11]

It was an uneasy separation. Greenberg met personally with the FP staff to explain the parting and to discuss the division's future. Afterward,

Greenberg named as president Thomas Savage, who had a PhD in mathematics and commanded a firm understanding of hedging devices and markets, and as chief operating officer Joseph Cassano, an experienced member of the FP team. Most of the FP staff remained in place, including its risk management personnel. The formal structure was changed from a joint venture to an AIG subsidiary, though FP's senior managers invested capital in the business, commonly done in joint ventures but not with subsidiaries.

FP was a resounding success for almost two decades. It was an unusual unit within AIG, because, like ILFC, it was not an insurance company. That meant that FP was not required to maintain liability reserves the way that insurance companies must. But it also meant that FP needed capital to run daily operations in a way that insurance companies usually do not. AIG's risk with FP therefore differed from those at insurance subsidiaries. Thus, it was important to assure that FP's capital needs or risks did not tilt AIG's overall risk profile.

To address that concern, in 1996, Greenberg recruited Charles M. Lucas, a longtime official at the Federal Reserve Bank of New York, where he had most recently directed its risk assessment and control operations. Lucas, who served as AIG's director of market risk management through the end of 2005, helped to create a state-of-the-art risk enterprise system that addressed both credit risk and market risk.

The internal controls and risk management tools AIG created to regulate FP concerning market risk and credit risk were both tighter and more elaborate than those elsewhere in AIG. FP managers, other independent AIG units, the company's outside auditors as well as the board of directors consistently monitored FP's risk portfolio. Additionally, AIG maintained a separate off-site program that mimicked FP's books, mirroring all trades; PricewaterhouseCoopers (PwC), the company's outside auditor, also monitored the business. Three reports regularly reached Greenberg's desk: FP's, the mimic, and PwC's. Headquarters could readily evaluate the soundness of FP's risk management and accounting, including how it allocated profits over time.

In addition to these tools, Greenberg and Matthews hosted a weekly meeting on hedging, investment, and income to review FP's risk, positions, and performance. AIG required FP to submit any new product proposals and transactions greater than a stated size to AIG's chief credit officer for approval. Similarly, Greenberg and Matthews cleared new products before FP was authorized to launch them. FP's operations were also subject to internal supervision by AIG's Enterprise Risk Management team, headed by Robert Lewis. Lewis reported to AIG's chief financial officer, Howard I. Smith. The reporting line thus ran outside FP—from one senior AIG official to another, more senior, AIG executive. AIG's Enterprise Risk Management service had to approve many contracts and commitments made across AIG, including all material contracts FP proposed. It had direct knowledge of risk management and concentration across the company and regularly reviewed and reported the information to AIG's top management.

After a relatively modest opening six years, earning $700 million in aggregate, FP's business soared from 1994 to 2004, when total earnings accumulated to nearly $5 billion.[12] Even more impressively, it never suffered a loss, and no serious problems ever occurred with its business, internal controls, or risk management. FP's book of business as of the end of 2004 consisted predominantly of high-quality, fully hedged positions mostly offered to corporate clients. From April 2005 to September 2008, however, AIG's corporate governance and control, along with FP's fortunes, would change dramatically with disastrous consequences.

Chapter 12

Governance

AIG's founding corporate board in 1967 included luminaries who made AIG into the largest insurance company in the world: insurance industry Hall-of-Famer Jimmy Manton; the old Asia hand Buck Freeman; the quintessential MOP John Roberts; the life insurance builder Ernie Stempel; and Starr's loyal long-time confidant, K. K. Tse. In the ensuing decades, AIG enlisted some of its most distinguished corporate officers to serve on its board of directors. Those traditional officer-directors not only knew the company and the insurance business well but were world travelers who understood the demands of building a global financial services company.

The early board appreciated the appeal of nominating some directors from outside AIG for election by shareholders. Such nonemployee directors offered fresh perspectives, opened doors to business opportunities and made decisions when employee directors faced conflicts of interest. Among early outside directors was Greenberg's first mentor,

Mil Smith (1969–1984), who brought years of valuable experience and connections as an innovative industry leader with a broad worldview.[1] Outside directors who served during the 1970s through the 1980s included former cabinet officials,[2] international business executives,[3] foreign service officers,[4] central bankers[5] and financial accountants.[6] In general, these outside directors served as senior advisors, without tending to second-guess managerial judgments, particularly concerning arcane insurance industry matters beyond their expertise. Outside director Dean P. Phypers (1979–1999), chief financial officer of IBM, noted that this was the standard corporate governance model of the period, at AIG and elsewhere: a collegial body operating in an atmosphere of trust and informality.[7]

That model began to change in the 1970s—just as American Home launched its thriving directors and officers (D&O) insurance business. Routinely ever since, in response to national scandals involving corporate misconduct, Congress passed new legislation and the New York Stock Exchange—where AIG listed its shares in 1984—adopted rules that increasingly required corporations to add outside directors to the board. The authorities also first suggested and later required increasing numbers of committees whose membership was limited to outside directors. These changes were aimed at checking management shirking and enhancing corporate performance, though empirical research never provided much support that such reforms achieved such objectives.[8] Legislators, regulators, and judges seemed to believe that, at the very least, outside directors would be able to exercise independent judgment. On that basis, as a "reform" to respond to crisis, elevating the number and power of outside directors helped forge political consensus. It did not matter whether directors had knowledge of a company's operations or industry or any other expertise.

Letting political expediency dictate business practice is always dangerous and such universal regulation necessarily overlooked variation among companies. Concerning AIG, its roots as a private company, its long-standing entrepreneurial culture and engagement in the complex field of international insurance all pointed in favor of an inside board. Nevertheless, throughout this period of increased enthusiasm for outside directors on corporate boards, AIG successfully recruited capable people who added the value of their business judgment and experience and put the interests of AIG and shareholder prosperity first.

From 1985 until his death in 1990, AIG's board boasted William French Smith, President Reagan's personal lawyer, a partner with the law firm of Gibson, Dunn & Crutcher and former attorney general of the United States.[9] A similarly esteemed outside director from 1991 until his death in 2003 was Barber B. Conable Jr., a pragmatic professor and congressman for two decades, before becoming a reforming pioneer as president of the World Bank.[10] Yet another impressive independent director was Lloyd Bentsen (1994–1998), former U.S. senator from Texas, secretary of the treasury, and Democratic vice-presidential candidate. In 1955, Bentsen had founded the Consolidated American Life Insurance Company, which he ran until 1967, and later created a billion-dollar private investment firm that formed global infrastructure funds, especially in Latin America.[11] His obituary in the *New York Times* observed that none of his colleagues in government could "recall a single instance in which he let his emotions get the better of him."[12]

With outside directors like these—experienced, informed professionals who understood what they could add and appreciated the limits of their expertise—the practice of nominating such directors for election by shareholders made sense. Despite such esteemed appointments, some corporate activists—from institutional investors, such as the California Public Employees' Retirement System (CalPERS) and Teachers Insurance and Annuity Association–College Retirement Equities Fund (TIAA-CREF), to coalitions such as the National Association of Corporate Directors—campaigned in the 1990s and early 2000s to overthrow the AIG board's traditional approach to director selection. These campaigns were part of a national mission to amplify "shareholder voice" in American boardrooms and targeted large corporations. Some campaigns sought to promote diversity or affirmative action, but many urged greater numbers of outside directors, trumpeting their unique ability to render independent judgments rather than having any particular knowledge or expertise.[13]

One activist AIG shareholder, the Presbyterian Church, submitted proposals to adopt a formal board nominating committee staffed by outside directors. It said this would support a public policy of "equal employment opportunity and workforce diversity."[14] It complained that AIG's practice of having the full board screen and nominate directors "clouded" the process and that an independent nominating committee would "uncloud" it—apparently echoing the period's perception, among corporate governance gurus, of the purity of outside director "independence."

AIG's board opposed such proposals, citing the company's decades-long record of profitability and tremendous growth in shareholder value. Consider the accompanying tables (Figures 12.1 and 12.2) depicting AIG's net income and shareholders' equity from 1969 to 2004.[15]

AIG's board had from 15 to 20 serve as directors in any given year, each a full-fledged member entitled to participate without distinction between inside or outside status. Every director could make, discuss and vote on nominations. Management's views on director identity and qualifications were invaluable, and AIG's management directors were substantial AIG shareholders, aligning their interests with those of its legions of loyal shareholders, which included a large number of public pension funds. In a 2001 response to such proposals, the board noted that management directors owned or controlled, principally through SICO, 500 million AIG shares then worth $48 billion (of 2.3 billion total shares outstanding).[16] Excluding them from the nomination process seemed absurd.

An individual shareholder presented a more subtle "shareholder democracy" argument supporting an independent nominating committee.[17] He posited that, regardless of the board's strong arguments about AIG's track record, selection criteria and management-director ownership, shareholders should get to exercise their vote, rather than have the board preempt that privilege. AIG's board responded that its job was to propose nominees to shareholders based on qualifications. It was not its job to "create a political environment" in which "nominees compete for the available directorships." If people knew they had to campaign for the position, such an approach would reduce the pool of candidates. Besides, such campaigns can distract the board from its duties and cause divisions within it.

Another activist targeting AIG was an AFL–CIO affiliate, which proposed that AIG adopt a policy requiring that a majority of directors be outsiders. The argument contended that a corporate board is a "mechanism for monitoring management."[18] Labor union officials

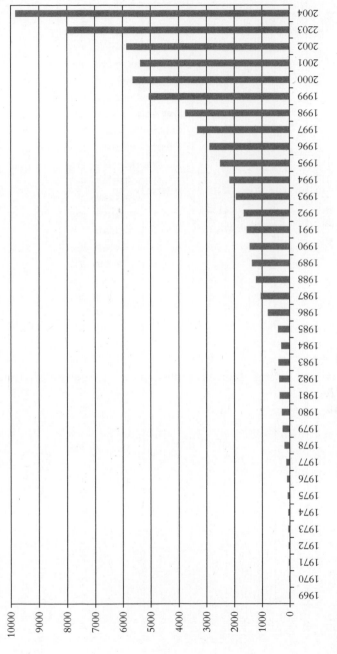

Figure 12.1 AIG's Net Income (1969 to 2004) (in millions)

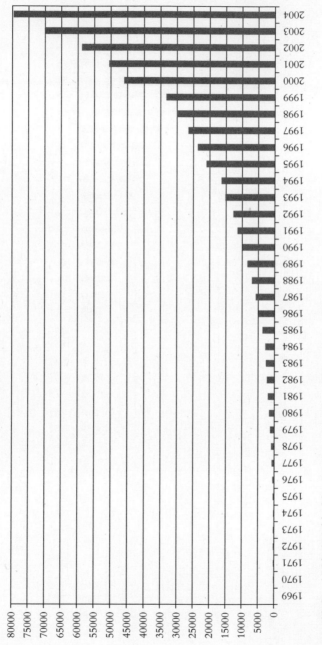

Figure 12.2 AIG's Stockholders' Equity (1969 to 2004) (in millions)

argued that meeting a strict test of independence enables directors to "challenge management decisions and evaluate corporate performance from a completely free and objective perspective." It cited a lone study arguing that "corporations with active and independent boards enjoy superior performance"[19]—though many more studies show that director independence has no effect on corporate performance.[20] The objective in such campaigns was not always to improve performance as much as to strengthen outside directors while weakening management and the CEO.

The overwhelming majority of AIG shareholders voted such proposals down, with only about one-fourth of shares voted in favor of them, low even by the standards of activists who considered such losing votes a victory. AIG's board and most of its shareholders favored governance that had delivered sustained long-term growth in shareholder value. AIG had thus earned a reputation as a "core stock holding" for many portfolios, including those of the proverbial "widows and orphans."[21] AIG shareholders preferred to have the existing directors and management identify directors for nomination and shareholder election, with enviable results.

By the early 2000s, AIG's board included a combination of inside and outside directors who respected each other and worked well together with Greenberg. Besides Greenberg, management directors were the long-serving Edward Matthews, who had been with the company from its inception and advised it on many transactions through his retirement in 2003,[22] and Howard Smith, the second chief accounting officer in AIG's history, having succeeded Peter Dalia in 1984. Other insiders included two younger executives being groomed as successors to Greenberg: Martin J. Sullivan and Donald P. Kanak.[23]

The board included 10 outside directors—a majority of the 18-person group as stock exchange rules by then required. The most senior was M. Bernard Aidinoff, the partner in the law firm of Sullivan & Cromwell who had represented AIG in its initial public offering, the establishment of Starr International Company (SICO), and many other transactions.[24] Some held impressive internationalist credentials, such as Carla Hills, former U.S. trade representative with whom AIG had worked on trade in services.[25] Ambassador Hills is a trained lawyer and

Washington-based international consultant, with expertise that includes risk management. From that same walk of life, and also a trained lawyer, was William S. Cohen, former U.S. senator from Maine and secretary of defense, a committed internationalist with sound business judgment and expertise in Asia.[26]

Others brought a diverse range of viewpoints. Ellen V. Futter, elected in 1999, ran the American Museum of Natural History and had been president of Barnard College. Futter, yet another lawyer, had chaired the Federal Reserve Bank of New York during a term when Greenberg was vice chair before succeeding her as chair. Elected in 2001 was the internationalist Richard C. Holbrooke, a senior U.S. diplomat who served in the Carter and Clinton administrations, including as ambassador to Germany, where AIG was eager to expand. Greenberg believed that Holbrooke's knowledge of Germany would prove useful to AIG. Also elected in 2001 was Frank G. Zarb, who had significant experience in international matters and the financial sector, having led both Smith Barney and the Nasdaq stock market—although Greenberg would later discover that he had not distinguished himself in those roles. Greenberg had several years earlier assisted Zarb in becoming president of an insurance brokerage firm, Alexander & Alexander, in which AIG had taken a minority interest.

Throughout any given year, board members coordinated informally as issues arose and met at scheduled meetings four times annually. An executive committee was formed to make official decisions between regular meetings. It kept the large company nimble in a dynamic world where opportunities come and go quickly. If senior officials in Malaysia or Shanghai needed a prompt response on an extraordinary matter, AIG could provide it. Besides Greenberg, the 2004 executive committee members consisted of outside directors Aidinoff; Hills; Frank Hoenemeyer, a retired vice chairman of Prudential Insurance Company; and Zarb.

The audit committee, which AIG established in the early 1970s, oversaw internal controls and accounting processes to assure accountability and accuracy. To maintain management discipline, Greenberg and Matthews held weekly AIG-wide management meetings with 15 senior officers. Each reported on respective areas of operations, keeping everyone accountable and current on what was happening. AIG also held monthly meetings with all the company's divisional and subsidiary presidents, 30 in all, to conduct the same exercise on a different scale. Members of AIG's board were invited to join these monthly meetings and most did so often.

A corporate board's primary task is appointing senior officers. In keeping with longstanding corporate policy that Greenberg had established at the founding of AIG, no officers had employment contracts. The board likewise endorsed the long-standing corporate policy Greenberg started that individual compensation be modest, certainly by prevailing American corporate standards. Officers earned a salary—never more than $1 million annually for anyone—and pension benefits along with stock options for performance. The steadily rising AIG share value increased the worth of SICO's holding substantially, and SICO paid AIG managers additional compensation under the program that the "band of brothers" had begun in the 1970s. The upshot was that virtually all executive compensation at AIG was performance based, and there was little need for a board compensation committee.

AIG's senior officers maintained a comprehensive worldwide program to enable them to identify, promote and reward the most promising AIG employees across all businesses in every country. The system dated to the late 1980s, when one afternoon Greenberg summoned to his office the head of human resources, Axel Freudmann.[27]

"How many people do you know at AIG?" Greenberg asked.

"I'm not sure, maybe between 500 and 1,000?"

"Exactly. That's a problem. We don't know enough people. We need to know more of them and to know them better."

Freudmann established a program that involved a global search and communication protocol to identify outstanding employees in all fields, such as those who excelled at earning an underwriting profit. The human resources staff coordinated with profit center managers across the company to compare notes on employees, consult other managers with whom employees had worked for verification, and bring results to the attention of senior officers. Overcoming the corporation's vast scale, senior managers got to know the employees and were able to reward them for stellar performance.

Another distinctive feature of AIG's corporate governance: the board did not believe it was their prerogative to use corporate assets to make charitable donations. At most corporations, the CEO and board make discretionary allocations of the corporation's assets to charities of their choosing, at a cost to shareholders, who may not support the chosen charities. That was not the practice at AIG, where the board believed that if shareholders wished to allocate their wealth to charitable causes, they should be able to do so and not have the board or CEO usurp that right.

Many AIG directors endowed private foundations dedicated to causes they valued. Starr had begun that practice, endowing a foundation of modest size that was concentrated in AIG stock. The Starr Foundation would grow over three decades after his death to a value of several billion dollars. Other directors, including Freeman, Greenberg, Manton, and Stempel, followed suit by establishing private foundations to make charitable gifts, which aggregated to billions of dollars.[28] For his philanthropy, particularly toward the Tate Britain Museum, Manton was knighted by the Queen of England.[29]

Despite impressive people, policies and performance at AIG, its board did not pass muster with the corporate governance gurus of the day and their national campaign for "shareholder democracy." A 2000 report published in a trade magazine suggested as much, along with how misguided this campaign was. It listed what it called corporate America's "five worst boards" and "five best boards."[30] The report stressed that it was not interested in a company's financial performance, such as growth or profitability, but only in a dozen board attributes that then defined "good governance," such as size, ratio of insiders to outsiders, women, minorities, and committee processes.

This approach is akin to a ship captain stressing the arrangement of deck chairs while ignoring leaks that could sink it. Using this approach, after noting that AIG "enjoyed enviable profitability and growth," these "experts" listed AIG as having the "third worst board." The "third best board," under this approach, was that of Enron Corporation, which the next year was revealed to be a multibillion-dollar fraudulent cypher, with scarcely any assets, income, or substance.

In response to such debacles as Enron, in 2002, Congress passed the Sarbanes-Oxley Act. It adopted a one-size-fits-all regime of governance and auditing—including yet more power for outside directors.[31] The New York Stock Exchange marched in lockstep with an additional set of homogenous requirements. The new regime's added roles for outside directors led AIG's board to have a "Nominating and Corporate Governance Committee," which Aidinoff chaired and on which Futter, Hills, and Zarb served. The committee met often and quickly produced newly required governance guidelines, committee charters and ethics codes, and stricter conceptions of "independence." The latter had the effect of stripping Futter's "independent" status because the Starr Foundation had made substantial donations to the American Museum of Natural History that she ran, though the foundation would have supported the museum whether Futter or someone else headed it, as it had since 1973 when it made its first gift to the museum.[32]

A related novel requirement was an "executive session" of the board, a separate meeting to occur around regular board meetings but solely for outside directors. No management directors were permitted, under the theory that they wield too much power in the boardroom, resulting in the "structural bias" of the outside directors, compromising their capacity for "independent judgment." Another fashion begun in corporate America during this period was the "lead director," chosen from among the outside directors. At AIG, this job would go to Zarb.[33]

These changes and devices—enacting into law what activists had sought for a decade and AIG shareholders had rejected—upset the unity that AIG's single board historically demonstrated. It effectively incubated a group of outside directors with newfound inspiration to challenge insiders. Some of AIG's outside directors became more assertive, many beginning to ask questions on matters beyond their competence. Some questions struck Greenberg as naïve, uninformed, or worse, and he would say so. They might call for a tutorial on the ABCs of insurance, international trade, or corporate structure that was an inappropriate use of board time. The traditional mutually supportive and respectful relationship among board members frayed.

The era of Enron and Sarbanes-Oxley stoked such media and regulatory hyperbole about corporate malfeasance that law enforcement authorities became emboldened. President George W. Bush in 2002 formed the President's Corporate Fraud Task Force within the Department of Justice to intensify this area of law enforcement.[34] Eager to police corporations and ferret out offenders, officials added pressure on outside directors, as well as independent auditors. These new government priorities motivated corporate officials to surrender employees in exchange for prosecutorial promises of leniency toward them or the corporation. The government's rationale was famously outlined in a series of Justice Department memos about "getting tough" on corporate malfeasance, a 2003 version of which stressed "vigorous enforcement" of law against "corporate wrongdoers."[35] It contained at least one provision—restricting employer reimbursement of employee legal defense costs—that a federal court later declared to be unconstitutional overreaching by the government.[36]

Enforcement intensity, combined with shifting boardroom power from management directors to nonemployee directors, made it difficult to sustain AIG's traditional employee-centric culture. Respecting that culture, Greenberg had zero tolerance for employees he knew to have violated any law or withheld information from him about pending investigations. In an incident well known among AIG insiders, Greenberg learned that a senior executive had improperly interfered with an investigation by French authorities that jeopardized AIG's license and had not informed Greenberg. Greenberg summoned the executive to his office at 70 Pine and, with Manton present, asked the executive to explain. The executive lied about the existence of the investigation and its merits, so Greenberg excoriated and summarily fired the man, apparently ending his career. On the flip side, if an AIG employee was unjustly prosecuted, AIG mounted a vigorous defense.

One example came to a head in 2003 after the Securities and Exchange Commission (SEC) had been hunting companies that falsified their financial statements by abusing sophisticated insurance products. The target was Brightpoint, Inc., a small provider of services to the telecommunications industry. The SEC said Brightpoint had used an AIG insurance policy to disguise $12 million in business losses. After cracking down on Brightpoint and three of its executives, the SEC went after AIG. Matters involving such relatively small amounts in a subsidiary of a much larger company were not usually the basis for an SEC fraud prosecution of the parent company. But given the period's regulatory environment, the SEC aggressively pursued this case, and some of AIG's outside directors were inclined to capitulate.

During the proceedings, disputes arose between the SEC and AIG about whether certain documents had been deliberately or innocently withheld. AIG's outside counsel, Sullivan & Cromwell, acknowledged full responsibility for whatever objections the SEC had to the document production but the episode intensified the SEC's charges and caused some AIG board members to push AIG's management to settle. As a result, in September 2003, AIG agreed to pay a $10 million fine and provide SEC-appointed monitors to wander through the records of all its subsidiaries to look for other negligent action.[37] Greenberg was not happy with this result. The crevice between management and some outside board directors was widening.

The gap grew in a second case that began in September 2004 after the SEC raised questions about a transaction between AIG's Financial Products division (FP) and PNC Financial Services Group, Inc. To help PNC manage the volatility of some of its assets, FP arranged a deal in which PNC agreed to transfer nonperforming assets to an entity that FP created and controlled. Gains or losses on the assets would belong to FP, so PNC could remove them from its balance sheet. In exchange, FP charged PNC a fee. PNC transferred $762 million of such assets, removed them from its balance sheet, and paid FP fees of $40 million. FP vetted this concept with accountants, lawyers, and some AIG directors, and concluded that it was valid.

The SEC disagreed. To remove the assets from PNC's balance sheet, accounting rules required AIG to stake a minimum amount of capital in the deal. It did stake that minimum, the SEC acknowledged. But, it said, the fees FP received should count as a reduction in that amount. Under that approach, AIG's investment fell below the minimum. AIG and its advisers had been in many conversations over the years with SEC officials about complex deals like this and had never heard of this purported requirement. AIG's outside counsel advised that it had a strong case but, again, several outside directors were more inclined to settle. AIG paid $126 million and agreed to various corporate governance reforms, including appointing another monitor, this time to oversee FP's products to assure they could not be used by other parties to massage accounting results.[38]

Greenberg found this resolution disagreeable, though his objection was not whether the transaction was in fact correctly executed and accounted for by PNC. Nor was the issue what responsibility AIG should have for assuring that its products are not misused—matters about which people differ vigorously, as many Supreme Court opinions addressing the scope of "aiding and abetting" liability attest.[39] The question was a matter of corporate governance: how a board should evaluate and respond to governmental assertions of corporate and employee misconduct. The gradual capitulation of several outside directors was an important and regrettable sign that members of AIG's board were prepared to defer to government authorities. They might have presumptively believed the authorities, regarded mounting a defense as too costly, or simply disagreed with management and wanted to make that point. The rights and protections of employees were correspondingly diminished as outside directors at many American companies increasingly surrendered them in the name of cooperating with prosecutors.[40]

In this new environment, outside directors at companies across the United States began to further strengthen their hand and protect themselves by retaining their own lawyers to represent them. Outside directors had not historically hired their own lawyers, but Sarbanes-Oxley authorized audit committees to do so.[41] A specialty legal practice emerged: representing outside directors, especially advising them on disagreements with chief executives.[42] Experts on corporate governance and legal ethics saw this development as perilous, as it would cleave boards into factions, inject lawyers deeply into corporate deliberations and compromise the independence of directors. It was clear that at some point directors would be forced to choose between acting in the best interests of the corporation and acting to protect themselves.[43] So it was difficult to stem the flow of lawyers into the boardroom

In late 2004, AIG's outside directors, led by Zarb, opted for this form of empowerment and self-protection. They considered two prospective lawyers. Republicans among AIG's outside directors suggested Richard Thornburgh, former Republican Pennsylvania governor and U.S. attorney general during the administration of George H. W. Bush. But Thornburgh's firm, K&L Gates, had a conflict of interest that, under canons of legal ethics, prevented him from accepting the assignment. Democrats on the outside board supported Richard I. Beattie, chairman of Simpson Thacher & Bartlett, who had served in the Carter and Clinton administrations and represented one of the directors, Holbrooke, during Senate hearings on his nomination to be United Nations ambassador. The outside directors chose Beattie, and Zarb charged him with strengthening the outside directors' hand in succession planning.[44]

Succession is a challenging planning process for the board and CEO of any corporation, particularly one in which the leader has invested his entire career and identity. Nevertheless, knowing it was in the best interests of the company, Greenberg wrestled with succession in the early 2000s. AIG's board had focused on Kanak and Sullivan. As of late 2004, an understanding was reached that one of them would become CEO for a trial period beginning in June 2005, while Greenberg remained chairman. Greenberg planned to vacate the executive floor at 70 Pine while staying involved as needed.

Throughout his tenure, Greenberg adhered to the presumption of innocence for AIG employees, preferring to defend them vigorously, and expected the board to do so, too. He believed that firm defenses would have been mounted in cases such as Brightpoint and PNC by boards from earlier AIG eras, certainly the board comprised of inside directors—Freeman, Manton, Roberts, and Stempel—stalwarts who had all retired by 1997 (Manton in 1988) as well as the valiant outside directors of the earlier era, such as Lloyd Bentsen, Barber Conable, Dean Phypers, and William French Smith. Greenberg was growing impatient with the new universal regime in corporate America where outside directors came to rule over territory they did not always understand. He knew his corporate world had changed and believed it was not for the better. But the worst was yet to come.

PART

Two

Interlude

T he ensuing chapters recount a saga worth summarizing at the outset. In less than four years, from February 2005 to September 2008, AIG sailed from being an American icon, with nearly $1 trillion in assets and worth $180 billion, to the verge of destruction. It was saved only by the loyalty and tenacity of its valiant workforce.

In February 2005, at a time when financial scandals such as Enron made many citizens skeptical of big business, Eliot Spitzer, an elected public prosecutor in New York, sparked the process that would drive AIG to near destruction. After some examples of Spitzer's tactics, including airing allegations in the media where targets cannot defend themselves as they can in court, you will read how Spitzer turned his sword on AIG and Greenberg.

Without investigation, Spitzer rapidly raised the heat on AIG's outside directors so high that they, advised by lawyers with close connections to Spitzer, asked Greenberg to resign as CEO in March 2005, just months before his planned retirement. Even AIG's outside auditor, PricewaterhouseCoopers (PwC), faced such pressure that it decided to repudiate five years of its own certifications, threatening the directors by withholding a renewed certification unless they sought Greenberg's resignation. All these threats were made based on conjectures that an investigation, done afterward, would prove empty.

We cannot be certain why the outside directors, lawyers, and auditors behaved as they did, and our reflecting on this saga sometimes make us feel as if we have as many questions as answers: why did the outside directors knuckle under so quickly; why did the outside lawyers facilitate such upheaval; and what pressures did the auditors face that would make them repudiate their consistent certifications, knowing that such a position would wreak havoc? Did Spitzer's threats overwhelm the judgment of the outside lawyers, or did the outside lawyers welcome his threats in order to advance goals they had already set?

Whatever the reasons, with AIG's corporate governance apparatus under prosecutorial control, Spitzer staked out a bold position about what he thought his case targeting AIG would show. Having tasted triumph when Greenberg resigned, he felt confident enough to go on national television in April 2005 to boast of having fingered a great fraud—yet the facts revealed by late May that the assertions were not even close to correct.

After scores of accountants and lawyers scoured AIG's accounting records worldwide, all they could come up with was a set of highly contestable changes to the five previous years' books that reduced net income and owners' equity by 2 to 3 percent. That is not the kind of thing that warrants a board's asking a CEO to resign.

Indeed, the accounting restatement that PwC and these lawyers concocted, along with Greenberg's departure, cost AIG and its shareholders a huge drop in market value, a slashed credit rating, and huge payments to settle numerous lawsuits. Although it remains difficult to fathom why people succumbed to the pressures leading to Greenberg's resignation, it is easier to pinpoint the reason they pushed so hard to change the accounting, though they came up short: to justify their decision.

Greenberg's separation from AIG was more than a typical CEO departure. He had been the face of the company since founding it and leading its expansion over four decades. He and the Starr Companies had provided additional support, especially through the Starr International Company (SICO) compensation plan. That priceless resource of

SICO's, with access to up to $20 billion worth of AIG shares, enabled AIG to attract and retain the best workforce in the industry.

The separation erupted into civil war that added costs to the board's prosecution-stimulated resignation request. Commercial disputes dragged out for more than a year, through 2006, as animosity deepened and a rising sense of defensiveness seemed to pervade the company's senior leadership and outside advisers.

Legal battles would last many more years. In a naked show of animosity, the board made a 180-degree about face in a shareholders' lawsuit against certain directors. In 2003, based on a thorough outside legal investigation, the board had unanimously recommended that the case be thrown out. Citing "new strategic considerations," however, in 2006, they recommend going forward with it against Greenberg. In a striking example of defensiveness, AIG, reeling from the loss of the SICO compensation plan, whose significance the board had apparently failed to appreciate, waged a desperate but doomed legal action to wrest the shares from SICO.

Finally, as new leadership joined AIG's senior ranks, the animosity and defensiveness began to dissipate and the two resolved all their disputes. In laying down the hatchets, AIG paid Greenberg's legal fees up to $150 million—revealing at last where the equities fell.

While Greenberg fought the civil war against AIG on one front, he battled Spitzer on another. In May 2005, still boasting publicly about the strength of his case against Greenberg, Spitzer tried to bludgeon him into submission by offering to settle on any charges Greenberg wished to admit to. Greenberg rejected the blackmail out of hand and Spitzer soon began to see his case unravel. A civil suit that Spitzer had drummed up and advertised to the media with great fanfare looked increasingly weak and, by Thanksgiving 2005, he quietly acknowledged that there was no criminal case.

His attack unraveling, Spitzer found a new target to hound in the media: the Starr Foundation. This foundation, which Starr had begun and Greenberg nurtured over the decades into one of the five largest charitable foundations in the United States, owned assets worth more than $3 billion. As with Spitzer's other assaults, this one would fail, though not before Spitzer saturated the media with wild statements that the Starr Foundation had to defend in the press rather than in court.

Back at AIG, during 2005 and early 2006, Spitzer had stimulated a variety of changes in corporate governance that would soon backfire, too. The man charged with making recommendations, a friend of the lead outside director, endorsed a set of off-the-rack changes without studying what made AIG tick and what kinds of governance would be most effective for it. These cosmetic changes put form over substance, stressing the motions of governance rather than the management of business risk.

As AIG's new management team mired themselves in the forms and talk of corporate governance, they lost control of the company. From mid-2005 through late 2007, the company accumulated $80 billion worth of risky financial bets without hedging its exposure. When the financial crisis of 2008 erupted, these deals were among those at the heart of it, requiring AIG to come up with enormous amounts of cash it simply did not have.

In September 2008, AIG thus faced a severe liquidity crisis at a time when its management and controls were in disarray. Sensing weakness, the U.S. government intervened on punishing terms not imposed on any other company facing similar problems. The government *both* loaned AIG money, $182 billion in all, meaning AIG had to repay it, *and* took ownership control of AIG's stock. The deal was akin to one in which your bank lends you $182,000 to buy a home, which you must repay, while the bank takes full title to the house.

More audaciously yet, the government then transferred $63 billion of those funds to other financial institutions instead of letting AIG use the money. Those companies thus avoided being tagged as recipients of "taxpayer bailouts," the pejorative label given to AIG during this national meltdown. Instead, to repay the "loan," the government put AIG on a selling spree, divesting on the cheap many of the prized assets that Greenberg and AIG's employees had toiled so hard to develop over the previous four decades.

The U.S. government would not have been able to exploit AIG in this way but for the disarray that plagued the company, which followed as a direct and foreseeable result of the unfounded claims that Spitzer first broadcast to the media in February 2005. The only reason AIG has not been utterly destroyed is that its loyal employees working in the lines it retains are so talented. Thanks to them, AIG may survive despite this extraordinary adversity visited on it by its own government.

Date 1972
Description Greenberg, Stempel and Freeman

PH.MRG194

Maurice R. ("Hank") Greenberg with Ernie Stempel and Buck Freeman

Date 11/1970
Event Dinner with President and Mrs. Marcos
Description President and Mrs. Marcos attending dinner with the Greenberg's and other American International executives in Manila, November 1970. Dinner was possibly hosted in the home of Earl Carroll. The photographs were sent to the Greenbergs by C.S. Roco, Philamlife per Mr. Carroll's request.
(13) Stempel, Greenberg, and President Marcos walking in front of Zalamea and Carroll

PH.MRG193

...with President Ferdinand Marcos of the Philippines, Ernie Stempel
(background left), and Earl Carroll (background right)

...with Chinese leader Deng Xiaoping

Date 1978
Description 16. MRG and an unidentified man, outside.   PH.MRG610

…with Sung Guohua of PICC

Date 4/24/2001
Event AIA's 70th Anniversary Celebration
Description (L to R): Mrs. Greenberg, Chee-hwa Tung, and MRG   PH.MRG533

…with wife Corinne and Chief Executive Chee-hwa Tung of Hong Kong

…with Premier Zhu Rongji of China

...with Secretary Henry A. Kissinger

...with President Richard M. Nixon

To Hank Greenberg
With best wishes,   Ronald Reagan

...with President Ronald Reagan

...with President George H. W. Bush at an ASEAN Meeting

To Hank Greenberg
Best wishes, Bill Clinton

...with President Bill Clinton

...with Senator Lloyd Bentsen

...with President Boris Yeltsin of Russia

...with Prime Minister Mahathir Mohamad of Malaysia

…with Commerce Secretary Ron Brown and
Ratan Tata of India

…with Secretary Kissinger and President Soeharto of Indonesia

AIG Building—Otemachi, Tokyo

AIA Building—17 The Bund, Shanghai

Shanghai Center

Chapter 13

Hostile Change

In July 2002, President George W. Bush gushed that the Sarbanes Oxley Act made the "most far-reaching reforms of American business practices since the time of Franklin Delano Roosevelt."[1] Adding to the hype, critics lambasted public prosecutors, including those at the Securities and Exchange Commission (SEC) and Department of Justice (DOJ), for allowing such abuses to fester into billion-dollar calamities.[2]

These prosecutors got the message. They escalated high-profile suits against esteemed corporate directors and prominent auditing firms.[3] A symbol of the seismic shift in enforcement intensity occurred when 20 outside directors of Enron and WorldCom paid $31 million out of their own pockets, unreimbursed by insurance or indemnification, to settle suits against them personally.[4] Directors across corporate America, including those exalted as independent, began to fear for their personal liability.

For auditors, a stunning result occurred when the DOJ filed criminal charges for obstruction of justice against the venerable independent accounting firm of Arthur Andersen, whose Houston office had signed off on Enron's books. During the government's investigation into it, two senior employees reinvigorated an ignored firm policy of destroying drafts of documents relating to the work. For that, the government indicted the entire firm, then employing 85,000 people and earning annual revenue of $10 billion, and won a fine of $500,000. Though a unanimous U.S. Supreme Court eventually overturned that result,[5] by then the prosecutorial enthusiasm had destroyed the firm.

When Sarbanes-Oxley was passed, Eliot L. Spitzer was the attorney general of New York, with his sights set on the governor's mansion. As attorney general, Spitzer drew on an obscure New York law, the Martin Act, which Greenberg calls "a legal weapon of mass destruction," at least when in the wrong hands.[6] As Spitzer portrayed the Martin Act, businesspeople can be liable for wrongdoing by employees without any finding that they actually knew about it at the time it was occurring. This reading would expose people to enormous and uninsurable damages in lawsuits brought by the New York attorney general. If a court agreed with that view of the law, all senior executives in New York (and possibly elsewhere) would face claims that could run to the billions of dollars, whether or not they were aware of misdeeds when they happened. In fact, however, no court had ever permitted the attorney general to do so—and for good reason, since the federal securities laws preempted this approach by requiring proof not only of knowledge of wrongdoing but of intent to deceive.[7] That did not stop Spitzer from invoking the Martin Act in his campaigns, however, which one lawyer aptly tagged as the "Sword of Spitzer"—the "legal equivalent of King Arthur's Excalibur."[8]

AIG enjoyed a reputation for following conservative accounting in the insurance industry. That tradition continued through February 2005, when AIG's auditor, PricewaterhouseCoopers (PwC), was completing its audit of AIG's 2004 financial statements and controls. Auditors found them in order, as they had for decades. PwC always approved AIG's financial controls, which Sarbanes-Oxley now required to be audited separately, entailing 50,000 hours of start-up work and costing AIG $12 million in the initial year.[9] AIG held a conference call with securities analysts on February 9, 2005, reporting earnings of $11 billion despite a difficult year for the insurance industry. Asked about the prevailing regulatory environment—and the still hotly debated Sarbanes-Oxley Act[10]—Greenberg expressed concern that excessive regulation could put a drag on the U.S. economy. Greenberg also criticized overzealous prosecutors. Using a common tennis term, Greenberg challenged those who "look at foot faults and turn them into a murder charge."

That afternoon, Spitzer turned to his computer to catch up on the day's news. One site featured Greenberg's remarks about prosecutors and "foot faults," which the AG apparently took as a reference to him, as he was then probing certain insurance practices industry-wide. Spitzer instructed his staff to dispatch subpoenas to AIG and Greenberg demanding various documents. Spitzer had earlier received, but not acted upon, information concerning AIG and many other insurance companies involved in transactions with General Reinsurance Co. (or Gen Re), a company acquired by Berkshire Hathaway, Warren E. Buffett's company, a few years earlier.

Virginia state authorities were investigating a medical malpractice firm that had gone bankrupt amid criminal activity that left two of its senior managers serving lengthy prison terms.[11] Gen Re's involvement with that firm led authorities to scrutinize numerous Gen Re reinsurance transactions that looked suspicious. Gen Re's lawyers cooperated by providing documents not only to the Virginia authorities that requested them but to other authorities across the country, from the SEC to New York. Documents addressed numerous Gen Re deals involving "finite insurance," a form of reinsurance used for a variety of accounting and operational reasons. AIG was one among many insurance companies that had entered into finite transactions with Gen Re.

After ordering staff to get the subpoenas out on the evening of February 9, Spitzer dashed across Lower Manhattan to the headquarters of Goldman Sachs to give a speech. Attending were Goldman's elite, including Henry Paulson, its chairman, who would a year later become U.S. Treasury Secretary.[12] Just before Spitzer rose to address the New York financial executives, a deputy entered and whispered in his ear that the subpoenas had been faxed. Moments later, during his remarks, Spitzer referenced Greenberg's comments of earlier in the day, mentioning him by name to the assembled audience. Spitzer then threatened

Greenberg and vaguely accused him of wrongdoing, declaring to the crowd: "Hank Greenberg should be very, very careful talking about foot faults. Too many foot faults and you lose the match."[13]

For Spitzer, whose campaign for governor of New York in 2005–2006 was seen by Democratic champions as a prelude to a White House run,[14] the prosecutorial environment of the post-Enron era was ripe. His campaign themes, as well as his attorney general speeches, were morality and righteousness, especially when challenging business practices. He assailed high-profile citizens, hounding prominent corporate leaders, in speeches like those at Goldman Sachs, in press conferences and on national television. The effect made him a regular in the media which branded him with such titles as "Top Cop of Wall Street" and "Sheriff of Wall Street."[15] By thus increasing pressure on targets, Spitzer induced high-publicity settlements, yielding favorable press without the need to conduct a trial, which takes time and can be lost.

Many were alarmed by Spitzer's trial-in-the-media strategy, however, which sometimes threatened to undermine the presumption of innocence by vilifying his targets.[16] They worried that some of Spitzer's comments infringed on the rights of Americans to due process, such as the right to a fair jury trial. Such outbursts tend to inflame public opinion and may disparage the reputation of an innocent person. His comments often appeared to violate Spitzer's duty as a prosecutor not to speak prejudicially about pending investigations[17] or publicly condemn the accused.[18] Writers at *Forbes* summarized the modus operandi: "The hallmark of a Spitzer trophy is victory by intimidation."[19]

In 2001, Spitzer targeted investment banks for misleading securities research. When Merrill Lynch resisted Spitzer's civil suit, he appeared on the *CBS Evening News* to warn of possible criminal charges, inducing the firm to settle the civil case.[20] The business writer Peter Elkind said the following about Spitzer's handling of the Merrill matter:

> Spitzer had engaged in considerable saber rattling along the way—at one point telling the media, in a scary phrase that would become of one of his favorites, that Merrill's behavior "bordered on criminal." Yet no firm or individual involved in the research scandal would face criminal charges. While Spitzer would regularly wield criminal prosecution as a threat during his

investigations, it was usually just a bludgeon. He viewed his power to criminally indict a big company as a weapon of mass destruction, too horrific to deploy except in the most extreme circumstances of corporate perfidy and defiance.[21]

In the fall of 2004, Spitzer aimed at insurance brokers for allegedly rigging the bidding process to channel customers into high-priced insurance contracts in return for fees. He filed a civil case against Marsh & McLennan, one based on assertions that conflicted with guidelines that New York insurance regulators had issued at Greenberg's request.[22] Again, he threatened criminal charges against the firm as a bludgeon, this time expressly to pressure its board to seek the resignation of its CEO, Greenberg's son, Jeffrey, in order to avoid such charges.[23] Spitzer declared, with "obvious anger," that he would not negotiate with the Marsh board so long as Jeffrey remained chief executive.[24] Such pressure, which was very controversial, forced the resignation of the CEO.[25]

Spitzer's ultimatum in the Marsh & McLennan case expanded the circle of his critics to include corporate lawyers, such as Richard Beattie, the lawyer AIG's outside directors had retained and would soon represent them in the coming drama over Hank Greenberg's forced early resignation from AIG. In the Marsh case, Beattie regarded Spitzer's move as overstepping the attorney general's bounds into the realm of corporate governance.[26] After all, appointing and removing a CEO are among the most important board decisions, a sacrosanct prerogative.[27]

One Spitzer victim who fought back was Kenneth R. Langone, the financier and philanthropist famous for helping to found Home Depot and for supporting the hospital at New York University medical school that bears his surname. He also served as chairman of the New York Stock Exchange's board of directors. In 2004, Spitzer second-guessed the NYSE board's decision to pay the NYSE's chief executive, Richard Grasso, up to $190 million over five years, at a time when popular antipathy to high executive compensation was on the rise. Without producing evidence of wrongdoing, at a press conference, Spitzer charged Langone with hiding things from fellow directors. He then promptly called Langone's lawyer to propose a settlement. Langone refused to take the bait. Spitzer would have to file the case, which lasted for several years, until New York's highest court threw it out.[28]

Langone alleged that Spitzer's case was politically motivated—intended to boost his position in the 2006 gubernatorial election. In response, Spitzer accosted a friend of Langone's, Jack Welch, former head of General Electric. At the Democratic convention in Boston in July 2004, Spitzer cornered Welch and requested that he urge Langone to settle the case. According to Welch:

> Spitzer got in my face, and he really wanted me to give Langone a message that he isn't backing down. Spitzer was really angry. He got himself in a tizzy. He wanted to make sure Langone knew he was in the fight of his life and he was going to get him. Spitzer said he was so mad that he is going to put a spike through Langone's heart.[29]

Spitzer also used the media to cajole other law enforcement authorities. In one instance, Spitzer publicly reproached his federal counterparts, asserting on *60 Minutes* that he felt compelled to act because of the lackadaisical stance of the SEC.[30] SEC officials did not appreciate Spitzer's grandstanding, which mischaracterized its operating procedure.[31] The practice at the SEC, as with most federal agencies,[32] is to investigate possible cases carefully and confidentially to determine where they lead and then decide whether to proceed with public statements or not.[33] To do otherwise would irresponsibly jeopardize reputations of innocent citizens. In contrast, Spitzer broadcast his cases as he went, making public statements about theories and inquiries he proposed to pursue before investigating. Nor did the SEC appreciate the substance of Spitzer's behavior, which in one case it described as having "no legitimate basis."[34]

In choosing cases, Spitzer favored targets where broad vague principles of criminal law could be used, as opposed to arcane regulatory tools.[35] But while criminal cases often offer the prosecutor greater publicity value, selecting cases for those reasons can prove misguided. While Spitzer was occupied with securities research and compensation packages, Wall Street and many banks were manufacturing a housing and credit infrastructure that would soon bring the global financial system to the brink of collapse. The FBI warned in September 2004 that banks and other mortgage lenders were ginning up fraudulent loan applications and junk consumer housing credit was being packaged and peddled as high grade.[36] Spitzer did not police those matters or pursue the wrongdoers, which may have seemed dull compared to the cases he brought, which had flash and publicity value.[37]

Spitzer's interest in Greenberg, which seemed to be personal, arose as early as the fall of 2004, just around the time when Spitzer demanded the resignation of Jeffrey Greenberg as CEO of Marsh & McLennan. In September of that year, Dennis C. Vacco, Spitzer's predecessor as attorney general then in private practice, represented an insurance broker which had become concerned about Spitzer's attack on Marsh & McLennan. Vacco, who lost a close and bitter race against Spitzer for attorney general, wanted to discuss Spitzer's inquiries. In Spitzer's office at 120 Broadway in Lower Manhattan, Spitzer abruptly changed the subject from Marsh & McLennan and the industry by launching into a tirade about AIG's Hank Greenberg. According to Vacco:

> Mr. Spitzer was upset over statements [Hank Greenberg] had recently made, commenting on [Spitzer's] "over prosecution" of minor infractions . . . . Mr. Spitzer gratuitously made several derogatory, deeply personal and highly inappropriate expletive-laden comments about [Hank and Jeffrey Greenberg] . . . . Mr. Spitzer stated that he planned "to take those mother fuckers down" . . . It was evident to me that Mr. Spitzer was motivated by some unexplained personal animus. I was very uncomfortable with the conversation and viewed it as unprofessional but did not say anything because Mr. Spitzer was very emotional about the topic and I did not want to compromise my client's position.[38]

Spitzer claimed that his interest in AIG was not a drive for political publicity or a personal vendetta against Greenberg but was based on a finite insurance transaction that AIG had done with Gen Re five years earlier. He said it was invalid because it lacked sufficient risk to count as reinsurance—a stretch when accounting interpretations required as little risk as 1 percent to qualify as reinsurance. Spitzer based this conjecture on notes about the transaction that were among reams of other documents Gen Re provided to authorities. The notes referenced a telephone call of October 31, 2000, that Greenberg placed to Gen Re's chief executive, Ronald E. Ferguson.[39]

Greenberg might have spent a total of 15 to 20 minutes on the entire transaction back in 2000 when it occurred. Right around the time of a lengthy overseas trip in October that year, Greenberg had held a meeting of senior colleagues to catch up on ongoing matters. This included updates on the financial results of the current quarter. Amid a wide-ranging discussion, some colleagues indicated a slight reduction in the level of reserves, by about $59 million at a time when total reserves were $24.9 billion. Most of that reduction, moreover, totaling $43 million, was due to unusually large claims paid by Trans Re, covering catastrophes it had insured against. Trans Re had become a majority-owned sub of AIG that quarter, and therefore its results, including these reductions in reserves, would be consolidated on AIG's books.

The group noted alternative solutions, including entering into a finite cover transaction or terminating reinsurance policies it had written for others (called "commuting" in industry parlance). A finite cover transaction would not only address the reserve reduction but enable expanding AIG's business at a relatively low cost. Commuting policies would regain the related premium income along with the reserves. The consensus was to find a finite deal. After discussing candidates to contact, they settled on Gen Re, because it was AIG's largest reinsurer. In deciding who should make the contact, Greenberg said he knew Ferguson and would be happy to give him a call, which he did. Greenberg explained the proposal to Ferguson and senior AIG personnel and then had nothing else to do with the deal. As it turned out, AIG's negotiators left the details up to Gen Re employees. They were to choose which exact risks Gen Re would transfer by identifying particular insurance policies the deal covered.

The Gen Re transaction had zero effect on AIG's equity or net income. True, one of the affected accounts was the company's "loss reserve liability" account, an important item in an insurance company's financials. But AIG's total reserves then were $24.9 billion, an amount 50 times the size of the Gen Re transaction. Nevertheless, Spitzer and the media spoke as if the Gen Re transaction had *increased* AIG's income, but that is not how transactions such as this ever work. When an insurance company increases reserves upon underwriting new insurance, the increase in reserves is treated as an expense, a cost of doing business, which *decreases* income.

Despite such flaws, the DOJ, apparently in part due to Spitzer's taunting, eventually made a criminal case out of it against Ferguson, five other Gen Re employees and one AIG employee—but not Greenberg.[40] Early in the case, the government made plea deals with two Gen Re employees who agreed, in exchange, to testify about steps they took to make the deal fraudulent and to inculpate other targets. A court later found that the testimony of one of these had been inconsistent on important points, was "suspicious" and signaled to the government's lawyers that they should "approach [his] revised recollections with a more skeptical eye."[41] During the hearing, one judge asked the government's lawyer about how they saw Greenberg's role in the case, and the lawyer explained that they had no evidence of his being involved at all—no e-mail, no phone calls, no substantial witness.[42]

The remaining targets, including Ferguson, maintained their innocence to the end. The case against them, which included a jury trial followed by an appeal, dragged out for six years. The government finally settled it when each employee paid fines ranging from $100,000 to $250,000.[43] In settling, these employees did not admit guilt but did acknowledge that the deal turned out to be fraudulent, was unusual and was accompanied by "red flags" that they should have spotted in order to stop the deal rather than help see it through.[44] Mistakes were apparently made, but not by AIG, and back in March 2005 a sense of proportion was missing, as Spitzer used his exaggerated conjectures about the deal to gain leverage against AIG and Greenberg.

On Monday, March 7, 2005, AIG's audit committee met with PwC to review the company's now-completed 2004 annual report. Carla Hills, the former U.S. trade representative and veteran AIG director and audit committee member, asked Barry N. Winograd, the PwC partner in charge of the AIG account, to see the schedule of disagreements between management and the auditors.[45] Winograd shared this routine document that auditors prepare in their audits. On the list were assorted quotidian matters that, Winograd observed, involved professional disagreement over immaterial topics. Winograd said that AIG's internal controls were effective and that PwC expected to issue a clean audit opinion.[46]

It was at this time that the threats Spitzer uttered at his Goldman Sachs speech, echoed in the press, reached AIG and its board, along with

Spitzer's subpoena.[47] A faction of the outside directors—led by Zarb and joined by Aidinoff, Futter, and Holbrooke—swung into action. The faction, which did not include Secretary Cohen or Ambassador Hills, minimized contact with AIG management.[48] Zarb and Aidinoff worked closely with Richard Beattie, the lawyer retained four months earlier to strengthen the directors' hand in dealing with succession, which Spitzer's regulatory inquiries would soon provoke.

Despite having criticized Spitzer for his handling of the Marsh & McLennan case, Beattie viewed many of Spitzer's methods as effective, including his tactic of getting private law firms to conduct investigations for him.[49] Throughout the next several months, AIG's outside directors, led by Zarb and represented by Beattie, went to work for Spitzer, producing the fundamental shift in corporate governance that experts had warned about: no longer were the interests of AIG, its board, and Greenberg aligned. A faction of outside directors stood on one side and Greenberg on the other. In the balance hung the interests and fate of AIG and its shareholders—among them "widows and orphans," public pension funds, and legions of loyal AIG employees.

Representing AIG was the law firm of Paul, Weiss, Wharton, Rifkind & Garrison ("Paul Weiss"). AIG's general counsel had retained Paul Weiss on an earlier matter after canvassing a few other firms.[50] One such firm, Cravath, Swaine & Moore, declined due to conflicts of interest, as it represented companies then engaged in insurance litigation against AIG.[51] Paul Weiss stayed on to defend AIG against Spitzer, though it had close ties to him that posed some appearance of a conflict. Spitzer had once worked at Paul Weiss as an associate; one of Spitzer's top prosecutors in the AIG matter was also a former associate of the firm;[52] and many Paul Weiss partners supported Spitzer's political campaigns and contributed money to his election efforts.[53] (Later, a chief Spitzer deputy went to work there after her stint with him; and Spitzer later retained the firm when facing charges of criminal solicitation of prostitution and attempted evasion of federal banking laws.[54])

Of course, it is not uncommon for a defendant to retain a lawyer thought to be close to the prosecutor. But increasingly over the course of the firm's involvement with AIG, Paul Weiss lawyers stated in formal legal documents and internal e-mails that AIG's interests were aligned with Spitzer's and were not adversarial.[55] This orientation seemed to reflect not only the cozy relationship between Paul Weiss and Spitzer but, consistent with the changing spirit of the times, a sense that AIG's interests would be better served by capitulating to government demands rather than defending the corporation and its employees.

As for PwC, the auditing firm, its role is also complex. Auditors are retained and paid by a corporation, but intended to hold a public trust in assessing the veracity of financial reports. Auditors balance the fear of liability for breach of duty with the fear of losing a client, a balancing act whose delicacy became acute for PwC in early March 2005 as it sought both to cooperate with the authorities and keep its role as AIG's auditor.[56]

All these forces came together during the week after the March 7 audit committee meeting where PwC reviewed AIG's financials and indicated that it expected to deliver a clean audit opinion on them.[57] Barely a month after Spitzer casually indicted Greenberg during his Goldman Sachs speech, Zarb called an emergency meeting of AIG's outside directors for Sunday, March 13, 2005. The meeting was not held in Lower Manhattan at AIG's 70 Pine Street boardroom, but rather midtown in a conference room on the 30th floor of Beattie's firm; the outside directors would seek no reports from AIG managers, who were directed to sit in an adjacent room until summoned; and it was chaired not by Greenberg, but by Zarb.

Zarb knew that Greenberg was out of town that weekend and arranged to have him call in to the meeting at designated intervals during his trip back to New York. Although Greenberg planned to step down as CEO and hand the baton over at the upcoming annual meeting two months hence, the meeting's purpose was to propose his early resignation—along with that of Howie Smith, the company's chief financial officer (CFO) since 1984. Motivations were mixed, however, since there had not been any investigation about the vague allegations Spitzer first aired at his Goldman Sachs speech five weeks earlier—not by Spitzer or Paul Weiss, the directors or Simpson Thacher, the SEC or DOJ, or PwC, though AIG had begun preliminary inquiries.

To prepare for the March 13 meeting, Beattie called Spitzer at the request of some of the outside directors. Beattie, who knew Spitzer professionally, saw Spitzer out running in Central Park in Manhattan. Walking together, Beattie wanted to find out where Spitzer was on the

AIG matter, which Spitzer said "looked grave."[58] Spitzer alluded to some tape recordings of phone calls among Gen Re employees. Such material was third-party hearsay possibly inadmissible in court,[59] both the experienced lawyers knew, and the tapes, it would be clear later, vindicated AIG and Greenberg.[60]

Beattie's second task ahead of Sunday's special board meeting was to host a gathering of AIG outside directors to vet their intended successor to Greenberg, Martin Sullivan. Under the succession plan put in place earlier, Sullivan knew he might be tapped to assume the CEO role on a trial basis while Greenberg facilitated a smooth transition. Meeting at Simpson Thacher's offices that Saturday, Zarb and the rest of the faction wanted to know if he was ready to step up sooner and on a permanent basis. Sullivan signaled that he was all set.

The next morning, Zarb and the faction met at 10:00 A.M. in Beattie's office to review their plan. The rest of the outside directors joined them at noon in a large high-tech boardroom of Simpson Thacher. At the meeting, Zarb invited Beattie to speak. Beattie referenced the tapes Spitzer had vaguely cited and told the board that Spitzer thought he "had damaging evidence" in the Gen Re matter.[61] Mark Pomerantz, a lawyer from Paul Weiss, spoke next, elaborating on the prevailing law enforcement intensity that had been stoked after Enron and Sarbanes Oxley, warning of associated perils.[62]

A somber mood set, the emotional intensity in the room was about to rise, as Winograd, PwC's partner in charge of the AIG account, took the floor. In a tone of distress, Winograd dropped a bombshell: the firm may be unable to deliver PwC's clean audit opinion on AIG's 2004 financial statements. That astonished most of those present, since there had been no hint of such a thing and the financial statements were due to be filed in a matter of days.[63]

Ambassador Hills, who had served on AIG's audit committee for many years since joining the board in 1992, was incredulous. "What happened," she asked, "since our audit committee meeting to warrant this reversal?"

Winograd cited questions about the accounting for the Gen Re transaction of 2000 raised in the six days since that committee meeting.

"What? But you signed off on that in 2000 and every year since."

"Well, we're not sure that we should have."

Secretary Cohen, who had joined AIG's board just the year before, pushed Winograd to explain. Winograd said Gen Re had not transferred the required risk to AIG for the deal to count as reinsurance.[64]

"But what is the effect of that difference on the financial statements?"

"Well, it just means that the liability was entered in the wrong account—it should be a *general liability* rather than a *reserve liability*."

"So, what effect does that have on shareholders' equity or net income?"

"None."

"Suppose," Secretary Cohen then suggested, "that you isolate the Gen Re transaction—now four years old, modest in size, and of no consequence for equity or income—and add a caveat to the financials explaining that, at this point, PwC has decided to reconsider its earlier opinion on that. Then you can certify the rest of the financial statements on time and in order."

Winograd balked at this solution. He explained that PwC's national office, rather than he, was taking this position. The directors could readily surmise that the firm's partners felt pressure, perhaps to avoid the fate of their friends from Arthur Andersen.[65]

Ambassador Hills found this ordeal to be painful, as she observed the dire situation: When a company like AIG is unable to file financial statements on time, equity traders sell off its stock, sending its price tumbling, and capital markets shun the company, cutting its access to funds required for daily operations.

So Hills and Cohen continued to request isolating the Gen Re transaction, and Winograd continued to resist that solution for reasons that remained nonsensical. Finally, Winograd made a suggestion that struck Hills and Cohen in particular as a nonsequitur: that PwC might be able to give its opinion if Greenberg resigned as CEO and Smith resigned as CFO.

The logic of that option was elusive. AIG's 2004 financial statements either were or were not fairly presented and the 2000 Gen Re transaction either was or was not accounted for properly. PwC's professional opinion about those matters had nothing to do with the identity of the company's top officers. And it is not the prerogative of the outside auditor to usurp a corporate board's sacrosanct authority to appoint its officers—anymore than it would be legitimate for an attorney general to do so. Such a suggestion reinforced an eerie sense that what the board was hearing from Winograd was not an independent PwC making accounting judgments but a PwC under pressure to throw Greenberg overboard. It is not clear why PwC might have done this, but prose-cutorial pressure would have led it to minimize liability risk that could threaten its survival, as happened with Arthur Andersen; business pressure would have stoked a desire to keep the AIG account as power at the company shifted from Greenberg to Zarb.*

With the directors startled, Zarb focused on the subject of Greenberg's employment and patched him in by telephone. After Zarb summarized what the board was discussing, Greenberg's voice must have boomed through the speaker phone. He stressed his belief in the accuracy of the Gen Re accounting, the immateriality of the amounts and the importance of standing by AIG employees, including those who implemented the Gen Re transaction. He argued that succumbing to prosecutorial pressure amounts to abandoning AIG's employees and surrendering its culture. The more you capitulate, the more they will target you, he contended, emphasizing that such a weak posture would ruin AIG.

Zarb drew the board's attention to a subpoena that Spitzer had issued requesting Greenberg to testify under oath about Gen Re and possibly other matters. Spitzer would also schedule an interview with Buffett, whose Berkshire Hathaway owned Gen Re, the company initially investigated by the Virginia authorities, but not under oath.[66] One outside director posed a tricky question ostensibly founded on an AIG corporate policy requiring all employees to cooperate with gov-ernmental inquiries: would Greenberg answer all and any of Spitzer's questions or exercise his Fifth Amendment right to decline to be a witness against himself?

Lawyers invariably counsel clients in such settings to take the Fifth, even with nothing to hide. After all, a witness recounting the same

---

*In fact, days after this board meeting, Winograd confided to Greenberg that he personally had no problem with AIG's financials or with him or Smith. Winograd blamed PwC's national office for the ultimatum. Samuel A. DiPiazza, who was PwC's chairman at the time, declined Cunningham's request for an interview for this book.

events more than once rarely does so exactly and two witnesses recounting events to a prosecutor often contradict each other. Either such common pitfall exposes a witness under oath to charges of perjury or obstruction of justice.[67] In this instance, Spitzer had refused to let Greenberg see any of the documents that Gen Re's lawyers had supplied and refused to limit the scope of questioning. So Spitzer could pose questions on any subject under the sun on which Greenberg could not possibly be prepared. That is a tall order for the CEO of a global company that engaged in 40 million transactions annually. It was daunting given that Spitzer had singled out a transaction that had occurred five years earlier after Greenberg had spent perhaps 15 to 20 minutes on it—and Spitzer signaled interest in addressing other trans-actions as many as 15 to 20 years old. Nevertheless, Greenberg said he could precommit to answering every question if Spitzer would tell him the subject matter and provide related documents. Absent that, he could not guarantee there would be no questions so far afield or outside his knowledge that he would have to decline answering.

The risk of contradiction in such contexts was borne out by Buffett's later statements in Spitzer's suit against Greenberg when compared to testimony of successive Gen Re CEOs. Ferguson, CEO when Green-berg broached the transaction, e-mailed two colleagues on November 6, 2000, to report that he had vetted the deal with Buffett, who had blessed it.[68] Buffett denied that such a conversation took place.[69] Ferguson's successor, Joseph Brandon, testified repeatedly that on several occasions he and Buffett spoke about the possibility of terminating the deal ("commuting" it, in industry parlance) and that Buffett opted each time to let it run its course.[70] Buffett likewise denied that any such con-versations ever occurred.[71] Prosecutors may have eventually sided with Buffett rather than with Ferguson or Brandon, but the contradictions show the perils any witness faces in such complex cases.

At the March 13 AIG board meeting, without Greenberg present, the directors then debated his fate. Cohen and Hills stressed the merits of the case that Greenberg made for standing by the company and its employees; they noted how he spoke of the value of AIG's loyalties to its employees and pointed out that, in this situation, the relevant employee was Greenberg. Aidinoff and Zarb argued the opposite, averring the need to be assertive and defend themselves. They urged that this was an opportunity to implement a succession that, they felt, should have been done years before, and on which they had been working since retaining Beattie four months earlier.[72]

Cohen and Hills acknowledged that the pressure was overwhelming and the situation anguishing: Spitzer was intense, uncompromising and had demonstrated a propensity to portray his targets in the most negative possible public light; PwC, apparently under pressure, was saying it may withhold its audit opinion; lawyers all around them were hammering the hazards of the matter in the prevailing environment; AIG's stock price was sliding and could plummet; the company's cost of capital was inching up and access to capital could evaporate. Ultimately, the directors were put in an acute conflict of interest: either throw their leader overboard or risk personal liability and the company's immediate fate. As the law professor and former SEC Commissioner, Joseph A. Grundfest, wrote contemporaneously in the *New York Times*:

> If the government insists that A.I.G.'s chief executive be fired as part of the price of not indicting the firm, the chief executive is gone . . . . A.I.G. has no realistic choice but to cooperate fully with the government, even if evidence might later demonstrate that the government's theories were legally infirm or that factual allegations couldn't withstand cross-examination.[73]

In this milieu—anguished, awkward, conflicted, or painful, depending upon each participant's viewpoint—the directors opted to request Greenberg's resignation as CEO. Beattie and Zarb called Greenberg with the news, indicating that he could continue as chairman until the annual meeting two months hence. Greenberg accepted the ultimatum to resign as CEO but said he would not continue as chairman if there were any time limit—it would have to be possible to be reelected at the next annual meeting and serve additional terms as well. Greenberg was stunned by what he heard next: that the men would check with Spitzer on that.[74] Afterward, they assented, though Aidinoff and others did not like the idea, for fear that Greenberg would overshadow Sullivan, whom the board named as his successor CEO.

Greenberg was already weighing the pros and cons, to AIG and to him, of staying on as chairman or simply resigning that post, too. He would continue to mull over that question in ensuing days after he returned to New York and then embarked for a long-scheduled 10-day business trip to Asia on a variety of AIG matters along with two other AIG executives.[75] On that trip, the Chinese government awarded Greenberg its Marco Polo Prize for promoting American-Chinese relations; the Malaysian government agreed to extend AIG's right to maintain its historical level of ownership in its operations there for another five years.[76]

After those meetings, Greenberg changed his itinerary, canceling the India leg of the trip and heading instead for Switzerland, where he and his wife, Corinne, spend two weeks each August hiking together. There they pondered the upheaval. Greenberg now thought it was probably best for him, and for AIG, to resign as chairman. He had several conversations with colleagues and advisers during this time, including David Boies, his personal lawyer who became a trusted confidant. During that trip, Greenberg decided to resign entirely.[77]

It was clear to Greenberg that AIG's governance was firmly, fully, and candidly in lockstep with Spitzer, whom Greenberg came to regard as a preening scion of outsized ambition. At the same time, Greenberg formed the opinion that Beattie was a political opportunist in lawyer's clothing—not simply protecting a client's interests but promoting an outcome shaped by New York politics, which then meant supporting Spitzer. As for lawyers at Paul Weiss, Greenberg concluded that they represented not so much AIG but Spitzer's views of what was good for AIG.

Under pressure and facing conflicts of interest, the directors had ceased defending employees or the company they had built. Senior AIG officials even pleaded with Spitzer to tell the media that they were cooperating with him, and Spitzer obliged this unusual service in a public statement of April 4, 2005,[78] to the continuing dismay of the other governmental agencies just beginning to look into the bold claims Spitzer would increasingly broadcast publicly.[79] An unorthodox hostile takeover of AIG by its outside directors had thus been completed.[80]

No justification for the decision had been given, however, as neither Spitzer nor anyone else had investigated the matters in speculation, about the Gen Re transaction or otherwise[81]—all of which had been certified for years by PwC based on its annual audits. Faced with the challenge of justification, those in control would resort to stretches of the accounting imagination.

Chapter 14

Restating History

Promptly after resigning in mid–March 2005, Greenberg directed his lawyers to begin separating AIG from SICO and C.V. Starr & Company, always independent companies but with commercial ties that now needed to be severed. The exercise should have been an ordinary matter of housekeeping, as employees of the two companies had worked together side by side for decades. In a sign of things to come, however, lawyers at Paul Weiss adopted a belligerent attitude. During the weekend of March 27–29, at an office in Bermuda that AIG and Starr International Company (SICO) had shared, SICO's lawyers were securing SICO corporate documents. A team of AIG lawyers segregating its files accused the SICO lawyers of removing documents illegally. Instead of resolving the matter between the two teams of lawyers, the usual practice, Roberta A. Kaplan of Paul Weiss reported it to Maria Filipakis in Spitzer's office, who informed the boss.[1]

Spitzer was livid. From the Vail, Colorado, resort where he was skiing, Spitzer called a lawyer at Paul Weiss, who then called Beattie, the lawyer representing AIG's outside directors, who called Spitzer to try to calm him down. Spitzer proclaimed this to be "criminal wrongdoing."[2] Screaming into Beattie's ear at about 10:00 P.M., Spitzer threatened to pursue a criminal case against AIG for obstruction of justice. Beattie contacted Boies and the two lawyers worked out a way to secure the documents and resolve the impasse. Though they patched Spitzer into the call to explain the resolution and calm him down, Spitzer's office, meanwhile, had threatened to arrest a SICO lawyer involved in the document gathering exercise, at the urging of Paul Weiss lawyers.[3]

AIG's board had a previously scheduled meeting planned to discuss whether Greenberg should continue as chairman, which Beattie believed that they would oppose. That meeting turned out to be very short, however, because minutes into it a messenger delivered a copy of Greenberg's resignation letter to Beattie, ending his nearly 40 years of service at AIG.[4]

To court public opinion, Spitzer intensified his media campaign. Under one telling headline of April 4, 2005, in the *New York Times*— "How a Titan of Insurance Ran Afoul of the Government"—an article recounted Spitzer's allegations and regaled readers with a dramatic tale of corporate wrongdoing.[5] But the piece was published before any investigation had occurred, before notice of any charges had been given, and before Greenberg had a chance to rebut the insinuations circulating in the press.

Spitzer's ambitions soon appeared to extend beyond the state lines of New York, as he went on national television to make more accusations. On Sunday morning, April 10, 2005, Spitzer appeared on ABC's network talk show, *This Week*, hosted by George Stephanopoulos. Spitzer asserted that fraud had occurred at AIG and that Greenberg was to blame. Spitzer's statements shocked many people, including other prosecutors.[6] His assertions repudiated the presumption of innocence by vilifying Greenberg, infringed on his constitutional rights to due process, and violated Spitzer's prosecutorial duty not to speak prejudicially about pending investigations[7] or publicly disparage the accused.[8] In response, Spitzer's office denied that he meant what the audience heard.[9] The program transcript reads as follows.[10]

Stephanopoulos: You mentioned Hank Greenberg, the former chairman of AIG. His lawyer, David Boies, was on *Charlie Rose* just the other day. Here's what he had to say.

(BEGIN VIDEO CLIP) *David Boies:* If the accounting's wrong, the accounting's wrong. But what I'm trying to make clear is that this is not something where it is a capital offense. It's not the kind of thing that's greatly influenced the market or misled people.

Charlie Rose: Do you believe that Mr. Greenberg thought he was violating the law when he made this?

Boies: No, absolutely not . . . .

(END VIDEO CLIP)

Stephanopoulos: Bad accounting, but no crime?

Spitzer: Well, obviously I disagree with that . . . . The evidence is overwhelming that these were transactions created for the purpose of deceiving the market. We call that fraud. It is deceptive. It is wrong. It is illegal.

Stephanopoulos: So does that mean you're moving toward an indictment?

Spitzer: No, I didn't say that. It depends what we will prove or can prove that Mr. Greenberg knew at the time. We have powerful evidence . . . . These are very serious offenses, over a billion dollars of accounting frauds . . . . That company was a black box run with an iron fist by a CEO who did not tell the public the truth. That is the problem.[11]

Fraud is a legal term of art, denoting *intent* to deceive, so that fraud cannot occur by accident. It requires a conscious mental commitment to mislead. There was not remotely any circumstance under which Greenberg committed fraud. In New York, however, the Martin Act has been seen, especially by Spitzer, to define fraud more loosely, to include not only misstatements intended to deceive, but misstatements that occur unintentionally, due to accident, carelessness, or negligence. That can mean that a senior manager, such as a CEO, can be guilty of "fraud" even for misstatements made by subordinates. Defined that way, "fraud" is not the "four-letter" word that listeners to this program would have heard—akin to financial murder—but something no worse than a traffic violation—akin to foot faults in tennis.

Prompted by Spitzer's loose allegations on national television, John C. Whitehead, a distinguished diplomat and financier, who had served as deputy secretary of state under President Reagan and chairman of Goldman Sachs before that, published an op-ed in the *Wall Street Journal*.[12] Whitehead was concerned that Spitzer was out of control. His op-ed of April 22, 2005, began:

> Something has gone seriously awry when a state attorney general can go on television and charge one of America's best CEOs and most generous philanthropists with fraud before any charges have been brought, before the possible defendant has even had a chance to know what he personally is alleged to have done, and while the investigation is still under way.

That afternoon, Whitehead and his wife were traveling from New York to Texas to visit friends for the weekend. Spitzer had called Whitehead's cell phone during the flight so Whitehead returned the call in the taxi from the airport.[13] Spitzer opened with a blast, which Whitehead reports as follows:

> Mr. Whitehead, it's now a war between us and you've fired the first shot. I will be coming after you. You will pay the price. This is only the beginning and you will pay dearly for what you have done. You will wish you had never written that.[14]

Whitehead tried to interrupt to say, "See, what you are doing to me now is what I objected to in the piece—threats without charges or proofs." But Spitzer ranted on. It was a two-minute diatribe, after which Spitzer hung up without giving Whitehead a chance to speak. Unbeknownst to Spitzer, Whitehead's wife was sitting beside him and heard everything, as Spitzer was shouting into the phone. After the Whiteheads arrived at their destination, they took a half-hour break to write down what Spitzer had said. Whitehead had it typed and sent it to a lawyer for safekeeping.

As time passed, Whitehead was content to leave it at that. But a few months later, as Spitzer ramped up his campaign for governor, a reporter called Whitehead seeking to verify a rumor that Spitzer had made a menacing call to him. Rather than churning the gossip, Whitehead thought he should establish the formal public record. So he wrote a follow-up for the *Wall Street Journal* explaining what happened and publishing his transcript. The conclusion: "It was a little scary."[15]

Spitzer acknowledged making the angry phone call and said he regretted it, but disputed some of the words, including "war."[16] His office said Spitzer ended the call by directing Whitehead to "focus on your day job."[17] Another eyewitness, a Spitzer political aide who was sitting next to Spitzer when he made the call, verified Whitehead's account: Spitzer spewed exactly the threats Whitehead reported, his "eyes narrowing to slits" as he threatened a citizen for criticizing his prosecutorial excesses.[18] Spitzer never apologized.

Spitzer's nationally televised accusations on April 10 staked out ground that he would not be able to sustain. He was making claims, now quantified at "over a billion dollars," without having facts to back them up. As the investigation got under way through April and May, Spitzer's allegations about accounting "deception," "fraud," "illegality," and "not tell[ing] the public the truth" proved incorrect.

The investigation was conducted for Spitzer by Paul Weiss, supposedly representing AIG, and PricewaterhouseCoopers (PwC), with assistance from Simpson Thacher. They would use an increasingly routine procedure in corporate accounting called a "restatement."[19] The restatement would collect and show differences between how AIG, with PwC's certification, had reported transactions during the previous five years, and how PwC and the others wished to present them after requesting Greenberg's resignation.

Having PwC run the investigation seems a bit like auditing your own tax returns. PwC had been AIG's outside auditors for decades and its staff had been spent hundreds of thousands of hours over those years assuring that AIG's accounting was true and fair. Although PwC used different personnel for the restatement than had been on the account previously, firms such as PwC face competing incentives when corporate clients propose an accounting restatement. On one hand, it is difficult to do a thorough job of second-guessing your own firm and publicly restating positions colleagues have taken in the past; on the other, ceding the investigation to another firm puts the firm's continued engagement at risk. Ultimately, the optimal self-interested balance may be to pursue an investigation with enough restatement to satisfy incoming management, validating the exercise, while laying all blame on outgoing management, keeping the assignment. Still, if a firm vouches for one treatment one day then repudiates that in favor of a different approach the next, one must wonder which position to believe.

Such conflicting forces seemed to plague PwC in AIG's case, as it adopted a rule at the outset of the process that it insisted the lawyers and every AIG employee obey: in scouring AIG's worldwide books, find as many potential accounting anachronisms, errors, or misjudgments as possible, and attribute them to Greenberg and Smith.[20] Indeed, some language in drafts of PwC documents was so combative that lawyers involved told them to tone it down.[21] Zarb and the board endorsed PwC's rule[22] and company management, led by Sullivan, told employees to cooperate fully with PwC.[23] For three months, teams of lawyers and accountants pored over AIG's books, spending tens of thousands of man-hours studying one million pages of documents and interviewing scores of AIG employees.[24]

AIG employees reported badgering by PwC partners. One claims manager, Jeff Johnson, received a phone call during this period.[25] The caller introduced himself as a PwC partner and got right to the point: "Did Mr. Greenberg or management ever ask you to suppress reserves?"

"No, of course not," Johnson replied.

The caller paused briefly before saying: "Let me ask you again, did Mr. Greenberg ask you to suppress reserves?"

Johnson considered that insistence odd, but figured the caller may have wanted to be crystal clear. So he repeated: "As I said, no, of course not."

The caller persisted yet again, however, pressing a third time: "Did Mr. Greenberg ever ask you to suppress reserves."

Johnson now considered this method of questioning to go beyond mere clarification or confirmation and to become badgering and repeated his answer yet again. As he hung up the phone, Johnson was disturbed and perplexed. He immediately called the company's chief actuary to report it. The badgering tone had all the earmarks of a witch hunt, Johnson said.

Paul Weiss and Simpson Thacher reported regularly to Spitzer, consistent with instructions from Sullivan and Zarb to cooperate fully with him.[26] The firms gave Spitzer chronologies based on their review of documents, provided notes that Paul Weiss attorneys made of interviews with AIG employees and reported on their conversations with Greenberg's lawyers.[27] On May 9, 2005, at the offices of Paul Weiss, lawyers gave Spitzer a "sneak preview" of the contents of the interim accounting report they were compiling.[28] The firm refused to let Greenberg see a copy. In the court proceedings where Greenberg sought access to the document, lawyers from Paul Weiss, in formal papers and in open court, wrongly denied giving Spitzer a "sneak preview" of it.[29] No judge appreciates such duplicity, as it bears on a firm's credibility and the opponent's right to see documents. When ordering Paul Weiss to share it with Greenberg, the judge noted with contained fury: "I know we are in the post-Enron world, but people are entitled to due process."[30]

Sharing this information with Spitzer, while hiding it from Greenberg, was characteristic of how Paul Weiss worked concertedly with Spitzer from the outset, though nominally representing AIG. Paul Weiss characterized Spitzer and AIG as "not actual adversaries."[31] In that spirit, Spitzer and Paul Weiss held weekly conference calls together,[32] and Paul Weiss performed numerous legal services for Spitzer's office, drafting legal documents, conducting research, and monitoring court proceedings. Paul Weiss lawyers even gave Spitzer's office the dial-in numbers to telephonic interviews they conducted with AIG employees.[33]

At the time, Greenberg's lawyers objected to Paul Weiss's actions, stressing that AIG and Spitzer were not on the same side. They believed that Paul Weiss had acted more like Spitzer's agent than as defense counsel for AIG and said that Spitzer appeared to control AIG's actions.[34] In response, while Kaplan disputed that AIG was controlled by Spitzer, she rejected the rest of the argument, stressing the unique relationship that AIG and Spitzer had that created a shared interest. All agreed, then, that there were not two "sides" to the matter, as one would expect there to be, with the government on one side and the defendant corporation on the other. Rather, as Kaplan repeatedly acknowledged, it was AIG and Spitzer against Greenberg.[35]

Greenberg was continually kept in the dark about the investigation. On May 25, 2005, while he was on a business trip in Ireland, Spitzer told one of Greenberg's lawyers that Greenberg would be criminally indicted upon his return to the United States unless Greenberg agreed to settle before he returned by paying a $750 million fine. Remarkably, Spitzer refused to answer questions about what Greenberg had supposedly done or what possible charges he could settle. "Hank Greenberg knows what he did wrong," was all Spitzer would say.[36]

When Greenberg was told of this bizarre threat and proposal, reminiscent of Spitzer's treatment of Langone, Greenberg told the lawyer to respond by requesting that Spitzer name the court where he should appear. Immediately after, Greenberg called each of his four children to say that Spitzer had just threatened to indict him.

Spitzer never followed through on his threat to criminally indict Greenberg. On the contrary, the Friday after Thanksgiving 2005, Spitzer publicly acknowledged that no criminal charges would be brought against Greenberg.[37] However, Spitzer never apologized for his public allegations that Greenberg had engaged in criminal conduct, or for his attempt to use the threat of a criminal indictment to coerce a settlement—a tactic which ran afoul of New York ethics rules then in effect, which prohibited prosecutors from threatening criminal action to obtain a settlement in a civil suit.[38]

On May 27, 2005, AIG released its restatement.[39] Beattie had sent Spitzer a highlighted copy, apparently trying to show the legally helpful parts, circled in felt-tip marker.[40] But the results affirmed Boies's point—this was "not the kind of thing that's greatly influenced the market or misled people." Despite all efforts, even Spitzer found most of the changes made in the restatement did not amount to a violation of law. They certainly did not provide "probable cause" for a criminal case, which he never filed; Spitzer's civil case, filed contemporaneously, was initially based solely on seven changes reflected in the restatement, and he soon voluntarily withdrew five of those, leaving solely the Gen Re matter and one other issue.[41]

Greenberg and his lawyers spent the next two months examining every change made in the restatement. Completed on July 26, 2005, their detailed memorandum challenges every change point by point. (Interested readers can see the full analysis, reproduced as Appendix D on this book's companion web site.) The following highlights a few of the most consequential points.

In the restatement, the changes added up to reducing shareholders' equity, cumulatively across five years, by 2.7 percent in total, or $2.26 billion, and net income by 2.1 percent per year, or $4 billion for that entire period. For perspective on the dollar amounts, AIG's assets totaled $800 billion, annual income exceeded $10 billion and it engaged in 40 million diverse transactions annually concerning premiums, reinsurance, financial exchange, investments, leasing, and other complex matters. Given that many accounting decisions involve judgments, from consolidating subsidiaries to estimating reserves, it would be relatively easy for a competent accountant, scouring AIG's records, to identify issues of judgment that could go either way and quickly add up to several billion dollars. Concerning the percentages, a long-standing rule of thumb in corporate accounting treated variations of less than 5 percent as immaterial. Although that custom was abandoned in 1999 at the behest of Securities and Exchange Commission (SEC) chairman Arthur Levitt,[42] auditors signed off on accounting reports so long as they were within 5 percent of their calculations of a fair financial picture, as AIG's clearly were.

A look back at the charts in Figures 12.1 and 12.2 (pages 153–154) adds perspective: the figures presented there are those appearing *after* the restatement, not before. In other words, even after giving effect to the restatement, AIG's position and performance were that of a fortress of financial prosperity and strength, giving lie to the idea that cutting accounting corners was a part of its master plan.

The item in the restatement that had the least accounting significance imposed the greatest human toll: the Gen Re transaction that Spitzer used to ignite this saga, and that the Department of Justice (DOJ) used to pursue four employees of Gen Re and one AIG employee for six years before settling it, did not affect shareholders' equity or net income by one cent. It merely required reclassifying one item as a "reserve liability" rather than a "general liability" and the item amounted to one-fiftieth of the total reserves on AIG's books at the time.

One change in the restatement to net income—12.6 percent of the total—was a decision to treat as an expense the compensation that SICO had for three decades paid to selected AIG employees. That reversed 30 years of well-known AIG practices in which everyone had concurred, including directors, officers and internal and external accountants and lawyers. In all those years, the SEC never raised any questions about this program or its accounting treatment and PwC signed off on this treatment year in and year out. After all, SICO made the payments, not AIG, and they cost AIG nothing, and so were properly treated as an expense of SICO, not AIG. AIG and its auditors and counsel had regularly discussed the accounting treatment and repeatedly decided the amounts were immaterial to AIG, let alone a cost to it, as Winograd reminded AIG's audit committee on March 7, 2005. Everyone also knew that, if AIG were required to expense SICO's payments, SICO would simply stop the program, since it was designed to save AIG money not cost it money.

Even so, beginning in 2001, AIG had added disclosure about the SICO plan to its financial statements, including descriptions of the history and amounts. After all, this was one of AIG's greatest strengths: it provided costless compensation that enabled AIG to attract and retain among the best workforce in the industry, a point about which peer executives were rightly jealous. AIG's disclosure was prompted by the broader political environment, when executive compensation became a hot button issue at many companies, though never at AIG. Stock option compensation had proliferated in corporate America and, until this time, accounting rules did not require it to be listed as an expense, since it did not cost a company anything, but at best, on exercise, rearranged the ownership of its equity. Further, even if anyone thought that the SICO payments should be AIG expenses, that would be a disagreement of principle, not a violation of accounting or law.[43]

The wildest entry in the restatement was also the largest single item, reducing shareholders' equity by $951 million, 42 percent of the total reduction. It addressed whether a special purpose company, Union Excess, should have been consolidated on AIG's books. The company's purpose was to take insurance risks from AIG, with SICO backstopping most of the shareholder risk of loss. Either AIG or SICO would have to consolidate Union Excess on their books, according to which of them bore the related risk of loss.[44] Since the mid-1990s, both AIG and Union Excess had submitted claims for loss to SICO for payment, which was proof positive that SICO bore the risk, not AIG. In addition, a separate independent audit by outside accountants for SICO confirmed that Union Excess was required to be consolidated on its books,[45] which was also the position that PwC had consistently taken as AIG's auditor. Accordingly, Union Excess properly would and did appear on SICO's consolidated books, not AIG's.

Yet the restatement consolidated Union Excess on AIG's books. At best, the restatement rested on differences of opinion among accountants and a change of opinion within PwC.[46] Suggestive of how this item was more a matter of accounting judgment than any clear-cut instance of error or trick, as late into the process as April 21, 2005, at an AIG board meeting, the directors were still scurrying to determine "the appropriate accounting for items such as Union Excess."[47]

Another large part of the restatement concerned the level of liability reserves for asbestos and environmental insurance, which was increased by $850 million, resulting in an after-tax drop of $552 million in both net income and shareholders' equity, a significant percentage of the total. Setting such reserves are judgment-laden exercises and there was nothing about the estimates that AIG had made requiring revision. PwC, as recently as February 8, 2005, had tested and found them appropriate, as they had in every prior year in memory. Again suggestive of what was really going on, it was only in late May that the board chose to inflate these figures, as they continued to debate the item at AIG's board meeting of May 18, 2005, nine days before the restatement was released.[48]

Insurance liability reserves are made to reflect a reasonable estimate of claims that may come due under policies; they can only be estimates, never exact figures. AIG had historically used two estimation methods, one based on its market share relative to estimated industry-wide exposure as published by recognized analysts, and one on AIG's actual claims experience in the period. This is a rigorous actuarial exercise conducted regularly by experts in AIG's actuarial department in consultation with officers in the relevant claims unit. The goal was to assure that reserves were within a reasonable range defined by the outer limits of these methods. AIG's chief actuary signed off on these estimates, as did PwC.[49]

In short, after AIG spent three months and tens of millions of dollars in professional fees, the investigation led to making contextually modest changes in AIG's shareholders' equity and net income, based on what amounted to changes of accounting policy or disagreements in accounting judgment. Spitzer had determined as early as June 2005 not to file any criminal charges in the matter, recognizing that he simply had no case; but rather than publicize his lack of evidence, he quietly leaked it to the press in November, over the four-day Thanksgiving weekend.[50]

Overall, Spitzer ultimately brought only a few high-profile cases, though publicly threatening many more. On the campaign trail when running for governor, Spitzer used the media adulation, and crusading speeches about virtue and morality, to win the New York governorship, which he took over in January 2007. In March 2008, however, Spitzer's political career came to an abrupt end when he resigned the governorship amid criminal investigations into his patronizing a prostitution ring and attempting to evade federal law by devising a paper trail to disguise the source of funds he used to pay for it.[51] Peter Elkind, the business writer, summarized the irony of Spitzer's downfall:[52]

> Spitzer's entire political strategy was based on his projection of an image as a moralist. That he broke numerous laws, so furtively and mischievously, to engage in extramarital sex with young [prostitutes] blew his cover. He was not what he portrayed himself to be. At best, he was a hypocrite. His tactics in the cases he brought underscored that he was not, in fact, the devotee of the rule of law or proponent of justice he and his media friends projected. But in their zeal to condemn, Spitzer and his fans overlooked many principles of legal ethics designed to prevent prosecutors from harassing citizens and unfairly or wantonly destroying reputations.*

---

*Federal prosecutors in the Spitzer case kept it open for nearly eight months before announcing that they would not bring charges. Their reasoning, however, was somewhat curious. Spitzer had admitted guilt and resigned the governorship, yet the prosecutors, in explaining why they were not going to charge him, said "we have determined that there is insufficient evidence to bring charges." See Danny Hakim and William K. Rashbaum, "No U.S. Prostitution Charges against Spitzer," *New York Times* (November 7, 2008).

In the end, the accounting restatement did not vindicate the decision to seek Greenberg's resignation. And AIG's board, management and advisers who created it failed to appreciate the immense costs the restatement inflicted on the company and its shareholders. The restatement resulted in AIG's paying fines to the State of New York, the SEC, and the DOJ—totaling $1.6 billion—giving credibility to unfounded claims in a series of class-action lawsuits, some by shareholders and others by competitors, all of which generated enormous increases in legal fees, fines, and settlements in aggregate exceeding $1 billion.[53]

The changes prompted rating agencies to downgrade AIG's credit, driving up its interest costs and impairing all strategic operations that relied on that rating, especially at AIG's financial products division.[54] Total direct costs to shareholders over the short term measured several billion dollars in reduced market capitalization. The long-term costs would prove incalculable. It was easy to wonder: who was watching out for the shareholders' interest?

The revisions were also a remarkable turnabout for all the directors involved. Every AIG director then in office, from Aidinoff to Zarb, both audit committee members, had repeatedly signed off on many of the accounting treatments they now revised—on SICO's compensation plan, Union Excess's consolidation, asbestos and environmental liability reserves. PwC, the company's outside auditors for decades, also reversed its opinions, many it had consistently held year after year.

Greenberg viewed the entire set of allegations to be trumped up. Most were dropped unilaterally and every one contested vigorously. After all, PwC had certified all the financial statements that reflected all the accounting choices that had been made. In Greenberg's view, AIG and all its advisors wanted Spitzer to look good and the participants worked toward achieving that optic. For the billions of dollars wasted in this fiasco, Greenberg holds responsible Spitzer, Beattie, Paul Weiss, and the defecting outside directors—Aidinoff and Zarb along with Futter, Holbrooke, and others. For standing up against the onslaught, he commends outside directors Bill Cohen and Carla Hills.

The accounting restatement made a lot of money for the law firms involved—and that was just the beginning of an extremely lucrative engagement. Paul Weiss proceeded to represent AIG in a commercial war against Greenberg. In legal battles over everything from the ownership of fine art to rights to famous insurance names such as American International and C. V. Starr, the war would produce legal fees on AIG's side alone exceeding $1 billion—more than the amount of any single item in the restatement.[55]

Chapter 15

Civil War

When Greenberg returned from abroad in late March 2005, he found his office on the 18th floor of 70 Pine Street cordoned off as if it were a crime scene. Apparently under orders from Spitzer's office, AIG guards refused to let Greenberg enter or retrieve even his personal property, which included memorabilia from world travels, letters from his mother when he was fighting in the U.S. Army, and medical files for his dog, Snowball.[1] Since no one at AIG had employment contracts, not even Greenberg, his lawyers and AIG's had been discussing a standard executive severance package, which would include office facilities. Before March was over, however, Paul Weiss abruptly ended the talks without explanation, and AIG would never provide Greenberg with any form of severance compensation.[2] AIG had also isolated Greenberg's staff, denying them access to their usual workstations in favor of banishment to remote reaches of 70 Pine on the 63rd floor, accessible only by a separate elevator, assuring they would not encounter any other AIG personnel.

A civil war had thus begun, with AIG first freezing out Greenberg and his staff and then gradually escalating into outright hostility. Battles would be fought on a dozen fronts, span five years, and consume billions of dollars. Greenberg's first task was to find an office. He worked from temporary quarters in a townhouse near Lexington Avenue and 75th Street that C. V. Starr & Company had owned for several decades and used to host guests and store company cars. In the townhouse, he huddled with his small team—Matthews, who returned from retirement to help, and Smith and their assistants—to plan business strategy on behalf of C. V. Starr & Company and Starr International Company (SICO). To plan legal strategy, Greenberg's top lawyer, David Boies, soon created a "war room" at his midtown Manhattan office.

A primary objective was separating AIG from C. V. Starr & Company and SICO. SICO owned about 12 percent of AIG's outstanding shares, although it did not have any insurance operations; C. V. Starr & Company operated several subsidiaries which acted as general managing insurance agents in specialty lines such as aviation, marine and technical risks. These agency businesses were left out of the corporate group when AIG was created because they were small at the time and would not have added value to the public offering. By March 2005, almost 30 years later, the C. V. Starr & Company agencies were worth perhaps $1 billion and employed 300 people, though trivial compared to the scale of AIG, then employing 92,000 and worth some $180 billion. The three companies— AIG, C. V. Starr & Company, and SICO—had been involved in thousands of transactions with each other over several decades. They shared information systems and office space and had overlapping directors and officers and some common shareholders. Severing these relationships, which had always been disclosed in AIG's regulatory filings, would be a significant task under the best of circumstances. Among uncooperative sparring partners, it became a battle of David versus Goliath.

Separating the directors of the two corporate sides was an initial step, one Greenberg had instructed SICO's lawyers to begin before he left on his overseas trip. Those lawyers, working in Bermuda in late March to segregate AIG and SICO documents, did their research in the business center of a hotel in Hamilton, after AIG lawyers had ejected them from the office space SICO had shared.[3] With little to go by but a thumb drive containing fragments of SICO corporate records, the lawyers determined that the swiftest and surest procedure was to convene a shareholders' meeting. The meeting's purpose would be to remove SICO directors who were also directors of AIG, including Kanak and Sullivan. The lawyers coordinated calling this shareholders' meeting to occur in Bermuda, SICO's headquarters, on March 28, 2005. All directors seemed to be cooperative, agreeing with the purpose of separating AIG from SICO.

SICO had only 12 voting shareholders, among them Greenberg, Matthews, and Smith, whom the lawyers contacted by cell phone to assure their availability. But SICO's voting shareholders also included four long-retired members of the band of brothers, now well into their 80s and 90s, frail and residing in different time zones: Stempel, who retired in 1995 was local, still living in Hamilton; Freeman, who retired in 1993, was in Hawaii; and Manton, who retired in 1988, and Roberts, who retired in 1997, were on the East Coast of the United States. Compounded by a lack of experience with prevailing technology such as teleconferencing and e-mail, the logistics were not easy. But all were determined to help Greenberg in this circumstance. Manton, the towering Brit, was so upset over these developments that he broke down in tears occasionally and could not speak.[4]

The lawyers managed to get all 12 shareholders on a call to discuss and give their unanimous consent to remove the directors, as well as to elect Freeman, Roberts, and Stempel. (Manton, the eldest of the four, protested that he was too old to serve.[5]) The lawyers also obtained resignations from the board of C. V. Starr & Company of those directors who would be continuing to work for AIG.[6]

The companies mutually agreed to end the historical practice of distributing SICO's shares of AIG as incentive compensation for AIG employees. With the directorships separated, SICO first fulfilled all compensation commitments it had outstanding and then terminated the plan. AIG thus lost one of the keys to its historical success and one that defined its culture: a huge free asset used to attract and retain a peerless employee base. AIG began to search for ways to replace those historical sources of employee compensation, which Sullivan said were essential to maintaining employee morale.[7]

Greenberg turned to the insurance agencies that C. V. Starr & Company owned. He was prepared to sell the agency businesses to AIG

if fair terms could be agreed. Greenberg and advisers he retained estimated their value at about $1 billion. In May 2005, they initiated
negotiations with Sullivan about the possibility of a deal. AIG seemed
receptive, and advisers spent most of the summer and early fall working
towards a pact. Discussions broke off toward year-end, however,
because AIG was ultimately unwilling to offer more than $600 million
for the businesses. Another bidder, Warren E. Buffett of Berkshire
Hathaway, offered a higher price, but Greenberg finally decided he
would prefer to retain all of the businesses and build them up rather than
sell them off.

Given the decision to retain C. V. Starr & Company intact, both
sides agreed that it was best for its diverse group of shareholders to part
ways, too, ending share ownership by any AIG executives. To that end,
in December 2005, C. V. Starr & Company offered to repurchase all its
shares from AIG executives. Referred to as a "self-tender offer" in the
jargon of corporate finance, all the targeted shareholders accepted
the offer and C. V. Starr & Company bought all their shares. The price
included a "gross-up," meaning payments that covered the costs to
recipients of income taxes on the sale. C. V. Starr & Company offered
the gross-up voluntarily, not through negotiations, because it believed
that the recipients, all long-time AIG employees, deserved that. The
AIG executives were richly rewarded. Sullivan received $14 million in
the deal, and several received payments exceeding $10 million.

Moving to build those businesses, Greenberg proposed to Sullivan
extending all existing contracts between AIG and the C. V. Starr &
Company agencies. Sullivan demurred on this proposal, however,
which Greenberg took as a signal that AIG did not want to continue the
relationships. So Greenberg began to expand the range of insurance
companies with which C. V. Starr & Company's agencies had long-
term general agency agreements. Over the next several months, C. V.
Starr & Company would enter into such agreements with several
insurers, including both ACE and Berkshire Hathaway on February 28,
2006; Everest National Insurance on April 6; Chubb on June 19; and
National Liability and Fire Insurance Company on July 21.

But Sullivan's rebuff of Greenberg's extension offer signaled
something more. Separation anxiety had apparently been gradually
growing among AIG executives during the course of severing the

director relationships, negotiating over the sale of the agency businesses and the self-tender offer. AIG management began to act as if it was in AIG's competitive interests either to control C. V. Starr & Company and SICO—and Greenberg—or to destroy them. Greenberg was not about to let any of those things happen. As a result, when the Starr companies began to generate business for other insurers rather than AIG and to sever their shared resources, AIG responded with a combination of aggressive business tactics and disruptive lawsuits and arbitrations.[8]

On January 6, 2006, AIG officials stormed the London office of a Starr Aviation unit called Redholm, which AIG and Redholm employees had long shared, and ousted two dozen Starr employees from the premises. The officials then commandeered all equipment and records in the office, whether belonging to AIG or Redholm. It denied employees access to e-mails and electronic documents, and tried to induce the employees to quit Redholm and go to work for AIG. On January 9, AIG terminated its managing general agency agreement with Redholm, cutting off Redholm's principal line of business. Redholm fought back by filing an arbitration proceeding challenging AIG's tactics and the validity of AIG's termination of the agency agreement. It objected, in short, that AIG was illegally trying to destroy it—a case that Redholm would eventually win.

AIG also targeted Starr Tech, the company created in 1967 after the explosion at the Cities Service refinery in Louisiana, still providing insurance services for complex engineering concerns in several industries. On January 27, 2006, AIG locked Starr Tech employees out of shared offices in New York and blocked access to Starr Tech files. On January 31, AIG sent letters to 32,000 insurance brokers advising them to stop doing business with Starr Tech. Starr Tech responded to such tactics by obtaining a court order barring AIG from poaching its employees and disrupting its customer relations.

AIG would repeat such campaigns against other C. V. Starr & Company businesses at several locations around the world. The result was a series of lawsuits or arbitrations filed by the two sides in various locales, from New York to Atlanta to London. Among the numerous allegations traded in these cases, the most significant was AIG's claim that the Starr agencies were not allowed to place insurance for other insurance companies. In the case of Starr Tech, AIG charged that it had become AIG's exclusive agent under a 1992 contract that barred Starr Tech from placing insurance with any other company. It called Starr Tech a "rogue agent" acting against orders from AIG.

In response, Starr Tech and the other Starr companies alleged that AIG was engaged in an illegal pattern of interfering with its contracts and business relationships. Starr Tech insisted it had the right to work as agent with any underwriter it chose. The 1992 contract did not create any exclusive agency arrangement. To the contrary, Starr said in a reply suit, AIG was trying to destroy Starr's business.[9]

Throughout 2006, the Starr companies won most of these legal disputes, as nothing in any of their agreements with AIG restricted their right to engage in the insurance business with other companies. Finally, in December 2006, the parties settled all of their commercial feuds, as well as trademark battles concerning use of the Starr and American International names.

With many of the commercial battles resolved, it remained for Greenberg to wrest control of his personal property from AIG, which it continued to hold, along with an art collection that belonged to SICO. The collection consisted of 80 works of fine art, including several paintings worth at least $6 million each.[10] They had been displayed or stored at offices around the world that SICO and AIG shared, mostly at 70 Pine Street, but also in such remote locales as Mt. Mansfield in Stowe and the Philamlife Tower in Manila. Several were by famous artists, such as Vincent Van Gogh and Winslow Homer, while others had more idiosyncratic value, including sculptures by two of Starr's favorites, David Aronson and Milton Hebald—the latter being the sculptor commissioned to render the tributes to Starr reposed at Morefar and at AIG's Tokyo building.[11]

During this standoff, AIG's general counsel, Ernest Patrikis, personally investigated the ownership of the disputed property and confirmed that it all belonged to Greenberg or SICO, not AIG.[12] Nevertheless, at Spitzer's direction, AIG refused to surrender the art, or Greenberg's personal papers and memorabilia.[13] Greenberg and SICO were forced to sue to recover this property, which led to their return, though at significant cost in time and legal fees.[14] Once reclaimed, Greenberg placed the sculptures by Aronson and Hebald on display in the boardroom of the Starr companies, by then in a proper office in midtown Manhattan.

Never recovered was a set of dining room chairs that had belonged to Starr, located successively in his office at 102 Maiden Lane, then Greenberg's at 70 Pine Street. AIG had agreed to deliver the chairs, and matching table, in exchange for SICO giving AIG documents to support income tax deductions worth $150 million. SICO delivered the documents to a senior AIG tax lawyer, who confirmed their veracity and custody to AIG's general counsel's office.[15] Anastasia Kelly, an in-house AIG lawyer, said the chairs were on their way, but the next day only the table arrived. Kelly said the chairs were withheld at the behest of Roberta Kaplan, the Paul Weiss lawyer. Later, AIG lawyers claimed that the dining room chairs had vanished.

As part of the civil war, AIG's new management and its lawyers turned a shareholder lawsuit that all had agreed should be thrown out into a competitive weapon against Greenberg and C. V. Starr & Company. The suit, filed in December 2002 against AIG directors, claimed that AIG paid C. V. Starr & Company agencies above-market commissions. It supposed that by having Starr overcharge AIG, the directors would gain more as Starr shareholders than they would lose as AIG shareholders. Following corporate practice, AIG had the claim evaluated by two independent directors who hired outside advisers, including the law firm of Weil, Gotshal & Manges. Their 146-page report, prepared over the course of eight months, concluded that the allegations were baseless.[16] Most commissions the Starr agencies charged for placing insurance with AIG were *more* favorable to AIG—they were *below*-market. Those above-market were priced to reflect services Starr provided to AIG that other market participants did not. The independent directors informed the judge in 2003 that the case should be dismissed.

Ordinarily, that would have been the end of it, but the events of early 2005 led the plaintiffs to renew their suit in May 2005;[17] ordinarily, a board would reply to such a renewal by referencing its report and repeat its request to dismiss the case, but the events through late 2005 led AIG's board to change tactics. At a June 2005 board meeting, lawyers from Simpson Thacher and Paul Weiss addressed this and other pending legal battles by speaking of "different strategic considerations now involved."[18]

AIG's new "strategic considerations" now made it expedient for AIG to join in the lawsuit against Greenberg, Matthews, and Smith, rather than oppose it, throwing the merits aside. Hence, it ran a new investigation, spearheaded by two directors and using new lawyers as well as reengaging Weil Gotshal. Within two months during the holiday season—in December 2005 and January 2006—this second team produced a new report with different conclusions.[19] Based on this report, the new board offered a deal plaintiffs' lawyers usually only dream of: drop the case against current AIG directors in exchange for their endorsing the case against Greenberg, Matthews, and Smith. The directors thus turned a legal sword pointing at them into a business dagger pointed at their newfound competitors.

The evidence in the case, developed during the next two years based on one million pages of documents and testimony of 62 witnesses,[20] showed that commissions were *below*-market, meaning AIG potentially owed Starr for those, in all but one policy class and in that class commissions were above-market because Starr did additional work on the matter. After extensive skirmishing as a result of this turnabout in "strategic considerations," Greenberg and Starr found it expedient to settle the lawsuit, partly due to the vagaries of litigation, especially the well-known uncertainties of court battles in Delaware, where the case was filed.[21] Another reason: an even bigger battle in the civil war, with stakes in billions of dollars, was coming to a head.[22]

The billion-dollar battle involved the SICO compensation plan, which Sullivan and the others had finally come to realize could not be replaced though it was among the most important features of the company. Rather than settling for legitimate substitutes for it, AIG decided to take a big gamble and file a lawsuit to wrest the shares of AIG that SICO owned for itself. Finding a legal theory to support such an effort was extremely difficult, as the case was frivolous at worst and a long shot at best. The minutes of a May 18, 2005, AIG board meeting state: "Mr. Beattie noted that counsel is hampered in determining what arguments are available to seek to impose a constructive trust over the AIG shares held by SICO because they have been unable to review relevant documents."[23]

The review of related documents that followed would last several years in the protracted process called "discovery." Teams of lawyers spent those years gathering and studying several millions of pages of documents covering the history of SICO and the compensation plan used for 30 years to provide billions of dollars in rewards to AIG employees. Scores of people involved with SICO for three decades answered written interrogatories or provided sworn testimony under cross examination by lawyers. AIG's general counsel, Patrikis, said that the case had less than a 50-50 chance of success.[24] He sought to settle the case early on, as part of an overall settlement of the civil war. But lawyers at Paul Weiss told AIG that it was strong so Sullivan decided to wage another losing battle.[25]

The dispute culminated in a three-week trial in New York federal court. Greenberg spent more than a week on the witness stand from morning to night answering questions of Paul Weiss lawyers about documents, speeches, and writings that went back 35 years. The jury concluded deliberations in less than a day, easily finding for SICO; the judge, Jed Rakoff, said Paul Weiss had "not come close to shouldering" its burden of proof in the case.[26]

Besides the ludicrous claim, much about this litigation was surprising. Every AIG director and senior officer had always known that SICO, an independent company controlled by a dozen people, owned a sizable block of AIG's stock and distributed shares annually to deserving AIG employees. Sullivan testified that he had never seen any document saying the shares that SICO owned actually belonged to AIG.[27] Patrikis, general counsel, whose responsibilities included preserving all documents, likewise testified that there was no document to support Paul Weiss's theory.[28] Zarb testified to the same effect, acknowledging that multibillion-dollar deals are rarely made without something in writing.[29] However, the AIG directors and officers avoided stating the obvious fact that SICO owned the AIG shares and stuck with the story that AIG owned them. Some testified vaguely that they could not recall relevant information about the arrangement.

The scale of the case, and its contest between two prominent trial attorneys, Boies and Theodore V. Wells Jr. of Paul Weiss, drew the attention of many local lawyers, filling the courtroom daily. Among these, oddly enough, were lawyers from Spitzer's office. Their actions attested, once more, to the cozy relationship between Spitzer's lawyers and those of Paul Weiss. One Spitzer lawyer, Alisha Smith, e-mailed

Paul Weiss lawyers who would be sitting at counsel's table in the front of the courtroom. Smith wrote: "Would it look strange if I sat up there with you guys??? Kidding. . . ."[30]

We have no way to determine exactly what motivated lawyers at Paul Weiss or the directors and senior executives at AIG who supported this lawsuit.[31] Most likely, however, it was due to the lingering effects of their defensive need to justify the extraordinary upheaval they had caused when requesting Greenberg's resignation. With the SICO compensation plan at stake, moreover, participants lost one of the company's most valuable resources—a key to AIG's strength in recruiting and retaining top talent. Tellingly, after losing the trial, Paul Weiss and AIG did not appeal.

On the bright side, after the lawsuit, the environment at AIG began to change with new leadership, including a new CEO, Robert Benmosche. Benmosche was the former chairman and CEO of MetLife and exactly the kind of highly qualified, experienced executive that Greenberg wanted as a successor. Confronted at the outset with Boies's assertion that AIG had no case against SICO, and Paul Weiss' assertion that AIG had a strong case, Benmosche decided to trust the company's lawyers. However, after AIG's decisive loss at trial, Benmosche concluded that it was time to bring the whole civil war to an end. In a comprehensive settlement—reached only in December 2009—AIG agreed to reimburse legal fees that Greenberg and the Starr companies incurred up to $150 million, reflecting the overall equities of this entire saga.[32]

Chapter 16

Saving the Starr Foundation

T he drama Spitzer generated around AIG in February, March, and April of 2005—with escalating threats and portrayals of great frauds he had discovered—had vastly overpromised. AIG's accounting restatement turned out to be a modest event; the threat Spitzer made to Greenberg in May was rebuffed; most of the claims in the civil suit Spitzer filed that month would later be dropped; and by November 2005 he affirmed that there was no criminal violation to pursue. With his case unraveling, Spitzer staked out another line of attack, this time against the Starr Foundation. Endowed mostly by the bulk of Starr's estate on his death, which was valued at about $15 million, Greenberg nurtured the Starr Foundation over ensuing decades to become one of the largest private charitable organizations in the United States. In December 2005, its assets exceeded $3 billion, and it made annual donations of hundreds of millions to charities worldwide, many in New York.

Spitzer's assault on the Starr Foundation claimed that it had received less value from Starr's estate for corporate shares it owned than it was entitled to—contending that the shortfall would now amount to $6 billion,[1] a facially preposterous assertion considering that Starr's entire estate was valued at about $15 million. To refute this claim, on Wednesday, December 9, David Boies, the lawyer representing Greenberg, brought all the original documents to a meeting with Spitzer's staff. He walked them through the entire administration of Starr's estate, showing how the executors did exactly what Starr intended in accordance with all relevant corporate requirements. Documents included validation of the arrangements by both federal and state authorities. At one point during the meeting, Spitzer stuck his head in to say hello. As he did, Boies tried to engage Spitzer in the discussion of this evidence, but Spitzer refused the invitation, saying Boies had to deal with the staff.[2]

Undeterred by the facts that Boies laid out, two days later, on Friday December 11, just before the close of business, Spitzer called a lawyer representing Starr International Company (SICO). Spitzer said he had concluded that the Starr Foundation had received less than it should have. Without explaining the basis for his belief, Spitzer offered not to disclose his claims publicly if Greenberg agreed immediately to pay a $770 million fine to resolve the unrelated charges that Spitzer had brought against him earlier in the year. Spitzer warned that if Greenberg did not agree to this by Saturday at noon, Spitzer would file a lawsuit based on these allegations. Greenberg refused to be blackmailed and declined to pay any such fine.

Lacking evidence to file a lawsuit, on Monday, December 14, Spitzer published what he called a "report" alleging breaches of fiduciary duty by Starr's executors. Without first giving the document to Greenberg or the foundation's president, Florence A. Davis, Spitzer distributed it to the media. Davis first learned of it when the press began calling her for comment.[3]

Spitzer's press release announcing the report made it sound as if a suit had been brought and won: "Attorney General Eliot Spitzer today released a report detailing Maurice 'Hank' Greenberg's conflict of interest and self-dealing as executor of the estate of his mentor, Cornelius Vander Starr."[4] Spitzer also sent copies directly to many others, including lawyers at Paul Weiss and Simpson Thacher and the judge presiding in Spitzer's unrelated accounting case against Greenberg—the latter an act of dubious ethical probity, as canons of legal ethics strictly prohibit lawyers from unilateral communications with the judge in a pending case.[5]

Despite regarding the assertions as frivolous, the Starr Foundation promptly ordered a full and independent investigation of Spitzer's conjectures by a special committee composed of Davis, the Starr Foundation's president; one retired New York state judge; and one retired New York surrogate court judge experienced in estate law and administration. The committee retained two outside law firms with similar independence and expertise.[6] The committee's investigation took more than a year, involved reviewing 650,000 pages of documents, and interviewing every participant and witness who was still alive. It cost the foundation $4 million in professional fees and out-of-pocket expenses.[7] These costs were incurred despite duplicating work done two generations earlier, when Starr's will was probated by New York's surrogate court, following standard procedures, and signed off by state and federal authorities, after numerous hearings, as well as scrutiny by and litigation with the Internal Revenue Service.

The committee found that all of Spitzer's conjectures were utterly off-base. On the contrary, the committee determined that Starr's executors—nine of his best friends and closest associates, named executors because he had made them the directors of C. V. Starr & Company—acted in good faith and prudently in carrying out his will.

Spitzer's charges against the executors—including Freeman, Greenberg, Manton, Roberts, Stempel, and Tse—concerned three share transfers from Starr's estate, two to the companies that had issued them, C. V. Starr & Company and SICO's predecessor, and the third to an affiliate of an Asian life insurance venture Starr co-owned with Tse. In each case, the executors simply carried out the transfers in accordance with the charter documents of the respective company. For example, the charter of C. V. Starr & Company provided, as charters of closely held corporations commonly do, for mandatory redemption of shares upon the death of a shareholder at predetermined price levels.

The executors had essentially no discretion in executing the required transactions and followed the requirements punctiliously. In response to Spitzer's press release, the surviving executors in addition to Greenberg, namely Freeman, Roberts, and Stempel (Manton died on October 1, 2005, at age 96), issued a statement calling the report "shameful, outrageous and insulting."[8] They added:

> The people of New York deserve an attorney general who is intent on fighting crime and solving the state's problems, not harassing its citizens and philanthropic organizations. Each of us fulfilled our duty to Mr. Starr and the foundation without compensation and in accordance with his wishes and the law. Our decisions were reviewed and approved nearly 30 years ago by Mr. Spitzer's own office, the Internal Revenue Service and the New York State Surrogate's Court.

Spitzer's wild goose chase, which was based on the work of a summer intern plowing through records obtained from SICO's lawyers in Bermuda,[9] was misconceived for many reasons. The foundation's special committee noted how Spitzer's "report" showed no understanding of who Starr was; how he had organized his companies; why he chose the directors of C. V. Starr & Company to serve as executors; or the special relationship that Starr had forged with Freeman, Greenberg, Manton, Roberts, Stempel, Tse, and the other director-executors. It explicitly ignored how that band of brothers led AIG during ensuing decades to increase the value of the Starr Foundation from some $15 million at the time of Starr's death to $3.5 billion in 2005.[10]

Although Spitzer had not challenged the Starr Foundation's grant-making, the committee highlighted some of the grants the foundation made in the previous year alone: $100 million to create a consortium of five internationally renowned medical research institutions, all but one based in New York, to collaborate on finding a cure for cancer; $50 million to Rockefeller University to support collaborative medical and scientific research, extending research commitments on hepatitis C and the genetics of obesity; $25 million to the Harlem Children's Zone, a community development organization dedicated to creating opportunities for disadvantaged children; nearly $20 million in need-based scholarships for college and university students; $15 million to Alice

Tully Hall at Lincoln Center; $15 million to the New York Philharmonic; and $10 million to New York's Cooper Union to provide scholarships for engineering students.

The Starr Foundation allocates its assets according to principles consistent with those Starr held, in the areas of education, medicine, human needs, public policy, foreign affairs, culture, and the environment.[11] Examples: about $250 million has gone to institutions in China, investments in keeping with the pivotal role China promises in promoting global economic security and peace; $300 million has funded scholarships for needy students, reflecting the intrinsic value of education; and grants of close to $2 billion have helped diverse institutions in New York, headquarters of AIG and domicile of the foundation.[12] Biting the hand that feeds citizens of New York is probably not something most New Yorkers would wish their attorney general to do.

Davis could only speculate about the exact motives that induced Spitzer to publish such a baseless document.[13] True, New York law vests its attorney general with powers to enforce state law against charitable organizations operating in the state, but the power is discretionary.[14] Davis attributed Spitzer's motives to his frustration with how poorly his accounting lawsuit against Greenberg was going—a motive to harass Greenberg and pressure him into a settlement.[15] This explanation was supported by how Spitzer distributed his material in a press release that read as if the charges had been proven and sent directly to many parties, including the judge in his pending case against Greenberg. The press construed the report as part of Spitzer's campaign against Greenberg, with the *New York Times* reporting it "turns up the volume in an already vehement battle between Mr. Spitzer and Mr. Greenberg."[16] This explanation also accounted for the timing of Spitzer's Starr Foundation assertions, coming as they did just after he acknowledged that there was no criminal case and as his civil case was proving increasingly weak.

Davis also appreciated that the attorney general had the power to take over private foundations through New York's Charities Bureau. If that were the case, decisions on how to allocate the Starr Foundation's billions of dollars in assets would no longer be made by the Starr Foundation's board, but by New York state officials. As Spitzer was then running for and would soon become its governor, Davis supposed that

Spitzer may have relished the prospect of diverting the funds to charities he preferred, rather than those chosen by the foundation's directors, who knew Starr.

Ironically, considering Spitzer's behavior, the Starr Foundation supports important programs devoted to promoting the rule of law and principles of world leadership in the democratic tradition. One is a program in China that includes training local prosecutors in legal ethics. Topics feature limitations on prosecutorial discretion and the need for prosecutors to adhere to proper standards of conduct. Examples of basic imperatives taught in the program include bans against unilateral communications to judges in a pending case, publicly disparaging a defendant, and engaging in conduct prejudicial to the administration of justice.[17]

The Starr Foundation has devoted considerable resources to promoting the rule of law and related principles around the world. In 1995, Temple University sought funding from the Starr Foundation to support a novel program inspired by Deng Xiaoping, China's premier whose liberalizing reforms of the 1970s enabled AIG to help reopen China for business.[18] When presented by Temple's Robert Reinstein, the Starr Foundation welcomed the proposal and agreed to fund it. An initial grant enabled launching the program and several renewal grants adding up to $9 million have sustained it. As a result, the Temple-China rule of law program has educated more than 1,000 government officials in the subject, including many prosecutors who have been trained in legal ethics.

Peking University, among China's top schools, recruited former Cornell University president, Jeffrey Lehman, to open a new law school focused on teaching law in the traditional mode of U.S. law schools.[19] Peking University believed that this approach, unique in China, would be a valuable institutional way to begin to incubate a generation of law students—future lawyers, prosecutors, and judges—in the rule of law. Again, the Starr Foundation liked the proposal and helped to fund it. The Peking University School of Transnational Law is making distinctive contributions to developing the institutions and cultural conditions to anchor the rule of law.

Since 2003, the Starr Foundation has supported the World Fellows program at Yale University. It brings emerging leaders from diverse cultures and countries to its New Haven, Connecticut, campus each fall for seminars, study, and leadership training in the U.S graduate school tradition. Greenberg meets with them and introduces them to the leadership of the Council on Foreign Relations. As Yale's president, Richard Levin, put it, the program immerses Fellows in "work addressing major problems of the planet: nuclear non-proliferation, eradicating poverty, managing climate change—problems confronting all places in the world though with each place looking at them through a different lens."[20]

The Starr Foundation embraced this program because it would expose budding world leaders to the best of American values. People taking residence in U.S. universities experience critical thinking and analytical rigor, the quest to surmount or subordinate prejudices, the American spirit of questioning and, of course, the rule of law. President Levin attests that many Fellows arrive as critics of the United States or skeptical of its policies. But their time as Fellows teaches them a lot about America's virtues, which they take back to their home countries.[21] One alumnus is Alexy Navalny, a young Russian lawyer who was imprisoned for 15 days after leading protestors challenging the validity of elections conducted by Prime Minister Putin in December 2011.[22] Of the program, Navalny said: "There is tremendous value in gathering rising world leaders to a great American university to study principles, such as the rule of law, as each of us return to our home countries with a greater appreciation of such principles and the credibility to promote them."[23]

Many other Starr Foundation commitments likewise support the goal of a civilization anchored in the principles of democracy and capitalism. A prominent long-standing recipient of the Foundation's money is the Council on Foreign Relations, founded in 1921 by a group of internationalists interested in the stabilizing potential of American involvement in the world.

The Starr Foundation has also long supported the Asia Society, founded in 1956 by John D. Rockefeller III. It pursues the twin goals of increasing knowledge about Asia in the United States and about the United States in Asia. The Asia Society's headquarters are in New York City, where the foundation helped finance the construction of its building.

Similar interests inspired the Starr Foundation to support the Japan Society of New York, which Rockefeller reopened in 1952 after it had been shuttered due to the hostilities of World War II. The Society features a rich array of groundbreaking exhibitions on all aspects of Japanese culture, including topics addressing corporate and policy issues.

Greenberg was personally involved in the creation of the Center for the National Interest, originally known as the Nixon Center. At first, the former U.S. president did not embrace the idea of a think tank, as it was not the kind of institution that appealed to him. But over dinner one night in late 1993 at President Nixon's home in Saddle River, New Jersey, Greenberg persuaded him otherwise. They were discussing Nixon's foreign policy accomplishments, epitomized by reopening relations between America and China. Greenberg suggested making the American national interest the basis for the center. Greenberg became the founding chairman, joined by board members Henry Kissinger, Brent Scowcroft, and James Schlesinger. The Starr Foundation was a leading benefactor. Devoted to promoting mutual understanding, the center is committed to educating the world about American values.

Other beneficiaries of the Starr Foundation include New York–Presbyterian Hospital, among today's most successful medical centers. A trustee since 1979, Greenberg was asked by fellow directors to take over as chairman in 1988 with the goal of turning the hospital around when it had been reeling from criticism about its quality of care and losing $1 million a week. The board recruited a new president of the hospital, Dr. David B. Skinner, who had been teaching at the University of Chicago's Pritzker School of Medicine for 15 years.[24]

Skinner and Greenberg put the hospital back on a solid footing. They installed more effective control systems governing both medicine and finances. They developed alliances with other area hospitals to form an efficient network for medical services. And they raised substantial sums of money by tapping into New York's philanthropic community. Funds were used to construct a world-class hospital building completed in 1997 at a cost of $760 million: the 11-story, 850,000-square-foot building near the East River extending over Franklin D. Roosevelt Drive—kindly named for Greenberg and his wife, Corinne, in recognition of their leadership and personal contributions made along with those of the Starr Foundation. Greenberg created a "Doctor of the Year" award and event attended by several hundred donors to raise funds and showcase the physicians at the hospital, the largest private employer in New York City.[25]

Before and since Spitzer's failed effort to usurp the Starr Foundation, the Foundation's roster of beneficiaries has included many other world class institutions in New York. A shining example is Weill Cornell Medical College, Cornell University's medical school, working at the forefront of medical research. In 2007, the Starr Foundation helped lead a fundraising effort of $1 billion, to support constructing a new medical center on the East Side of Manhattan. Groundbreaking occurred in May 2010 for the 18-story, 480,000-square-foot building.

Spitzer's failed intervention in the Starr Foundation's affairs wasted $4 million of its assets that could have funded scholarships for needy students, been invested in promoting the rule of law, or supported medical research. Greenberg and Davis found the purported justification for Spitzer's report to be preposterous. The independent committee's stinging rebuke of the report supports that characterization.[26] The Starr Foundation never received any response from New York authorities.

Chapter 17

Chaos

When AIG's new CEO, Martin J. Sullivan, first met with senior management in March 2005, he cheered colleagues on by saying: "Don't forget to have fun."[1] In contrast, Greenberg's CEO speeches to managers struck a disciplinary note, stressing things like risk analysis, control, and accountability. That command-and-control culture was on its way out, and nothing would replace it, as AIG became "directionless."[2]

As the old culture at AIG began to fade, Sullivan reported two accomplishments to the board: "keeping the management team together and losing very few customers."[3] Despite the low bar, at a mid-2005 board meeting, Zarb, acting chairman, declared that AIG's management, led by Sullivan, was doing "one hell of a good job."[4] Zarb cited how management was working with PricewaterhouseCoopers (PwC) to upgrade internal controls and improving its relationships with regulators in unspecified ways. For himself, Zarb trumpeted that he had been meeting with institutional investors, including the AFL-CIO.

Meanwhile, Paul Weiss was negotiating with Spitzer about radical corporate governance reforms at AIG.[5] The terms endorsed Greenberg's early retirement and how the board had already added three new outside directors. The deal contemplated a host of other requirements, ranging from numerous new board committees to new approaches to internal controls. A pivotal requirement, also later contained in the settlement with the SEC, called for the board to hire a special advisor to identify additional outside director nominees and to advise the board about "best practices and governance issues."[6]

The board retained Arthur Levitt, who had been chairman of the Securities and Exchange Commission (SEC) when the Enron-era debacles festered. Levitt, who had hired Zarb to run Nasdaq a decade earlier,[7] would spearhead a project for radical change at AIG. Levitt's job was to review AIG's corporate governance profile and recommend "reforms." Levitt believed in having a powerful group of outside directors control corporations as best for the public interest, rather than having strong managers run them.[8]

Under Zarb, the board began making changes almost immediately. Among first steps was increasing further the number and role of outside directors, ultimately resulting in an AIG board with only two management directors amid a dozen or more outsiders. To further dilute the power of management in the boardroom, AIG opted to separate the identity of the board chairman from the chief executive. That meant having two coequal leaders in the boardroom, initially Zarb and Sullivan, until Zarb nominated another of his old friends, Robert B. Willumstad, formerly an executive at Citigroup, to join AIG's board and succeed him as chairman.[9]

In his report, reprinted in Figure 17.1, Levitt began by congratulating Zarb for his "courageous leadership," and then recommended every corporate governance device that advocates and experts who shared his views then championed, which AIG's board embraced in full.[10] Levitt endorsed changes the board made, especially stripping the chief executive of power as well as holding "executive sessions" of the board that excluded any management directors. Levitt also recommended eliminating the executive committee, which he said was "often a symbol of board cronyism"; mandating retirement of directors at age 73; and barring any former chief executive from serving on AIG's board.

Arthur Levitt
43 Owenoke Park
Westport, Connecticut 06880

March 21, 2006

Board of Directors
American International Group, Inc.
70 Pine Street
New York, N.Y. 10270

Dear Members of the Board:

After nearly eight months of coordinated efforts by AIG's board and management, I wish to comment upon the progress of our efforts to develop governance standards that will be responsive to investor concerns. I say "our" because under Frank Zarb's courageous leadership—and prior to my retention as a special advisor to the board—the board of AIG had already commenced the process of implementing important reforms, including: the separation of the roles of Chairman and CEO as well as an intense effort to recruit strong, independent directors. My role has been to work with the board and its Nominating and Corporate Governance Committee and AIG senior management to continue and accelerate the pace of change with the ultimate goal of making AIG a company whose governance, transparency, and ethical standards are second to none.

An essential foundation for sound governance is a strong and engaged board that approaches its important role as a steward for shareholders with a sense of mission and commitment. Its members must have a determination to work with and assist management through constructive skepticism, not "nit-picking" interference. Guided by this belief in a strong board, we have canvassed the views of directors, shareholders, governance experts, and shareholder activists for recommendations.

Fortunately, changes in the make-up of the board since the beginning of 2005 have added the fresh perspective of a group of experienced professionals, who can provide management insights and guidance drawn from the wealth of their experience. I am confident that this diversified and multi-faceted group will be supportive of management, while creating a healthy environment of constructive criticism, when desirable.

As part of our dialogue, the board has adopted, or in some cases modified in an acceptable fashion, and then adopted, substantially all of my recommendations and initiated a number of corporate governance measures on their own.
These include:

- Each regularly scheduled board meeting will be accompanied by an executive session of outside directors, presided over by the Chairman of the Board
- An emphasis on providing timely and relevant information to members of the board and the development of a focused program on director orientation

Figure 17.1 Arthur Levitt Governance Letter

- A mandatory retirement age of 73 for all directors
- The elimination of the executive committee, often a symbol of board cronyism
- Strengthening the board's focus and independence by limiting the number of boards on which a director can serve; requiring attendance at a minimum of 75 percent of board and committee meetings; improving the process of self-assessment of the board, of committees, and of individual members; and providing that no former CEO can serve as a director of the company
- Reinforcing, recognizing, and detailing the critical functions of the Chairman of the Board who will be selected from among the directors and who will receive additional compensation for his or her vital services
- Evaluating the amount and form of compensation payable to directors in a way that will further align their interests with shareholders

Additional responsibilities:

- A commitment by the board to full, fair, and transparent disclosure of executive compensation, a critical element of sound governance
- A series of important guidelines on charitable giving and improved reporting of charitable and political contributions

One subject merits a separate and specific comment – the topic of shareholder participation in the nomination and election of directors. As you know, companies, regulators, academics, and shareholder advocates have been actively exploring and debating different approaches to afford shareholders with a more meaningful role in the election process. The guidelines recognize the benefits of a dialogue between the Nominating and Corporate Governance Committee and shareholders in the selection of nominees. Moreover, I recommended and the board has adopted, the so called "Pfizer Paradigm" under which, in an uncontested election, if a nominee for director receives a greater number of votes "withheld" from his or her election than votes in favor of it, that nominee must submit his or her resignation to the Nominating and Corporate Governance Committee for its review.

I believe that this will be a reasonable and potent weapon for shareholders to exercise oversight of directors. For a number of reasons, I did not now recommend the adoption of a majority voting system or shareholder access to the company's proxy statement. Clearly this is a very important subject to be thoughtfully revisited in a dialogue between investors, management and the board.

Figure 17.1 (*Continued*)

"Now" is a small, but critical word in my conclusion on this topic. Do not forget that corporate governance principles are neither engraved in stone tablets for the ages nor written in erasable ink. Governance is an evolutionary process and should take into account changing best practices, new challenges—whether technological or financial—and the strengths and weaknesses of management and of the board itself. Indeed, what may appear to be a superb governance regime will almost certainly not stand the test of time.

That is why periodic reviews and testing of guidelines as to their function in the "real" world are critical. Governance standards must be adapted to the genius and the unique culture of each company.

Nevertheless, while today's wisdom may quickly become tomorrow's foolishness, there are some enduring principles for good corporate governance in the modern corporation: the role of managers as custodians acting on behalf of shareholders, the commitment to full and fair disclosure, and compensation plans that fairly reward the creation of real value for the company and its shareholders.

In sum, the remarkable transformation of AIG's board of directors and of its corporate culture is proof of what is possible in today's corporate environment of chastened investors, active shareholder advocates, interested media, and careful regulators. The events of the past few years have created a culture in which the good governance practices adopted by the AIG board are both demanded and praised. In addition, it has put a premium on a certain type of leader - thoughtful, ethical, tough-minded and determined. The AIG board is fortunate to have Frank Zarb as its Chairman, a man whose decency and respect for the public interest is reflected by his constant advocacy of the significant corporate governance changes that have been implemented.

I also wish to acknowledge the vital contribution of M. Bernard Aidinoff, the Chairman of AIG's Nominating and Corporate Governance Committee. The timely participation of the board and management in the implementation of broad and far reaching change would not have been possible without Bernie's insight, wisdom and knowledge of AIG.

I am gratified to have been part of this extraordinary exercise in leadership, responsibility, and respect for the public interest.

Sincerely,

Arthur Levitt

cc: Eric N. Litzky
     Vice President—Corporate Governance
     and Special Counsel and Secretary to
     the Board of Directors

Figure 17.1 (*Continued*)

None of these changes had anything particularly to do with AIG or its needs. In fact, Levitt chose his recommended reforms after consulting shareholder advocates, corporate governance experts and selected directors[11]—but not AIG's management, employees, or largest share-holders.[12] The ideas were the off-the-rack notions of "good governance" then in fashion. Consider the recommendation to eliminate the executive committee, which Levitt supported by saying they are "often a symbol of board cronyism." At AIG, the executive committee in 2004 had consisted of Greenberg and four outside directors, including Aidinoff and Zarb. Its purpose was to enable AIG to operate nimbly in between full scheduled board meetings. There was nothing of cronyism about it, symbolic or otherwise. Abolishing it would simply make AIG slower and cost it lucrative opportunities.

Splitting the functions of CEO from board chairman had become fashionable, too. It was backed by the same rationale for adding outside directors, a desire to check the boardroom power of the CEO. This maneuver was slower to catch on, and probably with good reason. As an empirical matter, like board independence, most evidence shows that companies that split these functions do not perform better than those which keep the roles united.[13] Splitting the functions can also cause corporate schizophrenia and a sense that no one is in charge—exactly what would soon happen at AIG.

Age limits were another rage during this period, with some 40 percent of Fortune 1000 companies adopting them in response to urgings from governance gurus such as the California Public Employees' Retirement System (CalPERS). But a company that forbids older people from serving on its board ordains the exclusion of talent from its reach. At AIG, Levitt's 73-year-old cap would have compelled early retirement of such luminaries as Freeman, Manton, Roberts, and Stempel. More broadly, age limits would bar many venerated businesspeople from serving as directors, such as Warren E. Buffett at Berkshire Hathaway (who vociferously opposes age limits) or John C. Bogle at Vanguard (who was forced to retire at age 70 despite founding and leading that successful company that had invented the index fund). Age limits for directors at AIG also contradicted the company's long-standing nondiscrimination policy, which had prohibited discrimination on the basis of any demographic factor, whether race, religion, national origin, gender, or age.

Levitt said his goal was "making AIG a company whose governance, transparency, and ethical standards are second to none." Referencing the AIG board's embrace of his ideas throughout 2005, Levitt wrote:

In sum, the remarkable transformation of AIG's board of directors and of its corporate culture is proof of what is possible in today's corporate environment of chastened investors, active shareholder advocates, interested media, and careful regulators. The events of the past few years have created a culture in which the good governance practices adopted by the AIG board are both demanded and praised.

That passage would prove to be a regrettable one, akin to the captain of a ship celebrating the arrangement of the deck chairs when the ship is sinking. The passage did correctly note a link between board-level governance changes and corporate culture. Zarb boasted, in September 2006, on the occasion of Willumstad becoming chairman, that he and the board had "[o]ver the past 18 months transformed the company in many ways, most particularly in the area of corporate governance, composition of the Board of Directors, transparency, regulatory compliance and the installation of a new management team."[14]

When PwC and the new management team scoured AIG's internal controls in April and May 2005, they confirmed the effectiveness of internal control systems governing its financial products division.[15] AIG's risk management systems were likewise strong. As part of AIG's transformation, significant changes were made to its internal control and risk management systems, particularly as applied to the financial products division. Moreover, at the end of 2005, Chuck Lucas, the former New York Fed executive whom Greenberg had recruited a decade earlier to implement state-of-the-art risk management systems at AIG, left the company.

The internal control and risk management systems that AIG had maintained over its Financial Products (FP) division served several purposes. Above all, they were intended to promote AIG's creed of accountability under the profit center model, which entailed careful management of risk and calibrated product pricing. In particular, the systems at FP were designed to assure that no transaction ever jeopardized AIG's AAA credit rating. The rating enabled FP to operate profitably in the volatile world of financial products because it assured counterparties of its ability to make good on its obligations. AIG's AAA credit rating, a rare competitive advantage in corporate America, permitted AIG to provide its customers needed comfort cheaply without having to use costlier sources of security such as posting collateral or pledging assets.

Without the AAA rating, however, AIG would have to vouch for its financial strength in those more costly ways. The costs of operating FP absent the AAA rating were so high, Greenberg had always said, that a rating downgrade would prompt withdrawal from the business. But the new AIG seemed unaware of the role that its AAA rating played. Rating agencies stripped AIG of the AAA rating during the second quarter of 2005, thanks to Spitzer's actions, Greenberg's departure and new management's accounting restatement. AIG described resulting risks in a routine regulatory filing, noting adverse effects on FP's operations and competitive position.[16] Yet instead of curtailing FP or shutting it down, AIG's new management dramatically expanded it.[17]

AIG's internal systems were also intended to assure that FP hedged its exposure in these transactions. For any risk it took, managers would find an offsetting position to mitigate it. AIG would profit from the difference between what it charged for protection and what it paid to hedge. Hedging must be done in advance, usually when a position is created, rather than after the risk environment changes, when hedging becomes more costly or unavailable. Careful hedging was a factor that supported AIG's AAA rating, a feature of its business model for which the rating agencies gave credit. After Greenberg left, FP abandoned this hedging principle, committing to cover increasing volumes of unhedged risk, adding up to $80 billion.[18]

The third purpose of AIG's traditional controls and risk management systems was to keep the professionals at FP—who were bright, ambitious, well-paid risk takers—on a short leash. The contracts FP wrote had to be carefully vetted and limited to terms that AIG's senior managers could understand. An important example concerned credit default swaps, which could be complex, but were based on a relatively simple idea: they were akin to insurance policies covering customers against the risk that a third-party borrower would default in repaying obligations. FP historically offered customers such contracts only after scrutinizing the borrower's ability to repay. It limited commitments to the most creditworthy borrowers, such as blue-chip American corporations or European banks whose credit was also rated AAA.

More tangible examples of AIG's transformation concerned the board's new practice of giving employment contracts to executives, including Sullivan and chief financial officer (CFO) Steve Bensinger, a practice AIG had never followed in the past, preferring that managers not be given security that could impair performance.[19] Historically, every AIG employee was an "employee at will," from the CEO to underwriter trainees. Further, after SICO halted its historical practice of providing performance-based compensation in the form of AIG shares that could not be sold until retirement, AIG adopted new bonus policies that moved from that long-term orientation toward short-term results, including at FP.[20]

AIG's new corporate culture, defined by diminished internal control and risk management, a detached outside board, and short-term incentives set the stage for the debacle that followed. In April 2005, after Greenberg's departure from AIG, FP began writing credit default swaps on increasingly risky pools of mortgage-related debt, called "subprime," and increased the scale of this commitment throughout the year. These were pools of loans taken by homebuyers with relatively poor credit histories. Though such loans had an increased risk of default, those who sold pools of such loans, led by investment banks such as Goldman Sachs, sliced them into groupings with varying degrees of risk. FP backstopped the groupings that Goldman and other deal designers called "super senior," denoting that the risk of default was remote. In contrast, Goldman and others who had hand-picked the loans bet that the pools would default, leaving AIG on the hook. In many cases, it appears that customers misrepresented the quality of the pools—what AIG was told were "super senior" were bottom of the barrel at the time.[21]

During 2005, FP's portfolio steadily transformed from high to low quality, early on containing a small fraction of subprime mortgage pools (perhaps 2 to 10 percent, depending on classification) to eventually consisting of almost all subprime (90 to 95 percent).[22] FP wrote more mortgage-related swaps in the last nine months of 2005 than in the previous seven years combined.[23]

By June 2007, AIG had written nearly $80 billion of swaps on the riskiest mortgage pools, quintupling its 2005 position, all unhedged.

Many swaps required AIG to hand over cash if AIG were downgraded from AAA or the prevailing value of covered contracts declined, not merely pay only on default. In market parlance, this allowed customers to make "collateral calls" on AIG and required AIG to "post collateral" in response.

A financial crisis was brewing due to a combination of forces, including: (1) U.S. policy overstimulated appetites for home ownership and kept interest rates low for too long; (2) regulation of financial institutions was poor, as commercial banks fed the appetite for home ownership with generous mortgages while investment banks churned demand with complex financial products and increasing leverage; (3) rating agencies failed to analyze many financial products adequately and the lack of trading in such products on organized markets made them difficult to value; and (4) regulators at the SEC failed to monitor the leverage of many financial institutions, whose debt levels rose to as much as 30 to 40 times capital and, in AIG's case, regulators at the Office of Thrift Supervision, which had authority because AIG owned a savings and loan association, simply ignored any signs of trouble.[24]

During 2007, the U.S. housing market began to falter, leading to a cascade of economic problems that precipitated a global financial crisis.[25] Problems included rising mortgage default rates, falling home values, failures of various funds that concentrated in mortgages, and bankruptcies of many subprime mortgage lenders. Mortgage-related assets began to decline in value. From mid-2007 to late 2008, these problems gathered momentum and spread worldwide. For AIG, the events first produced collateral calls against it in late July 2007 and ultimately drained it of liquidity one year later.

At the same time, a securities lending program operated by AIG insurance subsidiaries added liquidity pressure. Consistent with industry practice, AIG insurance subsidiaries historically had lent securities to borrowers in exchange for cash collateral, which would be invested in short-term/low-risk investments to gain a few hundredths of a percent in interest (each hundredth called a "basis point"). After Greenberg left AIG, company employees without proper oversight decided that the goal of these programs was to earn not merely a few basis points but as many as 30, an increase of substantial magnitude that led to making investments in longer-term, riskier assets, including mortgage-backed securities.[26]

In 2007, AIG began to face a growing gap between its duty to return that cash collateral to counterparties and the fair value of the mortgage securities the subsidiaries bought with it.[27] The combination of this gap and the escalating collateral calls facing FP squeezed AIG's liquidity. True, it had abundant net assets, but in businesses whose sale would require many months to close and whose prices were temporarily depressed by the financial crisis.

An early sign of coming turmoil occurred on July 26, 2007, when Goldman submitted its first collateral call to FP, seeking $1.8 billion based on asserted value declines. Later, AIG's top management would deny being aware of this. If true, that underscores that a radical transformation had occurred, in which the new board and executives went through the motions of internal controls instead of insisting, as Greenberg had, on substantive accountability in fact. During Greenberg's tenure, he would have learned of such a colossal matter promptly or else heads immediately would have rolled. Inexplicably, senior AIG management and some top FP executives later testified to being unaware, until July 2007, that FP's contracts required posting collateral based on value declines. Yet the company's routine regulatory filings, signed by senior managers, specifically disclosed information about the terms of these contracts, including the need to post collateral in certain situations.[28] Such discord reveals how the dismantling of AIG's risk management system exposed the company to staggering losses.

How much collateral AIG was required to post for customers depended on the exact value of the securities the contracts covered. But these securities had become hard to value and did not trade on an organized market. Instead, participating firms—including Goldman Sachs and FP—prepared models to estimate value, called "marks," which varied widely. Firms developed reputations for establishing high or low marks, with Goldman well known for quoting the lowest. This led to disagreements: Goldman presented low marks to FP, seeking greater collateral; FP responded by pointing to high marks. In the case of Goldman's July 26, 2007 collateral call, FP's managers were able to resist to an extent, negotiating for a reduction in the amount to $450 million, which it posted on August 10. But this began a series of skirmishes between Goldman and FP about valuation and collateral requirements that would last for most of the next year and result in AIG posting billions in cash collateral to Goldman and others, culminating in total illiquidity.

Obscuring these perilous developments, during the second half of 2007, FP and AIG management made public statements that omitted mention of the mounting risk. At AIG's earnings conference call hosted by Sullivan on August 9, 2007, Joseph Cassano, then head of FP, infamously declared: "It is hard for us, without being flippant, to even see a scenario within any kind of realm or reason that would see us losing $1 in any of those transactions."[29] On the same call, Robert Lewis, AIG's chief risk officer, responsible for risk management at FP, said: "It would take declines in housing values to reach depression proportions, along with default frequencies never experienced, before AAA and AA investments would be impaired."[30]

The company's new internal control and risk systems apparently impaired information flow from the division to corporate headquarters. A recently hired AIG internal auditor, Joseph St. Denis, a former SEC accountant, grew concerned in September 2007 when FP received a large collateral call. St. Denis wondered about the valuations FP assigned to the securities it covered. But as St. Denis tried to investigate, Cassano reportedly discouraged him and blocked his access to report up the corporate chain to AIG's senior management or its board. St. Denis grew so frustrated that he resigned in October 2007.[31]

These and other problems were apparently also missed by the special monitor that AIG had installed several years earlier when settling the SEC's case over the PNC matter. The monitor, James Cole, a lawyer at Bryan Cave and later Deputy Attorney General in the Justice Department in charge of the President's Corporate Fraud Task Force, was charged with overseeing internal controls and compliance programs.[32] Cole spent 2005, 2006, and 2007 filing periodic confidential reports about AIG on such topics, for which AIG paid some $20 million.[33] Given the monitor's powers and cost, one would have expected those reports to call the brewing problems to the attention of AIG's board or senior management but that apparently did not occur.[34]

In disclosing interim financial results on November 7, 2007, AIG declared that management "continues to believe that it is highly unlikely that [FP] will be required to make payments with respect to its [financial products]."[35] On a November 8, 2007, conference call,

Sullivan said: "While U.S. residential mortgage and credit market conditions adversely affected our results, our active and strong risk management processes helped contain the exposure." Goldman, of course, did not give up, demanding on November 23, 2007, that AIG post another $3 billion in collateral. FP agreed to post half that.

Meanwhile, on November 29, 2007, PwC met with AIG's senior executives to discuss risk management problems it perceived to be growing at FP. During the meeting, PwC raised questions about a contradictory quality of AIG's operations. FP had come to recognize that the mortgage securities market was very risky and had ceased doing new business in it. But AIG's securities lending business increasingly invested the cash it received from borrowers of its securities in subprime mortgage pools. The questions PwC raised struck at the heart of AIG's new approach to corporate governance, internal control and risk management. Apparently, nothing was done.

Two months later, on February 6, 2008, PwC reported these festering problems to Willumstad, AIG's board chairman. PwC's appraisal, reprinted in Figure 17.2, was chilling, highlighting a pervasive problem at the new AIG: an appreciation of risk and risk management, once the company's defining spirit, had seeped out of its corporate culture.[36] PwC declared that AIG lacked leadership. Before detailing scathing criticism of Sullivan, Bensinger, and Lewis, PwC stressed that it was the board's job to select and remove corporate officers, referencing the normal practice, which contrasted, of course, with what PwC had done at the March 2005 AIG board meeting when the firm all but demanded Greenberg's resignation.

The auditors' blistering late 2007 critique of Sullivan stated that "some of [his] weaknesses [include] a difficulty in holding people accountable for internal control related matters, making difficult decisions, experience with large scale change, and lacking in execution skills." Their blistering critique of Bensinger stressed that those were "among [his] weaknesses as well," citing an example of the resulting problems: the imminent crisis concerning credit default swaps. Even the chief risk officer, who had been with AIG for many years, received a stinging review, PwC concluding that he lacked core skills of risk analysis and management. In short, the auditors told Willumstad, these officers were in over their heads and desperately needed help.

American International Group, Inc.,
Meeting Notes
February 6, 2008

Auditor 2 (A2) and Auditor 1 (AI)

On February 6th, 2008 A2 and A1 met with Bob W. to discuss the status of our material weakness consideration and our views as to remediation steps that the Company might want to consider. Below is a summary of the topics discussed.

We informed Bob that we had thought over nite about whether steps that AIG might take between today (Feb 6th) and the filing of the 10K might change our MW [material weakness] views and concluded that while steps that AIG might take during that time period will be helpful to the ultimate remediation, that implementing these steps at this point would not be enough to remediate the material weakness that exists at December 21, 2007. Bob understood this answer and indicated that AIG [would take] the necessary remediation steps regardless of the MW or not.

Bob then asked for our views as to possible remediation steps. We indicated that we had gathered our thoughts into two buckets—non people changes and people considerations. Below are the items that we shared with Bob.

Non People Changes
1. We indicated that the Board and the Company needed to address the reporting lines for ERM [Enterprise Risk Management]
2. ERM's interaction with the Finance Committee and how the Committee will oversee ERM needs to be addressed [as] to date, the primary focus of the Finance committee has not been on ERM, despite its charter
3. We indicated that the Company needed to review risk, transaction and other limits across the Company
4. We indicated that the Company should consider direct reporting (versus the dual reporting that has not been working consistently across the company) in ERM and Finance—we discussed that dual reporting—done substantively could be an alternative and agreed that this path should not necessarily be closed.
5. We indicated that the Board and management should consider separate compensation programs for control functions (ERM and Finance) that are non stock and non EPS driven
6. The Company should ensure that business units should also be incented on internal controls and compensation programs should be adjusted as appropriate.
7. We indicated that the FP compensation plan should be revisited to incent investments in internal controls.
8. We indicated that the Company needs to define its overall risk appetite
9. We suggested that the Company should form a operations and control Comprehensive Program into this Committee

Figure 17.2   PwC Auditor Notes

10. We suggested that the Company form a senior risk committee of the company
11. We suggested that the Company form a valuation control group in ERM that monitored valuation across the enterprise
12. We suggested that the outstanding issue with the ILFC CFO and controller be addressed
13. We indicated that the urgency and rigor with respect to remediating the remaining SD's need to be increased

People Considerations

As it relates to people, we indicated that among the skill sets that AIG needs include leadership, execution skills, change management skills, the ability to hold people accountable and experience in dealing with large scale improvement and change effots.

1. On the topic of Martin Sullivan—we indicated that it is the Board's decision in terms of what to do with Martin, we indicated that if the Board chooses to stay with Martin that they needed to be assured that he was truly committed to changing the way the Company is run and managed from an internal control perspective.
2. On the topic of Bensinger, we indicated that we viewed it as important that a CFO— particularly one with Steve's responsibilities (i.e., effectively the number two person in the company) compensate the CEO's weaknesses. We indicated that we viewed some of Martin's weaknesses to be a difficulty in holding people accountable for internal control related matters, making difficult decisions, experience with large scale change, and lacking in execution skills. We indicated that Steve does not compensate these weaknesses (i.e., these are among Steve's weaknesses as well). We indicated that as an example a significant contributing factor for the current situation regarding the super senior credit default swaps is because of the lack of leadership, unwillingness to make difficult decisions regarding FP in the past and in experience in dealing with these complex matters.
3. As it relates to ERM we indicated that there are two key skill sets that we would expect an ERM head to have—the first being the ability to understand, assess and evaluate risk (i.e., risk appetite) and second the ability to build an infrastructure to manage and monitor risk throughout a company like AIG. We commented that we were not sure that Bob Lewis had these skills. We also raised concern with his willingness to speak up as was evidenced by Willumstad's questions that he asked Lewis at the Dec AC meeting where Lewis was clearly uncomfortable discussing his reporting lines. Similarly, we pointed to the lack of access that ERM has into units like AIG Investments and others and that this arose thru the MW/SD discussions and that Lewis had not aggressively addressed these issues in the past.
4. We discussed Cassano. We indicated that the decision on Joe is that of the Board but that from our perspective the culture at AIGFP had to change.

Figure 17.2 (*Continued*)

5. We indicated that the lack of leadership and involvement by the AIG FP CFO in the valuation process was concerning and that this should be reviewed and—at a minimum the Company needs someone like Elias on top of the AIGFP CFO until her true capabilities are understood.

6. We indicated that it continues to be our view that the span of control and workload that Steve and Martin have is too great and that AIG needs a fulltime CFO without many of the responsibilities that are currently under the CFO. Bob agreed with both points and indicated that while Martin may not be amenable to a COO, that a CAO might be necessary.

7. We indicated that Jerry De St Pierre was struggling to get traction in the Company and that his effectiveness should be reviewed.

8. We indicated that Roemer was a key control but that the pressure lately has been relatively high from senior management (i.e., super senior valuation process, material weakness related to super seniors, mw/sd discussions related to access and roles and responsibilities of key control functions and other matters) and that the Board should ensure that Roemer knows he has their support.

We indicated that we would continue to think of other potential steps. Bob indicated that he was going to review these matters with Martin.

No other significant items were discussed.

A1
February 13, 2008

Figure 17.2   (*Continued*)

AIG's "good governance" board had failed in discharging its most important job.

On February 11, 2008, AIG publicly disclosed PwC's concern about control weaknesses, prompting immediate credit rating downgrades and slicing 12 percent off its stock price. On February 28, AIG reported its quarterly results: a $5.3 billion loss, driven mostly by an $11 billion valuation drop in FP's portfolio. As bad as that sounded, these figures were small compared to the losses to come. The reforms initiated by Levitt and adopted by Zarb and the other AIG directors had not only "transformed AIG's culture" as they heralded, but led it to the verge of self-destruction. For that, Greenberg concluded that Levitt had acted as a supercilious regulatory zealot.

Amid this turmoil, AIG opted to seek additional capital from the public markets. It prepared an offering of securities to raise up to $30 billion in a combination of debt and common stock. Strikingly, the prospectus describing the securities and the company, first dated July 13, 2007, and supplemented on May 12, 2008, nowhere mentioned PwC's concerns about managerial qualifications or internal control and risk management defects.

Shareholders grew anxious. On May 11, 2008, Greenberg, the company's largest individual shareholder and representing the company's largest shareholder group, detailed some concerns in a letter to the board.[37] The company was in crisis, he said, most obvious due to its financial and capital problems but more fundamental and pervasive deteriorations were occurring across all businesses. The May 2008 letter* highlighted the following changes since March 2005, besides the growing cumulative losses unprecedented in AIG's history:

- Losing AIG's unique leading positions in China and Japan.
- Eroding the leading position of AIG's Asian life operations.
- Releasing capital by converting overseas branches into subsidiaries.
- Allowing U.S. life insurance operations to stagnate.
- Increasing the number of employees by 24,000 ("the equivalent of two Army divisions," from 92,000 to 116,000).
- Bloating the expense ratio from 20 to 26.
- Bloating the loss ratio from 64 to 71.
- Therefore, bloating the combined ratio from 84 to 97.

In other words, AIG's healthy underwriting profit of 16 percent had shrunk to 3 percent and was vanishing. Gone were venerable employee-centric values and concepts such as profit centers, underwriting profit, risk analysis, expense control and long-term compensation programs. As PwC echoed, effective board oversight had disappeared along with competence among senior management. Significant costs were being incurred for legal fees, consultancy fees, and accounting fees—the latter

---

*The full text of this letter appears as Appendix E on this book's companion web site.

alone soaring from $35 million in 2005 to $108 million in 2008 without any obvious benefit.[38]

The board ignored Greenberg's warning letter. It sent a curt formal note in reply that did not address any of the substantive points raised. Although the note's salutation said simply "Mr. Greenberg," it read more like a form "Dear Shareholder" letter to a remote owner of a few shares than a response to the founder, former chairman and chief executive officer, and largest shareholder representative.[39]

But as later independent research reports would confirm, Greenberg's diagnosis of AIG's problems was spot on. According to a Congressional oversight report produced by Elizabeth Warren, the law professor and consumer advocate who became a Democrat U.S. senator from Massachusetts in 2012, AIG's risk management and internal control systems failed, especially in 2007 and 2008.[40] AIG's new management had overlooked the risks that FP and the securities lending group were taking. The practice of concentrating on "super senior" groupings had made managers complacent. When problems mushroomed in 2007, AIG lacked management and technical resources to address credit concerns, Warren's report concluded.

The board belatedly responded to the mounting evidence of danger in June 2008, when it requested that Sullivan resign as chief executive officer and asked Willumstad to succeed him—becoming both chairman and CEO, sensibly repudiating the Levitt-Zarb policy of separating those functions.[41] On his departure, AIG gave Sullivan a severance package worth $47 million.[42] Willumstad, who had been serving as chairman for nearly two years, held a conference call, telling investor analysts that he would conduct a strategic planning study of AIG "within 60 to 90 days, and hold an in-depth investor meeting shortly after Labor Day to lay it all out for you."[43] Pity that AIG's seasoned chairman could not complete such an exercise in a shorter period, however: before that deadline passed, the company would be nearly destroyed.

Warren's report noted discussion among experts about whether, had Greenberg remained in office, these problems would never have arisen or been solved at the outset. Insurance industry legend John J. ("Jack") Byrne, famous for turning around Fireman's Fund and GEICO, is among those convinced that AIG would have averted its fate had

Greenberg stayed on board. In an interview for a retrospective on the insurance industry from 1981 to 2011, he said:

> Hank Greenberg was the most amazing manager I ever saw. Just by dint of his personality and his fierce drive he turned AIG from a medium sized company into a giant, until the day it wasn't a giant anymore. It is quite remarkable the story of how AIG grew and grew, spread its tentacles around the world and developed enormous relationships. The end result was they forced Greenberg out and brought the company down. I continue to believe that if Hank had been there for that last five years he never would have let the risks taken on by those derivative traders get so out of hand.[44]

Comparing the history of AIG that Greenberg led to the changes wrought by the Levitt–Zarb reforms, it is hard to gainsay Byrne. Directors and senior managers seemed unaware of how AIG's previous culture defined its success and how their changes doomed it. Warren's report, after acknowledging inherent difficulties in making such "what if" judgments after the fact, quoted one comment that may be distressingly apt: former AIG in-house counsel Anastasia Kelly said that at AIG after March 2005, "no one was in charge."[45] Shortly after Labor Day in 2008, as chaos engulfed AIG, the U.S. government would take charge.

Chapter 18

Nationalization

I n July 2008, Robert Willumstad, AIG's chairman and chief executive, informed its board that the company would soon face a
liquidity problem.[1] During July and August, AIG continued to
pursue routine negotiations with customers, including Goldman Sachs,
to settle disagreements about valuations given market uncertainty. The
two would compromise by AIG paying a discount from the face value
of the contracts, something less than 100 cents on the dollar, and
reducing posted collateral accordingly. From late July through early
September, Willumstad pursued extraordinary discussions with officials
of the Federal Reserve Bank of New York about the possibility of
the Fed lending AIG money by opening its "discount window," the
liquidity resource it uses to support the nation's banking system.[2]

None of these overtures produced desired results. By mid-September,
AIG was in a liquidity crunch, needing $9 billion in cash to survive
the week—astonishing for a company commanding $800 billion in

assets.[3] On Friday, September 12, AIG was unable to access a routine source of funds, the commercial paper market, as collateral calls rose, reaching $7.6 billion from Goldman alone and totaling $23.4 billion.[4] In late August, Greenberg and Willumstad had dinner in Greenberg's apartment building in New York. Greenberg offered to assist AIG in any way that he could. Willumstad declined the assistance, expressing concern that he said the board shared, that allowing Greenberg to help would "overshadow" him—the same concern some board members expressed three years earlier at the time of Greenberg's resignation.[5]

During the global financial crisis of 2008, many institutions, domestic and foreign, faced illiquidity or insolvency as the world financial system teetered. The Fed opened its discount window to nearly any applicant, dispensing hundreds of billions of dollars in loans to scores of U.S. banks and many foreign ones, including Dexia of Belgium, Depfa Bank of Ireland, the Bank of Scotland, and Arab Banking Corporation, then 29 percent owned by the Libyan central bank.[6] All these arrangements were made at market interest rates with the borrowers posting reasonable security. The Fed lent Bank of America $91 billion and Morgan Stanley $107 billion—at a market interest rate of 1.5 percent, in exchange for the customary borrower promise to repay, without the government taking any equity owner- ship; it lent Citigroup $99 billion on such terms, though also taking nearly 30 percent of its equity[7] while guaranteeing $300 billion of its debt.[8] The Treasury supplied some $200 billion to others through its Troubled Asset Relief Program (TARP), often using creative man- euvers to grant requests. The Hartford, an insurance company, bought a small bank (for $10 million) in order to characterize a $3.4 billion loan as eligible for TARP, which was earmarked for banks—the Hartford sold the bank two years later.[9]

The Fed and Treasury were running a kind of soup kitchen for financially strapped institutions, so many and varied that the Treasury Secretary, Henry M. Paulson Jr., a former chairman of Goldman Sachs, wondered in bemusement, "Who are these guys that just keep com- ing?"[10] Americans recoil at government assistance to failed private enterprise, though such incidents recur in U.S. economic history. A few recent episodes include the Chrysler Corporation of the late 1970s, the savings-and-loan industry in the 1980s, and both the automotive and

financial sector in 2008–2009. Even as officials orchestrate vital stabilizing efforts, the public, politicians, and media strenuously protest.
Often using strident rhetoric, critics object that the "taxpayers" are
"bailing out" irresponsible corporations. Government officials charged
with the unloved task of executing the mission avoid using words like
bailout; some try earnestly to show that they are punishing rather than
rescuing. In the 2008 financial crisis, though government's intentions
were kept opaque, the result both vilified and victimized AIG: government made AIG the "poster child" for the unpopularity of bailouts
while also imposing the most punishing terms imaginable unlike those
imposed on any other financial institution.

. Through the weekend of September 13–14, 2008, AIG continued
to appeal for access to the Fed's discount window, as it had been
requesting since late July, on terms that would be routinely granted to
others. Willumstad dispatched vice chairman Jacob Frenkel, a dean of
international finance and former head of the Israeli central bank, who
maintained professional relationships with many senior officials of the
Fed and Treasury.[11] Frenkel told the officials that AIG would run out of
liquid funds in 5 to 10 days. To help AIG survive, it sought an emergency loan from the Fed. Timothy F. Geithner, president of the Federal
Reserve Bank of New York, overseer of New York–based banks, sent
members of his staff to AIG to study the matter.[12] But the officials
would make no commitments at that point, as the top brass, Geithner
and Paulson of the Treasury, were preoccupied with the fate of Lehman
Brothers, the investment bank that would soon fail.

So AIG kept seeking nongovernment solutions.[13] Attempts, begun
during the last week of August, included assembling private equity
investors, strategic buyers, and sovereign wealth funds to discuss
investment options.[14] The government discouraged AIG from pursuing
foreign sources, however, such as sovereign wealth funds or private
investors, though many such prospects knew AIG very well.[15] AIG's
management also considered an insolvency filing under state insurance
laws, which would continue to segregate the insurance companies, all
liquid, solvent, and well capitalized.[16] The process would isolate AIG's
disastrous noninsurance businesses, especially the financial products and
securities lending divisions, thus protecting policyholders while potentially cutting shareholder losses as well.

On Monday morning, September 15, Lehman filed for federal bankruptcy, wiping out its shareholders' equity.[17] The global financial crisis took another tailspin. Turning their attention to AIG, Paulson and Geithner hastily brokered talks between it and a consortium of domestic banks led by Goldman Sachs, JP Morgan Chase, and Morgan Stanley.[18] Greenberg, on behalf of himself, Starr International Company (SICO), then AIG's largest shareholder, and the Starr Foundation, another large shareholder, asked to attend these meetings, but representatives of Paulson's and Geithner's offices refused the request. There Greenberg would have seen conflicts of interest that would be widely documented after the fact: a global financial intervention being orchestrated using a coterie of firms representing multiple clients and opposing interests all at once.[19]

That Monday afternoon, rating agencies downgraded AIG's long-term credit rating, and its stock price plunged. AIG could not access short-term liquid funds in the credit markets and was prepared to take the ultimate step of drawing down its back-up lines of credit, which Willumstad analogized to a captain abandoning ship.[20] Geithner opposed this move.[21] He and Paulson decided that the government would step in, though eschewing any sense that government's overtures toward AIG would be any sort of "bailout."[22]

The next day, Tuesday, September 16, Geithner and Paulson called Willumstad to inform him of their decision and the terms, which—true to Paulson's commitment that this was no "bailout" of AIG—were mandatory, nonnegotiable, and punishing.[23] The government would take 79.9 percent of AIG's ownership, initially in the form of a new preferred stock that could be issued quickly and massively dilute existing common shareholders; separately, it would also lend $85 billion, at a 14 percent annual rate, vastly exceeding the prevailing market interest rate of 1.5 percent, fully secured by 100 percent of AIG's assets and to be repaid within two years.[24] The only way such a loan could be repaid was by selling substantial assets.

Willumstad received a formal statement of those terms at 4:00 P.M., ahead of an emergency board meeting set for 5:00 P.M. The terms were bizarre: there was no relationship between the stock and the loan, as the government would keep the stock even after AIG repaid the loan in full. It was as if your bank lent you money to buy a home, and even if you repaid the loan, the bank took ownership of your home as well. The government had "rescued" a number of institutions during the financial crisis and not one was subject to such arbitrary and punishing terms.

At 4:40 P.M., minutes before the AIG board meeting, Paulson and Geithner called Willumstad to add yet more pressure: "This is the only proposal you're going to get," Geithner threatened, making it clear that the government was giving more an ultimatum than an opportunity.[25] Paulson gave a further order: the government was replacing Willumstad, effective immediately.[26] Aware that he had scant legal authority to fire Willumstad or commandeer AIG's equity, Paulson that evening succumbed to a bout of the dry heaves.[27] Geithner worried that his terms were draconian.[28]

Within three hours of receiving the government's ultimatum, AIG's board capitulated. Yet it lacked detailed information about the matter. No one—not the board, nor the government—had made any assessment of AIG's business value. No one could make even a rough guess about whether what the government was providing was proportional to what it was taking.[29]

During the earlier call, Willumstad learned from Paulson that his successor would be Edward M. Liddy, causing Willumstad and his advisers on the phone to wonder: *Ed Liddy?* Liddy, a former head of Allstate Corporation, a domestic firm specializing in car insurance, was a strange choice to run AIG, as AIG directors at the emergency board meeting observed.[30] Liddy had presided over the break up in the 1990s of Sears, Roebuck & Company, from which Allstate had been spun out. Paulson and Liddy, fellow Chicagoans, were also friends. Several years earlier, when Paulson ran Goldman Sachs, he nominated Liddy to join that firm's board of directors, where Liddy still served[31] and in which he owned millions of dollars' worth of stock.[32] Goldman and AIG were then engaged in multibillion-dollar negotiations over the value of securities AIG had insured, revolving around how much collateral AIG was required to post to Goldman and what ultimate payments would be due. Liddy would effectively become a one-man creditor's committee, following orders from Paulson and Geithner, not advocating for the interests of AIG or its shareholders.

Willumstad had promptly called Greenberg to report the government's punishing terms, stressing that they did not resemble any of the financial support the government dispensed to hundreds of other financial institutions. On the contrary, as one senior Fed official explained, the security that Paulson and Geithner demanded for the loan—100 percent of AIG's $800 billion in assets—was enough to secure the entire debt held by the Federal Reserve.[33] Greenberg immediately tried to contact Paulson and Geithner. Paulson's assistant said that the Treasury Secretary was unavailable but would return the call. Paulson ducked the discussion, leaving a message on Greenberg's office voicemail at 5:30 A.M. the next morning. The two never spoke.

Determining why Paulson avoided Greenberg requires speculation. It cannot be simply because Paulson was too busy, or struck by panic or fear, as his memoirs reveal an intense daily work schedule. Every day he made scores of calls and participated in dozens of meetings addressing vexing challenges. Perhaps Paulson's avoidance was due to his awareness of the dubious legality of his actions concerning AIG. He may have felt uncomfortable knowing that the decisions would benefit Goldman Sachs, his former firm, by inflicting pain on AIG, both in dollar-for-dollar terms and in terms of incalculable damage to corporate reputation. One can only wonder, however, as Paulson's lengthy memoirs do not discuss it or mention Greenberg.

Reaching Geithner later that Tuesday, Greenberg spoke plainly: "As the representatives of AIG's largest shareholders, we want a seat at the table in any discussion of the company's future." Greenberg said they urgently needed to explore alternative solutions to FP's liquidity needs, finding the planned government takeover deplorable for many reasons, including the massive dilution of existing common stockholders and draconian loan terms. Greenberg specifically suggested adding foreign investors, which the government had earlier discouraged, or providing partial government guarantees of FP's obligations, as Paulson and Geithner had arranged for Citigroup and others. Either would solve FP's liquidity crunch, Greenberg explained, reminding Geithner that AIG as a whole, and every one of its insurance companies, had ample capital and was healthily solvent. "I hear you," Geithner said, indicating that he would get back to Greenberg. He never did.

At 8:30 A.M. on Wednesday September 17, Liddy appeared at 70 Pine Street, along with Dan H. Jester, Paulson's aide at the Treasury Department and also a former Goldman banker, as were many of

Paulson's aides at Treasury. Willumstad asked the two how he could be helpful in the impending transition. They said he could sign a document authorizing the government's takeover of AIG. Willumstad immediately declined. Besides finding the terms of the deal unattractive for AIG, Paulson had fired him the night before and anointed Liddy his successor.[34]

Liddy signed the first batch of formal takeover papers on September 23; Goldman Sachs announced his resignation from its board on September 26, stating the resignation was effective as of September 23.[35] The conflict of interest was clear but ignored: a Goldman director signed over AIG to the government, which would then call the shots in settling fateful negotiations between the two companies.

Willumstad had expected that when FP resolved disputes with customers over how much it owed, they would give concessions and settle disputes at a discount from face value—something less than 100 cents on the dollar.[36] Any rational party in the strained commercial situation of global capital markets would have asked for a discount, and any reasonable party in the trying financial circumstances would have granted it.[37] One FP customer made it clear that it believed it was only right to reach such a compromise.[38] Another developed a range of discounts for negotiation, indicating a reasonable range might extend as low as 40 cents on the dollar, given prevailing severe credit market conditions.[39]

Paulson and Geithner, however, engineered the opposite. AIG paid 100 cents on the dollar to every one of FP's 16 largest financial product customers, a clique of Wall Street firms and foreign banks, led by Goldman Sachs.[40] The actions made it clear that government's interest was not so much to help AIG but to use AIG to flood the market with capital, without publicly tarnishing the image of the recipients as "bailout" bandits. Government officials began to implement the plan on November 5 and 6. They created a special conduit, called Maiden Lane III. (The name reflected the location of the offices of the New York Fed, but was an ironic choice considering that 102 Maiden Lane was the location for many years of the offices of both Starr and Greenberg.)

Government officials funded the conduit in part by equity that AIG staked and in part by loans the Fed added. The officials then contacted FP's 16 largest customers and offered to pay off their outstanding contracts, by surrendering previously posted collateral and covering any shortfall in cash via the conduit. The officials did not broach possible discounts in half of those contacts.[41] To the half given that suggestion, officials asked the customer to make a proposal within 24 or 48 hours. None did.[42] As for the two customers who had volunteered to give a discount, officials insisted on paying them 100 cents on the dollar anyway.[43] Officials transferred $63 billion of funds nominally at AIG's disposal to the following banks, with no strings attached:[44] Société Générale $16.5 billion; Goldman Sachs $14 billion; Deutsche Bank $8.5 billion; Merrill Lynch $6.2 billion; Calyon $4.3 billion; UBS $3.8 billion; and another 10 at an average of $1 billion each.

To ordinary observers, the government's decision sounds like a waste of AIG's corporate assets. Geithner subsequently offered a strained rationale for his actions:[45]

> If we had sought to force counterparties to accept less than they were legally entitled to, market participants would have lost confidence in AIG and the ratings agencies would have downgraded AIG again. This could have led to the company's collapse, threatened our efforts to rebuild confidence in the financial system, and meant a deeper recession, more financial turmoil, and a much higher cost for American taxpayers.

Government officials invested considerable effort in hiding these arrangements from the public. They succeeded, in part, as it would take three months before outsiders began to learn what the government was up to with AIG—and several years to learn the full scale of funding made to essentially every financial institution other than AIG. Among government's efforts at secrecy, in December 2008, after these payouts were completed, AIG's lawyers drafted and filed with the Securities and Exchange Commission an investor disclosure document that described how AIG had settled all these contracts at 100 cents on the dollar.[46] Before the filing was publicly released, AIG's general counsel reviewed it with the Fed, the company's controlling shareholder. The Fed objected to disclosing these facts, insisting that AIG's lawyers remove the statements. The SEC said it would only allow that if AIG filed a formal request for confidentiality, which the Fed insisted that it do.

Not until March 15, 2009, after snooping from the press and pressure from Congress, did the government reluctantly disclose these clandestine payouts.[47] Howls of criticism resulted, as the government's actions in this matter were condemned in all official reports[48] and most media.[49] The scheme distorted markets and rewarded those who made bad bets on risky trades.[50] That created what is often referred to as "moral hazard," providing downside protection for peoples' excessively risky decisions. Nor was the scheme necessary: negotiating commercially reasonable discounts would have inflicted limited pain on the banks—which were substantially hedged on these trades[51]—and alleviated the punishing effects on AIG. To critics, it appeared as if cronyism rather than commercial sense drove government decisions.[52]

Not only did the government keep the terms of its dealings quiet, AIG was prohibited from speaking about them as well. The prohibition emanated from congressional grandstanding during debates about the government's intervention amid the crisis. One week after Paulson's decision to inject capital into AIG, Representative Harry Waxman of California showed a photograph during an open committee session of what he said was an AIG executive retreat at a lavish resort in Monarch Beach.[53] As other committee members and journalists piled on, Americans recoiled in disgust, venomously protesting the obscenity of "taxpayer money" funding such luxury. The party may have been today's version of the three-martini lunch that Greenberg decades ago squashed at AIG, though insiders say it was a party not for AIG executives but agents it relied on for business and was paid by insurance subsidiaries that did not receive government funds.[54] But it was one of a dozen examples of public protest against uses of funds by AIG—the ultimate revolt arose in March 2009 over bonuses AIG paid its FP executives.[55]

Responding to such uproars, AIG's government relations department decided to suspend its traditional activities, such as lobbying or edifying public opinion. The government liked AIG's reticence policy and insisted that the company commit to it in the takeover documents that Paulson and Geithner proposed and Liddy signed.[56] The clause cannot be changed without government approval.[57] AIG is therefore barred from publicly challenging any terms that government imposed, whether the taking of 79.9 percent of its equity, the appointment of Liddy as chief executive or any term of the loans. The clause, which remains in effect to this day, provided political cover to the officials, something they could point to as showing that government was controlling how taxpayer funds were being spent. The constraint on AIG remained tight, though by consultation between AIG's general counsel and the Fed, AIG is allowed to participate in limited lobbying on major pending legislation.

Another device the government used to protect the arrangements it implemented was even more extraordinary and permanent: the payout agreements the government had AIG sign with Goldman Sachs and the other banks contained AIG's binding release of the other side from any liability.[58] AIG surrendered any right to sue Goldman and the others for any reason.[59] On their face, such provisions seem out of place in the transactions. True, a settlement of claims would ordinarily include a release of liability, but in this case AIG was paying out 100 cents on the dollar, warranting recipients releasing AIG, not the other way around.

A possible explanation is that AIG had rights against Goldman and other customers for any misrepresentations to AIG about the quality of mortgage securities pooled for coverage. In April 2010, the Securities and Exchange Commission filed a case against Goldman alleging it had fraudulently misrepresented the quality of similar pools in a transaction called Abacus. Goldman settled the case by paying $550 million.[60] The releases AIG signed, at the government's behest, seem to prevent AIG from filing similar claims against Goldman and other recipient banks, such as the $10 billion fraud suit AIG filed against Bank of America, which was not among the government-favored banks.[61]

The government went to great lengths to secure control over AIG, riding roughshod over state corporate law in the process. The preferred stock it demanded on day one was easy enough for the corporation to issue without the need for shareholder approval. But at the time, AIG's corporate charter did not authorize it to issue the large number of common shares the government sought. The charter authorized issuing 5 billion common shares, 3 billion of which were outstanding. One way to enable the government to own 79.9 percent of the total shares would be to increase the number of authorized shares to above 5 billion and issue all the unissued shares to the government. (For example, increasing the total authorized to more than 12 billion and issuing all but the 3 billion already outstanding to the government.) Changing AIG's corporate charter to increase the number of authorized common shares required a vote of the existing common shareholders voting as a separate group—not counting the government's preferred shares. That requirement is designed to protect the common shareholders because increasing the number of shares decreases each shareholder's percentage ownership interest (called "dilution" in corporate parlance).

Knowing this, the government's agreement with AIG called for proposing to amend AIG's corporate charter to increase the authorized common shares. A vote of the common shareholders would occur at the company's next annual shareholders' meeting set for June 2009. Company officials assured the shareholders, as well as a judge, that it would submit a proposal for a vote of the common shareholders voting as a group.[62] The company listed such a vote on the agenda for the meeting.[63] Expectably, the shareholders voted it down, since the dilution would be massive: someone owning 10 percent of the outstanding common shares before the vote would own only about 2 percent if the new shares were issued.

Anticipating that outcome, the government-directed AIG had added a second proposal to achieve its objective, one that it believed did not require a separate vote of the common shareholders but a vote in which it could cast its preferred share votes as well, guaranteeing victory. Rather than increasing the number of authorized shares above 5 billion, this approach would reduce the number of outstanding shares to significantly less than 3 billion. Called a "reverse stock split," the government proposed to reclassify each existing common share into one-twentieth of a share. As a result, only 150 million shares would be outstanding, leaving 4.85 billion that could be issued to the government. By that subterfuge, government forced formal shareholder "approval" of its equity takeover of AIG.[64]

Geithner subsequently offered different accounts of his thinking in all these decisions about AIG. He once contended that his purpose was to protect AIG policyholders.[65] AIG's policyholders, however, were not at risk, as its insurance subsidiaries were segregated by state law and under little financial pressure: they were liquid and solvent.[66] In fact, AIG's insurance subsidiaries were so safe and sound throughout its liquidity crunch that the New York State Insurance Department authorized the parent company to use $20 billion of subsidiary capital to ease the liquidity pressure.[67]

Ultimately, Paulson and Geithner chose a "public purpose" rationale for their actions. They said that their decision to seize AIG, impose punishing terms, and then exercise total control over it—including transferring substantial capital to Goldman Sachs—was to protect America from a financial meltdown, though without explaining exactly how that would occur. Testifying before Congress in January 2010, Paulson said,[68] "If AIG collapsed, it would have buckled our financial system and wrought economic havoc on the lives of millions of our citizens." Geithner echoed the testimony at the same time:[69]

> [We] were motivated solely by what we believed to be in the best interest of the American people. We did not act because AIG asked for assistance. We did not act to protect the financial interests of individual institutions. We did not act to help foreign banks. We acted because the consequences of AIG failing at that time, in those circumstances, would have been catastrophic for our economy and for American families and businesses.

By refusing to lend to AIG through the standard route of the Fed's discount window, the government failed to exercise its valid authority. An important purpose of the discount window is to provide short-term liquidity during credit crunches that threaten the economy. Lending helps healthy firms needing short-term bridges during a crisis period and is neither intended to sustain failing firms nor limited to banks. During the 2008–2009 crisis, however, the discount window was used to fund at least 100 banks that failed within a year and was closed to AIG despite its abundant long-term capital and ownership of a savings and loan association. Experts detected politics playing an inappropriate role in the Fed's decisions.[70] Had the Fed opened the discount window to AIG, FP's liquidity crisis would have been nipped in the bud.

There was no legal authority to permit the government to oust Willumstad or commandeer 79.9 percent of AIG's equity. Officials had authority to lend money to AIG, or anyone else, under the pre-Depression era statute creating the Fed. But while this statute also allowed the Fed to assume control of banks in extraordinary circumstances, it did not authorize the Fed to seize ownership of insurance companies or replace their senior executives. Nor did any laws Congress passed abruptly during the financial crisis, such as TARP, provide such authority. (In any event, TARP was not enacted until October, after Treasury's intervention at AIG.)[71]

Paulson, in his memoirs, suggested the shaky ground for his and Geithner's actions concerning AIG.[72] He recounted warnings he gave to President Bush about needing congressional authority as well as inconclusive meetings he held with congressional leaders.[73] They raised doubts about the legality of this seizure and told the Secretary he was acting not by the authority of Congress but on his own.

Paulson was correct that his actions were not a "taxpayer bailout of AIG," at least not entirely. In significant part, they were a covert bailout of Goldman Sachs and Wall Street and foreign banks. Had officials in other countries seized property in similar circumstances, U.S. authorities, including Secretary Paulson and President Bush, would have cried foul, classifying it as nationalizing and expropriating private assets.[74] They would declare the action a violation of the rule of law and basic principles of a free society—values AIG embraced and projected worldwide for many decades and now found, paradoxically, its own government flouting.

Having ousted Willumstad and commandeered voting control of AIG, Paulson and Geithner's installation of Liddy as chief executive was effective for them. Liddy embraced the rationales Paulson and Geithner testified to, believing that his duty was not to AIG and its shareholders but to the public. Liddy testified:[75] "The U.S. government determined that a collapse of AIG and the consequent blows to our counterparties and customers around the world posed too great a risk to the global economy, particularly in the context of the near or actual failure of other financial institutions." Liddy went on:

> Because of its size and substantial interconnection with financial markets and institutions around the world, the federal government and financial industry immediately recognized that an uncontrolled failure of AIG would have had severe ramifications. In addition to being the world's largest insurer, AIG was providing more than $400 billion of credit protection to banks

and other clients around the world through its credit default swap business. AIG also provides credit support to municipal transit systems and is a major participant in foreign exchange and interest rate markets.[76]

Days after the takeover, Paulson announced on *Meet the Press*, a national television show, that AIG was to be liquidated.[77] The selling of AIG's assets, which Liddy promptly began under what he called "Project Destiny,"[78] would continue for years. Such action became necessary due to the combination of punishing terms the government imposed and its decision to divert considerable capital to others. AIG had a greater need for liquid capital after government's intervention than before.

To obtain it, AIG was forced to sell substantial assets—at a time when global market conditions meant that they would fetch discounted prices. This put AIG on a debtor's treadmill: more payments due the government, in a short period of time at high interest rates, than its business generated. It had to keep selling assets, which further reduced revenue, ad infinitum. This prompted some experts to wonder whether, as structured, AIG could ever repay the government's loans and escape its clutch.[79] The compulsory sale of assets at discounts to repay the government was anguishing for the legions of AIG employees worldwide who dedicated their careers to building the businesses.[80]

Among the assets sold:

- AIA, the flagship Asian insurance company that was among AIG's most valuable assets.
- Philamlife, the crown jewel life insurance company in the Philippines, which AIG divested by first folding it into AIA for reasons that remain mysterious.
- ALICO, the prized global life insurance company.
- Trans Re, the reinsurance company acquired in 1968 and then grown into a force in reinsurance.
- Nan Shan, the life insurance company in Taiwan acquired in 1970 with the help of K. K. Tse.
- Hartford Steam Boiler, the fabled engineering and industrial equipment insurer that AIG acquired in 1999.
- AIG's investment in the Blackstone Group and ILFC.

- Most of AIG's iconic buildings around the world, including its landmark 70 Pine Street headquarters building in New York and its storied Tokyo locale featuring a monumental sculpture of Starr installed at the 1974 dedication ceremony.

Many of these sales were made at prices the buyers considered a steal. AIG sold 70 Pine in 2009 for $150 million to a Korean investment firm; not two years later, that firm flipped the building, for $205 million, to a New York real estate developer for conversion into residential condominiums.[81] HSB was sold in 2008 for $742 million, down from AIG's 1999 purchase price of $1.2 billion, which the buyer's CFO said on a conference call was "very low."[82] The *Wall Street Journal* lampooned the very low price as reflecting a "giant neon 'fire sale' sign" hanging on AIG.[83]

Senior executives of Nippon Life Insurance Company, buyer of the Tokyo building, told Greenberg that they regarded the deal as an unbelievable bargain. For AIG employees in Japan, this sale to a competitor was an extraordinary loss of face. Nippon proceeded to tear the building down with plans to erect a larger more modern structure on the plot and adjoining land. It is not known what the parties did with the commemorative bust of Starr.

The piecemeal selling of discrete businesses, such as Nan Shan in Taiwan or HSB in the United States, neglected to capture the synergistic value of those operations within the broader AIG family. Sold as stand-alone entities, the going price was less than their value within broader business segments at AIG. Management initially ran away from the AIG brand, rebranding many retained companies as "Chartis." Rebranding exercises are costly, likely reaching tens of millions of dollars, and of uncertain value.[84] AIG's decision must have assumed that 40 years of brand development became worthless or worse in a matter of months. That would prove short-sighted. The move did not support favorable valuations of the AIG businesses being sold out of the family. These decisions attested to the short-term view AIG was operating under, which contradicted its traditional long-term horizon based on notions such as patient capital that were its trademark worldwide.

Hope eventually emerged that AIG could avert the course toward destruction. In early 2009, it had become clear that AIG needed new senior management. Greenberg urged Robert Benmosche, the distinguished former head of MetLife then in retirement, to take the position of CEO. After several discussions that met considerable resistance, Greenberg finally persuaded Benmosche to consider the job. In searching for a new CEO, the Fed took a leading role, and Geithner asked Greenberg for his assessment of Benmosche. Greenberg gave a ringing endorsement.

Benmosche became CEO of AIG in August 2009. He immediately began returning the company to its traditions and cultures and even restored the AIG brand name. He said that the company's ability to weather all the upheaval of the Spitzer assault and the U.S. government takeover was due to the outstanding workforce that Greenberg had assembled and left behind.[85] Those employees—the innovative, entrepreneurial and loyal backbone of AIG for decades—continue to give it promise today.

■ ■ ■

The government's takeover of AIG prompted SICO, AIG's largest shareholder after the government, to challenge the government action in a lawsuit. The Fifth Amendment of the U.S. Constitution directs that the U.S. government cannot deprive anyone of "property without due process of law" and forbids the government from appropriating private property "for public use, without just compensation." The government is not empowered to trample shareholder and property rights even in the midst of a financial emergency, SICO stressed. True, public policy goals can justify the taking of private property, the company acknowledged, but that does not change the requirement that government pay fair price for what it takes.

It may be necessary for government to intervene in private enterprise to rescue the country's financial system, but that does not change the constitutional mandate. Perhaps especially in the exigent circumstances of the financial crisis, government must not ignore basic legal and constitutional rights. The government's taking of a 79.9 percent equity stake for essentially no compensation, while separately providing loans that the company had to repay, and without a required shareholder vote, demanded due process and just compensation, SICO contended.[86]

SICO also challenged how the Fed, as controlling shareholder of AIG, operated the company after assuming control. Under state corporation law, controlling shareholders such as the Fed owe fiduciary duties to their fellow shareholders, which SICO alleged the Fed breached.[87] The Fed breached these duties by causing AIG's credit default swap counterparties to be paid 100 cents on the dollar when they could have been compromised for substantially less than that, SICO argued. The government apparently wished to help recipients weather the crisis and do so in a way that avoided any need for the government to confront the public and political opposition its program almost certainly would have engendered, SICO said. That may or may not have been good public policy, but using AIG funds to assist other troubled financial institutions violated the Fed's duties as the controlling shareholder of AIG to its fellow shareholders. SICO also contended that the Fed likewise violated its duties when concealing these dealings for several months and in helping to orchestrate the issuance of a massive number of new common shares to deliver to the government in violation of state corporation law.[88]

In both cases, SICO acknowledged that government had a legitimate interest in resolving the financial crisis but stressed that this interest did not give it a license to rob Peter to pay Paul. One objection to SICO's lawsuits against the government is that all government did was force AIG and its shareholders to bear the costs of risks it undertook in operating its business. But that is not an accurate or faithful account of what happened. The government's approach imposed on AIG the costs of the risky businesses engaged in by Goldman and the others. True, the public should not be obliged to pay for the costs of private risk taking, but neither should a private company be obliged to pay for the costs of private risk taking of other companies.

One might ask how AIG allowed itself to be treated as it was by the government. There appeared to be little push back. Granted, Willumstad and Frenkel sought feverishly to find liquidity sources. But they were rebuffed and seemed simply unable to persuade authorities of the dire straits. When it was finally AIG's turn for assistance, Paulson and Geithner gave an ultimatum to which the board surrendered within hours.

Greenberg would not have allowed any of this activity to proceed, and had he been in the boardroom that night, he simply would have told the government no. But suppose that the particular AIG board assembled that night felt that it had few choices. If so, that would be due to many decisions made during the previous 42 months. Those began in early 2005 with Eliot Spitzer's decision to threaten AIG without investigating and the capitulation to that pressure by PwC and the incumbent AIG board, with the assistance of lawyers from Paul Weiss and Simpson Thacher. These were followed in late 2005 and early 2006 by the radical changes in corporate governance and culture initiated by Arthur Levitt and embraced by Frank Zarb. A board and management ceased to exercise the disciplined, systematic methodologies that made AIG great, plunging the company into chaos. Paulson, a wise man of Wall Street who heard Spitzer's speech indicting Greenberg back in February 2005, surely detected this disarray in September 2008. Like dogs sensing weakness, he and the Goldman alumni on his staff may have found it convenient to roll over AIG in order to prop up their old firm. Geithner, who implemented much of the nationalization of AIG, may have found it appealing to protect the favored financial institutions he oversaw as president of the New York Fed. But he did not act alone.

Epilogue

fter a 10-day Asian trip in 1984, Greenberg and Freeman, the Asia hand among the band of brothers, were flying back from Tokyo, along with an old friend and insurance broker, Mel Harris. They had stopped in Anchorage to refuel and headed for Miami to meet their wives for a weekend getaway. Captain Davis was about to begin the descent.

Bang—a loud explosion rang through the cabin, jolting the passengers. Davis reported that the jet's left engine had blown, but that they could manage, as the right one was running. Yet five seconds later, *bang*—the right engine failed, too. At about 43,000 feet, the engineless jet was in peril.

Calmly but quickly, Davis and Greenberg conferred on alternatives. They had two viable choices: glide to Miami, probably within range, but a complex approach at a busy airport, or drift to a private airfield in Tampa, further away but easier to hit. Without power, the crew would have only one chance at a safe landing. They opted for Miami, got emergency clearance, and started a hopeful approach. On course for a harrowing landing, at 27,000 feet, the flight engineer managed to recover the right engine. With power, the pilots regained full control, and the AIG executives reunited with their wives for the weekend.

To Greenberg, the unnerving experience of losing both engines and then regaining power paralleled the loss of AIG and the ensuing recovery of the Starr companies. After losing AIG, Greenberg began building C. V. Starr & Company and SICO, along with a growing stable of subsidiaries, some predating AIG, such as Starr Aviation, Starr Marine, and Starr Tech.[1] The Starr Companies, as they are now called, are doing business in all lines of insurance throughout the world in Australia, China, Great Britain, Japan, Latin America, the Middle East, and Turkey. They also maintain investment businesses in China, Russia, and the United States, and have real estate interests worldwide. They are becoming another unique franchise, characterized by some of the same traits that traditionally distinguished AIG and were critical to its success.

Greenberg envisions building a powerful insurance and investment business with the sophistication and capital resources to insure any kind of property/casualty risk anywhere in the world. The Starr Companies attract employees eager to develop new products and open markets, using the profit center model focused on accountability, expense control, risk analysis, and generating an underwriting profit. Staffing is lean, there are neither employee manuals nor employment contracts; compensation is incentive based and geared toward long-term performance. Travel schedules remain grueling, with Greenberg taking monthly trips to China and elsewhere in Asia and the occasional swift trip halfway around the world and back—New York to Oman on Friday, back on Sunday. Where opportunities for opening new markets and products exist, the Starr Companies are at the forefront.

The leadership is experienced and involved, all directors being deeply versed in the insurance business, and senior management boasting a team of internationally minded entrepreneurial executives akin to the MOPs of AIG's heyday. They lead by example and attempt to infuse the corporate culture with a sense of passion about building this business, committed to developing an employee-centric atmosphere stoked by healthy competition, with a strong sense of camaraderie and mutual loyalty. Maintaining that capability requires flexibility in company design and oversight, starting with the board of directors and how it interacts with management. The approach is simple: all directors are also members of management, and all are devoted to helping the team build the company.

Relationships remain vital. In the fall of 2011, Greenberg invited the mayor of Shanghai to spend the weekend at Morefar, Starr's old estate in Brewster, New York. The visit would be one stop on an international trip that took the mayor from Shanghai to India, Argentina, and the United States, there to visit not only the Starr Companies but also area neighbors General Electric and IBM. The New York leg included a visit Friday morning to the New York Stock Exchange. Greenberg had arranged to meet the mayor and his entourage there and take the group up to Morefar by helicopter.

A driving rain pounded the New York region that day, however, making flight impossible. Greenberg proposed to drive his car downtown and pick them up, but the mayor said they would prefer to rent a coach bus for the ride so they could sleep. En route, first the downpour prompted closing the Hutchinson Parkway, causing a detour, and later the bus broke down. The group finally reached Brewster at 10:00 P.M. The chef had managed to keep their dinner warm and delicious. After eating in the clubhouse at Morefar, Greenberg escorted the mayor to his room. It was Cornelius Vander Starr's master bedroom where the mayor of Shanghai got a good rest that rainy night, 92 years after the Starr Companies got their start in the mayor's hometown, Shanghai, the Paris of the Orient.

Notes

Preface

1. See C. J. Prince, "CEO of the Year 2003," *CEO* (July 1, 2003).

Chapter 1   Independence

1. Greenberg enlisted in the U.S. Army during World War II. See Tom Brokaw, *The Greatest Generation* (New York: Random House, 1998), 319, 323–326. Officially, Greenberg held the rank of first lieutenant on the day he returned to the United States from North Korea, and shortly thereafter received a promotion to the rank of captain, the rank he held when he completed his service.

2. Today, the relevant law appears in Section 4237 of the New York State insurance law.

3. See Farnsworth Fowle, "Pool of Insurers in State Offers Plan for Elderly," *New York Times* (August 17, 1962).

4. For a summary overview of many insurance innovations of the 1940s and 1950s industry-wide, see James J. Nagle, "Health Insurers Gain on 3 Fronts: Advances Made in Medical Expense, Income, Senior Citizen Coverage," *New York Times* (May 22, 1960).

5. Starr followed the practice, still common in that period for aspiring young lawyers, of obtaining the required legal training by serving as an apprentice to

an admitted practicing lawyer. See "Taking Risks: The Story of American International Group, Inc." (AIG manuscript), chap. 1, p. 2.

6. See Thomas J. Neff and James M. Citrin, *Lessons from the Top* (New York: Currency Doubleday, 1999), 158 (quoting Greenberg). Starr and Smith had become acquainted when Starr sold one of his trademark insurance companies, U.S. Life, to a Continental Casualty subsidiary. This point is discussed in Chapter 9.

7. At the 1956 Olympics in Cortina d'Ampezzo, Italy, Igaya won a silver medal; he also won a bronze medal at the 1958 World Ski Championships. Years later, Igaya was elected to the executive board of the International Olympic Committee, a select group of 11 people who oversee the Olympic movement worldwide. See "AIG's Igaya Elected to International Olympic Board," *Contact* (February/March 1997): 3.

8. Cunningham interview with T. C. Hsu, New York, December 20, 2011.

9. Another unit, ALICO, had a modest presence in Japan at the time, licensed to sell life insurance to American military personnel stationed there. ALICO is discussed in detail in Chapter 9.

10. See Carlos Rodriguez Celis, "Selling PA and Life Simultaneously," *Contact* (October 1966): 4.

11. See "AIU Belgium Teams Up with Caltex in Special PA Program," *Contact* (May 1966): 5.

12. See "Worldwide Personal Accident Team Exceeds Contest Goals," *Contact* (June 1964): 2.

13. The company had been known as Globe & Rutgers Fire Insurance Company, the second-oldest insurance company in the United States (after the one founded by Benjamin Franklin). It had been a member of the AIU for decades, lately holding about 10 percent membership participation. It also happened to be the first U.S. insurance company to give Starr agency authority to write insurance back in 1921 Shanghai.

14. 15 U.S.C. §§ 1011–1015.

15. See *Contact* (November 1969): 3 (noting American Home's expense ratio in 1962 of 43 percent).

16. See "AIG Education, A Short History of American International Group" (March 24, 1978): 11, written by Edward A. G. ("Jimmy") Manton.

17. See "Taking Risks," chap. 6, p. 9.

Chapter 2 Innovation

1. See "Taking Risks," chap. 9, p. 6.

2. Ibid., chap. 7, p. 2.

3. Ibid., chap. 7, pp. 2–3.

4. Ibid., chap. 7, p. 3.

5. See Myles Mace, *Directors: Myth and Reality* (Cambridge, MA: Harvard Business School Press, 1971).

6. See Melvin Eisenberg, *The Structure of the Corporation: A Legal Analysis* (Boston and Toronto: Little, Brown & Company, 1976).

7. Cunningham e-mail from Chuck Dangelo, The Starr Companies, July 16, 2012.

8. See Tom Baker and Sean J. Griffith, *Ensuring Corporate Misconduct: How Liability Insurance Undermines Shareholder Litigation* (Chicago: University of Chicago Press, 2010).

9. Comment, "Law for Sale: A Study of the Delaware Corporation Law of 1967," *University of Pennsylvania Law Review* 117 (1969): 861 (note 167) (referencing 1968 interview of R. Brian Jarman, Assistant Vice President, American Home).

10. *Wall Street Journal* (March 21, 1968): 6, cols. 4–6.

11. See Sam Tarleton and Wayne Owens, "Plant Fires Still Raging," *Lake Charles American-Press* (August 8, 1967): 1.

12. See "CVSCO Forms Agency for Oil Risks," *Contact* (January 1968).

Chapter 3   Succession

1. See Walter Guaazardi, Peter Grose, et al., "Worth the Risk: The Story of American International Group, Inc." (AIG March 2009 draft), chap. 13, p. 3.

2. Ibid., chap. 13, p. 4.

3. See "C. V. Starr & Co. Elects Leaders," *New York Times* (August 19, 1968).

4. Among notable golfers who have played at Morefar are PGA veterans Tom Kite, Gary Player, Tom Watson, Doug Ford, Hubert Green, Curtis Strange, Willie Turnesa, and Gary McCord. (Strange holds the course record: 63.)

5. These descriptions of the artwork appear in "C. V. Starr & Co., Cornelius Vander Starr: 1892–1968" (1970), p. 15 (memorial tribute to Mr. Starr prepared by the company he left behind).

6. Ibid., p. 31.

7. See "Cornelius Vander Starr Dies; Founder of Insurance Group," *New York Times* (December 21, 1968).

8. The other two directors at the time of Starr's death, and therefore Starr's executors, were John Ahlers and Francis Mulderig.

9. See "Report of the Independent Committee of the Starr Foundation" (March 1, 2007).

10. See "In the Business of Downhill, Mt. Mansfield Races to New Heights," *Contact* (October/November 1991): 4.

11. "Skiing: A Builders' Year," *Sports Illustrated* (December 19, 1955), http://sportsillustrated.cnn.com/vault/article/magazine/MAG1130572/1/index.htm.

12. American Home shareholders were offered 2 AIG common shares per share; New Hampshire holders either 1.78 AIG common shares or 0.68 of a share of AIG $4 convertible preferred per share; and National Union holders $42 in principal amount of a convertible debt security. (This was chosen instead of

common shares to enable holders to defer recognizing tax in the exchange until conversion; the other two exchange offers were nontaxable anyway.)

13. New York had a cash-out statute at the time; Pennsylvania and New Hampshire enacted them at the request of those companies. See "Taking Risks," chap. 7, p. 7.

14. See "Insurance Group Sets Stock Offer," *New York Times* (December 5, 1968).

15. The arrangements were finalized in a valuation agreement among the participants dated September 19, 1970, in accordance with opinions and advice of Morgan Stanley as to business issues and Sullivan & Cromwell as to legal matters. See "Report of the Independent Committee of the Starr Foundation" (March 1, 2007), appendices 116, 118, 121–124.

16. Compare Sanjai Bhaga and Roberta Romano, "Reforming Executive Compensation: Focusing and Committing to the Long Term," *Yale Journal on Regulation* 23 (2009): 659 (footnote 23 highlights AIG's approach to executive compensation begun in the 1970s as akin to the authors' contemporary proposal designed to avoid the pitfalls that plagued executive compensation plans of the early 2000s).

17. Cunningham interview with Carla Hills, Washington, September 1, 2011 (reporting on statements made by PricewaterhouseCoopers to the AIG audit committee in March 2005); John F. Love, *McDonald's: Behind the Arches* (New York: Bantam Books, 1995), 363 (also noting debate over financial accounting for such an arrangement); U.S. Treasury Regulations 1.83-1 through 1.83-8 (addressing the tax consequences of such arrangements).

18. Louis Kelso pioneered the ESOP in 1956 and elaborated on its significance in several later books, including *The Capitalist Manifesto* (New York: Random House, 1958), coauthored by Mortimer J. Adler; and *Democracy and Economic Power: Extending the ESOP Revolution Through Binary Economics* (New York: Ballinger, 1986), coauthored by Patricia Hetter Kelso. See Andrew W. Stumpff, "Fifty Years of Utopia," *Tax Lawyer* 62 (2009): 419. ESOPs gained momentum after passage of 1974's Employee Retirement Income Security Act (ERISA), which provided favorable tax treatment.

19. A decade after the triple exchange offer that took AIG public, it switched its listing to the New York Stock Exchange (on October 10, 1984); it subsequently listed in other international stock exchanges as well: Tokyo in 1987, London in 1988, the Paris Bourse in 1990, and Zurich and Geneva in 1991. See *Contact* (October/November 1993): 11.

20. See "The Conglomerate War to Reshape Industry," *Time* (March 7, 1969).

21. A good discussion of the Leasco-Reliance takeover by Judge Jack Weinstein appears in the case of *Feit v. Leasco Data Processing Equipment Corp.*, 332 F. Supp. 544 (E.D.N.Y. 1971).

Chapter 4   Vision and Culture

1. Decades later, the inverse notion of the black swan was popularized in the 2007 book of that title by Nassim N. Taleb.
2. "Taking Risks," chap. 9, p. 16 ff.
3. Michael Loney, "30 Years in Insurance: Learning the Hard Way," *Reactions: Euromoney Institutional Investor* (April 1, 2011).
4. See Richard Witkin, "Methods to Avert Hijacking Studied," *New York Times* (September 8, 1970).
5. Politically motivated destructions were within those policies, not excluded by war-related exceptions. *Pan American World Airways, Inc. v. Aetna Casualty and Surety Co.*, 368 F. Supp. 1098 (S.D.N.Y. 1973), aff'd, 505 F.2d 989 (2d Cir. 1974).
6. See Christopher Lydon, "Nixon Names Gen. Davis to Head Hijacking Fight," *New York Times* (September 21, 1970).
7. See Robert J. Cole, "Personal Finance: A Hijacking Rider on Travel Insurance Is Planned to Pay for 'Inconvenience,'" *New York Times* (July 20, 1972).
8. Getty died in 2011 at the age of 54, after spending a life battling alcohol and drugs.
9. *Proof of Life*, starring Meg Ryan and Russell Crowe, is a fictional adaptation of a factual *Vanity Fair* article called "Adventures in the Ransom Trade" and the book by Thomas Hargrove, *The Long March to Freedom* (New York: Ballantine Books, 1995).
10. In the film, *Proof of Life*, the character played by Russell Crowe, the hostage rescuer, is based on Mr. Clayton.
11. These were, in addition to American Home: Metropolitan Tower, Swiss Re, Walton Insurance, United States Fidelity and Guaranty, Daido Mutual, Nichido Fire & Marine, and Compagnie Financiere et de Reassurance du Group.
12. Michael Loney, "30 Years in Insurance: Learning the Hard Way," *Reactions: Euromoney Institutional Investor* (April 1, 2011).
13. Ibid.
14. See Del Jones, "Some Firms' Fertile Soil Grows Crop of Future CEOs," *USA Today* (January 9, 2008) (though not listing AIG in a ranking of 19 progenitors of CEOs in corporate America, noting 26 GE alums became CEO elsewhere from an employee base of 300,000 and 18 such IBM alums from among 366,000).
15. Evan was the third AIG alum to become CEO of ACE, having been preceded by John Keogh and Brian Duperreault—the latter also having been CEO of Marsh, as was yet another AIG alum, Dan Glaser. In addition to those five are seven other AIG alums who have served as CEO of other insurance companies: Joe Taranto, Everest RE; Scott Carmilani and Gordon Knight, AWAC; Dinos Iordanou, Arch Capital; Stan Galanski, Navigators; Tony Galioto, York Risk Services; and Kevin Kelley, Ironshore.

16. See www.insurancehalloffame.org/laureates.php. Other notable inductees mentioned in this book include Guy Carpenter (2001) and, another AIG executive, Edmund Tse (2003).

17. This discussion of the system of internal controls AIG established during the 1970s is based on Cunningham telephone interviews with Peter Dalia, August 30, 2011, and October 13, 2011.

18. See Carter B. Horsley, "Insurance Concern to Buy Skyscraper Headquarters," *New York Times* (May 7, 1976).

19. See Christopher Gray, "Streetscapes/70 Pine Street; An Art Deco Tower with Double-Deck Elevators," *New York Times* (March 8, 1998).

Chapter 5   The Internationalist

1. *Contact* (November/December 2002): 11.

2. Founding AIG IAB members in 1981 (and their years of service) included: Kenneth H. J. Clarke (1981–1987); Yuet-Keung Kan (1981–1995); Baron Leon Lambert, (1981–1987); Hong-koo Lee (1981–1987) (a Korean scholar who served as South Korea's minister of national unification and prime minister); Aritoshi Soejim (1981–1989); Edwin Stopper (1981–1987); and Washington Sycip (1981–1996) (a Chinese-Filipino accountant, founder of the Asian Institute of Management, and chairman of the prestigious Filipino professional services firm, Sycip Gorres Velayo).

   Over the years, Greenberg added to the IAB such energetic internationalists as Lord James Prior, who had been a deputy secretary of state in the United Kingdom, chairman of England's General Electric Company, and chancellor of Oxford University; Dr. Pierre Languetin, former chairman of the Governing Board of the Swiss National Bank; Otto Graf Lambsdorff, an influential German political figure and economist; and Jacques de Larosière, adviser to the French bank, BNP Paribas, and distinguished head of the World Bank for many years.

3. See "Baron Leon Lambert; Banker Collected Art," *New York Times* (June 1, 1987).

4. "Tata AIG Risk Management Services Ltd. Is Formed in India," *Contact* (November/December 1998): 3.

5. See Guaazardi, Grose, et al., "Worth the Risk," chap. 15, p. 12.

6. All these organizations are discussed further in Chapter 16.

7. Cunningham interview with Peter G. Peterson, New York, November 4, 2011.

8. Cunningham interview with Dimitri Simes, Washington, January 24, 2012.

9. In more recent years, Greenberg became an active member of the board of BENS—Business Executives for National Security.

10. See Thomas J. Neff and James M. Citrin, *Lessons from the Top* (New York: Currency Doubleday, 1999), 161 (quoting Greenberg).

11. Cunningham interview with Charlene Barshefsky, Washington, August 31, 2011.

12. Cunningham interview with Henry A. Kissinger, New York, December 6, 2011.

Chapter 6 Raising the Iron Curtain

1. See Nicholas M. Horrock, *New York Times* Archives (January 14, 1976). The story of this venture has been recounted in numerous books. Among recent books is Norman Polmar and Michael White, *Project Azorian: The CIA and the Raising of* K-129 (Annapolis, MD: Naval Institute Press, 2010).

2. The agency's full name was Upravleniye Inostrannogo Strakhovaniya SSSR (Administration for Foreign Insurance of the USSR). See "American International Groups Expand Business with U.S.S.R.," *Contact* (August 1968).

3. Ibid.

4. This discussion draws on Guaazardi, Grose, et al., "Worth the Risk," chap. 15, pp. 24–28.

5. Ibid., chap. 14, p. 27 (quoting Nicholas Walsh, an employee working for Roberts).

6. A detailed account of a parallel escape from political imprisonment in Iran of this period, involving the company EDS and the leadership of its CEO, Ross Perot, appears in Ken Follett, *On Wings of Eagles* (New York: Signet, 1984).

7. AIG filed and won a claim against Iran in international court to obtain compensation for the expropriation of its assets.

8. Cunningham interview with Dimitri Simes, Washington, January 24, 2012.

9. Ibid., and Cunningham telephone interview with Simes, March 19, 2012.

10. Guaazardi, Grose, et al., "Worth the Risk," chap. 15, p. 8 (quoting R. Kendall Nottingham along the lines summarized in this paragraph).

11. See Thomas J. Cutler, *Brown Water, Black Berets: Coastal and Riverine Warfare in Vietnam* (Annapolis, MD: Naval Institute Press, 2000).

12. Ibid., 8–10. This is based on a contemporaneous report filed by Buck Freeman, speaking one month after the event from Anderson Air Force base in Guam. A variation of the story appeared in *Contact* magazine.

13. The AIU filed claims for compensation with the U.S. Foreign Claims Settlement Commission. "Taking Risks," chap. 8, p. 8.

14. See "AIG Responds after a Tragic Fire in Vietnam," *Contact* (November/December 2002).

15. Despite the tragedy, AIA's staff served its policyholders without interruption. Within 24 hours of the fire, the local staff launched the company's back-up systems located in the nearby Saigon Center. See ibid.

16. *Fortune* magazine listed AIG as the ninth largest company in the world at the time. *Forbes* magazine in July 2002 listed AIG as the third largest public company in the world using a composite of sales, profits, assets and market capitalization. See AIG Chairman's Letter 2002.

Chapter 7   Opening Trade in Services

1. Thanks to Franklin Davis, AIG's pilot and director of AIG's flight department, for relating this tale.

2. See "Nixon's Report to Congress on Foreign Policy," *New York Times* (February 19, 1970).

3. Subsequent presidents through Clinton routinely reappointed Greenberg to the post. See "Bush Reappoints M. R. Greenberg to Trade Panel," *Contact* (August/September 1992): 2. These appointments cross over presidential administrations.

4. See 88 Stat. 1996, §§ 102(g) ("the term 'international trade' includes trade in both goods and services"); 135; 163; 301(a) ("the term 'commerce' includes services associated with international trade"), codified in 19 U.S.C. 2411; see also AIG Chairman's Letter (1976) ("the fight against nationalism has been aided by a recent Commerce Department study on service industries.").

5. "The Realization of a Dream," *Contact* (June 1974).

6. Cunningham interview with Edward Matthews, Brewster, New York, September 12, 2011; Alison Tudor, "For Sale: AIG's Home Base in Japan," *Wall Street Journal* (February 13, 2009).

7. Michael Wines, "Bush in Japan; Bush Collapses at State Dinner with Japanese," *New York Times* (January 9, 1992).

8. Cunningham interview with Charlene Barshefsky, Washington, August 31, 2011.

9. That, of course, presented additional problems for Japan ahead of the WTO Financial Services Agreement. Having given concessions to the United States in those bilateral talks, under the WTO's MFN principle, Japan owed those same concessions to other WTO members. It didn't want to give them. Eventually, Japan did agree to extend them, and the stage was set for the WTO Financial Services Agreement.

10. See Clyde H. Farnsworth, "Washington Watch; Services Gain Lobbying Arm," *New York Times* (February 8, 1982).

11. See Maurice R. Greenberg, speech to the Empire Club of Canada, November 29, 1984.

12. Shelp also wrote the book *Beyond Industrialization: Ascendancy of the Global Service Economy* (New York: Praeger, 1981), which explored how changes in the world and U.S. economies mandated rethinking trade in services.

13. Cunningham interview with James D. Robinson III, New York, July 28, 2011.

14. See International Investment and Trade in Services Survey Act, 22 U.S. Code § 3101.

15. See Clyde H. Farnsworth, "What's New in Trade: The Drive Is On to Change the Rules," *New York Times* (November 7, 1982).
16. Many scholars and policy analysts contributed independent research that reached the same conclusions about the value of trade in services globally. See Geza Feketekuty, *International Trade in Services: An Overview and Blueprint for Negotiations* (New York: Ballinger, 1988), available at www.commercial diplomacy.org; Jagdish N. Bhagwari, "Trade in Services and the Multilateral Trade Negotiations," *World Bank Economic Review* 1 (1987): 549.
17. David Ricardo, *The Principles of Political Economy and Taxation* (London: John Murray, 1817).
18. See Joseph E. Stiglitz and Andrew Charlton, *Fair Trade for All* (New York: Oxford University Press, 2006).
19. Cunningham interview with Charlene Barshefsky, Washington, August 31, 2011.
20. The reply, however, was faxed from the cockpit to the 70 Pine Street office in New York, where another fax, a 250-page document from the Business Roundtable, was already rolling in and blocked all others until it was completed. That delayed the news for another half hour before Nahapetian could relay word to Johnson.
21. But the AIG-Malaysia series of five-year accommodations would not last beyond Greenberg's tenure as CEO of the company, for reasons explained below in note 76 to Chapter 13 (p. 290).
22. In the words of the agreement, countries would "permit financial service suppliers of any Member established in its territory to offer in its territory any new financial service" and "ensure that financial service suppliers of any other Member established in its territory are accorded most-favored-nation treatment and national treatment as regards the purchase or acquisition of financial services by public entities of the Member in its territory."

Chapter 8   Reopening China

1. See Jacques Barrère, "Art d'Extrême Orient, Bronze Panels of the Tong Ting Summer Palace, Beijin" (1991) (catalogue description of the bronze panels); Brett Freese, "Bronze Panels Returned to China," *Archaeology* 47(4) (July/August 1994): 18.
2. The steps required to arrange for such a transaction are surprisingly complex, entailing more than one year of coordination among lawyers and officials from China, France, and the United States. Among issues, the Starr Foundation followed the standard practice of obtaining a formal written legal

opinion of U.S. tax counsel supporting the Foundation's judgment that a grant to the government of China would be consistent with U.S. federal income tax law. That law proscribes private foundation actions that might constitute "self-dealing," in the sense of donations that directly benefit affiliated entities. The Starr Foundation always took care that its giving would be consistent with these tax laws by never directly benefiting AIG. The opinion in the case of the window panels was delivered by the well-known firm of Caplin & Drysdale by letter dated December 21, 1992.

3. See K. K. [An Obituary], *Contact* (July 1964): 12.
4. R. W. Apple Jr., "Drinking Abroad; Diplomacy by Other Means: Getting Stinko on Kerosene," *New York Times* (June 28, 1998).
5. Cunningham telephone interview with John Degnan, August 31, 2011.
6. Ibid.
7. Zhu Rongji, *Zhu Rongji Meets the Press* (New York: Oxford University Press, 2011), 383.
8. "Taking Risks," chap. 10, p. 5.
9. Seth Faison, "Insurance for China, One Door at a Time," *New York Times* (April 4, 1995).
10. Rongji, *Zhu Rongji Meets the Press*, 383.
11. "Back to the Bund: AIA Leases Historic Building in Shanghai," *Contact* (February/March 1997).
12. "AIG Archives: Preserving a Visual Legacy of 17 The Bund and 70 Pine Street," *Contact* (November/December 1998): 10.
13. Rongji, *Zhu Rongji Meets the Press*, 383.
14. Cunningham interview with Henry A. Kissinger, New York, December 6, 2011.
15. Ibid.
16. For a brief summary, see David M. Lampton, *Same Bed Different Dreams: Managing U.S.-China Relations 1989–2000* (Berkeley and Los Angeles: University of California Press, 2001), 348–352.
17. Roxanne Roberts and David Montgomery, "The ABC's of the A-List: How People Wind Up with an Invitation to the White House," *Washington Post* (April 14, 1999).
18. See Maurice R. Greenberg, "Time for a China-U.S. Free Trade Agreement," *Wall Street Journal* (January 9, 2012).

Chapter 9   The Life Business

1. AIA also then became a subsidiary of AIRCO. In 1978, when AIRCO merged into AIG, AIG became AIA's ultimate parent.
2. On December 8, 1941, Seitz, whose father, Carl, had helped Starr found one of his early companies, had arrived in his Manila office ready for business as usual. But he soon heard that the Japanese were simultaneously bombing

Pearl Harbor in Hawaii (on the other side of the international dateline, where it was still December 7) and the Clark Air Base about 40 miles north of Manila. Communications between the Philippines and the outside world were cut off. But Seitz and Stramm managed to bury the books in Stramm's garden just before Japanese troops seized Manila on New Year's Eve and rounded up civilians, who were detained as POWs for the rest of the war. Guaazardi, Grose, et al., "Worth the Risk," chap. 6, pp. 4–7; obituary for Clayton L. Seitz, *Contact* (August 1974).

3. Ambassador McNutt, previously a law professor and governor of Indiana, held many diplomatic posts during the 1930s and 1940s, and later chaired the Philippine-American Trade Council, a business group. He achieved considerable distinction during the period, as he appeared on the covers of *Life* and *Time* magazines in 1939 on his return from the Philippines and again on the cover of *Time* in 1942.

4. "The Philamlife Story," *Contact* (September 1969).

5. "Home of Savings, House of Beauty," *Contact* (August 1961); "Philamlife Building Complemented in *National Geographic* and *Time*," *Contact* (November 1966).

6. Quoted from *Contact* magazine (September 1969).

7. Trade Agreement Renewing the Agreement of July 4, 1946, Sept. 6, 1955, U.S.-Phil., 6 UST 2981 (in effect until 1974).

8. Cunningham interview with Edward Matthews, Brewster, New York, September 12, 2011.

9. Stephen Miller, "Ernest E. Stempel 1916–2009," *Wall Street Journal* (April 18, 2009).

10. Diana B. Henriques, "Bernard Cornfeld, 67, Dies; Led Flamboyant Mutual Fund," *New York Times* (March 2, 1995).

11. See Charles Raw, Bruce Page, and Godfrey Hodgson, *Do You Sincerely Want to Be Rich? The Full Story of Bernard Cornfeld and IOS* (New York: Viking Press, 1971).

12. AIG Chairman's Letter, AIG Annual Report (1983).

13. This story is based in part on a Cunningham telephone interview with John S. Reed, May 7, 2012.

14. See Paul Laxalt, *Nevada's Paul Laxalt: A Memoir* (Reno, NV: Jack Bacon & Company, 2000), 271–280. Ahead of Senator Laxalt's overture in October 1985, officials suggested he reach out to Greenberg for a briefing, which Greenberg naturally obliged. Senator Laxalt found the briefing helpful as Greenberg offered insight from a businessman's perspective. Ibid., p. 273.

15. M.R. Greenberg Attends APC Meeting and Philamlife Tower Ground-Breaking, *Contact* (February/March 1997).

16. C.V. Starr & Company, "Starr Memorial Book" (1970), 34. The Helen Graham Park Foundation was established in 1994 to honor the life of Helen Graham Park, an internationally renowned architect who worked closely with Starr.

17. Ibid.
18. Ibid.
19. Rhodebeck was ALICO president from 1953 and chairman from 1963. Gordon Tweedy Succeeds Richard Rhodebeck As ALICO Chairman, *Contact* (February 1965): 8. He was an MOP and traveled extensively throughout the Middle East and the Caribbean, building ALICO's life insurance business. Richard Rhodebeck, *Contact* (November 1965): 2 (reporting his death from cancer on November 7).
20. Discussion draws on "AIG Seizes Opportunity in Thriving Latin American Markets," *Contact* (July/August 1997).
21. Guaazardi, Grose, et al., "Worth the Risk," chap. 17, pp. 14–18.
22. "AIG to Acquire SunAmerica, Opening a New Window in Growing Retiree Markets," *Contact* (November/December 1998).
23. AIG–American General joint proxy statement.
24. The AIG bid price of $46 in AIG stock was subject to a 5 percent collar. If AIG's stock price traded outside a 5 percent range within so many days ahead of the deal's closing date, the payment would be based on a fixed ratio agreed in advance rather than a dollar amount of share value.
25. See "AIG Reaches Agreement to Acquire American General," *Contact* (July 2001) (agreement in May 2001, paid in AIG stock valued at $23 billion).
26. AIG Annual Report (2005), 28.
27. AIG Chairman's Letter (2001).

Chapter 10   The Domestic Front

1. Joseph B. Treaster, "Hard-Edged Insurance Chief Is Taking On a New and Public Face," *New York Times* (October 31, 2001).
2. Cunningham telephone interview with John Degnan, August 31, 2011.
3. Cunningham telephone interview with Kevin Kelley, April 9, 2012.
4. Michael Loney, "30 Years in Insurance: Learning the Hard Way," *Reactions: Euromoney Institutional Investor* (April 1, 2011).
5. Superfund is the popular name for the statute, also called CERCLA, which stands for Comprehensive Environmental Response, Compensation and Liability Act of 1980.
6. For a classic and comprehensive illustration, see *New Castle County v. Hartford Accident & Indemnity Co.*, 933 F.2d 1162 (3rd Cir. 1991). Cases involving AIG companies include *Technicon Electronics Corp. v. American Home Assurance Co.*, 533 N.Y.S.2d 91 (N.Y. App. Div. 1998), aff'd 542 N.E.2d 1048 (N.Y. 1989); *Northville Industries Corp. v. National Union Fire Insurance Co. of Pittsburgh*, 636 N.Y.S.2d 359 (N.Y. App. Div. 1995), aff'd 679 N.E.2d 1044 (N.Y. 1997).
7. Concerning the language begun to be added in the 1970s and its interpretation, see Kenneth Abraham, "Catastrophic Oil Spills and the Problem of Insurance," *Vanderbilt Law Review* 64 (2011): 1769, 1785; William H. Rodgers

Jr., "The Most Creative Moments in the History of Environmental Law: 'The Whats,'" *University of Illinois Law Review* 1 (2000): 20–21; see also Sharon M. Murphy, "The 'Sudden and Accidental' Exception to the Pollution Exclusion Clause in Comprehensive General Liability Insurance Policies: The Gordian Knot of Environmental Liability," *Vanderbilt Law Review* 45 (1992): 161.

8. See Maurice R. Greenberg, "Financing the Clean-up of Hazardous Waste: The National Environmental Insurance Fund," Geneva Papers on Risk and Insurance 14 (April 1, 1989): 207–212.

9. See Lester Brickman, "Ethical Issues in Asbestos Litigation," *Hofstra Law Review* 33 (2005): 833, 836–839 (describing practices used by lawyers to screen potential claimants).

10. Lester Brickman, "On the Applicability of the Silica MDL Proceeding to Asbestos Litigation," *Connecticut Insurance Law Journal* 12 (2006): 289.

11. See *Ortiz v. Fibreboard Corp.*, 527 U.S. 815, 821 (1999) (the "elephantine mass of asbestos cases . . . defies customary judicial administration and calls for national legislation"); *Amchem Products, Inc. v. Windsor*, 521 U.S. 591, 628–629 (1997) ("The argument is sensibly made that a nationwide administrative claims processing regime would provide the most secure, fair, and efficient means of compensating victims of asbestos exposure.").

12. See "Coalition for Insurance Reform," *Insurance Journal* (April 22, 2005), available at www.insurancejournal.com/news/national/2005/04/22/54201.htm.

13. Cunningham telephone interview with John Degnan, August 31, 2011.

14. There would be an Office of Asbestos Disease Compensation administering an "Asbestos Injury Claims Resolution Fund."

15. See James Rowley, "Asbestos Fund Blocked in U.S. Test Vote," *Bloomberg* (February 14, 2006).

16. Guaazardi, Grose, et al., "Worth the Risk," chap. 17, pp. 18 ff.

17. See John Fabian Witt, Speedy Fred Taylor and the Ironies of Enterprise Liability, *Columbia Law Review* 103 (2003): 1 (discussing HSB and noting that boiler engineering "stood as a shining example of what rational engineering could do for workplace safety.")

18. For a thumbnail sketch of tort law and policy over the past 50 years along the following lines, see Richard Epstein, *Torts* (New York: Aspen, 2008).

19. See Jonathan D. Glater, "To the Trenches: The Tort War Is Raging On," *New York Times* (June 22, 2008).

20. See Anthony J. Sebok, "Dispatches from the Tort Wars: A Review Essay," *Texas Law Review* 85 (2007): 1465.

21. See Susan Saladoff, *Hot Coffee* (HBO documentary film 2011).

22. See "Reagan Hits Jury Awards," *Washington Post* (May 31, 1986); Steven Brill and James Lyons, "The Not-So-Simple Crisis," *American Lawyer* (May 1986), pp. 1, 16.

23. See Theodore Eisenberg, "Use It or Pretenders Will Abuse It: The Importance of Archival Legal Information," *UMKC Law Review* 75 (2006): 1.

24. Thomas H. Cohen, "Tort Bench and Jury Trials in State Courts, 2005" (U.S. Dept. of Justice, Bureau of Justice Statistics) (November 2009), available at http://bjs.ojp.usdoj.gov/content/pub/pdf/tbjtsc05.pdf.

25. See Robert L. Rabin, "Pain and Suffering and Beyond: Some Thoughts on Recovery for Intangible Loss," *DePaul Law Review* 55 (2006): 359; Joseph H. King, Jr., "Pain and Suffering, Noneconomic Damages and the Goals of Tort Law," *SMU Law Review* 57 (2004): 163; e-mail from Kenneth Abraham to Cunningham, March 26, 2012.

26. See Glater, "To the Trenches."

Chapter 11   Investments

1. AIG Chairman's Letter (1983).

2. Quoted in "AIG Acquires Major International Aircraft Lessor for $1.2 Billion," *Contact* (November/December 1990).

3. AIG Annual Report (2005), 39.

4. "AIU Pools Resources to Meet Infrastructure Demands in Emerging Economies," *Contact* (July/August 1996).

5. "AIG Seizes Opportunity in Thriving Latin American Markets," *Contact* (July/August 1997).

6. Some of the following discussion is based on Cunningham's interview with Moeen Qureshi in Washington on September 15, 2011.

7. E-mail from Moeen Qureshi to Cunningham, April 20, 2012.

8. *Contact* (February/March 1997): 2.

9. E-mail from Moeen Qureshi to Cunningham, April 20, 2012.

10. Cunningham telephone interview with Dean P. Phypers, November 28, 2011.

11. Some media accounts of the separation between AIG and Sosin mischaracterize the separation, including Robert O'Harrow Jr. and Brady Dennis, "The Beautiful Machine," *Washington Post* (December 29, 2008).

12. Globalization increased the value to companies worldwide of markets able to process, trade and hedge a wide variety of things, especially currencies, oil and metals. Ordinary market fluctuations, punctuated by bouts of high volatility, meant there was money to be made by firms able to help customers manage these commodities. AIG answered in 1990 by creating AIG Trading Corporation, recruiting a cadre of traders to operate a hedging and market-making operation. Likewise offering large corporate clients ways to manage increasingly global market risks and handling large amounts of capital, AIG governed AIG Trading with a tight set of internal controls and risk management systems. The unit was folded into FP in 2003.

Chapter 12   Governance

1. Another was John I. Howell (1969–1995), retired chairman of the executive committee at J. Henry Schroder Bank & Trust Company, whose global financial perspective added considerable value to AIG's corporate board.

2. Henry Kearns (1974–1984), head of the Export-Import Bank in the Nixon administration and assistant secretary of commerce for international affairs in the Eisenhower administration. See "Henry Kearns Is Dead; Headed Export Bank," *New York Times* (June 1, 1985).

3. Pierre Gousseland (1977–1993), the international mining company executive who ran AMAX Inc.

4. Ambassador Douglas MacArthur II (1972–1988) was a particularly distinguished member of AIG's board drawn from outside the company's executive ranks. A prominent Washington-based consultant on international affairs and nephew of General MacArthur, the ambassador served with distinction in many U.S. foreign-service posts from 1935 to 1972, including as ambassador to Austria, Belgium, Iran, and Japan.

5. Scott E. Pardee, a senior vice president at the Federal Reserve Bank of New York in charge of foreign exchange operations.

6. Michael N. Chetkovich, a prominent accountant and former managing partner of Deloitte Haskins & Sells, one of the "big eight" international accounting firms of the period. See "Michael N. Chetkovich, 81, Top Accountant" *New York Times* (April 30, 1998).

7. Cunningham telephone interview with Dean P. Phypers, November 28, 2011.

8. See Lawrence A. Cunningham, "Rediscovering Board Expertise: Legal Implications of the Empirical Literature," *Cincinnati Law Review* 77 (2008): 465–499.

9. Richard D. Lyons, "William French Smith Dies at 73; Reagan's First Attorney General," *New York Times* (October 30, 1990).

10. Conable had also served on AIG's board during 1985–1986, the period between his service in Congress and becoming president of the World Bank. See "Conable Elected to AIG Board," *Contact* (October/November 1991): 8; see also Wolfgang Saxon, "Barber B. Conable, 81, Congressman and Bank Chief, Dies," *New York Times* (December 2, 2003).

11. David E. Rosenbaum, "Lloyd Bentsen Dies at 85; Senator Ran with Dukakis," *New York Times* (May 24, 2006).

12. Ibid.

13. See Joseph B. Treaster, "Some A.I.G. Shareholders to Press for More Independent Board," *New York Times* (May 15, 2000); Joseph B. Treaster, "A.I.G. Head Will Consider Altering Board," *New York Times* (May 18, 2000).

14. AIG Proxy Statement (March 23, 2000), 18–20.

15. Cunningham e-mail from Howard I. Smith, July 19, 2012; "A Short History of AIG: 1919 to the Present" (March 2001), 23. The figures include the effects of the restatement of 2005 discussed in Chapter 14. Thanks to Sara

Westfall, George Washington University, for creating the images from the raw data.

16. AIG proxy statement (2001), 8.

17. AIG proxy statement (March 23, 2000), 23–24.

18. Ibid., 22–23.

19. Citing Ira Millstein and Paul MacAvoy, "The Active Board of Directors and Improved Performance of the Large Publicly-Traded Corporation," Yale School of Management Working Paper No. 49 (1997).

20. A sampling of studies, conducted after the proxy statement in question, include Sanjai Bhagat and Bernard Black, "The Uncertain Relationship between Board Composition and Firm Performance," *Business Lawyer* 54 (1999): 921; Sanjai Bhagat and Bernard Black, "The Non-Correlation between Board Independence and Long-Term Firm Performance," *Journal of Corporation Law* 27 (2002): 231; Benjamin E. Hermalin and Michael S. Weisbach, "Boards of Directors as an Endogenously Determined Institution: A Survey of the Economic Literature," *Federal Reserve Bank of New York Economic Policy Review* (April 2003): 7.

21. See Roddy Boyd, *Fatal Risk* (Hoboken, NJ: John Wiley & Sons, 2011), 45.

22. Matthews retired as an AIG officer at the end of 2002 and as an AIG director at the 2003 annual meeting.

23. The business press, some shareholders, and many directors, including Greenberg, began mulling a succession plan for the helm of AIG. See, for example, Joseph B. Treaster, "Still Secretive, A.I.G.'s Chief Promises Hints on a Successor," *New York Times* (April 25, 2002); Joseph B. Treaster, "A.I.G. Makes Plans for Post-Greenberg Era," *New York Times* (May 2, 2002); Joseph B. Treaster, "Market Place; When A.I.G.'s Longtime Chief Mentions a Successor, Wall Street Talks, and Keeps Talking," *New York Times* (January 29, 2003); Joseph B. Treaster, "Top-Level Reordering at A.I.G. May Set Up Succession," *New York Times* (December 5, 2003).

24. Other veteran outside directors were Marshall Cohen, former executive at Molson Companies Ltd., the Canadian beer company; Martin S. Feldstein, the Harvard professor, former economic adviser to President Reagan and president and chief executive officer of the National Bureau for Economic Research; and Frank J. Hoenemeyer, a retired vice chairman of Prudential Insurance Co. More recent appointees included Pei-yuan Chia, former vice chairman of Citicorp.

25. Hills was an AIG director from 1992 to 2006.

26. William Cohen was an AIG director from 2004 to 2006.

27. Cunningham telephone interview with Axel Freudmann, April 10, 2012.

28. Some activities of the Starr Foundation are noted in Chapter 16.

29. See E.A.G. Manton, "Knighted for 'Charitable Services,'" *Contact* (October/ November 1994); see also Manton, *Contact* (November 1969): 5–6; Nicholas

Serote, "Sir Edwin Manton: Businessman and Art Benefactor Who Donated Millions to the Tate Gallery," *The Guardian* (Oct. 16, 2005).

30. Robert W. Lear, "Boards on Trial," *Chief Executive* (October 31, 2000).
31. See Donald C. Langevoort, "The Human Nature of Corporate Boards: Law, Norms and the Unintended Consequences of Independence and Accountability," *Georgetown Law Journal* 89 (2001): 797; Jill E. Fisch, "Taking Boards Seriously," *Cardozo Law Review* 19 (1997): 265.
32. The committee did not declare nonindependent several other directors who had relationships with other beneficiaries of the Starr Foundation, including Feldstein, Holbrooke, and Zarb.
33. Zarb's designation as lead director was formalized at an AIG board meeting of April 21, 2005, though his role was widely recognized to precede that formal designation.
34. Executive Order 13271, 67 Federal Register 46091 (2002), available at www .justice.gov/archive/dag/cftf/. President Obama replaced this with a Financial Fraud Enforcement Task Force. Executive Order 13519, 74 Federal Register 60123 (2009), available at www.sec.gov/news/press/2009/2009-249-exec-order.pdf.
35. The memos were written by successive deputy attorneys general of the United States. See Memorandum from Eric Holder, Deputy Attorney General, U.S. Dept. of Justice, to Heads of Department Components and United States Attorneys, Bringing Criminal Charges Against Corporations (June 16, 1999); Memorandum from Larry D. Thompson, Deputy Attorney General, U.S. Dept. of Justice, to Heads of Department Components and United States Attorneys, Principles of Federal Prosecution of Business Organizations (January 20, 2003), www.justice.gov/dag/cftf/corporate_guidelines.htm; Memorandum from Paul J. McNulty, Deputy Attorney General, U.S. Dept. of Justice, to Heads of Department Components and United States Attorneys, Principles of Federal Prosecution of Business Organizations (December 12, 2006), www. usdoj.gov.dag/speeches/2--6/mcnulty_memo.pdf; Memorandum from Mark Filip, Deputy Attorney General, U.S. Dept. of Justice, to Heads of Department Components and United States Attorneys Principles of Federal Prosecution of Business Organizations (August 28, 2008), www.usdoj.gov.dag/readingroom/dag/dag-memo-08282008.pdf.
36. *United States v. Stein*, 541 F.3d 130 (2nd Cir. 2008).
37. See *Securities and Exchange Commission v. American International Group*, Litigation Release No. 18,340 (Sept. 11, 2003).
38. *Securities and Exchange Commission v. American International Group*, Litigation Release No. 18,985 (November 30, 2004); Deferred Prosecution Agreement between the U.S. Department of Justice and AIG-FP (November 30, 2004), available at http://lib.law.virginia.edu/Garrett/prosecution_agreements/pdf/AIG-FP_PAGIC.pdf.

39. See *Central Bank of Denver v. First Interstate Bank of Denver*, 511 U.S. 164 (1994); *Stoneridge Investment Partners, LLC v. Scientific-Atlanta, Inc.*, 552 U.S. 148 (2008). In 2007, Joseph Cassano, then heading FP, reportedly acknowledged at an investors' conference that FP had made mistakes in creating the PNC deal, which he regretted. See Brady Dennis & Robert O'Harrow, Jr., "A Crack in the System," *Washington Post* (December 30, 2008).

40. See Lisa Kern Griffin, "Compelled Cooperation and the New Corporate Criminal Procedure," *New York University Law Review* 82 (2007): 311.

41. Proposals to equip outside directors with power to retain independent advisors remained rare even after being ordained in 1994 by the American Law Institute. ALI, Principles of Corporate Governance § 3.04 (1994); see also James D. Cox, "Managing and Monitoring Conflicts of Interest: Empowering the Outside Directors with Independent Counsel," *Villanova Law Review* 48 (2003): 1077 (making a "modest" proposal that outside directors asked to approve interested transactions of other directors retain their own lawyer).

42. Among the earliest and most prominent examples of outside lawyers exerting power in the boardroom to oust a chief executive occurred when Ira Millstein, of Weil, Gotshal & Manges, played that role in 1992's dismissal of General Motors CEO Robert Stempel. See John A. Byrne, "The Guru of Good Governance," *BusinessWeek* (April 28, 1997): 100; Alison Leigh Cowan, "The High-Energy Board Room," *New York Times* (October 28, 1992).

43. See, for example, *Report of the American Bar Association Task Force on Corporate Responsibility* (March 31, 2003), 24, n. 54; E. Norman Veasey, "Separate and Continuing Counsel for Independent Directors: An Idea Whose Time Has Not Come as a General Practice," *Business Lawyer* 59 (2004): 1413; see also Geoffrey C. Hazard Jr. and Edward B. Rock, "A New Player in the Boardroom: The Emergence of the Independent Directors' Counsel," *Business Lawyer* 59 (2004): 1389 (offering tepid acceptance of the concept).

44. Beattie's biography on the Simpson Thacher & Bartlett LLP web site says he "specializes in counseling boards of directors and non-management directors on governance issues, investigations and litigation involving corporate officers and other crisis situations." www.stblaw.com/bios/RBeattie.htm (accessed February 28, 2012).

Chapter 13 Hostile Change

1. Elisabeth Bumiller, "Bush Signs Bill Aimed at Fraud in Corporations," *New York Times* (July 31, 2002).

2. See, for example, Richard A. Oppel Jr., "Two Republicans Join Ranks of S.E.C. Critics," *New York Times* (July 3, 2002).

3. See Opinion, "Spitzer's Latest Loss," *Wall Street Journal* (August 2, 2011) ("Enron created a political incentive [for prosecutors] to pursue white-collar defendants").

4. See Bernard Black, Brian R. Chefffins, and Michael Klausner, "Outside Director Liability," *Stanford Law Review* 58 (2006): 1055.

5. *Arthur Andersen LLP v. United States*, 544 U.S. 696 (2005).

6. New York General Business Law § 334; see Frank C. Razzano, "The Martin Act: An Overview," *Journal of Business & Technology Law* 2006 (2006): 125.

7. See *People v. Federated Radio Corp.*, 244 N.Y. 33, 164 N.E. 655 (1926). Under federal law and most state laws, proving business fraud requires "scienter," referring to a mental state evincing a deliberate intention to deceive. Some argue that the federal securities laws, enacted in 1933 and 1934, and requiring scienter, do or should preempt the Martin Act. See, for example, Steve A. Radom, "Balkanization of Securities Regulation: The Case for Federal Preemption," *Texas Journal of Business Law* 39 (2003): 295.

8. Nicholas Thompson, "The Sword of Spitzer," *Legal Affairs* (May/June 2004), available at www.legalaffairs.org/issues/May-June-2004/feature_thompson_mayjun04.msp.

9. E-mail to Cunningham from Howard I. Smith, April 27, 2012; see Kurt Eichenwald and Jenny Anderson, "How a Titan of Insurance Ran Afoul of the Government," *New York Times* (April 4, 2005).

10. See, for example, Henry R. Butler and Larry E. Ribstein, *The Sarbanes-Oxley Debacle* (Washington, DC: American Enterprise Institute, 2006); Roberta Romano, "The Sarbanes-Oxley Act and the Making of Quack Corporate Governance," *Yale Law Journal* 114 (2005): 1521.

11. Greenberg's lawyers have filed numerous requests to obtain related documents under Virginia's freedom of information laws. None of the documents specifically sought by them has been produced.

12. Brady Dennis & Robert O'Harrow Jr., "A Crack in the System," *Washington Post* (December 30, 2008).

13. This episode has been widely reported. See, for example, Brooke A. Masters, *Spoiling for a Fight: The Rise of Eliot Spitzer* (New York: Times Books, 2006), 231; Peter Elkind, *Rough Justice: The Rise and Fall of Eliot Spitzer* (New York: Portfolio, 2010), 84.

14. See Greg Sargent and John Benson, "El-iot! Can Spitzer Go to 1600?" *New York Observer* (October 21, 2002).

15. See, for example, "Adi Ignatius, Crusader of the Year: Wall Street's Top Cop," *Time* (December 30, 2002); CBS News, *60 Minutes*, "The Sheriff of Wall Street" (May 25, 2003), at www.cbsnews.com/stories/2003/05/23/60minutes/printable555310.shtml.

16. See, for example, Kimberly A. Strassel, "The Passion of Eliot Spitzer," *Wall Street Journal* (May 3, 2006).

17. See New York Rules of Professional Conduct, 4-109; New York Code of Professional Responsibility, DR 7-107 (in effect when Spitzer was in office).

18. American Bar Association, Model Rule 3.8(f) (criminal prosecutors "shall refrain from making extrajudicial comments that have a substantial likelihood of heightening public condemnation of the accused").

19. Daniel Fisher, Carrie Coolidge, and Neil Weinberg, "The Battle of the Titans over AIG: Superlawyer David Boies Takes on Eliot Spitzer," *Forbes* (May 9, 2005).

20. Ibid.

21. Elkind, *Rough Justice*, 57–58.

22. Greenberg asked New York insurance regulators to issue formal written guidance concerning the payment of contingent commissions to brokers and regulators did so. Those guidelines clarified that many of the practices that Spitzer challenged were legitimate. Vincent Laurenzano was the person Greenberg contacted; he was assistant deputy superintendent and chief examiner of the Financial Condition Property/Casualty Bureau.

23. Jeffrey Greenberg was succeeded by Spitzer's former boss at the New York District Attorney's office, Michael Cherkasky.

24. See Joseph B. Treaster, "Broker Accused of Rigging Bids for Insurance," *New York Times* (October 15, 2004).

25. See Kulbir Walha and Edward E. Filusch, "Eliot Spitzer: A Crusader against Corporate Malfeasance or a Politically Ambitious Spotlight Hound: A Case Study of Eliot Spitzer and Marsh & McLennan," *Georgetown Journal of Legal Ethics* 18 (2005): 1111.

26. Cunningham interview with Richard I. Beattie, New York, May 2, 2012; see Masters, *Spoiling for a Fight*, 236.

27. While sparing Marsh & McLennan as a firm, Spitzer nevertheless targeted employees, who were vindicated. Two whose cases were dismissed because of prosecutorial unfairness later sued Spitzer for defamation after Spitzer wrote an online article suggesting that, despite the dismissal, they were guilty as charged. See Eliot Spitzer, "They Still Don't Get It," Slate.com (August 22, 2010); Don Jeffrey, "Ex Marsh & McLennan Executive Gilman Sues Spitzer, Magazine for Defamation," *Bloomberg* (August 22, 2011). One of those defamation cases remains pending as of this writing while one was dismissed because Spitzer's statements appeared to concern Marsh rather than the particular employee. *See Gilman v. Spitzer*, 11 CV-5843 (S.D.N.Y. Oct. 1, 2012).

28. *People ex rel. Spitzer v. Grasso*, 893 N.E.2d 105 (N.Y. 2008); see also Ken Langone, "Drop the Case Against Hank Greenberg," *Wall Street Journal* (October 6, 2009).

29. Cunningham telephone interview with Jack Welch, March 6, 2012; Cunningham interview with Kenneth R. Langone, New York, October 3, 2011; see also Charles Gasparino, "Wall Street: This Case Is Personal," *Newsweek* (September 27, 2004); Opinion, "Spitzer's Rise and Fall," *Wall Street Journal* (March 11, 2008).

Spitzer has equivocated or obfuscated concerning this incident. For example, in a Fox Business News interview of November 9, 2011, after the moderator played a clip of Welch quoting Spitzer's menacing words—that he "will put a spike through Langone's heart"—the following exchange occurred:

Moderator: "Is that true or not?"
Spitzer: "Not true. But here's what are the facts."
Moderator: "Jack Welch is lying here?"
Spitzer: "Jack was not there. Look, Jack and I got along well most of the time. We also pursued GE. Silly little kids stuff. They had some dishwashers that burst into flames when they hit the dry cycle. . . ."

http://video.foxbusiness.com/v/1300170404001/spitzer-private-sector-should-determine-pay.

30. CBS News, "The Sheriff of Wall Street"; see also Patrick McGeehan, "With Critics at the Door, Funds Propose Cleaning Own House," *New York Times* (October 31, 2003) (reporting interview in which Spitzer called for "heads to roll" at the SEC for agency's failure to properly supervise the mutual fund industry, which became another Spitzer target); Jonathan R. Macey, "State-Federal Relations Post-Eliot Spitzer," *Brooklyn Law Review* 70 (2004): 117, 127 (quoting Spitzer as asking "the most obvious and embarrassing question: 'where has the Securities and Exchange Commission been while all of this . . . was going on?'"); Deborah Solomon and Ian McDonald, "Spitzer Decries Lax Regulation over Insurance," *Wall Street Journal* (November 17, 2004).

31. "Spitzer Blames the SEC; Donaldson Admits Mistakes," *The Corporate Reform Weekly: Citizen Works' Look at the Campaign for Corporate Reform* 2(41) (November 3, 2003), http://citizenworks.org/news/index.php?id=106.

32. See, for example, Peter Krug, "Prosecutorial Discretion and Its Limits," *American Journal of Comparative Law* 50 (2002): 643, 659.

33. Cunningham telephone interview with Cynthia A. Glassman, former SEC commissioner, April 6, 2012.

34. "Statement of the Commission Regarding the Enforcement Action Against Alliance Capital Management," *SEC News Digest* (December 18, 2003), at www.sec.gov/news/digest/dig121803.txt (objection to Spitzer settlement that involved setting mutual fund fees).

35. See William S. Laufer, *Corporate Bodies and Guilty Minds* (Chicago: University of Chicago Press, 2006), 40.

36. Terry Frieden, "FBI Warns of Mortgage Fraud 'Epidemic': Seeks to Head off 'Next S&L Crisis,'" CNN (September 17, 2004), available at www.cnn.com/2004/LAW/09/17/mortgage.fraud.

37. Spitzer's foray into subprime alleged that high-interest loans made by large national banks were disproportionately made to minority groups, violating

state fair lending laws. Federal banking authorities challenged the power of states such as New York to pursue such claims. The Supreme Court eventually rejected the federal argument, after Spitzer had left the attorney general's office. *Cuomo v. Clearing House Association*, 557 U.S. 519 (2009), www.supremecourt.gov/opinions/08pdf/08-453.pdf. Although the case is taken to speak for concern that the federal authorities had some responsibility for failing to investigate matters associated with the financial crisis of 2008, the claims that Spitzer raised were about fair lending laws.

38. See Paul Tharp, "AG Snit Has Hit the Fan," *New York Post* (July 10, 2012); CNBC, "Spitzer's Vendetta vs. Greenberg" (July 10, 2012), available at www.cnbc.com/id/15840232?video=3000102000&play=1; affidavit of Dennis C. Vacco in *Smith v. New York State Office of the Attorney General*, Index No. 3670-08 (Cahill, J.) (September 27, 2012). In this case, Howard Smith, former CFO of AIG, sought various records under New York's FOIL, including e-mails of Spitzer addressing official state business on nonstate computers. Despite resistance from Spitzer's successor, Eric Schneiderman, the court ruled in Smith's favor.

   On the program where Vacco appeared to report this meeting, Greenberg's lawyer, David Boies, was asked to comment. The program aired the following written statement from him:

   These are obviously very disturbing charges. Over the last seven years, almost all of the charges originally brought by the Attorney General against Mr. Greenberg have been dismissed. If these claims were brought with knowledge that they were without merit for the purpose of retaliating against a political critic, this was an even greater miscarriage of justice abuse of the legal system.

   Transcript at 5:42–5:43. Immediately afterwards, Spitzer called one of Boies's law partners, another of Greenberg's lawyers, and shouted into the phone:

   Because your firm is in bed with someone like Hank Greenberg, you have to bear the consequences and I have a bazooka pointed at David Boies, you and everyone else at your firm who is involved.

   E-mail from Nicholas Gravante to David Boies, July 10, 2012.

39. The theory had three elements. First, the two executives supposedly ordered underlings to fabricate a paper trail making it look as if Gen Re proposed the deal rather than AIG—since usually AIG wrote primary insurance policies and Gen Re specialized in reinsurance. Second, the theory went, the scheme involved creating a deal that looked as if Gen Re transferred some insurance risk to AIG in exchange for Gen Re paying AIG a fee. But, third, Spitzer and others surmised, Gen Re did not really transfer the required risk and the fee it paid was reimbursed by AIG through credits an AIG subsidiary gave to a Gen Re subsidiary.

40. Both companies agreed to cooperate fully in prosecuting their employees, in agreements reached long after Greenberg left AIG. See AIG-DOJ Non-Prosecution Agreement (February 7, 2006), available at http://lib.law.virginia.edu/Garrett/prosecution_agreements/pdf/aig.pdf; Gen Re–DOJ Non-Prosecution Agreement (January 2010), available at http://lib.law.virginia.edu/Garrett/prosecution_agreements/pdf/genre.pdf.

41. *United States v. Ferguson*, 654 F.3d 61 (2d Cir. 2011). Richard Napier, a former Gen Re vice president, who made a plea bargain, acknowledged in court testimony that some of the facts he supplied when negotiating his plea deal were incorrect and the rest of his testimony did not support the government's claims. Trial Transcript, *United States v. Ferguson*, vol. VIII (January 18, 2008), 1660–1668 (plea agreement recited as a fact that a no-risk deal was discussed in the October phone call but Napier acknowledges repeatedly in open court that that there was "no discussion about risk at all in that [October] conversation"); see also ibid. at 1678–1682 (acknowledging giving at least two and perhaps three different versions of events during the course of the case). A federal appeals court called Napier's testimony overall "less than reliable." *United States v. Ferguson*, 653 F.3d 61, 71 (2nd Cir. 2011) (referring to part of his testimony); see Mark Hamblett, "Circuit Reverses Five Convictions in Alleged AIG Insurance Fraud," *National Law Journal* (August 2, 2011).

42. Oral argument, *United States v. Ferguson* (November 17, 2010), at 11:59:45 A.M. to 12:03:46 P.M. In charging Ferguson and the others, the government had named Greenberg as "an unindicted coconspirator," an often gratuitous designation prosecutors assign to people for a variety of reasons, though the practice, popularized during the Watergate era, is frowned upon and discouraged by such authorities as the U.S. Attorneys' Manual.

43. Reuters, "Defendants in AIG/Gen Re Case Reach Deal with Government" (June 22, 2012).

44. See, for example, Deferred Prosecution Letter Agreement between U.S. Department of Justice and Christian M. Milton, 3:06cr137(VLB) (June 22, 2012), which recites that the defendant:

recognizes that aspects of the [Gen Re] transaction were fraudulent; and does not dispute that (a) the [Gen Re] transaction was highly unusual, (b) red flags suggested that the transaction would be improperly accounted for, which he disregarded, and (c) he should have attempted to stop it from going forward, but instead continued to participate in it.

45. These are technically called the "summary of unadjusted differences."

46. See Minutes of Meeting of the Audit Committee of American International Group, Inc. (March 7, 2005):

Mr. Winograd presented PwC's update on the audit since the earnings release date . . . He noted that among the most sensitive and judgmental areas of accounting utilized by the Corporation is the reserve for losses and loss expenses, and PwC remains comfortable with Management's estimates in this area. . . . He also indicated that the audit would not be complete until the investigation [stimulated by the subpoenas] was substantially complete. . . . Winograd reported that disclosure with respect to ongoing regulatory matters will be finalized this week. . . . Winograd next advised the Committee that no material weaknesses in internal controls had been identified. . . . PwC expects to issue a "clean" opinion . . . .

47. The press had begun to report the story, describing Spitzer's inquiry in ominous tones or attributing the information to "unnamed sources"—which made it easy to surmise that Spitzer's office was spinning the press, before an investigation was complete. See, for example, Alain Sherter, "Spitzer Exposes Crack in Greenberg's Armor," *Daily Deal* (February 18, 2005); "Regulators Eye Reinsurance, AIG Reserves," *CFO* (March 8, 2005) (noting stories in both the *Financial Times* and *Wall Street Journal* citing "unnamed sources" about the inquiry); see also Boyd, *Fatal Risk*, 135.

48. Cunningham interview with Ernest Patrikis, New York, January 23, 2012.

49. See, for example, Masters, *Spoiling for a Fight*, 262, quoting Beattie as follows:

What Eliot [did] very successfully [was] outsource his work by threatening people and subpoenaing them. . . . I think it is a very effective method. He [had] many law firms in the city working for him.

50. Cunningham sought to interview Paul Weiss lawyers involved in the AIG case but the senior Paul Weiss partner in the matter declined on the grounds of the firm's ethical duties to AIG.

51. In the interest of disclosure, Cunningham was an associate of Cravath, Swaine & Moore during the first six years of his legal career.

52. See Masters, *Spoiling for a Fight*, 202 & 207 (referencing Matthew J. Gaul).

53. See "Pataki, Spitzer Spar Over AIG Lawyer Contributions," *Insurance Journal* (April 13, 2005) (referencing widely reported story, that Spitzer's office affirmed, about 16 Paul Weiss lawyers financially backing Spitzer's campaign).

54. See Brian Baxter, "Paul Weiss Pro to Defend Spitzer," *American Lawyer* (March 12, 2008) (referring to Michele Hirshman, who was also Spitzer's former deputy).

55. See, for example, Defendant American International Group, Inc.'s Memorandum of Law in Opposition to [Greenberg's] Motion to Compel Production of Documents (September 12, 2005), 2, 22.

56. Cunningham sought to interview senior PwC officials involved in the AIG matter but they declined or ignored the requests.

57. See Minutes of Meeting of the Audit Committee of American International Group, Inc. (March 7, 2005) (quoted above).

58. Cunningham interview with Richard I. Beattie, New York, May 8, 2012; Masters, *Spoiling for a Fight*, 235.

59. Masters, *Spoiling for a Fight*, 236. There are many exceptions to the rule barring hearsay evidence, including one covering statements of "co-conspirators." So there is always some doubt about admissibility.

60. Some of the tapes surfaced in the trial against the four Gen Re employees and one AIG employee.

61. Cunningham interview with Richard I. Beattie, New York, May 8, 2012; Masters, *Spoiling for a Fight*, 235.

62. Masters, *Spoiling for a Fight*, 235.

63. This portrayal of the meeting is based on Cunningham interviews with a half dozen participants, not all of whom spoke on the record, as well as articles and books cited elsewhere.

64. He referenced a rule of thumb published by the head of the Financial Accounting Standards Board calling for risk measured as something like a 10 percent chance of a 10 percent loss—essentially a 1 percent net risk of loss.

65. See also Andrea Felsted, Ellen Kelleher & Stephanie Kirchgaessner, "Insurer Struggles to Sever Links with Starr," *Wall Street Journal* (April 4, 2005) (reporting that PwC was also a subject of regulatory inquiries and that the SEC had requested information).

66. See Greg Farrell, "Two Titans to Answer Questions in AIG Probe," *USA Today* (April 11, 2005).

67. Andrew Countryman, "AIG Chief to Take 5th in Spitzer Interview: A Wise Decision, Say Several Legal Experts," *Chicago Tribune* (April 12, 2005).

68. *People v. Greenberg*, deposition of Warren Buffett (April 15, 2009), Exhibit 2.

69. Ibid., 42–48.

70. For example, *People v. Greenberg*, deposition of Warren Buffett (April 15, 2009), Exhibit 9 (U.S. Department of Justice submission of "Brady materials" to employee defendants in case); *In re Certain Loss Mitigation Insurance Products*, SEC, Wells Submission on behalf of Joseph P. Brandon (October 7, 2005), 48.

71. *People v. Greenberg*, deposition of Warren Buffett (April 15, 2009), 57–63.

72. Cunningham not-for-attribution interview with a direct participant.

73. Joseph A. Grundfest, "Over Before It Started," *New York Times* (June 14, 2005).

74. Beattie does not recall saying that he told Greenberg that he and Zarb would have to check with Spitzer about this matter. Cunningham interview with Beattie; e-mail from Beattie to Cunningham, August 9, 2012.

75. AIG's board met the next day, Monday March 14, at which Greenberg formally resigned as CEO, Smith was removed as CFO, Greenberg was elected as nonexecutive chairman, Martin J. Sullivan was appointed CEO, and Steven J. Bensinger was appointed CFO. AIG Board Minutes (March 14,

2005), 4. At that meeting, Greenberg requested that Winograd explain further the issues surrounding PwC's audit opinion, on which a "lengthy discussion" ensued. Ibid. at 5.

76. In Malaysia, AIG's current five-year ownership agreement was about to expire and Greenberg had arranged for negotiating a permanent solution to the ownership issue with a new prime minister who had recently taken office. The day Greenberg arrived was the day of another state minister's funeral, causing a delay in their meeting. It also did not create the best atmosphere to negotiate a permanent solution so Greenberg proposed simply extending the existing deal for another five years and to take it up again later. The prime minister agreed. A few months later, Sullivan went to Malaysia to implement that new five-year deal, where the prime minister's office did not see him, instead shunting him off to a deputy minister of finance or banking. There he was told that the only way Malaysia would agree to another five-year deal was if AIG also agreed that it would be the last one. The upshot: relationships matter, especially in international business affairs, and must be nurtured in personal ways.

77. The resignation letter, and accompanying AIG press release, appears as Appendix B on the companion web site for this book, at www.wiley.com/go/theaigstory.

78. Greg Farrell, "Two Titans to Answer Questions in AIG Probe," *USA Today* (April 11, 2005) ("After the AIG board fired [Greenberg], Spitzer took the unusual step of issuing a statement praising the board for its actions and pledging that he would not take any legal action against the company itself.").

79. Ian McDonald and Theo Francis, "Spitzer Expects a Civil Settlement with AIG," *Wall Street Journal* (April 5, 2005).

80. A formal meeting of the "Outside Directors" of AIG was held on March 28, 2005, complete with the taking and filing of formal minutes, prepared and signed by Richard Beattie. AIG Minutes of Meeting of Outside Directors (March 28, 2005). Others have suggested that Spitzer effectuated a hostile takeover of the SEC. Jonathan R. Macey, "Positive Political Theory and Federal Usurpation of the Regulation of Corporate Governance: The Coming Preemption of the Martin Act," *Notre Dame Law Review* 80 (2005): 951, 951–953.

81. See AIG Board Minutes (March 14, 2005), 5 (asked about filing the pending annual report with the SEC, Bensinger, the new CFO, said "new management needs ample time to conduct an appropriate review and take any necessary remedial action."); Masters, *Spoiling for a Fight*, 237 ("No formal analysis had been done.").

Chapter 14 Restating History

1. See e-mail from Mark Pomerantz (Paul Weiss) to Spitzer's office, March 28, 2005 (chronology of events obtained by the authors under the New York Freedom of Information Law, No. 09777 002904-8).

2. This episode has been widely reported. See, for example, Masters, *Spoiling for a Fight*, 239 (saying Spitzer "blew his top"); Elkind, *Rough Justice*, 84–85.

3. Cunningham interview with Lee Wolosky, New York, February 6, 2011.

4. Cunningham interview with Richard I. Beattie, New York, May 8, 2012. Several published sources portray this sequence of events concerning Greenberg's resignation as chairman differently, including books written by Boyd, Elkind, and Masters. These appear to be otherwise credible and reliable sources.

5. See Eichenwald and Anderson, "How a Titan of Insurance Ran Afoul of the Government," *New York Times* (April 4, 2005).

6. Fisher, Coolidge, and Weinberg, "The Battle of the Titans over AIG"; Masters, *Spoiling for a Fight*, 278. The *Forbes* article quotes Hofstra University law professor Monroe Freedman, an ethics expert, calling Spitzer's television appearance "reprehensible conduct" and a "very serious violation of due process, in my view."

7. See New York Rules of Professional Conduct, 4-109.

8. American Bar Association, Model Rule 3.8(f) (criminal prosecutors "shall refrain from making extrajudicial comments that have a substantial likelihood of heightening public condemnation of the accused.").

9. See Timothy L. O'Brien and Jenny Anderson, "Greenberg, In Exile, Plots His Next Move," *New York Times* (May 22, 2005) (quoting Spitzer spokesman Darren Dopp as interpreting Spitzer's remarks as "not commenting on Mr. Greenberg specifically" but on "improper conduct" at AIG that they said the company had acknowledged).

10. Transcript of *This Week with George Stephanopoulos*, FDCH–eMedia, Inc. (April 10, 2005).

11. This dialogue continued to advance another characteristic of Spitzer's approach to the attorney general's office noted in the previous chapter:

> *Stephanopoulos*: In so many of your cases, you get to settlement before you go to court. Is that what you expect here?
>
> *Spitzer*: . . . I would certainly hope so. . . . Hank Greenberg had been one of the most powerful CEOs in America with a board that did what he wanted. The board looked at the evidence, forced him out [as] CEO, forced him out of the chair. The new board, the new leadership wants to reform the company . . . .

> The board, of course, had not "looked at the evidence," because no one had conducted an investigation up to that point.

12. John C. Whitehead, "Mr. Spitzer Has Gone Too Far," *Wall Street Journal* (April 22, 2005). Whitehead had submitted the piece to the *New York Times* as well, but that newspaper turned it down. Cunningham interview with John C. Whitehead, New York, October 3, 2011.

13. These passages are based on Cunningham's interview with John C. White-head, New York, October 3, 2011.
14. John C. Whitehead, "Scary," *Wall Street Journal* (December 22, 2005).
15. Ibid.
16. See Patrick D. Healy, "G.O.P. Finds Hope in Spitzer's Hard Edge," *New York Times* (January 8, 2006).
17. Jonathan D. Glater, "Executive's Article Revives Feud with Prosecutor," *New York Times* (December 23, 2005) (quoting Spitzer spokesman Darren Dopp).
18. See Elkind, *Rough Justice*, 93–94:

    [E]verything Whitehead had claimed about his conversation with Spitzer was true. Kristie Stiles, Spitzer's young national fundraiser, had been with him . . . on the day he spoke with Whitehead and had watched it all unfold. Shocked, she called Ryan Toohey, the AG's campaign manager, to tell him about it afterward. Eliot's eyes had suddenly narrowed to slits before he let loose. You'll wish you had never crossed me! "Eliot really lost it in the car," Stiles reported. "It was like Gunsmoke." Whitehead's account was verbatim.

    These reports seem corroborative in substance and tenor if not quite verbatim (compare "never written that" versus "never crossed me").
19. Accounting restatements became so increasingly common and ultimately routine during the mid-2000s, that officials cautioned about restatements that were themselves suspect. For example, speech of John White, SEC Director of the Division of Corporation Finance, "Corporation Finance in 2008: A Focus on Financial Reporting" (San Diego, 2008), 5–6, available at www.sec .gov/news/speech/2008/spch012308jww.htm (commenting on concern and proposals made by an SEC Advisory Committee); see also Marlene Plumlee and Teri Lombardi Yohn, "An Analysis of the Underlying Causes Attributed to Restatements" (June 2009) (noting growth in number of restatements during this period, up from 475 in 2003 to 1,538 in 2006).
20. Cunningham interview with Ernest Patrikis, New York, January 23, 2012.
21. Cunningham interview with Richard I. Beattie, New York, May 2, 2012.
22. See Ian McDonald and Theo Francis, "Spitzer Expects a Civil Settlement with AIG," *Wall Street Journal* (April 5, 2005) ("The company has told regulators it will hire forensic accountants to give the company's books an in depth scouring.").
23. See Monica Langley, "CEO School: Flung into Top Job, Sullivan of AIG Learns on the Fly," *Wall Street Journal* (July 21, 2005).
24. Defendant American International Group, Inc.'s Memorandum of Law in Opposition to [Greenberg's] Motion to Compel Production of Documents (September 12, 2005), 3.
25. Cunningham telephone interview with Jeff Johnson, July 12, 2012. Johnson continued to work at AIG for several years, through 2012, when he left to join the Starr Companies.

26. See McDonald and Francis, "Spitzer Expects a Civil Settlement with AIG."
27. Freedom of Information Law (FOIL) requests under New York law revealed extensive evidence of how Paul Weiss and Simpson Thacher did Spitzer's work. In addition to those cited elsewhere, examples include the following. On March 28, 2005, Mark Pomerantz of Paul Weiss emailed Spitzer's office a chronology that Paul Weiss prepared concerning what he called the "Bermuda documents," a reference to the events noted in the beginning of this chapter. FOIL 09777 002904-8. On April 4, 2005, James Gamble of Simpson Thacher sent a detailed seven-page letter to Michele Hirshman, Spitzer's top deputy, outlining "our understanding of SICO as of this time." FOIL 09777 002754-62. On April 6, 2005, John Carroll of Spitzer's office emailed Roberta Kaplan of Paul Weiss telling her that if she had any more discussions with other parties in the case, to call to discuss what was said. FOIL 09777 006712. On April 15, 2005, Paul Weiss sent David Brown in Spitzer's office extensive notes that Paul Weiss attorneys had recorded of their interviews with AIG employees. FOIL 09777 002763-5.
28. SICO Reply Memorandum in Further Support of Its Motion to Compel the Production of Documents, p. 6 (citing Declaration of Roberta A. Kaplan (January 12, 2006) ("On May 9, 2005, AIG permitted members of the Attorney General's Office to review a preliminary draft of the report in a conference room at Paul, Weiss' offices."), FOIL 09777 002478 (January 17, 2006).
29. Defendant American International Group, Inc.'s Memorandum of Law in Opposition to [Greenberg's] Motion to Compel Production of Documents (September 12, 2005) (repeatedly stressing delivery of the report on July 1 without mentioning earlier preview in May); Kaplan Reply Declaration; Transcript of Hearing in People v. Greenberg (Jan. 5, 2006), pp. 33-37, FOIL No. 09777 002453-09777 002457.
30. Transcript of hearing in *People v. Greenberg* (January 5, 2006), p. 40, FOIL No. 09777 002458 (statement of the Honorable Charles E. Ramos).
31. Defendant American International Group, Inc.'s Memorandum of Law in Opposition to [Greenberg's] Motion to Compel Production of Documents (September 12, 2005), 22; see also ibid., p. 2 ("AIG shared a common interest with the NYAG").
32. See e-mail from Spitzer's office to Paul Weiss attorneys, August 1, 2005 ("We have nothing that needs to be discussed tomorrow, and some people are out of the office. So, I thought we could just cancel this week's conference call. We will do it again next Tuesday."); FOIL 09777 006515.
33. For example, e-mail from Keeley Wettan of Simpson Thacher to David Szuchman of Spitzer's office, July 8, 2005; FOIL 09777 005008; FOIL 09777 006336.
34. SICO Reply Brief, 28–29.
35. For example, e-mail from Roberta A. Kaplan, Paul Weiss, to Peter Pope, Spitzer's office, August 30, 2005; FOIL 09777 004694–004721.
36. Cunningham interviews and correspondence with David Boies, September 2012.

37. See Ian McDonald and Leslie Scism, "AIG's Ex Chief Clears a Hurdle but Faces More," *Wall Street Journal* (November 25, 2005); Masters, *Spoiling for a Fight*, 278.

38. See New York Code of Professional Responsibility, Disciplinary Rule 7-105 ("A lawyer shall not present, participate in presenting, or threaten to present criminal charges solely to obtain an advantage in a civil matter."). The New York code of legal ethics was revamped in 2009, omitting this prohibition, but did not change the law retroactively. One critical issue is "probable cause." See New York Code of Professional Responsibility, Disciplinary Rule 7-103 ("A public prosecutor or other government lawyer shall not institute or cause to be instituted criminal charges when he or she knows or it is obvious that the charges are not supported by probable cause."). If a prosecutor has probable cause to believe that a defendant committed a crime, it is consistent with the prosecutor's public trust to threaten criminal charges. But absent probable cause, such threats are an abuse of public trust that border on misrepresentation and conduct prejudicial to the administration of justice, both prohibited by prosecutorial ethics. See American Bar Association, Model Rules of Professional Conduct, Rule 8.4 ("It is professional misconduct for a lawyer to . . . (c) engage in conduct involving dishonesty [or misrepresentation] [or] (d) engage in conduct that is prejudicial to the administration of justice.").

39. Defendant American International Group, Inc.'s Memorandum of Law in Opposition to [Greenberg's] Motion to Compel Production of Documents (draft of August 30, 2005), 3.

40. Letter dated June 27, 2005 from Richard I. Beattie to Eliot Spitzer (obtained under New York State's Freedom of Information Law, No. 09777, 002886–002896). This document is included as Appendix C on the companion web site for this book, at www.wiley.com/go/theaigstory.

41. *People v. Greenberg*, No. 401720/2005 (Sup. Ct. N.Y. May 2005).

42. See SEC, Staff Accounting Bulletin No. 99 (August 12, 1999).

43. Some read some provisions of an accounting standard adopted in 2004 to support the restatement's stance. Financial Accounting Standards Board, Statement 123R (2004).

44. Financial Accounting Standards Board, FIN 46R.

45. See Jenny Anderson, "A.I.G. and Related Insurer Set to Fight for Big Liability," *New York Times* (August 3, 2005) (noting independent audit of SICO by Lazard Levine & Felix).

46. Ibid. (quoting Robert Willens, an accounting policy expert with Lehman Brothers).

47. AIG Board Minutes (April 21, 2005), 9 (referencing report of Hoenemeyer).

48. Ibid., 5 (statement of Bensinger in response to question from Hoenemeyer).

49. For example, AIG Audit Committee Meeting Minutes (March 7, 2005).

50. See McDonald and Scism, "AIG's Ex Chief Clears a Hurdle but Faces More"; Masters, *Spoiling for a Fight*, 278.

51. For details, see Elkind, *Rough Justice*, 200–201.

52. Ibid. 260.

53. See *In re American International Group Inc. Securities Litigation* (S.D.N.Y. February 22, 2010). For details, see Labaton & Sucharow, Settled Cases, www.labaton.com/en/cases/In-re-American-International-Group-Inc-Securities-Litigation.cfm. In addition, Greenberg personally settled an SEC case asserting that, as a "controlling person" of AIG, he shared legal responsibility for some infractions. See SEC, Accounting and Auditing Release No. 3032 (August 6, 2009). He paid $15 million.

    During the investigation leading to the restatement in 2005, Spitzer reopened another subject, unrelated to accounting matters, dealing with the taxation of workers' compensation insurance policies. In 1992, AIG's general counsel had told Greenberg of potential problems in this line of insurance. Greenberg reported this concern to AIG's board, which authorized hiring two law firms—Sullivan & Cromwell and Cahill Gordon & Reindel—to investigate. The firms concluded that the concerns were exaggerated and in some instances erroneous but AIG nevertheless implemented additional controls to assure compliance with state laws.

    States impose taxes and assessments on workers' compensation policies. To calculate the correct amount, a company must classify policies internally. Not all policies are clearly delineated as workers' compensation and some may encompass general liability obligations. If classified as general liabilities, workers' compensation taxes or assessments would not be due, though other taxes may be—and these could be higher or lower.

    Despite thus resolving the matter internally a decade earlier, Spitzer included it in his charges against AIG. He made a state-by-state analysis for the period from 1985 to 1996 to identify errors and demanded that AIG create a special fund to pay those—totaling $343 million. State insurance regulators in other states were baffled by this, some observing that AIG had actually overpaid and others preferring to conduct their own investigation.

54. See "AIG Downgraded," *Insurance Journal* (June 30, 2005), available at www.insurancejournal.com/magazines/features/2005/06/20/150287.htm.

55. Cunningham interview with Lee Wolosky, New York, February 6, 2011.

Chapter 15   Civil War

1. Cunningham interview with Ernest Patrikis, New York, January 23, 2012 (stating that AIG cordoned off Greenberg's office and seized his property at

the direction of Spitzer's office); e-mail from Patrikis to Cunningham, August 26, 2012 (stating that Spitzer told AIG not to return any property associated with Greenberg).

2. Cunningham interview with Lee Wolosky, New York, February 6, 2011.

3. Cunningham telephone interview with Christopher Duffy and Lee Wolosky, March 7, 2012.

4. Ibid.

5. Ibid.

6. The effort was completed two weeks later when additional resignations were supplied by three other directors not removed at the shareholders' meeting: Thomas Tizzio, Robert Sandler and R. Kendall Nottingham.

7. AIG Board Minutes (April 21, 2005), 9; AIG Board Minutes (May 18, 2005), 2; see also ibid., p. 4 (statement of Marshall Cohen); AIG Board Minutes (June 16, 2005), 14 (referencing a "discussion" without naming individuals).

8. Many phases of the protracted dispute between AIG and the Starr companies were covered by general business journalists and the insurance press. For a sampling, see Jenny Anderson, "Suit by A.I.G. Adds to the Rancor of Breaking Up Old Times," *New York Times* (January 28, 2006); Jenny Anderson, "In Lawsuit, C. V. Starr Accuses A.I.G. of Hurting Its Business," *New York Times* (January 30, 2006); Judy Greenwald, "Greenberg Fights AIG over Starr Business in Battle for Control," *Business Insurance* (Crain's) (February 6, 2006); Rupal Parekh, "AIG, Starr Feud over Employee Defections," *Business Insurance* (Crain's) (August 14, 2006).

9. See Parekh, "AIG, Starr Feud over Employee Defections."

10. Joint pretrial order in *Starr International Co. v. American International Group*, 05-CV-6283 (BSJ) (MHD) (July 31, 2008), 4. Schedule A to this order contains an inventory of the artistic property.

11. The Van Gogh is *Little Streams* or *Le Petite Cours d'Eaul;* the Winslow Homer paintings were *Taking on Wet Goods* and *Sloop Bermuda;* the David Aronson was *The Singer;* and there were several sculptures by Milton Hebald, including *Mother with Two Children.*

12. Cunningham interview with Ernest Patrikis, New York, January 23, 2012.

13. Ibid.; e-mail from Patrikis to Cunningham, August 26, 2012.

14. *SICO v. AIG*, No. 05-CV-6283 (JSR) (MJD) (S.D.N.Y.) (complaint filed July 8, 2005).

15. Cunningham telephone interview with Roger Dinella, April 30, 2012.

16. See Stipulation of Settlement, *Teachers' Retirement Systems of Louisiana v. Greenberg*, C.A. No. 20106-VCS (Del. Ch. September 29, 2008).

17. See *Teachers' Retirement Systems of Louisiana v. Aidinoff*, 900 A.2d 654 (Del. Ch. June 21, 2006).

18. AIG Board Minutes (October 20, 2005), 5 (presentation by Stephen Radin, of Weil Gotshal). At the October 20 board meeting, a lawyer from Weil Gotshal,

Stephen Radin, after referencing the earlier report's conclusion "that the commissions paid by the agencies were fair to AIG," suggested that "one possible avenue for settlement of the lawsuit involves the purchase of the agencies by AIG." Sullivan echoed that possibility, saying the issues in the lawsuit could be resolved simply by AIG acquiring C. V. Starr & Company agencies.

19. See Stipulation of Settlement, *Teachers' Retirement Systems of Louisiana v. Greenberg*.

20. Ibid.

21. See, for example, William M. Carney and George B. Shepherd, "The Mystery of the Success of Delaware Law," *University of Illinois Law Review* vol. 2009 (2009): 1.

22. See Stipulation of Settlement, *Teachers' Retirement Systems of Louisiana v. Greenberg*.

23. Minutes of AIG Board of Directors Meeting (May 18, 2005).

24. Cunningham interview with Ernest Patrikis, New York, January 23, 2012; e-mail from Patrikis to Cunningham, August 26, 2012.

25. Cunningham interview with Ernest Patrikis, New York, January 23, 2012.

26. *SICO v. AIG*, 648 F.Supp.2d 546 (S.D.N.Y. 2009) (Rakoff, J.).

27. *SICO v. AIG*, Statement of Material Uncontested Facts (February 15, 2007), 40–41.

28. Ibid.; e-mail from Patrikis to Cunningham, August 26, 2012.

29. *SICO v. AIG*, Statement of Material Uncontested Facts, 40–41.

30. E-mail from Alisha Smith to Mark Ciani/Andrew Goldstein of Paul Weiss (June 2009); FOIL 09777 000909-911, FOIL 09777 000904-906.

31. Cunningham asked the senior Paul Weiss partner involved in the matter to discuss it in an interview for this book, but the partner respectfully declined, citing the firm's attorney-client relationship with AIG.

32. Memorandum of Understanding (November 25, 2009), reprinted in Russ Bleemer, "ADR Brief," *Alternatives to the High Cost of Litigation* 28 (2010): 8.

Chapter 16   Saving the Starr Foundation

1. New York State Attorney General Report (December 14, 2005), 18.

2. Cunningham interviews and correspondence with David Boies, September 2012.

3. Cunningham interview with Florence Davis, New York, November 28, 2011.

4. New York Department of Law press release, December 15, 2005.

5. American Bar Association Model Rule 3.5(b).

6. The members in addition to Davis were Hon. C. Raymond Radigan and Hon. William C. Thompson; the firms were Farrell Fritz, PC, and Heller Ehrman LLP.

7. Cunningham interview with Florence Davis, New York, November 28, 2011.

8. See Gretchen Morgenson, "Report Says Ex-A.I.G. Chief Defrauded Foundation 35 Years Ago," *New York Times* (December 15, 2005).

9. Masters, *Spoiling for a Fight*, 248.

10. Spitzer letter transmitting attorney general report, p. 2.

11. See Starr Foundation web site, www.starrfoundation.org/priorities.html.

12. See The Starr Foundation press release, "The Starr Foundation Announces Donation of $300 Million Since 1980 through the C.V. Starr Scholarship Fund Program" (March 3, 2011).

13. David Boies offered another explanation: "I think the attorney general may be the victim of not completely accurate staff work because if you read that report that was submitted by his staff, it's got a lot of errors in it." See Maria Bartiromo, "Hank Greenberg Speaks Out," *CEO Wire* (December 19, 2005) (CNBC live interview).

14. See Part 97 of Title 13 of New York Code of Rules and Regulations.

15. Cunningham interview with Florence Davis, New York, November 28, 2011.

16. Gretchen Morgenson, "Report Says Ex-A.I.G. Chief Defrauded Foundation 35 Years Ago," *New York Times* (December 15, 2005).

17. See American Bar Association, Model Rules of Professional Conduct, Rules 3.5, 3.6, 3.8 and 8.4

18. Cunningham telephone interview with Robert Reinstein, October 14, 2011.

19. Cunningham interview with Jeffrey Lehman, New York, January 30, 2012.

20. Cunningham telephone interview with Richard Levin, November 29, 2011.

21. Ibid.

22. See Ellen Barry, "Russia Cracks Down on Antigovernment Protests," *New York Times* (December 7, 2011).

23. E-mail from Alexey Navalny's press secretary, Anna Veduta, to Cunningham, April 27, 2012.

24. Tina Kelley, "Dr. David Sinner, 67; Oversaw a Hospital Merger," *New York Times* (January 26, 2003).

25. Cunningham telephone interview with Herb Pardes, October 31, 2011 (about 20,000 employees, including 5,500 doctors and 4,800 nurses).

26. In fact, the Starr Foundation continued to be a favorite target of Spitzer's successors, who sometimes mimicked his tactics while continuing for more than seven years the accounting suit against Greenberg. In June 2012, one successor, Eric Schneiderman, subpoenaed the Chamber of Commerce and a charitable affiliate, questioning political financing and lobbying activities. Questions addressed grants the affiliate received from the Starr Foundation which, the subpoena suggested, may have been used not for charity but to repay loans the Chamber took from the affiliate. Of course, the Starr Foundation lacks power over how the charity uses funds it provides and it is difficult to track the end use of

fungible dollars. It did not seem coincidental that the Chamber had filed a "friend of the court" brief in the accounting suit, siding with Greenberg by arguing that the Martin Act, the statutory basis of the case, was invalid.

Chapter 17   Chaos

1. Theo Francis & Ian McDonald, "'Hank-less' AIG: More Deliberative (and Fun)," *Wall Street Journal* (May 20, 2005).
2. Guaazardi, Grose, et al., "Worth the Risk," chap. 22, p. 10 (by May 2008 "The company seemed directionless.").
3. AIG Board Minutes (November 16, 2005), 3.
4. AIG Board Minutes (June 16, 2005), 2.
5. E-mail from Martin Flumenbaum of Paul Weiss to Eliot Spitzer et al., July 19, 2005 (attaching "a draft of a proposed settlement agreement" and asking if there were "any open issues"), FOIL 09777 011247–09777 011262.
6. AIG ultimately signed a deferred prosecution agreement with New York authorities dated January 18, 2006, in coordination with parallel settlements with federal authorities. See Stipulation, *In the Matter of AIG*, No. 2005-0262-S (January 18, 2006). The detailed terms differed from those of the drafts circulated in the summer of 2005, but still contained "business reforms," including the hiring of a consultant to advise the board on corporate compliance and governance "best practices." Ibid. pp. 29–34.
7. Jenny Anderson, "A.I.G. Role for Ex-Chief of S.E.C.," *New York Times* (July 6, 2005).
8. Levitt letter to AIG board of directors (March 21, 2006), reprinted in AIG 2006 Proxy Statement (twice endorsing the notion of AIG being run in the "public interest"), available at www.sec.gov/Archives/edgar/data/5272/000095011706001641/a41737.htm and reprinted in this book at pages 225–227.
9. AIG press release, "AIG Board Elects Robert B. Willumstad Chairman, Succeeding Frank G. Zarb" (September 20, 2006).
10. Levitt letter to AIG board of directors (March 21, 2006), reprinted in AIG 2006 proxy statement.
11. Ibid. ("We have canvassed the views of directors, shareholders, governance experts, and shareholder activists for recommendations").
12. Cunningham interview with Ernest Patrikis, New York, January 23, 2012.
13. See James A. Brickley, Jeffrey L. Coles, and Gregg Jarrell, "Leadership Structure: Separating the CEO and Chairman of the Board," *Journal of Corporate Finance* 3 (1997).
14. AIG press release, September 20, 2006.
15. The new board's restatement took issue with certain internal controls concerning accounting for derivative transactions at FP, but did not challenge any other aspects of FP's operations.

16. AIG 2005 10K, filed 3/16/06, p. 15.
17. See Michael Lewis, *The Big Short: Inside the Doomsday Machine* (New York: Norton, 2010), 71–72; see also "Financial Crisis Inquiry Report," 141–142.
18. AIG 2005 10K, filed 3/16/06, p. 14 (summarizing downgrades); AIG 2004 10K, filed 5/31/05, p. 90.
19. Cunningham interview with Ernest Patrikis, New York, January 23, 2012.
20. See Sanjai Bhaga and Roberta Romano, "Reforming Executive Compensation: Focusing and Committing to the Long Term," *Yale Journal on Regulation* 23 (2009): 659. The authors explain:

    But if, as Greenberg states, AIG did not write credit-default swaps in huge volumes until after he retired and the incentive compensation post-retirement vesting period changed, that is consistent with our contention that our proposal will more properly align executive incentives with shareholders' interest than existing shorter-horizon plans.

21. Robert Reich, the professor and former secretary of labor under President Clinton, wrote acerbically of the "tactic that Goldman used for (and against) American International Group (AIG): Hide the ball, and then bet against the ball and fob off the risk to investors and taxpayers." Robert Reich, "Where on Earth Has the SEC Been?" *Clusterstock* (March 31, 2010).
22. Lewis, *The Big Short*, 71–72. Some media accounts written while the financial crisis was still underway, before investigations had been conducted, incorrectly suggested that many of AIG's credit default swaps at the center of the crisis were created during Greenberg's tenure. See, for example, Robert O'Harrow Jr. and Brady Dennis, "Downgrades and Downfall," *Washington Post* (December 31, 2008).
23. James Bandler, "Hank's Last Stand," *Fortune* (October 13, 2008).
24. See, generally, Lawrence A. Cunningham and David Zaring, "The Three or Four Approaches to Financial Regulation: A Cautionary Analysis against Exuberance in Crisis Response," *George Washington Law Review* 78 (2009): 39.
25. The opening sentences of this paragraph are drawn from the complaint in *SICO v. Treasury*, p. 36.
26. Cunningham and Greenberg interview with Robert Willumstad, New York, May 16, 2012; see Bethany McLean and Joe Nocera, *All the Devils Are Here* (New York: Portfolio, 2011), 328 (noting that Robert Lewis approved the request of securities lending program chief to "raise the limit on the securities he was allowed to purchase" and "rev up the program itself").
27. U.S. Government Accountability Office, Review of the Federal Reserve System Financial Assistance to American International Group, Inc. (September 2011), 5, 17. This document is hereafter called the GAO Report.
28. See Financial Crisis Inquiry Commission Report (hereafter called the FCIC Report), 243 (noting testimony of Sullivan, Bensinger, and Lewis and noting that AIG's 2005 10K disclosed that collateral postings could be triggered by

downgrades without mentioning that they could be triggered by value declines); compare AIG, Annual Report on Form 10K (2007), 100 ("certain of the credit default swaps are subject to collateral call provisions. In the case of such swaps written on CDOs, the amount of the collateral to be posted is determined based on the value of the CDO securities referenced in the documentation for the credit default swaps.").

29. FCIC Report, 268.

30. FCIC Report, 268 (quoting AIG Earnings Call credit supplement, August 9, 2007, 28, 14, 21, 22).

31. See Transcript, House of Representatives, Committee on Oversight and Government Reform, Hearing on the Causes and Effects of the AIG Bailout (October 7, 2008) (testimony of Joseph St. Denis); letter from Joseph St. Denis to House Committee on Oversight and Government Reform (October 4, 2008), available at http://oversight.house.gov/documents/20081007102452.pdf.

32. See Peter Lattman, "The U.S.'s Fly on the Wall at AIG," *Wall Street Journal* (March 27, 2009).

33. Ibid.; Consent Order p. 3.a.1 (referencing products having "a primary purpose of enabling a Reporting Company to obtain an accounting or financial reporting result").

34. See Memorandum from Mark Jickling to the House Committee on Oversight and Government Reform, Independent Consultant Reports on AIG Accounting Reforms, Congressional Research Service (May 5, 2009). AIG and the SEC fought intensively to keep the reports confidential, denying the public access to them, until a journalist years later pried them open after filing a federal lawsuit. See *Securities and Exchange Commission v. American International Group Inc.* (D. D. C. April 16, 2012) (opinion granting motion to compel disclosure of the reports by journalist Sue Reisinger of Corporate Counsel), available at http://pdfserver.amlaw.com/cc/KesslerFOI_opinion.pdf. The journalist was represented by the Thomas Jefferson Center for the Protection of Free Expression, Charlottesville, Virginia, with help from a clinic at the University of Virginia Law School.

35. AIG 10Q.

36. See American International Group, Inc., Meeting Notes (February 6, 2008) (between "Auditor 2 and Auditor 1" and "Bob W." concerning material weaknesses in AIG's internal controls). These auditor notes are reproduced in this book at pages 236-238.

37. This letter is reproduced as Appendix E on the companion web site for this book, at www.wiley.com/go/theaigstory.

38. AIG proxy statement (2009); e-mail to Cunningham from Howard Smith, April 26, 2012.

39. This letter is reproduced as Appendix F on the companion web site for this book, at www.wiley.com/go/theaigstory.

40. Oversight Report: The AIG Rescue, Its Impact on Markets and the Government's Exit Strategy (Elizabeth Warren, chair, June 2010). This report is hereafter called the Warren Oversight Report.
41. AIG press release, AIG Names Robert B. Willumstad Chief Executive Officer (June 15, 2008).
42. Reuters, July 1, 2008.
43. Guaazardi, Grose, et al., "Worth the Risk," chap. 23, p. 2.
44. Michael Loney, "30 Years in Insurance: Learning the Hard Way," *Reactions: Euromoney Institutional Investor* (April 1, 2011).
45. Warren Oversight Report, 54, n. 144:

> Former AIG General Counsel Anastasia Kelly stated: "There wasn't focus on the fact that now that Hank's gone, what do we need, what kind of succession planning should we have in place . . . A lot of companies have very robust human resource-driven succession plans, have people identified. AIG didn't have that. Maybe they would have had Hank stayed as long as he wanted to and had done it himself." She continued, saying that when the crisis hit, AIG did not have the "infrastructure to call upon to respond" and that "there was no one in charge." Ian Katz and Hugh Son, "AIG Was Unprepared for Financial Crisis, Former Top Lawyer Says," *Bloomberg News* (March 13, 2010) (online at www.bloomberg.com/apps/news?pid=20601087&sid=aYq7MDFtelkc).

Chapter 18   Nationalization

1. GAO Report (September 2011), 19.
2. Willumstad made informal overtures to the Fed on July 29 and a formal application on September 9, with various informal efforts in between. Cunningham and Greenberg interview with Robert Willumstad, New York, May 14, 2012; see Andrew Ross Sorkin, *Too Big To Fail* (New York: Viking, 2009), 207–209, 235–237.
3. FCIC Report, 344.
4. Ibid.
5. Cunningham and Greenberg interview with Robert Willumstad, New York, May 14, 2012; letter from Greenberg to Willumstad, September 16, 2008 (appearing as Appendix G on the companion web site for this book, at www.wiley.com/go/theaigstory).
6. Bradley Keoun and Craig Torres, "Foreign Banks Tapped Fed's Secret Lifeline Most at Crisis Peak," *Bloomberg* (April 1, 2011); Neil Irwin, "Files Shed Light on Fed Lending Activity," *Washington Post* (April 1, 2011); Luca Di Leo and Maya Jackson Randall, "Fed Disclosure May Hurt Banks' Discount-Window Use," *Dow Jones Business News* (March 31, 2011).
7. See Bradley Keoun and Phil Kurtz, "Wall Street Aristocracy Got $1.2 Trillion in Secret Loans," *Bloomberg* (August 22, 2011).

8. David Ellis, "Citi Dodges Bullet," *CNN Money* (November 24, 2008).
9. See "The Hartford Sells Its Fla. TARP Bank," *Hartford Business* (November 14, 2011).
10. See Joe Nocera and Edmund L. Andrews, "Struggling to Keep Up as the Crisis Raced On," *New York Times* (October 23, 2008).
11. FCIC Report, 345.
12. Cunningham and Greenberg interview with Robert Willumstad, New York, May 14, 2012; see Sorkin, *Too Big To Fail*, 290.
13. FCIC Report, 347–349.
14. Cunningham and Greenberg interview with Robert Willumstad, New York, May 14, 2012; see Sorkin, *Too Big To Fail*, 224–227, 293, 316–317.
15. Factors Affecting Efforts to Limit Payments to AIG Counterparties, Office of the Special Inspector General for the Troubled Asset Relief Program (Nov. 17, 2009) (hereafter called the SIG-TARP Report), 8; GAO Report (September 2011), 21–22.
16. Cunningham and Greenberg interview with Robert Willumstad, New York, May 14, 2012.
17. See Peg Brickley, "Lehman Makes It Official in Overnight Chapter 11 Filing," *Wall Street Journal* (September 15, 2008).
18. FCIC Report, 349; SIG-TARP Report, 8.
19. Warren Oversight Report.
20. Cunningham and Greenberg interview with Robert Willumstad, New York, May 14, 2012; see Sorkin, *Too Big To Fail*, 388.
21. Ibid.; Sorkin, *Too Big To Fail*, 393.
22. Paulson repeatedly urged all concerned not to call his decisions concerning AIG a "bailout," stressing that he was throttling shareholders, and protecting American taxpayers. Henry M. Paulson Jr., *On the Brink: Inside the Race to Stop the Collapse of the Global Financial System* (New York: Business Plus, 2010), 233, 240.
23. See David Wessel, *In Fed We Trust: Ben Bernanke's War on the Great Panic* (New York: Crown Business, 2009), 196–197.
24. The odd ownership percentage figure was chosen for accounting reasons—so the government would not need to consolidate AIG on its own books. Later, the government would adjust some of these terms, doubling the loan amount, reducing the interest rate somewhat, and extending the repayment period to five years.
25. Cunningham and Greenberg interview with Robert Willumstad, New York, May 14, 2012; see Wessel, *In Fed We Trust*, 196; Sorkin, *Too Big To Fail*, 401, 406.
26. Paulson, *On the Brink*, 239 (Paulson recounting that he called Willumstad "to tell him that he was being replaced"); Sorkin, *Too Big To Fail*, 403.
27. Paulson, *On the Brink*, 241.
28. Sorkin, *Too Big To Fail*, 402.

29. SIG-TARP Report, 6.

30. Sorkin, *Too Big To Fail*, 404 (noting comments of AIG directors Virginia Rometty and James Orr).

31. Liddy resigned from the Goldman Sachs board on September 26, 2008, effective as of September 23, 2008. See Goldman Sachs press release, "Edward Liddy Resigns from Goldman Sachs Board of Directors" (September 26, 2008).

32. See Timothy P. Carney, "AIG Head's $3 Million in Goldman Stock Raises Apparent Conflict of Interest," *Washington Examiner* (April 8, 2009).

33. GAO Report (September 2011), 35–37; SIG-TARP Report, 6; see Wessel, *In Fed We Trust*,196–197.

34. Cunningham e-mail from Willumstad, July 23, 2012.

35. AIG press release, "AIG Signs Definitive Agreement with Federal Reserve Bank of New York for $85 Billion Credit Facility" (September 23, 2008); press release, "Edward Liddy Resigns from Goldman Sachs Board of Directors" (September 26, 2008).

36. Cunningham e-mail from Willumstad, July 23, 2012.

37. Warren Oversight Report, 9.

38. See SIG-TARP Report, 30, 19.

39. GAO Report (September 2011), 72.

40. Warren Oversight Report, 9; SIG-TARP Report, 19, 29–30; FCIC Report, 378 (noting that that government's decision to pay 100 cents on the dollar "has been widely criticized").

41. GAO Report (September 2011).

42. Ibid. 71.

43. Ibid.

44. See FCIC Report, 353.

45. U.S. Treasury Press Center, Secretary [Geithner] Written Testimony before the House Committee on Oversight and Government Reform (January 27, 2010).

46. GAO Report (September 2011), 94–101.

47. Gretchen Morgenson, "At A.I.G., Good Luck Following the Money," *New York Times* (March 14, 2009); Andrew Frye and Hugh Son, "Geithner Says AIG Rescue Avoided 'Utter Collapse,'" *Bloomberg News* (January 27, 2010).

48. Warren Oversight Report, 9–10.

49. See, for example, Richard Teitelbaum and Hugh Son, "New York Fed's Secret Choice to Pay for Swaps Hits Taxpayers," *Bloomberg* (October 27, 2009); Serena Ng and Carrick Mollenkamp, "Goldman Fueled AIG Gambles," *Wall Street Journal* (December 12, 2009); David Skeel, "A Nation Adrift from the Rule of Law," *Wall Street Journal* (August 21, 2012).

50. Warren Oversight Report, 10.

51. FCIC Report, 202.

52. Warren Oversight Report, 9–10.

53. See, for example, Peter Whoriskey, "After Bailout, AIG Executives Head to Resort," *Washington Post* (October 7, 2008).
54. Cunningham telephone interview with Axel Freudmann, April 11, 2012.
55. See Lawrence A. Cunningham, "AIG's Bonus Blackmail," *New York Times* (March 18, 2009).
56. The AIG Lobbying Policy appears as Appendix H on the companion web site for this book, at www.wiley.com/go/theaigstory.
57. AIG Lobbying Policy; Section 6.04(e) of the Treasury-AIG Recapitalization Agreement.
58. See FCIC Report, 376 ("A condition of [the 100 cents settlements] was that AIG waive its legal claims against those counterparties.").
59. Louise Story and Gretchen Morgenson, "In U.S. Bailout of A.I.G., Forgiveness for Big Banks," *New York Times* (June 29, 2010).
60. See *Securities and Exchange Commission v. Goldman, Sachs & Co.*, Litigation Release No. 21489 (April 16, 2010).
61. See Louise Story and Gretchen Morgenson, "A.I.G. Sues Bank of America Over Mortgage Bonds, *New York Times* (August 8, 2011).
62. *Walker v. AIG*, Civil Action No. 4142-CC, Stipulation and Order of Dismissal, premised upon the following undertaking:

AIG's counsel stated that any amendment to the Restated Certificate of Incorporation to increase the number of authorized common shares or to decrease the par value of the common shares would be the subject of a class vote by the holders of the common stock, and, based on this representation, plaintiff's counsel agreed that the plaintiff's request for an order granting this relief is moot . . . .

63. Press release, "AIG Announces Voting Results of Annual Meeting of Shareholders" (June 30, 2009).
64. In late 2012, SICO filed a lawsuit challenging this subterfuge. The Delaware corporate statute states that charters can be amended, including to effectuate a reverse stock split, § 242(a), and amendments require both board and shareholder approval. § 242(b)(1). Separate shareholder votes by class are required whenever an amendment "would increase or decrease the aggregate number of authorized shares of such class" or "alter or change the powers, preferences, or special rights of the shares of such class so as to affect them adversely." § 242 (b)(2). A reverse stock split "increase[s]" the "number of authorized shares of [the common stock]" and therefore should require a class vote. See also *Sellers v. Joseph Bancroft & Sons Co.*, 2 A.2d 108 (Del. Ch. 1938).

   AIG promised in the settlement of the lawsuit to hold such a class vote but failed to do so. The government might argue that its purpose in effectuating the reverse stock split was proper, intended to restore luster to the battered stock, putting its trading price back in double rather than single digits.

Relatedly, that may have been necessary to maintain its NYSE listing, where rules provide for delisting of stocks that trade below $1 for sustained periods as AIG common threatened. But while that purpose might help defend or explain the motives, SICO argued that it does not satisfy the Delaware statute's requirements. Shareholder voting rights are sacrosanct in corporate law. See *Paramount Communications v. QVC Network Inc.*, 637 A.2d 34, 42 (Del. 1994) ("Because of the overriding importance of voting rights [we] have consistently acted to protect stockholders from unwarranted interference with such rights.").

65. Joint Economic Committee, Hearing on Financial Regulatory Reform (November 19, 2009); see http://big.assets.huffingtonpost.com/geithnertestimonyaig.pdf.

66. See Arthur D. Postal, "NAIC Disagrees with Geithner and Paulson On AIG," *National Underwriter Life & Health Magazine* (February 4, 2010) (referencing letter from state insurance regulators challenging Geithner's position).

67. Cunningham and Greenberg interview with Robert Willumstad, New York, May 16, 2012; see FCIC Report, 348; Sorkin, *Too Big to Fail*, 382. The New York Insurance Department was later reorganized and merged into a new Banking Department.

68. Testimony by Henry M. Paulson before the House Committee on Oversight and Government Reform (January 27, 2010).

69. U.S. Treasury Press Center, Secretary [Geithner] Written Testimony before the House Committee on Oversight and Government Reform (January 27, 2010).

70. See Binyamin Appelbaum & Jo Craven McGinty, "Fed Help Kept Banks Afloat, Until It Didn't," *New York Times* (April 4, 2011) (noting failure of 111 banks despite Fed discount window funding and quoting Charles Calomiris, Columbia University finance professor and historian of the Fed's discount window operations: "the Fed has become more politicized than at any point in its history, and I do worry very much that a lot of Fed discount window lending may just be part of a political calculation.").

71. The government officials were thus acting under the authority of their offices but engaged in unlawful conduct while doing so. See *Starr Int'l Co. v. United States*, No. 11-779C (Ct. Fed. Claims, July 2, 2012) (opinion denying most of the government's motion to dismiss and addressing the distinction between unauthorized conduct and authorized but unlawful conduct).

72. Paulson, *On the Brink*, 236-241.

73. Paulson explained that on Sunday September 14, when addressing the failing Lehman Brothers, he "warned [President Bush] that we might have to ask Congress for broader powers to stabilize the financial system [but two days later when addressing] the fire-alarm emergency of AIG, I didn't raise the issue of going to Congress again." Paulson, *On the Brink*, p. 237. Paulson recounts that he "next had to make arrangements to go to the Hill . . . as we

probably would need to meet with congressional leaders to discuss [the takeover of AIG]." P. 239. Paulson met with Congressional leaders, including Harry Reid, Chris Dodd, Judd Gregg, John Boehner, and Barney Frank. Ibid., p. 240-41. Paulson reports that "Dodd asked twice how the Fed had the authority to lend to an insurance company and seize control of it." Paulson says Ben Bernanke, Fed chairman, "explained how Section 13(3) of the Federal Reserve Act allowed the central bank to take such actions under 'unusual and exigent' circumstances.' It was the same provision the Fed had used to rescue Bear Stearns." Ibid. Section 13(3) of that statute did not authorize the Fed to seize control of private property and the constitutionality of any such provision would be doubtful. It authorizes making loans to anyone, banks or others. Paulson reports candidly: "In the end, [Senator] Reid said: 'You've heard what people have to say. But I want to be absolutely clear that Congress has not given you formal approval to take action. This is your responsibility and your decision." Ibid., p. 241.

74. Only a handful of such exertions of government power have occurred in the United States—the Tennessee Valley Authority, Amtrak, and Conrail are the prime examples.

75. Testimony by Mr. Edward M. Liddy before the House Committee on Oversight and Government Reform (March 18, 2009).

76. Ibid. Federal Reserve chairman Ben Bernanke joined the chorus:

[The AIG takeover was] a difficult but necessary step to protect our economy and stabilize our financial system [as AIG's] failure under the conditions then prevailing would have posed unacceptable risks for the global financial system and for our economy. [AIG's] failure could have resulted in a 1930s-style global financial and economic meltdown, with catastrophic implications for production, income, and jobs.

Chairman Ben S. Bernanke, Before the House Committee on Oversight and Government Reform (March 24, 2009).

77. Transcript, Tom Brokaw, "The American Financial System in Deep Crisis," *Meet the Press* (Sept. 21, 2008).

78. Guaazardi, Grose, et al., "Worth the Risk," chap. 23, p. 7.

79. Warren Oversight Report, p. 10.

80. Guaazardi, Grose, et al., "Worth the Risk," chap. 23, p. 8 (asset sales "represented a very deep blow to the morale of AIG employees around the world").

81. C. J. Hughes, "Rentals Offered, with Bragging Rights," *New York Times* (March 22, 2012).

82. Associated Press, "AIG Sells Hartford Steam Boiler for $742 Million" (December 22, 2008). The price was about 4.6 times earnings and no more than 1.5 times book value.

83. Heidi N. Moore, "AIG: Paying Off a $60 Billion Loan, One $742 Million Deal at a Time," *Wall Street Journal*, Deal Journal Blog (December 22, 2008).

84. See Ed Leefeldt, "AIG Rebrands Itself, But at What Cost?" *CBS News* (March 23, 2009).

85. Cunningham interview with Robert Benmosche, New York, September 12, 2012.

86. In SICO's case against Treasury, the Court of Federal Claims mostly denied the government's early motion to dismiss the case. *Starr Int'l Co. v. United States*, No. 11-779C (Ct. Fed. Claims, July 2, 2012).

87. The facts of the government takeover of AIG are unprecedented and the setting raises a host of novel issues. See Barbara Black, "The U.S. as 'Reluctant Shareholder': Government, Business and the Law," *Entrepreneurial Business Law Journal* (2010); J. W. Verret, "Treasury Inc.: How the Bailout Reshapes Corporate Theory and Practice," *Yale Journal on Regulation* 27 (2010): 283.

88. In an 89-page opinion, the federal judge who initially reviewed SICO's claims against the Fed rejected them, saying the Fed was not a controlling shareholder of AIG and, even if it were, as a federal actor, it did not owe AIG fiduciary duties required by state law. *Starr International Co. v. Federal Reserve Bank of New York*, 11 Civ. 8422, (S.D.N.Y. November 16, 2012). The Starr Companies appealed that decision and the appeal was pending when this book went to press.

Epilogue

1. After five years of sustained business development, in March 2011, Greenberg released a video on the company's web site explaining a rebranding. The Starr Companies became the new name and umbrella for all the various insurance companies and agencies in the Starr family: beginning with C. V. Starr & Company and SICO, and including the several insurance agencies. Zaeem Shoaib, "Report: C.V. Starr, Starr International USA rebranding as Starr Cos.," SNL Insurance Mergers and Acquisitions (March 15, 2011).

About the Companion Web Site

This book is accompanied by a web site, which you can find at www.wiley.com/go/theaigstory. The site includes the following appendices:

Appendix A.   Structure and Businesses (an overview)

Appendix B.   Greenberg's Resignation Letter (see p. 290, n. 77)

Appendix C.   Beattie's Mark-Up for Spitzer (see p. 294, n. 40)

Appendix D.   Accounting White Paper (see p. 196)

Appendix E.   Greenberg's Letter to AIG's Board, May 2008 (see pp. 239 & 301, n. 37)

Appendix F.   AIG's Response to May Letter (see p. 301, n. 39)

Appendix G.   Greenberg's Letter to Willumstad, Sept. 2008 (see p. 302, n. 5)

Appendix H.   AIG's Anti-Lobbying Policy (see p. 305, n. 56)

The companion web site also features additional photographs and other material.

About the Authors

Maurice R. Greenberg, formerly chairman and CEO of AIG from its founding in the late 1960s through 2005, is chairman and CEO of the Starr Companies, a global insurance and financial services organization. An active member of the international business community, Greenberg is honorary vice chairman and director of the Council on Foreign Relations, a member of the U.S. China Business Council, a former chairman and current member of the U.S.-Korea Business Council, vice chairman of the Board of Directors, member of the Executive Committee of the National Committee on United States-China Relations, and a member of the Business Roundtable. Greenberg has received honorary degrees from a number of institutions, including Brown University, Middlebury College, New York Law School, and Rockefeller University. He lives in New York City with his wife, Corinne, and has four children.

Lawrence A. Cunningham is the Henry St. George Tucker III Research Professor at George Washington University Law School and director of GW's Center for Law, Economics and Finance (C-LEAF) in New York. Previous books include *What Is Value Investing?* (McGraw Hill) and *Contracts in the Real World: Stories of Popular Contracts and Why They Matter* (Cambridge University Press). His extensive writings—on a wide range of business and legal topics—have also appeared in leading scholarly journals and such periodicals as the *New York Times*, *Financial Times*, *Baltimore Sun*, and *New York Daily News*. He lives in New York City with his wife and daughter.

Index

AAA credit rating of AIG, xv, 140, 141, 145, 146, 229–232
accident and health insurance, 4–5, 7–12, 46, 82, 120
accounting:
  AIG's historical performance charts, 153–154
  consolidation of subsidiaries, 198–199
  insurance liability reserves, 130–131, 199
  reinsurance, 197
  restatement, of AIG, 168, 193, 196–202, 213, 230
  stock option compensation, 198
ACE, 49–50, 132, 206
A Civil Action, 135
acquisitions, corporate:
  American General Corporation, 123–124

American Home Assurance Company, 12, 38, 122
Chiyoda Mutual Life Insurance, 121
Commerce & Industry Insurance Company (C&I), 128
GE Edison Life Insurance, 121
Hartford Steam Boiler (HSB), 133–134
International Lease Finance Corp. (ILFC), 140–142
Nan Shan Life Insurance Co., 44
National Union Fire Ins. Co. of Pittsburgh, 21–24, 38
New Hampshire Insurance Co., 20–21, 38
Sun America, 122
Transatlantic (later Trans Re), 24, 48
U.S. Life, 124

Aeroflot, 65
AFL–CIO, 152, 223
Ahlers, John, 267 n. 8
Aidinoff, M. Bernard:
  accounting turnabout, 201
  AIG board member, 156, 159, 118
  AIG founding, work on, 38
  Greenberg's resignation, 185–186
  SICO compensation plan creation,
    work on, 155
  transformation of AIG, 227
AIG Financial Products (see
    Financial Products)
AIG Trading Corporation, 278 n. 12
airline passenger insurance, 46–47
Allied World Assurance Company,
    126–127
American Association of Retired
    Persons (AARP), 4
American Express, 85
American General Corporation,
    123–124
American Home Assurance
    Company, 12–17, 20–28,
    37–38, 46–47, 50, 65, 119,
    122, 127, 150
American International Assurance
    Company (AIA), 10, 77, 89,
    103–105, 112, 120, 256
American International Building
    (see 70 Pine Street)
American International Group (AIG),
    passim
American International Reinsurance
    Company (AIRCO), 6, 9, 12,
    31–33, 36–37, 41
American International Underwriters
    (AIU), 6, 8–9, 12–14, 16–17,
    20–22, 25, 28–29, 38, 41, 49,
    66, 74–76, 81–82, 96

American Life Insurance Company
    (ALICO), 37–38, 55–56,
    119–121, 256, 266 n. 9
American Museum of Natural
    History, 156, 159
Amin, Idi, 121
Andrus, Ethel Percy, 4
Aquino, Benigno S. Jr., 116
Aquino, Benigno, III, 119
Archdiocese of Boston, 13–15, 33
Arthur Andersen, 172, 183–184
Asia Society, 57, 219
Association of Southeast Asian
    Nations (ASEAN), 57
auditors' liability, xvii, 172,
    183–184

"backdoor" bailout, xii, 246,
    249–250, 254
Back O'Beyond, Inc., 33
"band of brothers" (AIG founders),
    39, 157, 205, 261
  AIG's first board of directors, 149
  Starr's executors, 215, 216
Bangladesh, 119
Bank of America, 244, 252
Bank of Scotland, 244
Barshefsky, Charlene, 62, 84, 91,
    106, 108
Beame, Abraham, 52
Beattie, Richard I., 162, 175,
    180–182, 186–187, 190, 196,
    201, 210, 282 n. 44
Belco Petroleum, 59–60
Belgium, 11
Benmosche, Robert, 212, 258
Bensinger, Steven J., 231, 235, 237
Bentsen, Lloyd, Sen., 151, 163
Berkshire Hathaway, 173, 184,
    206, 228

Bermuda, 6, 31, 189, 204–205, 216
Bernanke, Ben S., 307 nn. 73 & 76
Bhutto, Benazir, 56
Bhutto, Zulfikar Ali, 55–56
Blackstone Group, 139, 256
Bogle, John C., 228
Boies, David, 187, 190–191, 196,
    204, 211–212, 214
Boston College, 136
Brandon, Joseph, 185
Brazil, 87, 90
Brightpoint Inc., 160, 163
Broad, Eli, 122
Brock, William, 86
Bryan Cave, 234
Buffett, Warren E., 173, 184–185,
    206, 228
Bureau of Labor Statistics, 87
Bush, George H. W., 90, 98, 162
    as chief of U.S.–China Liaison
        Office, 98
    presidential Asian trip, 83–84
Bush, George W., 81, 125, 159,
    171, 255
    post–9/11 aviation insurance, 125
Business Executives for National
    Security (BENS), 270 n. 9
Byrne, John J. ("Jack"), 240–241
Byroade, Henry, 114

California Public Employees
    Retirement System
    (CalPERS), 151, 228
Calyon, 250
Caplin & Drysdale, 274 n. 2
Carmilani, Scott, 269 n. 15
Carpenter, Guy, 24, 48, 270 n. 16
Carroll, Earl, 113
Carter, Jimmy, 58, 68–69, 81, 98,
    156, 162

Cassano, Joseph, 147, 234, 237
Castro, Fidel, 65
Ceauşescu, Nicolae, debate with
    Greenberg, 67–68
Center for the National Interest,
    57, 220
Central Intelligence Agency (CIA),
    63–64, 69
Charlie Rose, 191
Charoui, Henri, 75–76
Chartis, 257
Chektovich, Michael N., 279, n. 6
Chen Yuan, 107
China Development Bank, 107
China Development Forum, 57
China, 95–109
    AIG insurance license, granting of,
        102–103
    Cultural Revolution, 97
    diplomatic relations with U.S.,
        98–99, 220
    infrastructure investments, 142, 144
    market position, 239
    Nixon–Kissinger trip, 97
    reopening, 95–109
    Shanghai Center, 99–101, 103
    Starr and, 6, 9, 33, 35, 111
    Starr Companies and, 262
    Starr Foundation and, 217–218
    Tiananmen Square, 97–99
    trade relations with U.S, 109
Chiyoda Mutual Life Insurance, 121
Chrysler Building, 52
Chrysler Corporation, 244
Chubb, 126, 132–133, 206
Cities Service Oil Co. 27–29,
    51–52, 207
Clarke, Kenneth H. J., 270 n. 2
Clayton Consultants, 47
Cleveland Crane Co., 66

Clinton, Bill, 84, 90–91, 106–108, 130, 156, 162
Coalition for Asbestos Reform (CAR), 132–133
Coalition of Service Industries (CSI), 86–87, 90
Cohen, Marshall, 280 n. 24
Cohen, William S., 156, 180, 183, 185–186, 201
Colby & Hewitt, 21
Cold War, 63–68, 70–72, 74, 77, 83, 97, 121
Cole, James, 234
combined ratio, 21, 239
Commerce & Industry Insurance Company (C&I), 128–130
Conable, Barber B., Jr., 151, 163
Consolidated American Life Insurance Company, 151
Continental Casualty Company, 3–5, 7, 9–10
Continental Insurance Co., 13–14, 17, 32, 41
Cooper Union, 217
Cornell University, 218, 221
Cornfeld, Bernie, 115
Corrigan, E. Gerald, 72–74
corporate governance:
    board of directors, 26, 149–150, 155–157, 180
    politics and, 150–151, 158–159
    shareholder activism, 151–152, 155, 158–159, 162
    traditional approach under Greenberg, 149–150, 157–158, 163
    transformation by Greenberg's successors, 223–232, 238–241
    U.S. government interference with, 246–247, 250, 252–254

Council on Foreign Relations, 56–58, 60, 219
Cravath, Swaine & Moore, 180
credit default swaps, 145, 230–231, 235, 237, 256, 259
cross–selling of products, 9, 11, 120, 124
Cuba, 6, 65, 119
Cuisia, Jose L., Jr., 119
C. V. Starr & Company, 8–17, 31–33, 215–216, 262
    directors of, 34, 36, 215–216
    reorganization of, 36–37, 39
    separating from AIG, 189, 204–209
    succession of Greenberg, 31–33
Czech Republic, 71

Dalia, Peter, 50–51, 155
Davis, Florence A., 214–215, 217, 221
Davis, Franklin, 62, 79–80, 261
deductibles, 13–14, 16
Defense Intelligence Advisory Board, 79–80
deferred compensation (SICO plan), 39–41, 45, 168–169, 197–198, 201, 210–212, 231
Degnan, John, 132–133
de Larosière, Jacques, 270 n. 2
Deng Xiaoping, 97–98, 218
Department of Justice (DOJ), 159, 171, 179, 181, 197, 201
Depfa Bank, 244
d'Estaing, Valery Giscard, 11
Deutsche Bank, 250
Dickinson, Elmer N., Jr., 128
Diner's Club, 11
DiPiazza, Samuel A., 184
directors and officers (D&O) insurance, 25–27, 126, 150

Drexel Burnham Lambert, 145–146
Duperreault, Brian, 49–50
duSaillant, Guy, 11

Elkind, Peter, 174, 200
Empire State Building, 52
employees, xvi, 25, 39–41, 43–45, 48,
        51–52, 62, 157–158, 161–162
    AIG executives who became CEO
        elsewhere, 49–50
employee stock ownership plans, 40,
        268 n. 18
employment–at–will v. contracts, xvi,
        157, 203, 231, 262
Enron, 158–159, 167, 171–172, 174,
        182, 195, 224
environmental insurance, 128–131
Environmental Protection Agency
        (EPA), 129
Erin Brockovich, 135
errors and omissions (E&O)
        insurance, 27, 126
Estonia, 71
European American Underwriting
        Agency in Vienna, 68
Everest National Insurance, 206
Executive Briefing Book, 61–62, 126
executive compensation, 39–41, 45,
        157, 175, 198, 203, 240
expense ratio, 15, 17, 20, 239
Exxon, 71

Fairness in Asbestos Injury Resolution
        (FAIR) Act, 133
Faulkner, Michael J., 11
Federal Reserve (the Fed), 243–245,
        248, 250, 252, 254, 258, 259
Federal Reserve Bank of New York,
        72, 147, 156, 229, 243,
        245, 259

Feldstein, Martin S., 280 n. 24
Ferguson, Ronald E., 177–179, 185
Fifth Amendment, 184, 258
financial crisis of 2008, xii, xvii, 170,
        232, 243–260
financial performance charts, 153–154
Financial Products (FP), xvii
    AIG Trading Corporation, 278
        n. 12
    changes after Greenberg, 230–232
    internal controls at, 147–148,
        229–230, 238–239
    origins, 145–146
    PNC transaction, 161
    results through 2004, 148
    role in financial crisis of 2008,
        234–235, 246
Financial Services Agreement
        (see trade in services)
Finland, 92
Fisher, Phil, 49
float, 15
Ford, Gerald R., 80, 98
Foreign Policy Association, 56
Foster, Tom, 76
founding of AIG, 37–38
    board of directors, 149
    (see also band of brothers)
France, 11, 95, 121
Franklin, Benjamin, 50, 266 n. 13
Freeman, Houghton ("Buck"):
    AIG board member, 149, 163, 228
    background, 9, 45
    band of brothers, 39
    charitable foundation of, 158
    China, 103
    China trips, 97–98, 261
    C.V. Starr & Co. director, 34
    executor of Starr's estate, 215–216
    Japan, 9

Freeman, Houghton ("Buck")
        (*continued*)
    SICO separation from AIG, 205
    Stowe year–end celebration, 35
    Tokyo building dedication, 82
    Vietnam report, 271 n. 12
Frenkel, Jacob, 245, 259
Freudmann, Axel, 157
Futter, Ellen V., 156, 159, 180, 201

Gailoto, Tony, 269 n. 15
Galanski, Stan, 269 n. 15
García, Alan, 59–60
GEICO, 240
Geithner, Timothy, 91–92, 245–251,
        253–255, 258–260
General Agreement on Tariffs and
        Trade (GATT), 81, 85–86
General Electric (U.K.), 270 n. 2
General Electric (U.S.), 6, 49, 71,
        176, 263
General Reinsurance Co. (Gen Re),
        173, 177–179, 183–185
Gen Re – AIG reinsurance
        transaction:
    accounting rules, 177
    board's questions about, 182–184
    immateriality of, 178, 184
    origins, 177–178
    Spitzer's role, 177, 185
    turnabout by directors, 201
    turnabout by PwC, 182–183,
        187, 197
Germany, 11, 120–121, 156
Getty, John Paul, 47
Glaser, Dan, 269 n. 15
globalization, xiii, xiv, xviii, 59–62,
        278 n. 12
Globe & Rutgers Fire Insurance Co.,
        266 n. 13

Glomar Marine, 63–64
Gonda, Leslie, 140–141
Gorbachev, Mikhail, 71–72
Gousseland, Pierre, 279 n. 3
Grasso, Richard, 175
Greece, 121
Greenberg, Corinne, 7, 54, 77, 97,
        187, 220
Greenberg, Evan, 50
Greenberg, Jeffrey, 50, 175, 177
Greenberg, Maurice R. ("Hank"),
        passim
Grundfest, Joseph A., 186
Guy Carpenter (see Carpenter, Guy)

Hai, Le Thanh, 78
Hammer, Peter, 76
Harlem Children's Zone, 216
Harris, Mel, 261
Harrison, William B., Jr., 73
Hartford Steam Boiler Inspection and
        Insurance Company (HSB),
        133–134, 256–257
Hartford, The, 244
Hazy, Steven, 140–141
Hebald, Milton, 33, 35, 82, 208
Hewitt brothers, 21–22, 24
Hills, Carla, 84, 104, 155–156, 159,
        179, 180, 182–183,
        185–186, 201
Hoenemeyer, Frank, 156, 280 n. 24
Holbrooke, Richard C., 156, 162,
        180, 201
Home Depot, 175
Homer, Winslow, 208
Hong Kong, 5–7, 10, 34, 57, 64,
        75–76, 96, 100, 103, 105, 111,
        114, 119, 146
hostile takeovers, 20, 39–41, 187
House of Savings, 113–114, 117

Houston, Lawrence G., 64
Howell, John I., 279 n. 1
Hsu, T. C., 7–8, 95
Hughes Aircraft, 25
Hughes Airwest, 140
Hughes, G. M. ("Barney"), 10–11
Hughes, Howard R., 63–64
Hungary, 66, 68, 70–71, 121, 140
  Hungarian American Managers
    (HAM), 68
Hurd, J. Victor, 14, 17, 32, 41

IBM, 35, 50–51, 145, 150, 263
Igaya, Chiharu ("Chick"), 7, 9,
    266 n. 7
Immelt, Jeffrey, 121
India, 55, 86–87, 90, 92, 144,
    186, 263
infrastructure funds, xv, 73, 92
  life insurance investments in, 89,
    101, 112–113
  sponsorship of, 142–144
innovation, xiv–xv, 5, 16–17, 24, 43,
    46, 49, 121, 127, 142–145
internal controls, xii, 50–51, 142,
    147–148, 156–157, 229
  breakdown after Greenberg,
    223–224, 229–231, 233–237,
    239–240
International Advisory Board (IAB),
    54–56, 60–61, 100, 142
international business councils, 57
  U.S.–China Business Council, 106
  U.S.–Japan Business Council, 84
  U.S.–Russia Business Council, 71
International Business Leaders
    Advisory Council (IBLAC)
    (Shanghai), 100–102, 106
International Insurance Hall of Fame,
    50, 149

International Lease Finance
    Corporation (ILFC),
    140–142, 147
international travel, 26, 53–54
investments, 39, 139–148
  AIG Financial Products (FP),
    146–148
  Blackstone Group, 139
  infrastructure funds, 142–144
  International Lease Finance
    Corporation (ILFC),
    140–142
  real estate, 114, 119
    Manila, 119
    New York, 51–52, 257
    Shanghai, 99–100, 105–105
    Stowe, 35–36
    Tokyo, 81–82, 257
Iordanou, Dinos, 269 n. 15
Iran, 68–70
Ireland, 195
Italy, 92, 121

Japan:
  accident & health insurance,
    9–11, 54
  Kobe earthquake, 78
  life insurance, 120–121
  market position, 81, 85, 121, 239
  opening trade with, 81–85
  third sector, 9, 82–84
  Tokyo building, 81–82, 257
  World War II, 96, 112–113,
    219–220
  yellow hats, marketing with, 9
Japan Society, 84, 219–220
Jester, Dan H., 248
Johnson & Higgins, 27
Johnson, Jeff, 194
Johnson, Oakley, 91–92

Jordan, 121
JP Morgan Chase, 246

Kajima Corporation, 99
Kanak, Donald P., 155, 163, 205
Kantor, Mickey, 84, 90
Kan, Yuet–Keung, 54, 270 n. 2
Kaplan, Roberta A., 189, 195, 209
Kaye Scholer, 145
KB Home, 122
Kearns, Henry, 279 n. 2
Kelley, Kevin, 269 n. 15
Kelly, Anastasia, 209, 241
Keogh, John, 269 n. 15
Kenya, 121
KGB headquarters, 65
kidnapping and ransom insurance, 47
Kissinger, Henry A., 54, 62, 89,
    97–98, 106, 143, 220
Knight, Gordon, 269 n. 15
Komisar, Gerald, 61, 126
Korea, 3, 57, 75, 83, 144, 257
Kroc, Ray, 40
Kuwait, 121

Lambert, Leon Baron, 54
Lambsdorff, Otto Graf, 270 n. 2
Langone, Kenneth R., 175–176, 196
Languetin, Pierre, 270 n. 2
Latin America, xi, 120, 141–142, 144,
    151, 262
Latvia, 71
Laurel–Langley agreement, 114
Laxalt, Paul, Sen. 118, 275 n. 14
Lebanon, 6, 119, 121
Lee, "Harry" (Lee Kuan Yew),
    143–144
Lee, Hong–koo, 270 n. 2
LeFevre, Louis D., 58, 121
Lehman Brothers, 245

Lehman, Jeffrey, 218
Levin, Richard, 219
Levitt, Arthur:
    relationship with Zarb, 224
    transformation of AIG, 224–229,
        238–241, 260
Lewis, Robert, 234
Lexington Insurance Co., 21–22, 127
L. Hammonds, 17
Liberty Mutual, 132
Liddy, Edward M., 247–249, 251,
    255–256
life insurance operations, 10–11, 32,
    77, 101–104, 111–124
    Africa, 121
    AIA, 89, 111–112
    ALICO, 37–38, 55, 119–121
    American General Corporation,
        123–124
    China based, 101–104
    Nan Shan, 44, 103
    Philippine American Life Insurance
        Company (Philamlife),
        112–119
    Sun America, 122
Lincoln Center, 217
Li, Peng, 102–103
Lloyd's of London, 13, 25–26, 47
Long, Robert L. J., Adm., 117
loss ratio, 21, 239
Lucas, Charles M., 147, 229

MacArthur, Douglas, Gen., 112
MacArthur, Douglas II, 279 n. 4
Mahathir bin Mohamad, 89–92
Maiden Lane III, 249
Malacañang Palace (Philippines),
    114–115, 118
Malaysia, 88–91, 103, 142–143, 156,
    187, 290 n. 76

Manton, Edwin A. G. ("Jimmy"):
   AIG board member, 149, 163, 228
   AIU president, 9, 14, 20, 22
   background, 14, 28
   band of brothers, 39
   charitable foundation of, 158
   China trip, 97
   C.V. Starr & Co. director, 34
   debate with Greenberg, 14–16
   executive interrogation, 160
   executor of Starr's estate, 215–216
   Insurance Hall of Fame
      member, 50
   knighthood, 158
   meeting with Hewitt brothers, 22
   SICO separation from AIG, 205
   Starr Tech, creation of, 28
   Stowe year–end celebration, 35
   Tokyo building dedication, 82
   Turkish joint venture, 61
Marcos, Ferdinand, 114–119
Marcus, Mickey, 10
Marsh & McLennan, 25, 50–51, 175,
      177, 180
Martin Act, 172, 191
Matthews, Edward, 23, 155, 205
McCarran–Ferguson Act, 13, 136
McCormack, Richard, Dr., 36
McDonald's, 40, 135
McNutt, Paul V., 112–113,
      275 n. 3
medical research, 216
Meet the Press, 256
Merrill Lynch, 51, 174, 250
Middle East, xi, 22, 29, 61, 69,
      120–121, 141–142, 262
military:
   AIG executive experience, 45
   assistance to U.S., 9, 11, 63–64, 75
   Greenberg's interest in, 67

insuring the Korean Army, 75
   U.S., 96, 117
mobile overseas person or personnel
      (MOPs):
   meaning, 50, 78
   recruitment, 112
   value, 59, 78
   (see also Charoui, Faulkner,
      LeFevre, Nottingham,
      O'Rourke, Rhodebeck,
      Roberts)
Morefar, 33–34, 71, 82, 208, 263
   notable golfers at, 267 n. 4
Morgan Stanley, 22–23, 37,
      244, 246
Mt. Mansfield Co., 35–36, 208
Mulderig, Francis, 267 n. 8

Nahapetian, Shaké, 92
Nan Shan Life Insurance Company,
      44, 50, 103, 256–257
Napier, Richard, 287 n. 41
Nasdaq, 156, 224
National Association of Corporate
      Directors, 151
National Environmental Trust
      Fund, 130
National Geographic, 113
nationalism, xiii, xvi, 80
nationalization of AIG assets:
   Iran, 69–70
   Nigeria, 58
   Pakistan, 55–56
   Peru, 59–60
   United States, 254–255
   Vietnam, 77
National Union Fire Insurance
      Company, 21–24, 27, 37–38,
      47, 127
Nationwide, 130

Navalny, Alexy, 219
negotiating strategies, generally, 93
    buy–sell, 36–37
    empathy, 89
    good–cop, bad–cop, 108
    international business, 74
    tenacity, 84
networking, 43–44
    (see also relationships)
New Hampshire Insurance Company,
    20–21, 25, 27, 37–38, 69
New York Law School, 3
New York Philharmonic, 217
New York–Presbyterian Hospital, 77,
    220–221
New York State Insurance
    Department, 4, 12, 175, 253
Nigeria, 58, 80, 121
Nippon Life Insurance Co., 257
Nixon Center (see Center for the
    National Interest)
Nixon, Richard M., 46, 54–55, 80,
    97–98, 220
Norton, Joe, 5
Nottingham, R. Kendall, 70, 120,
    296 n. 6
Nysco Shu, 104

Office of Thrift Supervision, 232
Oman, 262
102 Maiden Lane, 10, 14, 27,
    31, 52, 209, 250
Ongpin, Roberto V. ("Bobby"), 118
O'Rourke, Patrick, 76

Pahlavi, Reza (Shah of Iran), 69
Pakistan, 6, 55–56, 80, 119
Pan American World Airways (Pan
    Am), 26, 53, 86
Pardee, Scott E., 279 n. 5

Park, Helen Graham, 34, 275 n. 16
patient capital, 89, 101–102, 257
Patrikis, Ernest, 208, 211
Paulson, Henry M. Jr., 173, 244–249,
    251, 254–256, 259–260
Paul, Weiss, Wharton, Rifkind &
    Garrison (Paul Weiss):
    alignment with Spitzer, 180–181,
        193–195
    clashes with Greenberg, 203, 209
    Greenberg's resignation, 182
    relationships with Spitzer, 180
    reporting to Spitzer, 189, 195
    retention by AIG, 180
    SICO compensation plan case,
        211–212
    transformation of AIG, 224
    withholding documents from
        Greenberg, 195
Peat Marwick Mitchell, 51, 86
Pei–yuan Chia, 280 n. 24
Peking University, 218
Penn Central Railroad, 26
People's Insurance Company of China
    (PICC), 97–99, 102, 104
Peru, 59–60
Peterson, Peter G., 57, 139
Philamlife Tower, 119, 208
philanthropy, 157–158, 175, 192,
    216–221
Philippine American Life Insurance
    Company (Philamlife),
    112–119, 208, 256
Philippines, xiii, 12, 22, 57, 78, 91,
    112–119, 256
Phypers, Dean, 145, 150
PNC Financial Services Group, 161,
    163, 234
Poland, 68, 71, 121
    Polish American Managers (PAM), 68

political risk and insurance, xix–xx,
    59–61
(see also nationalization of
    AIG assets)
Pomerantz, Mark, 182
Portman, Jack, 99
Portugal, 92, 121
Presbyterian Church, 151–152
President's Advisory Committee on
    Trade Policy and Negotiations
    (ACTPN), 80–81
President's Corporate Fraud Task
    Force, 159, 234
PricewaterhouseCoopers (PwC):
    accounting turnabout, 167–168,
        182–183, 187, 193–195,
        197–199, 201
    AIG's auditor, 172, 179, 181
    criticism of Greenberg's successors,
        235–239
    Greenberg's resignation, 167,
        182–184, 186
    internal controls, 147, 223, 229
    liability risks, 181
Prior, Lord James, 100, 270 n. 2
probabilities in insurance
    business, 128
probable maximum loss method, 28
profit center model, xiv, 24–25, 28,
    44–45, 51, 120, 157, 229–230,
    239, 262
Proof of Life, 47
property and casualty insurance, 9, 50,
    61, 82, 104, 111, 134, 136
public policy, 127, 217, 258–259
    accidents, 133–134
    asbestos, 131–133
    Environmental Trust Fund, 130
    insurance regulation, 136–137
    Superfund, 128–131

terrorism, 125–126
torts, 135–136
public–private corporate conception,
    xiv, 39–41
Putin, Vladimir, 74, 219

Qureshi, Moeen, 55–56, 142–144

Radigan, C. Raymond, 297 n. 6
Radin, Stephen, 296–297 n. 18
Rakoff, Jed, 211
Reagan, Ronald M., 69, 119, 135,
    151, 192
real estate investments, 114, 119
    Manila, 119
    New York, 51–52, 257
    Shanghai, 99–100, 105–105
    Stowe, 35–36
    Tokyo, 81–82, 257
Redholm, 207
Reed, John S., 117–118
regulation of insurance industry,
    136–137
Reinstein, Robert, 218
reinsurance:
    accounting for, 177, 183
    after 9/11, 126
    China, 97–98
    commuting, 178
    concept and usage, 16–17, 29, 48
    eastern Europe, 67–68, 71
    finite, 173
    Gen Re, 173
    HSB, 134
    Soviet Union, 65
relationships:
    China, xv, 44, 96
    eastern Europe, 67, 70
    importance of, xv, xvi, xix, 43–44,
        53–54, 98

relationships (*continued*)
  networking, 43–44
  New York State Insurance
      Department, 4
  Soviet Union, 68, 72
  the Philippines, 112
Rhodebeck, Richard, 119, 276 n. 19
Ribicoff, Abraham A., Sen., 145
Ricardo, David, 88
risk management at AIG, xii, 134,
      145, 147–148, 229–230
  dismantling after Greenberg, 231,
      233–235, 239–240
Ritter, Dick, 76
Roberts, John J.:
  African trip, 121
  AIG board member, 149, 163, 228
  background, 22
  band of brothers, 39
  C.V. Starr & Co. director, 34
  eastern Europe, 65–68
  executor of Starr's estate, 215–216
  Hungarian trip, 70–71
  Iranian joint venture, 69
  military service, 22, 45
  mobile overseas person, 50, 78
  Moscow trips, 64–66
  SICO separation from AIG, 205
  Tokyo building dedication, 82
  Turkish joint venture, 61–62
Robinson, James D. III, 85–86, 90
Rockefeller, David, 69, 102
Rockefeller, John D. III, 219
Rockefeller University, 216
Romania, 67–68, 71, 92, 121
  Romanian American Managers
      (RAM), 68
Rose, Charlie, 191
Roussel, Louis, 20–21
Rubin, Robert, 107–108

rule of law, xix, 59, 72
  China, 218
  legal ethics, 200, 218
  Russia, 74
  Spitzer's attitude toward, 200
  Starr Foundation's support of,
      218–221
  U.S. nationalization of AIG, 255
  (see also nationalization of AIG
      assets)
Ruschp, Sepp, 35
Russia, 62, 65–66, 71–74, 79, 141,
      144, 219, 262

Sandler, Robert, 296 n. 6
Sarbanes–Oxley Act, 51, 158–159,
      162, 171–173, 182
satellite insurance, 25
Saudi Arabia, 121
Savage, Thomas, 147
Schlesinger, James, 220
Scowcroft, Brent, 220
Securities and Exchange Commission
      (SEC), 38, 50, 160–161, 171,
      197, 224, 250, 252
securities lending business, 232, 235,
      240, 245
Seitz, Carl, 274–275 n. 2
Seitz, Clayton L., 112
services, trade in (see trade in services)
17 The Bund, 104–105
70 Pine Street (American
      International Building),
      51–52, 61, 77, 145, 160, 163,
      181, 203, 208, 209, 248, 257
Shabani, Koshrow C. ("K. C."),
      69–70
Shah of Iran, 69
Shanghai Center, 99–101, 103
Shelp, Ronald K., 85, 272 n. 12

Simpson Thacher & Bartlett, 162,
   181–182, 193–194, 209,
   215, 260
Singapore, 77, 83, 103, 143–144
60 Minutes, 176
Skinner, David B., Dr., 220
Slovakia, 92
Smith, Adam, 87
Smith, Alisha, 212–213
Smith, Howard I. ("Howie"), 148,
   155, 181, 183, 184
Smith, J. Milburn ("Mil"), 5, 7,
   122, 150
Smith, William French, 151, 163
Socialist Countries Division, 66–68
Société Générale, 250
Soejim, Aritoshi, 54, 270 n. 2
Sosin, Howard B., 145–146
South Africa, 121
Soviet Union, 63–66, 71–72,
   74, 97
Spitzer, Eliot, L.:
   aggressive tactics of, 172–177,
      192–193, 203, 208
      Langone, Kenneth, 175–176
      Marsh & McLennan, 175, 177
      Merrill Lynch, 174–175
      New York Stock Exchange, 175
      Starr Foundation, 213–215
      Vacco, Dennis, 177
      Welch, Jack, 176
      Whitehead, John 192–193
   crimes of, 180, 200
   ethics of, 174, 185, 200, 215
   Gen Re transaction and, 177,
      179, 197
   media and, 174, 176, 190–191,
      200, 213
   relationships with Paul Weiss,
      180–181, 193–196, 211–212

rule of law, attitude toward,
      200, 218
   SEC, criticism of, 176
   temper, 175, 176, 190, 193
   threats, 173–174, 177, 190, 193,
      195–196, 214–215, 286 n. 38
Sports Illustrated, 35
Stamm, Werner, 112
Starr Companies, 262–263
Starr, Cornelius Vander:
   business vision and skills, 6–7
   China and, xiii, xv, 6, 96,
      104, 111
   death and funeral, xiv, 34–36
   estate, 213–214
   generosity, 7, 22, 158
   group concept in AIG name, 37
   Insurance Hall of Fame, 50
   international travel, 53
   legal training, 265–266, n. 5
   Philippines and, 112–113, 119
   pioneering spirit, xiii, 5–6, 62, 82
   recruiting savvy, 7–8, 45,
      112–113
   SICO name as tribute to, 38
   Tokyo building, 81–82, 208, 257
   U.S. Life, 122, 124
   wit of, 119
   (see also Morefar; Stowe, Vermont)
Starr Foundation:
   American Museum of Natural
      History, 159
   beneficiaries, 217–221
   China contributions, 95–96, 218
   growth, 213–214, 216
   philosophy, 216–217
   purchase of Chinese bronze
      window panels, 95–96
   Spitzer's attack on, 169,
      214–215

Starr International Company (SICO):
AIG shareholdings, 152, 157, 246
consolidation of Union Excess,
198–199
creation of, 38–39
deferred compensation plan,
39–41, 45, 168–169,
197–198, 201, 210–212, 231
fiduciary duty lawsuit against
Federal Reserve Bank of New
York, 259–260
separating from AIG, 189, 204–209
takings lawsuit against U.S.
Treasury, 258–260
Starr Tech:
disputes with AIG, 207–208
formation of, 27–29
independence from AIG, 39
ongoing business, 262
State Farm, 132
St. Denis, Joseph, 234
Steinberg, Saul, 41
Stempel, Ernest E.:
AIG board member, 149, 163, 228
ALICO expansion, 120
band of brothers, 39
charitable foundation of, 158
C.V. Starr & Co. director, 34
executor of Starr's estate, 215–216
life insurance expert, 32, 113
Marcos, 114
negotiations with Youngman, 32
SICO separation from AIG, 205
Stowe year–end celebration, 35
Tokyo building dedication, 82
Stephanopoulos, George, 190–191
Stiles, Kristie, 292 n. 18
Stopper, Edwin, 54, 270 n. 2
Stowehof, 35
Stowe, Vermont, 35, 208

Strauss, Robert, 81
Subprime mortgages, 231–232, 235
Sullivan & Cromwell, 38, 155, 160
Sullivan, Martin J., 186, 223
as candidate to succeed Greenberg,
155, 163, 182
cooperation with PwC, 194
separation from Starr companies,
205–207
severance received, 240
SICO compensation plan, 205,
210–211
transformation of AIG, 223, 231,
234–237
weaknesses cited by PwC, 237
Zarb and, 223–224, 240
Summers, Lawrence, 92, 107
Sun America, 122
Sung Guohua, 97–98
Superfund law, 128–131
Swiss Re, 126, 269 n. 11
Sycip, Washington, 270 n. 2
Syria, 121

Taiwan, 44, 50, 103, 256–257
(see also Nan Shan)
Taranto, Joe, 269 n. 15
Tata, Ratan N., 55
Temple University, 218
Thailand, 77, 91, 103
think tanks, 57, 220
This Week, 190–191
Thompson, William C., 297 n. 6
Thornburgh, Richard, 162
TIAA–CREF, 151
Tighe, Eugene, Jr., Gen. , 79–80
Time, 113
Tizzio, Thomas, 296 n. 6
Toohey, Ryan, 292 n. 18
tort wars, 135–136

trade in services:
    ACTPN, 80–81
    advocacy to open, 79–93
    benefits to open markets, 81
    Coalition of Service Industries
        (CSI), 86–87
    Financial Services Agreement,
        272 n. 9, 273 n. 22
    Japan, 81–85
    Malaysia, 88–91
    measurement of, 86–87
    opponents of open trade, 87–89
    World Trade Organization, 88–92
Transatlantic Company, 24, 48
Trans Re, 48, 178, 256
travel insurance, 50, 82
    airline passenger insurance, 46
    in the Soviet Union, 64
    Starr's vision of, 7
Travelers, 130, 132
Troubled Asset Relief Program
    (TARP), 244, 255
Truman, Harry S., 112
Tse, Edmund, 77, 103, 270 n. 16
Tse, K. K., 32, 34, 43, 149,
    215–216
Turkey, 61–62, 121, 262
Tweedy, Gordon, 14, 31–35

UBS, 250
Uganda, 121
underwriting discipline (see
        underwriting profit)
underwriting profit, 120, 127, 140,
    157, 262
    ALICO, 120
    business goal, 15, 45, 127
    China, 104
    competitive advantage, 127
    directors and officers insurance, 27

disciplining device, 19–20, 127
    erosion at AIG after Greenberg, 239
    HSB, 134
    Japan, 82
    profit center model and, 25
    property and casualty
        insurance, 111
Union Excess, 198–199, 201
U.S.–China Business Council, 106
U.S. government and AIG:
    AIG as national asset, 78
    aviation insurance after 9/11,
        125–126
    China, Nixon–Kissinger
        reopening, 97–98
    Korean Army, insurance for, 75–76
    Philippines, intervention with
        Marcos, 117–119
    Soviet Union, submarine recovery,
        63–64
    U.S. identity as AIG asset, 119–120
    Vietnam, 75–76
    (see also trade in services)
U.S.–Japan Business Council, 84
U.S. Life Insurance Co., 12, 122, 124
U.S.–Russia Business Council, 71
U.S. Treasury Department,
        244–245, 255
Uzbekistan, 71, 92

Vacco, Dennis C., 177
Vance, Cyrus, 58
Van Gogh, Vincent, 208
Vesco, Robert, 116
Vietnam, 62, 74–78, 92, 143
    evacuation of AIG personnel from
        Saigon, 76
    fire, 77–78
    War, 75–76
Vollreide, Bob, 3–4

Warren, Elizabeth, Sen., 240–241
Watson, Thomas J., Jr., 35–36
Waxman, Harry, Rep., 251
Weil, Gotshal & Manges, 209
Weill Cornell Medical
    College, 221
Welch, Jack, 176
Wells, Theodore V., Jr., 211
white blackbirds, 43
Whitehead, John C., 192–193
White, Robert, 10–11
Williams, Roy, 28
Willumstad, Robert B., 224, 235,
    243–247, 259
  liquidity squeeze at AIG, 243, 245,
    246, 259
  ouster by U.S. government, 249,
    254–255
  response to U.S. government
    pressure, 246–247, 249
  succeeding Sullivan, 240
  transformation of AIG,
    229, 235
Winograd, Barry N., 179,
    182–184, 198
Wolfensohn, James D., 140
workers' compensation,
    295 n. 53
World Bank, 60, 140, 143, 151,
    279 n. 10
WorldCom, 171

World Trade Organization (WTO),
    xiv, 90, 96, 106–109
Wu Yi, 108

Yale University, 218–219
Yeltsin, Boris, 72–74
Youngman, William, 8, 12, 14, 16,
    21–22, 31–33, 41
Young Presidents Organization, 22

Zalamea, Cesar, 115
Zarb, Frank G.:
  accounting turnabout, 201
  AIG board member, 156, 159
  background, 156
  control at AIG, 184, 186
  Greenberg's resignation, 181–182,
    184, 186
  lead outside director, 159, 162
  relationship with Levitt, 224
  relationship with Spitzer, 180, 184,
    194–195
  retention of Beattie, 162
  testimony in SICO compensation
    plan case, 211
  transformation of AIG, 223–224,
    228–229, 238–241,260
Zhu Qizhen, 102
Zhu Rongji, 99–102, 104–105,
    107–108
Zyuganov, Gennady, 73